Urban Legends

Urban Legends

The As-Complete-As-One-Could-Be Guide to Modern Myths

N.E. Genge

Three Rivers Press
New York

This book contains urban legends, accurate printed representations of stories that, although set in our time with characters, company names, and other references that might be real, are themselves works of fiction.

Published by Three Rivers Press, 201 East 50th Street, New York, New York 10022. Member of the Crown Publishing Group.

Random House, Inc. New York, Toronto, London, Sydney, Auckland

www.randomhouse.com

Three Rivers Press is a registered trademark of Random House, Inc.

Printed in the United States of America

Library of Congress Cataloging-in-Publication Data
Genge, N.E.
Urban legends : the as-complete-as-one-could-be guide to modern myths / by N.E. Genge.—1st ed.
p.   cm.
1. Urban folklore—United States.   2. Legends—United States.   3. Legends—United States—History and criticism.   4. United States—Social life and customs—1971–
I. Title.
GR105.G45   2000
398.2'0973'091732—dc21   99-41287
CIP
ISBN 0-609-80494-4
First Edition

For Peter and Michael—with love.

Contents

Acknowledgments

I'm delighted to have this opportunity to thank:

Patty and Kristen at Harmony, for not only doing their jobs brilliantly, but for having as much fun with this book as I did.

S. Weissman and P. Miller, for timely legal advice.

Lorna Sainsbury, for donating body parts, reading the drafts, and being honest enough to say "I just don't get this part" whenever necessary.

John, Joanne, Monty, Clair, Julianne, Maggie, Ben, and William, for digging up the odd and esoteric on less than a moment's notice; the Queen Elizabeth II Library, the Health Science Center Medical Library, the Truman Research Center, the Museum of Journalism, Clippings, and the BNIT may not know you're the real treasures in their collections, but I certainly do.

Phantasm1, CRowen, OddStuff, pmitchell, Kounter, JKLee, BarbieGirl, DustMote, and TallTale, for filling my e-mail box with chuckles, information, and encouragement.

The Folklore Department of Memorial University of Newfoundland, for pointers and inspiration.

The wonderful people at Gallery Pharmacy, Captain William Jackman Memorial Hospital, Pet City, Dow Chemicals (Montreal), the Royal Newfoundland Constabulary, and the RCMP Forensics Unit in Winnipeg, for letting me pick their brains and their files.

Michael, for being an all-around terrific kid who hands out hugs instead of complaints as deadlines loom.

And Peter, for a seemingly endless supply of patience, generosity, laughter, and love.

Thank you.

Introduction

T he ancient Greeks had morality plays. Aesop and his fables still teach, among other things, the value of being a persistent tortoise rather than a dilettante of a hare. The Brothers Grimm scattered bits of solid advice throughout their fairy tales. Modern television broadcasters get the rich and famous to tout the virtues of staying in school, off drugs, and away from the streets. Seems the notion of burying a sermon inside a good story with a strong cast didn't begin, or end, with a guy from Galilee and some parables. Of course, modern audiences aren't found hanging about the village square waiting for wandering troops of entertainers, or idling along the edge of salt lakes in the hope someone will come to hand out that week's public-service announcement.

Modern audiences, congregating around the office water cooler, the corner bar, the supper table, or the student union, would probably call security at the first sight of an unannounced bunch of jongleurs wandering through the cafeteria with stories of plague and the dangers of fornication.

"Crazies!"

"Religious freaks!"

"Nuts!"

"Yeah!"

Then heads would come together, voices would hush, and one of the group would begin with, "You know, reminds me of something I heard a few weeks ago. Friend of mine and her cousin, just in from Dayton I think, went up to that new movie place out on Pomenda Drive, The Royal. They were going to see *Dead Man on Campus,* I think, not that it matters, 'cause they didn't get to see anything!" A dramatic pause so the audience can quickly consider and discard a dozen reasons why two women mightn't get to see a film. "The cousin went to push down her seat and something jabbed her, right in the palm! It was hard to see in the theater, but they found something in the seat and took it out into the lobby." Another dramatic pause. Every storyteller knows the imagination of his audience is the strongest tool in his arsenal. "A used syringe! Propped right there in the seat! The manager freaked! Told her to get to the hospital, with the syringe, right away." The third, and last, pause. "The *last* one of these they found had a note curled up inside it: 'Welcome to the World of AIDS!'"

"No!"

"Yes! They're trying to keep it out of the papers while they follow up on some leads,

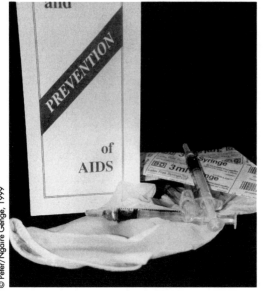

If they show up on beaches, why not on movie theater seats?

but you watch, it'll be all over the news soon!"

Move over, Aesop, you've got some serious competition here in the form of urban legends.

Urban legends?

More than the name of a recent popular film, urban legends, a form of folklore that's continued in the same basic style from the time of Boddeccia and Socrates and Xio Ming, fill, in modern times, the role of fairy tale and parable and grapevine—with twists.

Even when books like *Stories of Tales of Olden Times with Morals,* which included the most famous versions of such fairy tales as "Cinderella," were first circulated back in the 1690s, the audience of the day didn't *really* believe Charles Perrault's version of events.

Fairy godmothers, disappearing dresses, and magical shoes made for a good story, but no one took the tale as historically accurate.

Urban legends, on the other hand, are *intended* to be taken as tales of real events happening to real people in real locations—even if the events are more bizarre, more terrifying, and more farcical than anything dreamed of in fairy tales. For example, several reference books claim that Cinderella's slippers, in the original versions of the fairy tale, were actually made of fur, not glass, and that the only reason we tell our children about glass slippers is that, during translation from French to English, someone mistook *vair,* the French for "fur," for *verre,* the French for glass. The words, which sound very similar to English-trained ears, were, according to urban legend, never proofed by a native speaker and the error eventually became the accepted version.

The fictional *story* "Cinderella" is a fairy tale; the *belief* that a mistake made by a real-world human translator led to the inclusion of glass slippers in "Cinderella" is an urban legend.

The whole glass-slipper thing, just coincidentally, is also a load of hooey.

Perrault's original French text clearly reads, "pantoufle de verre," slippers of *glass*!

So why would anyone continue to claim the slippers were fur?

A number of reasons, all of which will rear their collective heads again and again as we investigate more legends: source, plausibility, and current *emotional* experience.

As in the case of the woman who supposedly found a contaminated syringe in a movie theater seat, urban legends are most often found in what has come to be known as the "friend of a friend" version. The victim was someone *known* to the storyteller, even if only by association. In the AIDS needle story, the woman whose hand is pricked is removed by only one person from the teller. The audience infers that, while not firsthand information, the story came from a source close enough that the veracity of the tale could easily be checked—and probably was!

The "probably" is, of course, a key point.

In the listener's mind, a train of thought starts as soon as the storyteller identifies himself or herself with the victim. Why would this person's friend tell such an outlandish story if it *wasn't* true? No one wants to be caught in a lie, especially an easily exposed lie, a stupid lie. The social embarrassment, the listener assumes, would heavily deter *anyone* from telling a stupid lie in the first place. If the victim is someone the storyteller could easily run into in the future, there's a similar deterrent in place for the person who told the story to the present storyteller. So, even without any direct evidence, a sense of veracity is already in place before further details come along.

The AIDS tale, if you read it closely, is filled with details. The name of the theater, the name of a local street the audience would be familiar with, the name of the film the women intended to see. All these details, also presumably verifiable, strengthen the audience's belief in the story. If 99.9 percent of a story is true, who'll seriously question the remaining tenth of a percent? As con artists reputedly say, the best place to hide a lie is between two truths.

A deeper examination, however, reveals startling gaps in the information presented. The storyteller never reveals the name of her friend, or her friend's cousin. She tells the audience the visitor is from Dayton, but not her name? Why? Unless the storyteller is in a very small population center, you'd also expect to know *which* hospital the woman was sent to, right? Especially if a particular hospital had treated the first victim.

Time frames are frequently confusing, or nonexistent, within an urban legend, though the listener may not realize this at the time. The cousin arrived from Dayton "recently," and a particular film, *Dead Man on Campus,* is supposedly playing. The listener, on a first pass of the tale, might think these were sufficient details to pin down the time frame, if necessary. Obviously they aren't. *Dead Man on Campus* was out in video long before it reached our tiny local one-screen cinema! "Just in from Dayton" tells us nothing about when the *event* actually took place. Was it a week ago? A month? How long might it take some mysterious "they" to track down leads? Unknown. So, even if this event, or a similar one, were later reported in local papers, it wouldn't help to identify the "when" aspect of the tale.

Only to someone actually trying to track down the incident, however, do these omitted details become truly apparent.

Plausibility plays into every good urban legend. Both the AIDS tale and the story of the fur slipper *make sense* to modern audiences. Who has seen, or even heard of, a real glass slipper? Our minds can immediately conceive of several very good reasons why glass slippers *wouldn't* exist. Glass is delicate, totally unsuitable for footware. A broken heel on a glass slipper could leave its owner bleeding to death instead of inconvenienced! Who would chance such a thing? And what about simple comfort? The thought of a rigid glass slipper encasing a foot after an evening of dancing leaves most women cringing in sympathy.

Fur, however, makes sense!

It's soft, unlikely to slice through the hamstring, warm, cozy, capable of accommodating a foot swollen after a night of dancing. Fur is also touched with a certain romance and elegance. Mink slippers peeking from under the hem of silk skirts, even if never seen before, are at least *plausible,* the sort of thing some highborn lady with too much money and a bit of imagination *might* come up with.

The AIDS tale isn't quite as simple, but plausibility can be built up over time from more than one source.

Inadvertent pinpricks have happened. For several summers in recent public memory,

tales of medical waste, including syringes, washing ashore at local beaches—and pricking the unwary—circulated through the popular, and supposedly reliable, media. Needle stabs on playgrounds, resulting from discarded drug paraphernalia, also make the news from time to time.

Needles can be sources of AIDS contamination. Warnings to that effect have bombarded the general population since the early 1980s, especially those public-service spots warning against the sharing of needles.

Some AIDS patients alleviate their anger by infecting unwary, innocent victims through deliberately unprotected sex. Several real-world cases, widely reported, planted the image of the murdering AIDS madman deep in the public psyche. Popular television programs like *Law & Order* explored the possibility in dramatic style.

In the mind of the average person, these three "facts" easily swirl together and create a *plausible* scenario of an enraged AIDS victim infecting yet more people with syringes scattered throughout the darkness of movie theaters. For those whose experience tells them that homosexual men, the group most closely associated with AIDS, often met for sexual encounters in the back rows of certain theaters, the connection between AIDS and theaters is drawn even more tightly.

Facts alone can't turn a what-if-style scenario into a full-fledged urban legend. If no one cares about a topic, or finds it relevant, legends about, and knowledge of, that topic slowly fade from public memory. The fact that AIDS continues to be one of the century's most terrifying diseases, that our efforts to conquer it have been more often stymied than successful, and that atypical cases, cases for which no known source of infection can be found, continue to arise, all combine to explain the emotional angle of the AIDS legend. AIDS is scary stuff. It hits us deep in the gut, it's the troll under our bridge, the plague waiting to take our children.

In fairy tales, the source of fear is obvious. If Cinderella, favorite daughter of a loving father, could end up in the ashes, couldn't we? If Red Riding Hood could be attacked by a wolf in her grandmother's house, presumably a place perceived as safe, it follows that someone else could be as well—if the wolf is taken symbolically, not literally. In one sense, urban legends resemble fairy tales. Though they are meant to be taken literally, as having really happened, they contain clearly visible warnings or lessons. The moral of the needle story is equally blatant: Letting your guard down, being less than 100 percent aware of your surroundings, can be deadly.

Sure, other tales could express the same sentiment, and dozens do, but it's the most effective legends that spread, and because "The Movie Theater Needle" came from a source perceived as reliable *by its audience,* was based on facts that lent it credibility *to that audience,* and spoke to a real fear *of that audience,* it will continue to be spread *by that same audience.*

Is twenty-five cents really worth it?

© Peter/Ngaire Genge, 1999

Variations of each story will also spread. Details within the story migrate with the stories, changing to keep the tale relevant for the next audience. The Royal Theater might become the Omni, the Troy, or whatever cinema is close at hand. The syringe might be just a needle next time around. Perhaps the girl actually sat on the needle instead of pricking her hand.

Larger changes occur, too. Another variant is "The Needle in the Coin Return." Everyone has probably checked the coin return on a pay phone or a vending machine to see if the previous user accidentally left a bit of change behind, so the plausibility factor of this tale is as high as, if not higher than, the original tale while maintaining all the source credibility and emotional factors, this version will also spread.

Students of folklore, of which urban legends are a part, trace both major and minor changes in the legends they encounter, and in some cases the changes in detail allow a researcher to follow one tale across an entire country. Other tales, seemingly similar in moral, with numerous coinciding details, have no apparent "root" tale, no common point of origin. Just as biological evolution equips several unrelated species to perform the same biological functions, like aerating soil, or breaking down dead matter, or weeding out the weakest members of a population, linguistic evolution can nurture legends that serve similar functions without any contact with any other tale.

What separates an urban legend from a rumor, or a bit of simple misinformation, or a fairy tale? Consistency of form. Though few apparent similarities exist between the tale of the contaminated needle and the story of the glass slipper, both narratives share key features.

First, they *are* narratives. Some legends are longer, some shorter, but they are all told as stories with once-upon-a-time-type origins. There's a beginning, a middle, and an end. The beginning sets the stage. In the AIDS tale, that's the introduction of the characters, their circumstances, the reason they were in the location, and some idea of their backgrounds. (You'll discover that legends frequently pick folk from places in the Midwest, like Dayton, Ohio, to illustrate their wholesomeness and contrast it with the situation they're about to encounter.) The middle, the part of a story devoted to rising action and complications, begins when the cousin from Dayton feels a tiny prick on her palm. The end, the climax, the finale of the story, is the revelation of the AIDS threat. A complete story in just a few paragraphs.

The glass-slipper tale also sets a stage: seventeenth-century France, when many people, even acknowledged giants in the field of literature, haven't agreed on just which spelling went with which words. The complications are simple in this one. One person claims a belief, another confronts that claim. The slippers are either fur or glass, but which? The denouement is the discovery that modern scholars were all too anxious to attribute sloppy scholarship to Perrault—but it was they themselves who started the myth!

Some tales will lend themselves to extravagant stories with considerable detail; others contain the whole legend in a single line: Mrs. O'Leary's cow caused the Chicago Fire by knocking over an oil lamp while being milked. Despite brevity, each tale's background is understood. In the case of the cow, Mrs. O'Leary clearly had to bring the lamp out, so we know it was night. Because no one would normally leave an oil lamp in a cow's stall, we can surmise that Mrs. O'Leary was careless, or called away unexpectedly, or whatever fits the case. The climax is history itself. The fire burned everything! We don't need to know any more than that the cow knocked over the oil lamp to get the point.

Another legend, that Charles Drew, the African-American man who developed the blood-bank system, bled to death outside a whites-only hospital, illustrates how much an audience can infer from a short tale. Though it's possible to expand on this tale—to include descriptions of the car crash that brought him to this hospital, to name the other prominent men who were in the car with him, to relate how traumatic the moment of impact must have been—none of those details can add to the essential moral of the story: Bad Americans once kept blacks, even blacks who helped them, down.

This tale, in particular, helps illustrate two other common elements in most urban legends. Legends frequently derive their punch from irony. That a man who helped establish a blood-bank system could die of blood loss himself hits us somewhere between the heart and the soul. Similar ironies explain the staying power of stories like "The Marlboro Man," which claims that every model to have posed as the Marlboro cowboy died of cancer. (It's not true, but lung cancer did claim the life of the man best known as the Marlboro cowboy.) Numerous tales of happy-faced child actors turning into pedophiles or serial killers or heavy-metal rockers also play into those same ironies.

We love twisted endings, and urban legends supply them.

The other element that the Charles Drew story illustrates is that the "truth" of a legend isn't necessarily all that important. The majority of legends either aren't true (based on inconsistencies within the story), can't be confirmed (owing to lack of detail), or can be considered apocryphal (told of so many, in so many different, unrelated locations as to be clearly impossible). There may well have been a Cinderella, but she's an archetype, an amalgam of dozens of female victims who somehow became something more at the end than they were in the beginning.

The Charles Drew story isn't true.

Drew was fatally injured in a car crash, but he didn't die outside a whites-only hospital. He was treated to the full extent of any hospital's ability, without success, inside the emergency room of Alamance General Hospital in North Carolina. The legend, however, creates an image that symbolically represents the fact that blacks have literally bled to death at the hands of white Americans. It's powerful on an emotional level, to both blacks and whites, and that power keeps it alive despite all evidence to the contrary. As recently as 1999, the novel *Dust,* an otherwise brilliantly researched piece of scientific horror, propagated this myth to yet another generation.

True stories become legends, legends are debunked, and other tales grow into legends, but the veracity of the legend itself is seldom the whole point. Legends grow based on their emotional impact, on the lessons the audience *believes* they've taken from the story. That a man like Charles Drew *might* have died outside a whites-only hospital on April 1, 1950, is all too possible—many blacks of that era *did*—and the lesson, if not its specifics, is something that certainly *should* be remembered.

Folklore is history, but it's often the history of how given people perceive themselves and others, not just of facts and dates. In the same way that psychologists are beginning to give credence to the concept of "emotional intelligence" as well as the already established "intellectual intelligence," historians now understand that decisions and actions frequently come from a society's perception of itself, which is most often reflected not in its textbooks but in its folklore.

Folklore, including urban legends, differentiates itself from fairy tales and history in two other significant ways: humor and minutiae.

Where history concerns itself with the powerful and famous, folklore elevates the tiny corners of life to prominence, frequently poking fun at our humanity, providing a welcome relief from the warnings.

One of my personal favorites, "A Little Cream?," demonstrates many of the unique qualities of urban legends within a single brief tale.

A woman returns to her job after her maternity leave to the congratulations and best wishes of all her colleagues, but soon finds herself with an unusual problem. Her solution, elegant and ironic, is carried throughout her office by e-mail!

> *To Whoever Used the "Cream" in the Office Fridge:*
>
> *Please don't admit it, at least not to me. I don't think I could spend the rest of our working days meeting your eyes over the computer printouts, across the cafeteria tables, or over the water cooler, without giggling—or gagging. So please don't feel any need to tell me it was you, okay?*
>
> *However, for your future consideration, please be aware that the milk you used was "express"-ly for my new son, not for the general use of everyone with access to the fridge. I know how easy it can be to forget to bring your own milk and nab a few drops of someone else's, so from now on I'll make sure my name is prominently displayed on the side.*
>
> *Hoping you enjoyed your coffee as much as my son enjoys his supper,*
> *Claire*

The visual image of someone reading this e-mail, thinking back to the spot of milk they snitched, and gagging at the memory, is completely irresistible! Any number of miffed employees who have discovered their own lunches missing will also appreciate the tiny feeling of vengeance that blooms with each hearing. The ironies are many (we'll share cow's milk, but choke on the notion of human milk), the humor high, all delivered in clean narrative style.

As this example shows, urban legends are

Real comfort food.

also flexible entities, quickly adapted to new methods of transmission, like e-mail, faxes, and in copy after copy, hand-carried from office bulletin board to office bulletin board. Urban legends are current in *content* as well. Storing expressed breast milk in the office fridge probably hasn't been mentioned in many employee handbooks, and new mothers recently returned to work sure as heck haven't until very recently been sending e-mail warnings to their co-workers to keep away from the breast milk!

Urban legends thrive on new technology, zipping along telecommunication lines to reach more people faster, incorporating the new "virtual realities" into their content (like the tale of two people who meet after months of e-mailing each other only to discover they used to date in high school), and frequently *using* these new media to create updated versions of old legends, like the belief that hitting a particular publisher's Web page a hundred times will mean one more book goes to inner-city libraries free of charge.

The quote, "I can't tell you what constitutes pornography, but I know it when I see it," could as easily apply to urban legends.

Some enthusiasts of the form happily open the field to include collections of jokes that comment on some aspect of current life; chain letters passed by conventional mail as well as electronic packets; "faxlore," those bizarre little items that turn up in your fax machine without any return information on the top, but a lot of laughs in the body of the message; and the numerous petitions asking readers to support some cause or other—regardless of how outdated the issue or clearly fictitious the problem.

Others, folkloric purists, embrace the field as a science, demanding stricter definitions of "urban legend." One professor at Memorial University of Newfoundland didn't include a legend in his collection unless it had popped up in the conventional media (print, television, or radio) at least three times. As urban legends remain largely *oral,* that severely limits the subject matter available to study.

Both approaches, however, bring something to the field. Careful collection, dated, investigated, and recorded contemporaneously with a legend's appearance, certainly makes it easier to track changes and grasp what events might spark its origins or mutations. Citations for every claim would certainly make tracing common misconceptions (like the "fact" that more women are beaten on Super Bowl Sunday than any other day of the year) to their source easier.

However, despite the designation of "urban" legend, many legends trace their roots back several centuries—before "urban" was even a word. The Cinderella story, without the slippers and other trappings, may have originated a thousand years ago—in China! If folklorists were to ignore first-person accounts, the faulty memories of variously assorted aunties, and the contents of such nonscholarly documents as personal letters, diaries, and speeches, they'd soon have nothing to study!

Likewise, the approach of different individuals to the field varies widely. Some simply collect and record the tales, some collect and interpret them, others try to debunk them or trace them to their original sources, while another group tracks the appearance of legends that have already been identified. Many try to integrate all of these functions, archiving, interpreting, tracing, and validating.

It's a huge task.

I'll debunk one claim here and now. Though this book's subtitle claims it to be a "complete" guide to urban legends, it would clearly be impossible to include every variant of every legend ever passed through the grapevine. In the time it took to write this volume, I added nearly as many new and unique legends to my hoard of stories! What I have tried to do is present a good selection of almost every *type* of legend. Here are tales that began as true stories from which, after years of retelling, the original details have fallen by the wayside. There are tales of warning as well as of humor, horror, the down-to-earth, and the supernatural. Tales that sprang to life full blown sit side by side with those that evolved over decades.

The content categories included in this volume cover those most popular in the field: sex tales, corporate tales, celebrity tales, and more. Some of the legends will be familiar to you. If a tale is a true classic, I've attempted to reproduce it in its most stable form—and thrown in a few of the most interesting variants for comparison. Because legends are mutable, you'll inevitably run into tales you recognize in part, but with twists and turns, complications and simplifications completely new to you.

The demands of fitting more than four hundred tales between these covers meant dispensing with the extensive footnotes and citations that are some folklorists' bit of heaven here on earth. In most cases I've provided enough material within the text to let researchers track down anything that particularly catches their eye. Everything else is available by request; simply drop me a note in care of my publisher, and I'll be delighted to pass along all the citations you might want.

In the case of legal references and medical records, you may find it more convenient, and faster, to go directly to the source. Though many incidents, such as the continuing efforts of the Procter & Gamble company to escape their legendary association with satanism, are well documented in the popular press, the real action (i.e., the rebuttals and legal arguments) is contained in court transcripts—which are publicly available.

Hundreds of medical journal articles were reviewed for this book in a search for underlying incidents that might have inspired a particular legend, or spurred an existing legend on to new heights. While I thank the staff of the Health Sciences Center's Medical Library for helping me round them up, those of you with access to the Internet can track down brief references through an online database called MedLine, and, through an associated service, obtain complete copies of many articles. These journal pieces, naturally, conceal the names of the patients, but will provide time-and-place information and other details, including the name of the author, usually the recording physician. (Ironically, the traditional urban legend is full of names, but light on time-and-place details!)

Throughout this volume, I've endeavored to make a clear separation between urban legends that may contain the names of real individuals and firms, and real-life incidents upon which a legend might be based. Not only is this an important issue from a legal and ethical standpoint, but from a folkloric viewpoint as well. In the final chapter of this book are a number of urban legends that have grown up around the fast-food industry. While it might be possible to tell any of these tales without naming any specific fast-food operator, it would also undermine the tales themselves.

Take, for example, any two tales of restaurants who served up cockroaches to their patrons. Without detail, the stories are simply gross and easy to dismiss the next time you go for takeout. If, however, story after story combines cockroaches with Taco Bell, then a storytelling pattern begins to emerge. A folklorist sensitive to the urban-legend tradition of associating cultural icons might well conclude that Taco Bell and cockroaches became linked in the public mind through a "south of the border" connection. Since cockroaches in food qualifies as an "invasion" tale, the next step in the interpretation process might well be to conclude that Taco Bell has been targeted as the star in this particular urban legend *because* a specific part of the legend's audience believes America itself is being invaded by "south of the border" people and/or culture.

Without including the name of the restaurant actually attached to the urban legend, no cultural study of the popular tale is possible.

Of course, relating an urban legend without identifying it as a legend would be an equally serious breach of responsible reporting, so, throughout this text, recognize that, *unless otherwise noted,* you are reading urban legends—stories that, although set in our time, with players that might well be real, the tales themselves are fictitious.

Are they lies, then?

No.

They are accurate printed representations of legends. The person who leans closer to her girlfriend on a Monday morning to relate the latest story heard in the bar the preceding Saturday night isn't trying to perpetuate a lie. She may actively believe the story, for all the reasons we've already explored. She may half-believe the tale. The adage "where there's smoke, there's fire" explains much of the mechanisms by which urban legends are passed along. If a story is repeated frequently enough, even the most implausible story can begin to take on a sheen of authenticity.

And don't we still tell our children that a tortoise's industry can overcome a hare's braggadocio?

Because we're liars?

Because we believe it?

Or because some part of us *wishes* it were true?

CRAZY LITTLE THANG CALLED SEX!

t heart, we're voyeurs. We love photographs; they let us stare at each other without getting caught. Water-cooler gossip about our co-workers delights us. Our neighbors' troubles invite us to press our ears against their walls. Their improprieties provide us with that wickedly sinful sense of moral justification as we peer into their lives—and yet another opportunity to pass along the tales of their falls from grace!

In light of the many taboos we've created about sex, it's no wonder nearly half of all urban legends, with their blatant moral warnings, feature the sexual antics of those around us. The more bizarre the story, the better—and the more persistent. Which explains why there aren't any urban legends about happily married couples who prefer the missionary position and live quietly in Ann Arbor!

No, what titillates us are tales of men substituting Hoover vacuums for living partners, couples caught in *flagrante delicto,* governments trying to legislate the state of our bedrooms as well as the union, women who *eat* contraceptive jelly, and the conundrum posed by the pregnancy of a woman without a vagina.

You'll find them all in the following stories.

Settle in, enjoy your sinful secret pleasure in the full knowledge that even though this section will come to an end, almost every urban legend has some tinge of sexual naughtiness.

ONE IS SUCH A LONELY NUMBER

Molière said, "If every man was born with a wife, every man would be a genius."

Not a believer in the adage that "behind every good man there's a better woman," the playwright simply bemoaned the time we humans waste pursuing love and sexual pleasure. Unfortunately, at least from Molière's viewpoint, most of us will spend ten years searching for Mr. or Ms. Right, investing in our carnal instincts all the time we might have devoted to philosophy or higher mathematics.

Urban legends, however, provide a third option for those who aren't willing to wait for that special someone and who just haven't the knack for calculus or navel contemplation. In one of the best-known sexual urban legends (certainly the most repeated locker-room tale), "Hot Dog," one young woman, tired of staring into her tub of Rocky Road ice cream while *Ally McBeal* moaned away on the tube, eyed something that looked, well, *sort* of phallic in the freezer. We won't go too deeply into her inner musings here, but it wasn't long before she'd abandoned her ice cream and, instead, taken a frozen hot dog back to her bedroom instead!

Most of us shudder at the thought of such a cold bedmate; this young woman, however, became so excited, and her thrashings so agitated, that she cracked off the wiener, losing her grasp on the upper half, which later, to her total embarrassment, had to be removed by a giggling emergency-room staff!

The moral is obvious: Do the socially/sexually unacceptable and get publically humiliated.

Variations on this story, reflecting our changing view of what's socially acceptable, do little more than up the ick-factor or the victim's level of humiliation. In some versions, she's discovered by friends or parents in mid-act. In another, the doctor who examines her turns out to be the guy she was fantasizing about while plying her hot dog. Gross-out renditions lose the wiener up her anus instead, or return it to the freezer—only to have it eaten by her roommate!

This legend rattled around middle schools for decades as just another harmless story before coming to the media forefront when

hooker, n., a person who engages in sexual activity for pay, a prostitute. Though the term is frequently associated with general "Fighting Joe" Hooker, who commanded the Army of the Potomac in 1863, "hooker" was in general use some twenty-five years earlier, and according to *The New York Public Library Book of Popular Americana*, the term originally arose in 1840 for prostitutes working in the Hook, a red light section of New York City.

© Peter/Ngaire Genge, 1999

Who knew the corner market was a secret sex shop?

parents of "Jane Doe" brought suit against a school counselor in the Petaluma, California, City School District. Their daughter had become the target of persistent and vocal rumors that she *was* the girl in the legend. Though there's absolutely no medical evidence that the hot-dog incident ever took place, in Petaluma or anywhere, the city of Petaluma settled the case for $250,000 in Jane Doe's favor in 1996, and inadvertently sent the tale off on yet another round of repetition by appearing in high-circulation magazines and papers like the *Los Angeles Times*.

Though sexually degrading urban legends usually cast women as the victim, these tales also reflect our current society, adapting to the times. Beginning in the early

1980s, tales of men caught in some lonely activity, and rushed to emergency rooms across the globe, began circulating.

If anything, these were told with even *more* glee than the forerunners featuring women, and the cross-your-legs-in-sympathy factor went absolutely off the charts.

In 1991 a Michigan State University senior was talking to his girlfriend in Toronto when she retold, with considerable relish, the case of a man in Detroit who'd decided to dabble in exotic masturbation aids by performing with a piece of spaghetti slipped into his penis. The lad evidently forgot that uncooked spaghetti is incredibly brittle or wasn't aware that it would, under rough handling, shatter into dozens of pieces! It was

THE VIBRATOR

While the modern electric vibrator is seen as something women order from Sears "for back pain relief" when its real purpose is clearly as a sexual toy, it has, according to Rachel Maines and others, a place in medical history. Used for "vulvular massage to orgasm," it was a serious tool in the physician's black bag for the treatment of "hysteria in females." The "hysterical paroxysms" it created were believed to short-circuit nervous indispositions, leaving the patient considerably more "calm and relaxed."

perhaps inevitable, at least in the realm of urban legend, where the naughty are always punished, that he would end up the brunt of many guffaws at the nearest emergency room.

While "Spaghetti Man" makes a fine water-cooler tale as is, women enjoyed some vindication when it was revealed that, unlike the hot-dog tale, the spaghetti story was *true*! It had even been written up in the prestigious *American Journal of Forensic Medical Pathology*'s September 1986 edition!

Whether men or women are the stars, the variations on this group of tales include an incredible smorgasbord of objects and locations substituted for hot dogs and spaghetti, and while veracity isn't necessary for any urban legend, it's amazing how many of these old chestnuts trace back to well-documented medical cases or are instances of legends coming true after the fact.

The legend of the woman who developed an affection for Coke bottles has circulated since the product first hit shelves, but it received a considerable boost when the *American Journal of Obstetrics and Gynecology* reported the case of a nineteen-year-old woman who'd been carrying a bottle cap around in her vagina for years! (The cap was removed after it perforated the vaginal wall and worked its way into her abdomen. This woman recovered completely, unlike the later urban-legend star of this story, who died. In the legend, the bottle cap was discovered at autopsy.)

All ages are well represented, as "One Banana, Two Bananas" proves. Two elderly widows who frequented Lar's Fruit and Vegetable Market in St. John's, Newfoundland, arrived for their weekly shopping trip. One woman ordered a bunch of firm bananas; the other ordered only one and was miffed when the proprietor didn't offer her a bag in which to carry it home.

"But, ma'am," he protested, "one banana? Who orders one banana if they don't intend to eat it now?"

The woman flushed furiously, demanded her bag, and slammed out of the store.

The fruit vendor looked at her companion in puzzlement.

"Well," says the other woman, "Elsie's not been a widow *that* long."

In another version, Lar is dispensing cucumbers. (This while the government was promoting a heavily subsidized—and ultimately unsuccessful—greenhouse enterprise specializing in cucumbers, a marginal seller in this market.) The cucumber tale, which poked fun at both the government and sexually frustrated old women, would, in this region, later bump into another old saw (well, at least as old as disco) in which a young man hoping to attract attention at the local discotheque rolls up a sock, washcloth, or whatever and stuffs it into the crotch of his Travolta-tight trousers to give the impression of being incredibly endowed.

Unfortunately for him, he slips on the dance floor, knocks himself out, and, while being cared for by paramedics at the scene, has his bulge revealed for the exotic object it is. In the days of Newfoundland's Sprung Greenhouse Project, the sock becomes—what else?—a cucumber!

Perhaps it's because some human beings seem capable of viewing almost anything as suitable for insertion in their genitalia (how *did* that guy manage to end up with the butt end of a partially melted candle in his bladder?) that these types of legends never die out. If there are true cases like that of the doctor who, while attempting to complete a patient's yearly Pap smear, discovered an aerosol can lid blocking the way are reported in such prestigious works as the *International Journal of Gynaecology and Obstetrics* (February 1996), who's to say

fuck, v., to engage in genital sexual activity. Figuring out the origin of this word is something of a process of elimination. We know what it *doesn't* mean. It doesn't stand for "Fornication Under Consent of the King" or "For Unlawful Carnal Knowledge." Both of these meanings have been suggested, but neither phrase predates 1503, to which the *Oxford English Dictionary* traces the first written sighting. As words generally exist for some time in oral form before turning up in writing—especially so when writing was a less common skill—this word may well have roots in the 1400s or earlier, perhaps in Old German, *focken,* to poke, or *ficken,* to strike. Part of the difficulty in following the word's route through time and geography relates to the social prohibition against putting it in writing. Until 1961 it was a restricted word that could not be printed with all four letters (no f*ck or f#ck) in any British Commonwealth publication.

that someone's friend of a friend *didn't* hear about it from her friend, who told . . .

Then again, it may be that real cases only spur urban legends to new heights, pushing our envelope of acceptability. Prior to 1970, the majority of odd-sexual-toy-lost-in-body-cavity tales were restricted to the vagina and, more rarely, the penis. Then, with gender equalization, the roles were distributed almost evenly between men and women. Most of the old tales received new, gender-opposite revivals—and quickly became stale. It seemed the time was ripe for a higher level of shock value and, of course, along came a new stream of urban legends to fill the gap—the *other* gap. Suddenly the rectum became star, and new urban legends took a darker, all too evidently homophobic, turn.

Previous urban legends, like those detailed here, seldom resulted in even imaginary individuals coming to lasting harm. While embarrassment and a certain amount of physical discomfort was meted out to anyone who strayed from society's public code of normalcy, the punishment was seen as fitting the crime. With the outing of America's gay community (Europe's outing made few if any urban-legend ripples), tales grew grimmer.

The urban legend of a girl hitchhiking, without her parents' consent, to a party with older kids, usually ends with the girl later discovering she'd taken a ride with an escaped convict and being so terrified that she vows never to hitch again. The tale's victim is never actually *hurt*. Not so in the hor-

rific tale of the young *man* who, also hitchhiking without his parents' consent to a party with older kids, is picked up by a gay trucker.

In one version the guy is left, tied hand and foot, on the side of the road with a wheel wrench protruding from his rectum to proclaim his "taken" status for anyone too stunned to figure it out any other way. In later versions, the youth dies of his injuries. This is a vastly different scenario, depicting a degree of violence that was unusual in such tales just a few years earlier.

Even when the first wave of homophobia was smothered by public censure, rectal tales, usually featuring single gay men who, through the lack of a partner or fear of AIDS infection, chose to keep their sexual activities to themselves, continued to make the rounds. Not content simply to adopt the already existing tales, a whole new set featuring new objects and fetishes, clearly more exotic than those favored by their heterosexual neighbors—straight hadn't already proven they were weird—sprang up.

The most bizarre tale by far contended that gay men, desperate for some sort of companionship, were resorting to an obscure practice called "gerbilling," in which the warm, furry body of a live gerbil was tucked inside the rectum—a sort of living vibrator! Cranking up the shock level was easy; just attach the story to whichever celebrity admitted to being gay—or to whichever celebrity society deemed most in need of being dragged down off his pedestal.

Needless to say, despite the rash of such incidents being reported around the world, not a single case was ever substantiated or reported in the reliable literature.

Lots of other things, however, *were* being lost and found in rectums, thus ensuring the continuous spread of gay-fearing tales. Harking back to the toolbox theme, screwdrivers were prominently featured; one case was even reported in a Bulgarian journal, *Khirurgilia* (1977), on the same day a large gay-rights march was making headlines back in the States. Barbie dolls, those icons of heterosexual adoration, required extraction on a regular basis, according to locker-room gossip, but, again, no leads panned out and it quickly became apparent that this was an urban legend of the usual sort—completely untraceable and unattributable.

Cases that could be pointed to with reasonable certainty, such as that of the sixty-seven-year-old man who presented himself to his local emergency room with not only a bottle lost in his rectum but the coat hanger he'd used in an attempt to dislodge it (*Australian and New Zealand Journal of Surgery*), inspired dozens of spin-offs that inevitably induced the person hearing the tale to dig out his latest "gay joke," as these lost-in-the-back-alley stories were being called.

And any story that combined the perception of homosexual frustration with one of society's more prevalent and immediate problems, such as drug abuse, flew through college campuses and over back fences

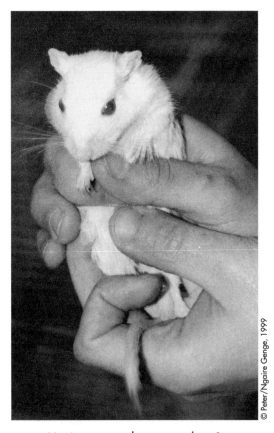

© Peter/Ngaire Genge, 1999

You're gonna shove me *where?*

before you could say, "Well, I have this friend, and he said . . ." Such was certainly the case when everyone began repeating the story of the gay man who, in his search for ever-more-exotic sensations, injected cocaine into his penis while masturbating. Depending on who told it, the unfortunate fellow immediately found himself with a permanent or recurring erection so painful he stumbled around for an entire night (or day or week) until the throbbing agony drove him to a hospital. Paltry embarrassment isn't a sufficiently disastrous ending to this tale. No, it ends when medical workers, on removing the man's trousers and hearing a thud near their feet, discover his penis has fallen off!

It wasn't until some time later that further, more conscientious investigations revealed that both the Bulgarian with the tool fetish and the elderly but inventive man who was now short a coat hanger were both *straight*!

The real roots of the "Lost Penis" didn't hurt the gay community, either. According to doctors at New York Hospital, both men and women, gay and straight, have been known to rub cocaine on their genitals, where the thin skin allows the drug to penetrate easily, much as the mucous membranes of the nose and throat do. The case that became so mangled in its numerous retellings was based on the experiences of a thirty-four-year-old New York City man whose priapism, the technical term for his permanent erection, began immediately after intercourse with his *girl-friend*! Gangrene in his extremities set in over the following week as a result of blood clots throughout his legs, genitals, arms, chest, and back, resulting in the loss of not only his penis but both legs as well as nine fingers. The incident, in reality, had no basis in homosexuality or exotic masturbation.

Perhaps the revelation that, even in the land of urban legends, straight folk are as lonely, or inventive, as gay folk explains why these next few legends are historically free of any reference to sexual orientation, or any real male-female gender bias. Or maybe it's because, unlike the previous legends, which focused on

things getting lost inside people, these next few relate tales of people getting stuck inside . . . well, you'll see. And there are, after all, only so many bits of human anatomy that can get stuck in anything else, right?

One urban legend out of Tokyo, "The Happy Sun Company," featured a lonely young man who limped into work for nearly a week before his boss was convinced the man was ill enough to leave work and see a doctor. You see, if the worker missed time, the supervisor had to fill out a report on the physical reason for absence—a reason the employee seemed curiously unwilling to provide.

The first day, Monday, he told his boss his illness was caused by a change in his diet.

The next day he said that he was sure his difficulty arose from the milk he'd drunk over the weekend.

By midweek his supervisor was beginning to have concerns about public health, and insisted the man identify the source of his milk. The employee couldn't say; all he knew was that the milk was being delivered in different bottles than previously.

On Thursday the employee reported that the milk came from the Happy Sun Company, but that he was sure there was nothing wrong with the milk itself. Confused by the contradiction between the employee's condition, by now pale, sweating, and limping, which he claimed stemmed from his new milk company, and the man's conviction that he hadn't contracted food poisoning, he suggested the employee see the company nurse. The employee refused, and insisted on seeing his own physician. Still not sure what to write on his form, the supervisor sent the man back to work if he wouldn't see the company's nurse.

On Friday morning the employee staggered into work and promptly collapsed. All things made sense when, on arrival at—you guessed it—the local emergency room, the doctor on call found the employee's dark and swollen penis stuck firmly inside the neck of a milk bottle with "Happy Sun Company" written on the side.

The quarter-inch-narrower opening of the new bottles had gone unremarked by the employee until it was too late.

Although no one knows for sure if this story has any factual basis at all—after all, Japanese employees are no less likely to make fun of their paper-bound supervisors than any other employees—it is true that, about the time this story circulated, a report in *Hinyokika Kiyo* (1988) related the case of a thirty-eight-year-old male patient who'd suffered an incarcerated penis inside a milk bottle for some seventeen hours before seeking help. It was reviewed as one of *fifty-seven* similar cases across Japan.

Maybe people really don't notice downsizing in packaging.

It may be only coincidence that shortly after the release of Stephen King's *Firestarter,* at least to judge by urban legends related to the phenomenon, a significant number of men suddenly developed the desire to get intimately friendly with motorized equipment of various types. No less eminent sources than *European Urology* (1980) and the *British Journal of Urology* (1985) claim that "36 cases of 'vacuum cleaner injuries' to the penis" were reported, with some so severe as to include the complete "loss of the glans penis." For the ultimate in do-it-yourself, there's the case of the machinist who, during his lunch hours when all his chums were away, habitually masturbated by rubbing his penis over the drive belt of some machine. While deeply engrossed in the feelings thus engendered, he failed to realize he'd swayed closer to the contraption than usual. Everything came to a sudden halt when his scrotum was yanked between the drive belt and one of its guide wheels.

Expecting the usual "and his embarrassment was made complete by having to present his torn scrotum at the local clinic" sort of ending?

Well, not just yet.

No, first he performed his own bit of field surgery, deftly stapling the tear together before resuming work at his usual time. However, in life as in legend, things seldom go smoothly and, yes, several days later, complaining of "male problems," he did seek real, licensed medical assistance. The physician was amazed to discover eight staples in the ugly mass that had developed in the intervening days; the machinist was amazed to discover that sometime during the accident, his left testicle had been snipped off and was evidently lost somewhere in the shop!

The case, written up in the July 1991 issue of *Medical Aspects of Human Sexuality,* has served as a cautionary tale, both in its true form and in the numerous folkloric renditions (how exactly you could up the shock- or ick-factor on this one is difficult to imagine, but, I'm informed, it includes a cat and a startled vet) ever since.

And how do these cases of mechanical mayhem and sexual accident relate to Stephen King? Well, according to yet another urban legend, it was King's image of the crazy psychiatrist, dressed in women's underwear, having sexual thoughts about his garbage disposal unit, and eventually killing himself by jamming one of his own body parts into the under-the-sink appliance, that inspired all the sexual-mechanic fantasies, and thereby the injuries, that followed. Neither the abovementioned machinist nor the domestically inclined men of Great Britain and Europe were available for comment on that one!

Considering that the most robust sexual legend of 1943 seems to have been the claim that Errol Flynn, already famous for being charged with two counts of statutory rape the previous year (now you know what "in like Flynn" really means!), had played a solo version of either "The Star-Spangled Banner" or "America the Beautiful" on a xylophone using his penis instead of a hammer, the only safe assumption to make about

sexual-antics-for-one urban legends is that the modern trend *isn't* toward boring!

A LITTLE SOMETHING ON THE SIDE

Remember that straight couple in Michigan? The one no one ever writes about? These next stories aren't about them, either, but you can probably see them nodding sagely and casting glances at their neighbors from the corners of their eyes as these tales prove that gettin' 'em ain't the same as keepin' 'em! *They* saw the plumber at Kittle Fistle's yesterday, oh yeah, and last Friday too!

Just as dozens of stories warn us not to "play with it," dozens more predict our fall into the pit of humiliation if, having been blessed with one loyal, wonderful partner, we seek to exceed societally imposed limits by having a little extramarital activity, too.

One of the oldest urban legends says people shouldn't be expected to adhere to all that "cleave only unto one another" stuff, anyway. After all, how many minutes after uttering those words are the bride and groom put on display in the receiving line, where every Tom, Dick, and Raoul in the place thinks it's perfectly acceptable to kiss the bride? And as Tom, Dick, and Raoul will assert, didn't all the nobility once have the right to more than a kiss on a bride's wedding night?

Historic legend has it that Edward I of England, in particular, enforced the *jus pri-*

mae noctis, his right to have the bride first on her wedding night, with particular zeal—as did Charles II (whose court inventor, Earl of Condom, is sometimes falsely linked to an invention of the same name), James I, and William of Orange, depending on who's doing the telling. Several of the French kings named Louis, as well as Charlemagne and an assortment of Scottish lairds, also famously exercised their royal prerogative.

A number of books, films, poems, and purported histories have either perpetuated the claim or been put forward as proof that the custom was firmly entrenched in our cultural and, by extension, societal consciousness. The film *Braveheart* suggests that Edward I proclaimed the practice as law in his efforts to demoralize the Scots.

Modern-day Lotharios—those who can read, anyway—will, however, soon discover their fantasies have little, if any, basis in fact.

The claim against Edward I falls flat on even the scantiest review of his reign. Proclamations and the adoption of laws were the sorts of things that tended to get recorded, even then, and while all of Edward I's other legal *faux pas* are archived in loving detail, no one has ever discovered any *jus primae noctis* clauses anywhere.

Further careful research would reveal that in the few cases where such laws may have been enacted, mostly in France, the intent was to leverage extra monies out of underlings, not to satisfy an affair of the heart.

So, with the gas let out of the historical-precedent argument, other, more modern urban legends can feel themselves all the more justified in humiliating the erring lovers of their tales.

A PEEK IN THE SHOWER

Guys have been eyeing one another from the corners of their eyes in showers since they were first told to wear pants. Curiosity being as human as lust, everyone wants to know how they stack up. Now you won't have to peek!

The average erect penis is how long?

Six inches. Almost every man on the planet falls into the five- to seven-inch range.

And the biggest would be?

If the data from all reliable studies is included, the longest erect penis measured was 12⅞ inches.

Has anyone ever measured the amount of semen per ejaculation?

Yes, about a teaspoonful.

Has anyone ever measured the velocity of semen?

Yes, 45 kph (28 mph).

One of the oldest, "Backseat Lovers," runs something like this:

Somewhere in England (it's almost always England, because the English have the smallest cars), a woman and her extramarital lover were desperately trying to make do with the limited space inside her MG when suddenly the man freezes and stares, horrified, into his lover's eyes.

"You'll never believe it, luv, but I've thrown out me back! I can't move!"

Discovering that neither of them can free themselves from the tiny car's tight confines, the woman squirms about under her heavier partner until she can press her foot against the horn and signal for help.

When the police arrive, they can't get the man out of the car, and they, in turn, send for the fire department, which notifies the hospital, which sends an ambulance. All these people are in excellent positions to watch as the fire department uses the Jaws of Life to remove the roof of the car, revealing its naked passengers in their compromising situation.

The most gentlemanly member of the group wraps the woman in a raincoat as her lover is carted away on the stretcher. So far gone is the woman's sense of propriety, however, that when one of the paramedics hurries over to assure her that her partner will be all right, she ignores him and simply wails, "So what? What do I tell my husband about the car?"

While many people, including couples, have been freed from cars on both sides of the Atlantic, tracing a true story that includes the skeleton of this legend proves difficult.

One may have occurred in Canada in 1967 when a honeymooning couple decided to celebrate the country's centennial as well as their wedding by driving from coast to coast. Just outside Winnipeg, their two-door car slid off a wide turn during a thunderburst and ended up on its side in a ditch. The couple were basically unhurt but couldn't get the topside door to open and were forced to wait an unusually long time for firefighters to arrive. The unseasonable weather had caused other accidents, and their situation was deemed the least urgent.

According to Constable George Thistle, who was the first on the scene, the couple took the wait in good humor, with the new groom assuring everyone present he was sure he could "find something to do" until help arrived.

The new groom in the "Plumber Legend" wasn't nearly as sanguine when the plumber, called in to unclog a persistently troublesome toilet, began pulling large numbers of used condoms from the drain. In fact, the plumber explained that it wasn't a good idea to dispose of them in this way, he couldn't understand the man's growing anger and agitation. "Sir, it's just that each time you flush, water fills the condoms, they swell, and block your drain."

"I can see that!"

"Well, sir, then there's nothing to worry about. As long as you don't throw them in there, you should have no further problems."

Could you buy them from your date's father?

He stopped as the man's face turned almost purple. "Sir? Is something wrong?"

"You bet there is! *I* don't use condoms!"

Oops.

That's the end of the story in most versions, but a few add a cuckold-seeks-revenge twist. After the man confronts his wife, she admits her guilt and implicates the milkman or the meter reader or the oil deliveryman as her lover. The enraged husband kills the lover, and, in you-ought-not-seek-revenge style, discovers the man he's killed is just filling in for the usual provider!

This, like the one about the couple stuck in the car, appears to be an honest-to-goodness, spontaneously arising, and endlessly repeated urban legend. Some works of fiction have incorporated the plotline, but this usage postdates the oral tradition, which, without the discovery-of-a-substitute

ending, is recorded in the private diary of Ellen Constable as being "heard at the table" during an evening out in 1945.

Constable's version does, however, have an interesting prequel to the story, in which one man is reading the warning leaflet from inside the condom packet to his wife. He notes two important items: "Do not puncture!" and "Do not flush!" It's at this point in the story that the second man begins the tale of the plumber and the clogged drain.

Condom jokes weren't just about the married man looking to get a bit on the side without being caught by the little woman. At about the same time, servicemen were returning home from the war to settle down, and were rediscovering the new latex condoms that were being perfected just before they went off to Europe, and another cautionary condom tale was making the rounds.

In this one, a young man, nervous while making his first condom purchase, adopts a braggadocio attitude, speaking loudly of how he is definitely going to "get some" tonight.

The druggist's attempts to point out the warnings on the side of the box are brushed off with claims of having "used plenty" and the declaration that everything would be just fine as long as they were the right size—the implication, of course, being big enough, not small enough.

He finally breezes out into the night, goes home to attend to his appearance—and read the instructions on packaging he's never actually seen before!

He arrives promptly at his blind date's home, but never does find out what his date might have looked like. The man who answers his knock, the young woman's father, is none other than the druggist!

Gender-switched versions of the tales sprang up during the 1960s and early 1970s, when birth-control pills gave women the same sexual freedom as men, and the relationship motto was no longer "till death do us part," but "love the one you're with."

CAUGHT IN THE ACT

Whether married, single, alone, gay, or straight, the ultimate sexual horror story would, for most people, include being caught in the act. According to a 1998 Heath and Melville survey in United States high schools, the most commonly reported nightmare among adolescent males was being caught naked, or in nothing but their underwear, by some authority figure. Mothers, teachers, ministers, and "peer group leaders" topped the list, and it's no surprise that scads of urban legends revolve around the many ways, likely or unlikely, that those old nightmares might come true.

Some are subtle, like "The Case of the Missing Clock" (a.k.a. "The Case of the Missing Gravy Ladle" and "The Case of the Missing Egg Timer"). In this one, a young couple, call them Jill and Jim, are living together but trying to maintain the illusion, at least for their parents, their grandparents, or their parents' friends, that they're nothing more than roomies.

They go to some fairly elaborate extremes to support their story. Each has a separate room with his or her things scattered about. His room doesn't even have what most couples would consider a basic necessity for cohabitation—a double bed. Both keep their clothes in their own sections of the apartment. Even their toiletries are kept in their rooms so as not to suggest any sort of intimacy by bumping up next to each other on the bathroom counter!

Parents, however, were once as young as their children and aren't easily fooled by such shenanigans, so, when Jill's mother comes to visit one afternoon, she's impressed more by the couple's attitudes to one another than by their decor. Still, she allows herself to be led about without question, merely commenting on what a lovely apartment they have, and stopping to admire a particularly elegant clock displayed in Jim's room. The couple sighs with relief when Jill's mother later leaves without asking any embarrassing questions.

A few days later, however, Jim notices that his clock, the one Jill's mother had been so obviously taken with, is missing! Neither of them have seen it since the visit.

Though it goes against the grain to believe her mother could steal anything, Jill is eventually forced to concede that no one else was in a position to take it. Reluctantly she calls her mother, and eventually gets around to "Do you remember Jim's clock?"

"Why, yes, it was lovely."

"Um, you didn't happen to . . . move it, did you? It's just that we can't find it."

The conversation trails off into miserable silence until her mother, not sounding in the least embarrassed, responds, "Of course, dear, but I'd have thought he'd have found it by now. I hid it in the middle of his bed!"

The beauty of this tale, of course, is that Jill endures all the embarrassment of being caught in the act, and her mother enjoys all the wicked thrill of proving she still knows a thing or two about love and lust without ever having to actually catch her daughter in the act!

Not all urban legends end so cleverly, however, and depend on the classic elements of farce and situation comedy to reduce the hapless victim to a quivering ball of embarrassment. In fact, many of these legends have found their way into sitcoms such as *I Love Lucy, Three's Company, Mad About You,* and *Will and Grace.*

Few young couples, especially those living at home, wouldn't take advantage of an evening alone at home for a little heavy petting, or more. "The Surprise Party" takes this natural tendency one step further by introducing us to a young woman, Margie, and her boyfriend, Robert, then leaving them alone in Margie's house by the simple expedient of sending her father off on a weekend business trip with her mother along to keep him company. Her parents' only regret is that they'll miss being with Margie on her birthday that Friday night, but, they promise, they'll make it up to her when they get back with a nice adult-type dinner out.

Margie, as she waves good-bye to her parents from the porch, is already working out an adult scenario for her birthday, and before her folks are around the corner, she's on the phone to invite her (not entirely suitable and therefore unknown to the parents) boyfriend over for the evening.

Well, one thing leads to another, and just as the couple manages to get rid of their clothes and start some serious petting on Margie's bed, the phone rings. It's her parents.

Margie doesn't let any guilt into her voice as she calmly listens to her mother explain that she's afraid she left the iron on downstairs. Would Margie run down and turn it off? Sure, no problem and, yes, everything's just fine.

As Margie is anticipating a quick return to her warm bed, she doesn't bother dressing for her dash downstairs. Neither does Robert, who chases after her. They're both giggling as they stumble down the steep basement stairs—right up to the point when Margie switches on the light to find the iron and discovers . . .

The basement is decked with balloons, streamers, and "Happy Birthday!" banners.

A huge cake and a veritable pile of presents are on a table center stage.

Music suddenly blares from a hidden speaker.

And in the second between flicking the switch and seeing all her friends and her parents jump out from behind the furniture, Margie realizes she's about to attend her surprise birthday party in her birthday suit!

As if to rub salt in the wound, many versions of "The Surprise Party" aren't satisfied with Margie's complete humiliation. One adds physical misery to her emotional trauma by having her so scared she falls down the stairs and breaks her arm (thus necessitating an emergency run to the hospital in nothing but her father's coat); another has her boyfriend taking off, leaving her to face the music alone; yet another particularly nasty one has the boyfriend *pushing* her down the stairs and breaking her arm as he hurtles toward the nearest door!

A neat reversal of "The Surprise Party" is found in "Trailer Tango." Ralph and Madge, a middle-aged couple with three children, take the kids on one of their favorite excursions, a camping trip to a nearby national park. The weather isn't with them this time, though, and, instead of a couple of days of freedom running around outside, everyone is trapped together inside the camper trailer by rain.

When the sky finally clears, Ralph and Madge happily send the kids off with their fishing poles and, as adults sometimes do when the kids are safely occupied elsewhere, engage in a little afternoon delight. Unfortunately, the bright spell is short-lived, and even harder rainfall sends the kids racing back to the trailer just as a heavy gust of wind flips the tent free, exposing their amorous parents to kids, neighboring campers, and any wandering bears!

A less innocent story, "Nothing But His Socks," features all the usual elements of the caught-in-the-act tales, but ups the naughtiness factor by moving past teenagers in the exploratory stages and happily married couples with bad timing, to casting a married man, George, as the leading character and his lovely secretary, not his wife, as the supporting lady.

One evening after a particularly long day, George's secretary suggests he stop by her place for a bite to eat and a drink before heading out on his long drive to suburbia. At first, anticipating exactly what was offered, he follows her home with nary a sexual thought in his head. On arriving at the apartment, however, she gives him a secretive little smile and immediately slips into the bedroom to "get into something more comfortable first."

Left alone in the living room, and sure that his most erotic fantasies are about to come true, George starts ripping off his clothes! He's down to nothing but his socks when his secretary, his wife, his kids, and all the other staff and partners from his office sally forth carrying presents and cake to help him celebrate the twenty-fifth wedding anniversary he'd evidently forgotten!

Oddly, in these days of sexual equality, the gender-reversed version of this tale, "Come and Get It!," re-creates the entire surprise-party scenario, even exceeding the already high level of humiliation, but it completely eliminates the adulterous component.

A Christian fundamentalist couple is about to celebrate their wedding anniversary. He's planned a big surprise party; she's planned a sexy evening at home—a real rarity. Obviously, neither tells the other of their intentions. As the husband is downstairs helping all the guests hide, the unknowing wife takes extra time with her shower and preparations, dabbing a little perfume here and there and planning her entrance. She smiles a wicked little smile as she imagines the surprise on her husband's face.

Of course, as in all urban legends, the surprise goes the other way when, standing at the top of the stairs, completely naked except for her perfume and a smile, she calls out, "Come and get it!" just as her husband flicks on the lights downstairs!

A cruder version suggests that her actual words were, "Come and get it *while it's clean*!"

Perhaps it's the pervasiveness of the caught-in-the-act tales—it's possible to find versions featuring every imaginable relationship—that lead to "The Hairdresser's Dilemma," a sort of anti-caught-in-the-act tale, unique in that it's the only well-known tale where the *catcher* is caught out!

It all begins in a little town in Missouri, in a small beauty salon that seldom deals with male customers. It is just about to close, only one hairdresser still working, when an elderly man pokes his head in and asks if he can have a quick cut. He has a job interview first thing in the morning, and the barbershop has already closed. Nervous about being in the shop, alone, after hours, with a male client, the hairdresser hems and haws a little. The man, however, looks so innocent and so earnest that she eventually puts aside her fears and waved him inside.

She washes and conditions his hair, then drapes a cloth over him to protect his clothes from flying hair. As she is about to begin, she notices that, under the cape, in his lap, his hands are moving in a rhythmic fashion, back and forth, back and forth, back and forth.

Her previous fears return with a rush and with a scream of "Dirty old man!" she whacks him in the head with her blow dryer, knocking him unconscious!

She's still shaking when police and ambulance personnel respond to her frantic 911 call. Its mortification, not fear, though, that assails her moments later when paramedics pull the cape aside to attend to the unconscious man and discover his handkerchief and his glasses sitting in his lap, where he'd been cleaning them under the cape!

Speaking of capes, the release of *Batman* and all its sequels regularly resurrects one of the most visually compelling caught-in-the-act legends of all time, "The Lover and the Caped Crusader."

A perfectly ordinary couple, perhaps those two from Ann Arbor, are sitting out on their porch one evening, probably sipping home-made lemonade, when bloodcurdling screams cut the night air. The woman races for the phone to notify police while her hus-band, trusty baseball bat in hand, runs across the yard to the next-door neighbors. As the screams continue, he wastes no time breaking into the house and racing upstairs.

There, in the master bedroom, tied naked to the bed, is the lady of the house. On the floor beside her, a masked man is slowly lift-ing himself to his feet. Taking in the scene at a glance, the neighbor bashes the masked intruder. Much to his surprise, instead of relieving the woman, she screams all the louder! When she begins crying and babbling hysterically, he quickly grabs a blanket and drapes it over her naked body.

"Hey, okay, it'll be okay. The police are on their way. Nothing else can happen to you now."

Just then the man groans and once more tries to get to his knees.

An old-fashioned roundhouse punch puts the assailant down just as the woman starts screaming madly. The police burst into the room. Behind them, his wife peers cautiously around the doorway. She's the one who finally notices, and thinks to comment on, the fact that the man they're about to hand-cuff and drag away is wearing not only a mask but a Batman cape and black tights!

Everything stops for a second, just long enough for the woman on the bed to gasp, "Don't hurt him! That's my *husband*!"

Before the tale winds to its torturous end, the woman is forced to reveal that she and her husband often incorporate a little fantasy role-playing in their lovemaking. On this occa-sion her husband had tied her to the bed, slipped into his costume, climbed atop the dresser, and launched himself toward the bed, re-creating the save-the-captured-maiden scenario with himself as the hero. Unfortunately, he'd failed to allow for the arc of his flight, and, instead of landing on the bed, had slammed his head on the ceiling and fallen in a heap on the floor just out of his wife's line of sight. She, unable to get any response from him, and terrified he might have broken his neck or something, screamed to attract attention to their plight.

Realizing that the punishment in urban legends is rated against a scandal scale, it would be easy to assume that being caught in *flagrante delicto* would top any list. Modern mythology, however, is nothing if not ambitious and has at least two more scenar-ios that go beyond the nightmarish but sim-ple caught-in-the-act stories.

"The Case of the Captive Lover" doesn't

even really start until *after* the poor couple has been caught! In an urban legend perpetuated, if not inspired, by an 1884 letter that appeared in the eminently prestigious journal *Philadelphia Medical News,* via the editor of *The Canadian Medical and Surgical Journal,* we are introduced to the condition known in scientific circles as *penis captivus.* In the author's own words:

Wow.

Dear Sir:

The reading of an admirably written and instructive editorial in the Philadelphia Medical News *for November 24 on forms of vaginimus [spasms of the muscles of the vagina], has reminded me of a case in point which bears out, in an extraordinary way, the statements therein contained. When in practice at Pentonville, England, I was sent for about 11:00 P.M., by a gentleman whom, on my arriving at his house, I found in a state of great perturbation, and the story he told me was briefly as follows:*

At bedtime, when going to the back kitchen to see if the house was shut up a noise in the coachman's room attracted his attention, and, going in, he discovered to his horror that the man was in bed with one of the maids. She screamed, he struggled, and they rolled out of bed together and made frantic efforts to get apart, but without success. He was a big, burly man, over six feet, and she was a small woman, weighing not more than ninety pounds. She was moaning and screaming, and seemed in great agony, so that, after several fruitless attempts to get them apart, he sent for me.

When I arrived I found the man standing up and supporting the woman in his arms, and it was quite evident that his penis was tightly locked in her vagina, and any attempt to dislodge it was accompanied by much pain on the part of both. It was, indeed, a case "de cohesione in coitu." I applied water, and then ice, but ineffectively, and at last sent for chloroform, a few whiffs of which sent the woman to sleep, relaxed the spasm, and relieved the captive penis, which was swollen, livid, and in a state of semi-erection, which did not go down for several hours, and for days the organ was extremely sore. The woman recovered rapidly, and seemed none the worse.

*I am sorry that I did not examine if the sphincter ani was contracted, but I did not think of it. In this case there must have been spasm of the muscle at the orifice, as well as higher up, for the penis seemed nipped low down, and this contraction, I think, kept the blood retained and the organ erect. As an instance of Iago's "beast with two backs," the picture was perfect. I have often wondered how it was, considering with what agility the man can, under certain circumstances, jump up, that Phineas, the son of Eleazar, was able to thrust his javelin through the man and Midionitish woman (*vide *Exodus); but the occurrence of such cases as the above may offer a possible explanation.*

Yours truly,

Egerton Y. Davis

Ex. U.S. Army

The only problem with the tale is that Egerton Y. Davis was actually the alter ego, the pseudonym, of one Sir William Osler! Now, Dr. Sir William Osler was indeed a lettered man of science, an expert in his field, and his field was indeed the one he was commenting on—even if pseudonymously. So, even if the source wasn't this "Egerton Y. Davis," surely the real author was perfectly qualified to make the necessary observations, record them properly, and report them accurately, right?

Sure—if the incident happened at all.

Which it didn't, as Dr. Osler was well aware before submitting his letter, via a third party in Montreal, to a publication that would be read by thousands of trusting souls.

Why'd he do it? As a joke, as a commentary on what he believed was a bit of fluff published anonymously by a colleague in a previous issue. A bit of academic revenge. He freely confessed to the crime against Knowledge, never intended it to be accepted into the realm of the profession's precedents.

Unfortunately, his prank wasn't widely recognized at the time. In years to come, it was quoted in numerous other publications that took the journal at its word, thereby passing the tale farther than intended, to an audience ill-equipped to judge its merits. And when the farce *was* revealed, it muddied the entire issue to the point where any further reports, or any references to incidents previously reported, were met with immediate mockery. Whether or not a physician believed he had an actual case to report, he was unlikely to hold himself up to public and professional ridicule.

Considerably better reported, both as legends and as fact, are the numerous tales of men and women who fall victim to the biggest caught-in-the-act scenes ever, the ones that leave one party, or both, dead! Despite numerous attempts, it's incredibly difficult to hide a case of *in delicto flagrante morto*—especially among the more adventurous.

Witness the tale of "The Gift-Wrapped Lover." Thinking to surprise his girlfriend with a gender-reversed version of the jumping-out-of-a-cake trick, William Boney reportedly stripped naked, tied a pink bow to his private parts, hid in a large box, and had himself wrapped in shiny Mylar for delivery to his lover's apartment. She was undoubtedly surprised to open the package and discover his dead body curled under the tissue paper.

He'd neglected to provide himself with any ventilation!

Slapping a "return to sender" stamp on the box must have been a tempting option.

Although no factual case exactly matching that one has ever turned up—perhaps others realized the wrapping paper of choice, the same shiny material used in helium balloons, was airtight—two other "wrapped in plastic" stories were widely circulated and, despite arising spontaneously and contemporaneously in two different states, could easily have inspired the later story.

The first occurred in New Orleans and was dutifully reported in the *American Journal of Forensic Medical Pathology* in June 1985. A man with a liking for autoerotic asphyxiation scenarios had evidently realized the potential of wrapping oneself in plastic as a method of inducing the supposedly intensely erotic sensations that result from the combination of oxygen starvation and sexual arousal. He had no intention of ending up dead, though, and, while wrapping himself in the plastic, provided an emergency airway through a common snorkel. Evidently something went terribly wrong, and despite the snorkel and obvious attempts to cut himself free, the man died. While the article's author clearly believed he was reporting a unique incident unlikely to be repeated, a second article, reported in the same journal in September 1987, depicted yet another "wrapped in plastic" death!

The *American Journal of Forensic Medical Pathology* isn't likely to be coffee-table material for most folks, so it's hard to imagine how these incidents could have inspired "The Gift-Wrapped Lover." Still, it's equally important to recognize that no instances of "The Gift-Wrapped Lover" had ever appeared before the first real-life case was reported, and three unique versions of the story appeared between 1985 and 1988, when these articles were released.

Slightly less bizarre are the numerous tales featuring a couple, one of whom, in mid-action, suddenly discovers that the other half of the partnership has chosen that particular moment to die of natural causes.

The urban version usually has an extensive setup, as this is the only area where the creativity so well known in these modern fables can be expressed. Regardless of which partner dies, what they were doing at the time of death, or how complicated the results may be, each story must, of course, end the same way.

One version that circulated through Columbia University during the summer of 1990 had an incredibly long buildup, detailing in loving vignettes the whole course of a young woman preparing for her date with an elderly professor who, she hoped, would allow her to slide on some of her course requirements. From the brush of perfume on the back of her knee, to the type of earrings she wore, to the order in which she put on her stockings (left, then right, if you're curious), nothing is left to the imagination. Published letters in *Penthouse* and *Playboy* seem amateurish compared with the highly erotic scene conveyed in this tale!

Considering that all this buildup ends with, "Then, as she stepped out of the bedroom to impress her elderly amour, the professor gasped, leaned forward—and died!" many researchers wonder if perhaps these intricately drawn settings aren't legends themselves but *examples,* proof, of yet another urban legend, "The Case of the Phone Sex Ring."

It's been said that in order to keep their

young men from straying while they're away for vacations, or during hectic spurts like exam week, young women at various campuses devised a simple strategy based on those enormously successful phone-sex lines. Instead of leaving their men with nothing to occupy their hands, these resourceful young women called them up each evening and encouraged their guys to masturbate to the sound of a sexy story she told. Of course, the girls still had to study, finish papers, and fulfill all the other obligations of college life, so, in order to come up with new tales as necessary, women who were in on this secret means of keeping their guys interested would regularly meet in the student union and, instead of trading history notes, exchange photocopies of their best phone-sex scenarios. Guys could easily recognize girls who provided this service to their dates by the thick red binders each girl carried. The thicker the stack of photocopied tales between those covers, so the legend goes, the better service they would get!

This comes back to the caught-in-the-act tales with poetic justice in "The Phone Message." Leo, one of those lucky enough to have a girlfriend happy to provide the phone-sex service indicated by her red binder, got the bright idea of recording her with his answering machine's memo function one night. Why not be able to reenact the scenario whenever he felt the need?

He didn't tell her, of course, or the roommate who accidentally discovered the tape when he arrived home and checked for messages. Thinking it was nothing more than an obscene phone call of a rather funny type, he copied the tape for himself, then carried it off to play before class for his buddies.

The tape was running when a group of girls hurried in, chattering away among themselves. The guys huddled over the machine freeze, recognizing one voice as identical to that on the tape. Not sure which girl among the group it had been, they simply turned up the volume and waited to see which one suddenly turned red and ran from the room. It didn't take long.

Circular tales like that trilogy, where one story leads to and seems to support the validity of the next, are relatively rare. The only other such case is, oddly, a further pairing of caught-in-the-act and died-in-the-act scenarios. Remember the case of *penis captivus,* in which the startled young woman's body reacts hysterically, spasming with sufficient force to trap her partner? Well, in several other articles of that historical period, such fits of hysteria were described as "resembling in nearly all its symptoms a case of tetanus." The common name for tetanus, both descriptive and easily remembered, is, of course, lockjaw, and it's this symptom of "hysteria" that appears in the legendary—and perhaps even true—story of the death of the President of France in 1899. That he did die while engaged in sexual antics with his mistress is taken as fact by most; no one has seriously contested that issue at all. The curious part of the story lies in what happened *after* his unfortunate demise.

According to some, the mistress, shocked to discover the man on whom she was performing her best oral sex had died without her being immediately aware of it, was so rattled by the thought of the scandal about to descend on her that she immediately suffered one of these "tetanus-like" fits of hysteria so often reported at the time and, as the name "lockjaw" does imply, couldn't open her mouth to release her lover! The tale ends with the by-now-familiar rush to the hospital, where she's released from her captivity by the miracle of chloroform or simply fainting, but not before her complete humiliation at the hands of the laughing staff, a victim of both *penis captivus* and having been caught in the act with a dead man!

You'd almost think that with dozens of similar stories making the rounds for centuries, people would seek medical certification of health before jumping in the sack with anyone, but it seems "dying in the saddle" is actually a fairly common way to go—for commoners and celebrities alike. It's tacitly acknowledged, if not openly admitted, that Errol Flynn and John Garfield died in the arms of their lovers. President Roosevelt (what, I wonder, are the statistics on sex-related deaths among presidents of any nation?) may well have died under the tender hands and attentions of a mistress. Nelson A. Rockefeller is rumored to have died in the

house of a lover, a lover who later received the house via a provision for her in the former New York governor's will. And, perhaps to prove that not all churchmen are prudes, a very prominent Roman Catholic cardinal was found dead within the walls of a notorious Paris cathouse. Amazingly, only one popular died-in-the-act tale featured a woman—and it was false. For many years, detractors of Catherine the Great claimed she died while trying to have intercourse with a horse. Catherine the Great died alone.

The substructure of every great caught-in-the-act legend is the presumption that people *don't* want to have their sexual proclivities displayed for all and sundry. A tiny proportion of caught-in-the-act tales, however, revolve around the absolutely opposite assumption—that there are people for whom doing it in public is the ultimate experience.

One tale, "On the Rails," tells of a young couple who boarded a train in Great Britain. Almost before they'd tucked their gear in the overhead compartment, they began sliding their hands in, over, and under one another's clothes without any apparent concern for the sensibilities of their fellow passengers. Complaints to the train's staff were ignored.

Before long, the heavy petting took a turn for the even more explicit, and passengers were shocked to find themselves the unwilling audience to a leisurely round of oral sex. Again, none of the complaints made to train employees produced any action to stop the couple.

Perhaps taking nonintervention as approval, the couple moved on to full-fledged sexual intercourse in front of a car full of strangers. Cries of outrage did nothing to move the train staff to interfere.

Only when the couple was finally satiated and sat back to enjoy a postcoital smoke, in a nonsmoking car, did train employees finally ask them to leave.

It has all the classic structure of a fairy tale, doesn't it? In all the best nursery stories, events always play out in three distinct acts. There are three little pigs and three houses for the wolf to attempt to destroy. There are three beds in "The Three Bears." Red Riding Hood asks about three of "granny's" facial features before the wolf finally attacks. This couple goes through three distinct stages of outraging their audience and, like all their fairy-tale prototypes, are never punished until the last.

The bizarre image created by the story, a juxtaposition of dour British passengers hurrying to work sitting next to these sexual athletes, is typical of urban legends that depend on coincidence or a blatantly weird setup being taken as normal for their plot. And, of course, the twist at the end, where it's the cigarette smoke that train personnel find offensive, not the sex, is the sort of irony that underwrites every good punch line. Taken together, these elements fairly scream "urban legend"! Right?

Nope.

This one's for real.

Guess they never had those nightmares when they were kids.

BEST SERVED COLD

It rather stands to reason that with all these folks out living and dying in the embrace of someone other than their significant other, eventually those significant others would decide it was time to get a little of their own back on their erstwhile partners. As we've already seen, when it comes to hanky-panky, most legends put the blame firmly in the men's camp. They're the ones off dying in their mistresses' arms, they're the ones wrapped in plastic, the ones getting their private parts caught in all manner of things—including women other than their wives. It's hardly surprising, then, that many revenge stories feature women turning the tables on erring men. Rarely overtly violent, women tend toward the inventive when considering how best to bury their ex-lovers in humiliation—which makes revenge legends some of the most entertaining of all.

"The Breakup" exists in at least a dozen different versions. In every case, the man decides he's bored with his present situation, usually a cohabitational arrangement with a woman who's been completely unaware there was any problem in the relationship until, out of the blue, she's told to take her things and go!

In most "Breakup" stories, this ultimatum is delivered just as the guy is about to go away for a week on business, or for a weekend of camping with the guys, or, in nastier versions, is about to head off to some lush tropical locale with a new paramour. The old girlfriend is to be out before he gets back.

In other words, our rejected woman has plenty of time to think out her revenge—and full access to her ex-lover's belongings!

An all-time favorite among those tales linked by the theme of a spurned woman's eventual revenge takes some time to play out. The lover arrives home, finds all the ex's stuff has been removed as requested, the apartment is spotless, even the plants have been watered. The key is left on the counter with a brief note along the lines of, "Oh, well, guess it wasn't meant to be. No hard feelings. Call me sometime."

Relieved at the smooth change in his living arrangements, the guy is hardly perturbed by the one thing out of place: The phone is slightly off the hook. When he picks it up, there's some recorded voice on the other end jabbering away in a language he doesn't understand. Figuring this is another case of that politically correct multilingual thing, he assumes he's probably hearing the "Your phone is off the hook" message in six different languages. He drops the receiver back in the cradle without another thought— until his phone bill arrives with charges in excess of $1,500 for a week-long continuous call to Tokyo's twenty-four-hour weather and traffic report!

Attacking both his pocketbook and his ego, a San Francisco version of "The Breakup" once again features the relieved man returning to his home from his tropical cruise to find the place empty of his former girlfriend's belongings and absolutely immaculate. Not a thing out of place, not even the phone off the hook! Since it's late and he has to be at work early the next morning, he unpacks by simply tossing all the clothes in his suitcase into the bag used by his laundry service, then throwing that in the collection bin before falling into his empty bed to dream of his Caribbean playmate.

The next morning he's awakened by an irate laundry owner who tells him in no uncertain terms that he'll wash no more laundry until he's paid for all the dry cleaning he's already done. Confused, the ex-lover promises to come by and pick up the dry cleaning, which he can't even remember dropping off, as soon as he gets free from work that evening. Mollified, the laundry

BITE ME!

One would-be rapist, apparently up on the new DNA techniques, integrated the use of condoms into his routine. The next woman he attacked, however, wasn't about to let him get away with that, and as he struggled with his prophylactic, she bit a piece off his ear.

owner promises to put the rest of his clothes in right away.

As the man showers and shaves, he racks his brain for some memory of the clothes that he's supposedly left at his service all this time. Of course he comes up empty until, reaching into his closet for his business clothes, he discovers there's absolutely nothing there!

A frantic search of the apartment confirms that the only clothes left in the place are the rumpled Hawaiian shirt and shorts he wore home yesterday.

In the process of tearing his place apart, however, he does find a note taped to his refrigerator:

"Hope you find everything nice and tidy. Too bad things didn't work out. Oh, by the way, I sent out all your suits for dry cleaning. P.S. Your boss called to tell you that meeting with that big client has been moved ahead to 8:00 A.M."

"On the Road Again" tells the tale of a married woman who'd suspected her husband of dallying with one of her neighbors but had never been able to figure out where the couple made their trysts until the day she saw a faint, rhythmic rocking in their RV. Saying nothing, she went back to the house and called the family lawyer. A few moments later she quietly slipped into the cab of the RV and eased out into traffic. Despite the immediate uproar somewhere in the back, she drove, without stopping, for over an hour along the nearest highway before retracing her route and parking just a few streets away from where she'd begun.

As she parked and stepped out of the cab, her irate husband and his lover jumped out of the back, just in time for her lawyer, who'd had time to go get his camera while she was driving, to snap their pictures!

One variant alters their destination to the woman's driveway, where the couple emerge to find not only the lawyer with his camera, but the straying wife's husband as well!

The quick-thinking driver got the house, the kids, the bank accounts, and the RV!

A considerably more risqué but equally embarrassing tale, "Dear John," arose while American troops were engaged in the Desert Storm skirmishes. Like many army wives, Joan had heard all the stories about husbands getting too intimate with the women of countries where they were stationed. She'd put the whole thing aside as big-boy fantasy until the wife of another serviceman in her husband's platoon received a video showing their camp, the flat desert countryside—and the party thrown after the United States declared they'd completed their objectives in Iraq and Mr. Hussein had been brought to heel. In the background was a clear picture of her hubby dragging some woman off into a tent! (A version of this scenario is also played out in the film *Major League*.)

As technology has improved over the years, it's become quite common for servicemen to send and receive videos instead of the usual letters of previous conflicts. These are often played in a common recreation area and are considered something of a highlight in the otherwise predictable routine of army life. So, when Joan's husband received a tape, he didn't hesitate to shove it in the machine. First came the usual greetings from family and friends back home, pictures of the latest snowfall, and two episodes of his favorite TV program. The last part of the tape, introduced by Joan telling him she thought he and his buddies might like this, featured a brief porno flick!

As his buddies hooted and slapped him on the back, telling him what a neat old lady he must have to send him this, something in the scene began to seem familiar. Instead of noticing how well the masked woman in the film serviced several faceless men, he noticed how similar the film set was to his own bedroom!

Before it sank in and he could switch off the tape, the woman pulled off her mask, told him how much she was enjoying his trip to Iraq, and that the divorce papers were on their way by regular mail. Cuckolded in front of his entire platoon, the husband could only slink off to the sounds of his buddies' catcalls!

Starting to see a theme in all these tales? Basically, boy meets girl, boy betrays girl, girl humiliates boy. You're likely starting to wonder if the poor husband is *ever* the victim who, through his own ingenuity, turns the tables on his wife. One legend, "The Concrete Caddy," comes close, but, as with all urban legends, there's a twist.

Our story starts with the woman who, over the course of twenty-five years of marriage, had, by dint of her incredible domestic savvy and the sharpness of her coupon-cutting scissors, managed to tuck away enough money to buy her husband the classic Cadillac Seville he'd always dreamed of. As their anniversary approached, her husband, driving by the house in the concrete mixer he operated for the city, couldn't help noticing the shiny red car parked in the driveway—or the man he could spy through the open kitchen window, leaning awfully close to his wife! Making an on-the-spot decision, he headed once around the block so he could pull in close to the curb on his next pass.

Meanwhile, back in the house, the car dealer finished pointing out the places the housewife must sign on the contract, tucked the finished paperwork into an inside pocket, then went outside, where he pulled a bike out of the Cadillac's trunk and pedaled off back to the dealership. The wife, delighted with her purchase, checked the lovely dinner waiting in the oven and headed off to pretty up before her husband got home.

Outside, hubby maneuvered in nice and close to the bright red car, swung the cement truck's chute around, and released yards and yards of concrete down and into the Caddy. Without a word to anyone inside, he then hurried away and finished his shift.

Imagine his surprise and dismay when, arriving home, he discovered the car he'd just ruined was his own!

It seems that in the land of urban legends, the husband is always wrong.

Many correlations have been drawn over the years between a man's ego and the car he chooses to drive.

"Big boys, big toys."

"Think he's overcompensating for a lack elsewhere?"

Rightly or wrongly, men are perceived as having much more intimate relationships with their transportation than women do with their vehicles. Which is why the next legend, though long in the tooth, never fails to bring a chuckle.

"The Hundred-Dollar Porsche" begins in typical revenge fashion with a middle-aged, unsuspecting wife suddenly discovering her husband has run off with his much-younger secretary. She is left to deal with not only her heartache but the lout's unfinished business as well. This particularly coldhearted Lothario left instructions for their home to be sold and the assets divided fifty-fifty; he'd "give" her the station wagon, but, since his Porsche was his before the marriage, she was to sell it and send all of that money to him at his secretary's address.

While packing her things, dealing with the realtor, and trying to find the pink slip for the wagon, she has time to consider the wording of the for-sale ad she plans to place in a local paper for the Porsche. A conversation with her lawyer has confirmed that because she didn't share title in the Porsche, and her husband's letter clearly made her his agent

in its sale, it is up to her to sell it and send him the money, even though there is no advantage for her in doing so. If she doesn't do it, that could be taken as a breach of agreement and she'd have to go to court—a lengthy and public process—just to get her half of the money from the house!

Eventually she runs the following advertisement:

FOR SALE
Cherry-red Porsche in like-new condition.
One owner only!
Price: $100 or best offer

Most people assume the price is a typo and simply ignore the ad. Out of curiosity more than any real hope of getting such a vehicle for such a ridiculous price, however, one young student does make an appointment to view the car, at which point the wife assures him there's no error in the ad, and asks him what he is willing to offer on the car. A quick rummage through all his pockets and his backpack turns up forty-eight dollars. She thanks him, hands him the keys, forwards the forty-eight dollars and the bill of sale to the secretary's address, then moved!

The attraction of these short tales of well-reasoned revenge has always been their ability to produce the desired effect without permanent damage to people or their property. Perhaps it's a response to the perception that we live in an increasingly more violent society, or that gender equality will inevitably make women more masculine, but the basically innocent tales of the past have, in recent versions, taken ever more nasty turns.

When Lorena Bobbit chopped off part of her husband's penis, it shocked the world as much because it was a woman who'd done it as because it was a truly horrific act. It also polarized opinions faster than a second-term election. While most refused to condone the violent physical assault regardless of extenuating circumstances, some segments of the general population were already claiming it "served him right." In the abstract, at least, many saw the act as a form of poetic justice. As "bobbitizing" entered the English lexicon, urban revenge legends turned dark.

According to a legend of that time frame, Joan, a college student, came back to her apartment early from a visit home to discover her boyfriend, Cal, in bed with her best friend, Kathy. Kathy stole the sheets, grabbed her clothes, and ducked into the bathroom, leaving Cal naked and sheetless on the bed to face Joan. Turning on her heel without a word, Joan left him to find his underwear while she started calling around to her friends for a place to spend the night.

That night away from home must, to Cal, have seemed to mellow her anger considerably. When he arrived home the next night, Joan was back, with a lovely supper on the table and dressed in her slinkiest lingerie. He responded in kind, swearing the night

> **The longest recorded case of priapism lasted three weeks, two days, eleven hours, and fifty-two minutes.**

with Kathy was an aberration, never to be repeated. They spent the meal cooing at one another, then retired to the bedroom together. Later, completely sated, Cal sprawled back and fell asleep.

His fantasy of cohabitational serenity died a swift death the next morning when he awoke to discover that Joan had superglued his penis to his leg!

The note she left him probably wasn't much comfort during the long hours of painful manipulations required to separate his body parts. "If you're wondering how I finished off the rest of the tube, check your car locks!"

Considering that an earlier variation ended with Cal awakening to find his girlfriend gone, his car intact, and only a red ribbon tied around his private parts "as a reminder of what Lorena might have done!" the superglue version seems even more unnecessarily violent by comparison.

Top award for the violent vengeful-woman scenario, however, has to go to "The Tale of the Curling Iron." The scorned woman in this legend, like Joan in the previous story, also discovers her husband and the woman she once believed to be her best friend in the most compromising situation possible. Like

Joan, she initially storms out, then appears to soften and eventually lets herself be lured back into her lover's bed. To "celebrate" their new start, she shyly suggests they try something different and brings out a pair of handcuffs and some silk scarves. Highly appreciative of his wife's new attitude, he agrees immediately.

His fantasy quickly turns to nightmare once the cuffs and scarves put him under her complete control. In this horrible scenario, she slips her curling iron into his rectum, turns it on, and leaves him!

Some psychologists, hearing this story, speak vaguely of "female penetration fantasies" and "phallic anger," suggesting that women are testing the limits of their capacity for violence in the relatively harmless venue of oral storytelling, basically seeing what level of brutality they can tolerate.

Another theory, however, holds that these tales aren't created by women at all, but are the constructs of *men* whose worst nightmare would be for women to adopt a *male* model of vengeance!

DON'T I KNOW YOU FROM SOMEWHERE?

We've already identified some of the elements that urban legends share with other story forms: the three-part structure of fairy tales, the elaborate setup of farce, and the compounding coincidence of situation comedy. The best combination of these elements pops up often in the urban sex legends that, in one way or another, relate to cases of mistaken identity.

The absolute classic is "The Halloween Party," sometimes called "The Costume Ball." A young couple is invited to the year's biggest shindig—well, next to the New Year's Eve costume ball—and the wife rushes out to find the perfect costumes before they're all taken. Hers is a little risqué, but, as most of the evening will be masked, she decides to be daring and maybe give her husband a few smiles when he sees it for the first time.

Unfortunately, as the day of the party dawns, the wife wakes with a terrible headache and flu symptoms. Still, not wanting her husband to miss the event, she insists he go without her while she curls up with some aspirin and hot milk. The quiet, the painkillers, and a good nap revive the woman, and on awakening and seeing it's not really that late, she eyes her sexy little costume and begins considering a new scenario. Since her lover hasn't seen her costume yet, she decides to go ahead and see just what sort of naughtiness he might be tempted into without her there to keep an eye on him.

The party is in full swing when she arrives in her flirty little French maid outfit and it takes her a few minutes to locate the costume she rented for him. Eventually she finds him dancing, rather closely, with a young woman dressed as Cleopatra. A little miffed that he seems to be having such a good time without her, the wife, to see just how far he might take his freedom, spends the next few moments casting come-hither looks his way until he comes hither. With only the slightest encouragement, she soon has him swaying and cuddling on the dance floor. A short time later they're petting in one corner of the main room, and within an hour of her arrival, they're making out in a bedroom upstairs—masked and all.

Jumping up before the midnight unmasking, she dresses and races home to be all tucked in bed when her husband finally wanders in some hours later. Pretending that she's never left the house, she asks him how the party went, if anything exciting might have happened.

Sighing, he crawls into bed and wraps an arm around her. "Not really, it's no fun without you. I ended up loaning my costume to some guy who ripped his, and I spent the whole night playing poker in a back room." As he feels her stiffening next to him, he quickly adds, "Don't worry, honey, I know it's a rental, so I made sure to get it back before I left. The guy said he had a great time with it, so I guess it wasn't a total waste, right?"

A more innocent version, completely eliminating the mistrusting-wife-who-tests-her-husband line of the plot, features two couples arriving in the same pair of costumes. The two couples get mixed up in the huge crowd and each wife, emboldened by her sexy outfit, comes on to the man she thinks is her husband. Sexual habits being well established in most relationships, each

husband is surprised and delighted by the "new" things they try in the darkened rooms of their host's house before heading home. The simple expedient of getting in the right car sorts the couples out once again. It's only later, in their own beds, when each husband asks his wife to "do what you did at the party," that they realize they must have been with someone else!

A similar tale with a far raunchier tone is "Swing," a cautionary tale aimed directly at the college students who star in it. According to this tale, a fraternity party in Houston gets out of hand when a keg of home brew is breached and a senior takes his enthusiastic girlfriend up to his room. Sometime during their fumbling, the senior finds himself in the embarrassing position of not being able to perform. Claiming he's forgotten his condoms, he staggers from the room with the lights still out and fetches one of the new pledges, whom he orders to protect his image with his girlfriend by "getting in there and giving her the time of her life!"

He does, then sneaks out to let the senior make his way back into the room.

Only when the pledge sees the senior and his girlfriend leaving the next morning does he realize the older student's date is his sister!

In "Double Trouble," another case of an urban legend coming true after the fact, a New York State youth was charged with the highly unusual crime of impersonating his twin brother for the purpose of having sex with the twin's girlfriend!

During the Desert Storm activity, a radio announcer calling herself "Baghdad Betty" did her best imitation of Tokyo Rose in an attempt to undermine the morale and confidence of American troops. Baghdad Betty obviously lacked her predecessor's savvy. While some few servicemen might have been concerned by her claims that Tom Cruise was sleeping with their wives, only laughter greeted her assertion that the cuckolding lover was Bart Simpson. (While dozens of servicemen claim to have heard these transmissions, no one seems capable of producing a tape of the broadcasts.)

The legend's straightforward plot introduces Kenny and Lenny, and Kenny's girlfriend Donna. As is sometimes the case with identical twins, though duplicates in appearance, the two were very different in temperament. Lenny found school a trial; Kenny breezed through. Lenny blushed when girls looked his way; Kenny charmed them. Lenny was by no means a nasty character, just not as outgoing or confident as his brother, who was older by two and a half minutes. Donna and Kenny, secure in their relationship and mature enough to see dating as more than another opportunity for sex, frequently asked Lenny to their various activities, often finding a fourth to fill out the group and keep Lenny from feeling like the fifth wheel.

Things went well until one evening when Lenny drank more than any of them realized, and fell into Kenny's bed instead of his own. He was already in a state of semi-arousal from Donna's attentions when he awoke with a start. Too shocked to speak up immediately, he floundered for the right words,

didn't find them, but discovered he was finding his brother's girlfriend all too hard to resist! The dirty deed was cut short when Kenny arrived from the shower to find the two in bed. Determining who was more upset, Donna or Kenny, would require one of the judgments of Solomon, but, in the legend, all was eventually forgiven when Lenny agreed to have "I'm not Kenny!" tattooed above his left nipple.

The real-life tale coincidentally (the court case occurred two decades after "Double Trouble"'s popularity peaked) featured another Lenny, this one the brother of Lamont Hough. According to the complaint against him, this Lenny deliberately, and with forethought, assumed his brother's identity in order to obtain sexual favors from his brother's girlfriend. The jury, however, may have seen things differently. Lenny's claim, that his only encounter with this woman had been completely honest and aboveboard, that she'd been a fully informed and consenting partner, and that the first and only indication to the contrary had been her call to police after the fact, carried the day and he was acquitted of all charges!

In a considerably different take on mistaken identity, there's the "Slice of Life" legend, a tale of gender-confused twins with unusual overtones of scientific horror. As technologies progress too fast for the layperson to follow and comprehend, it's possible that this is the type of urban legend that will become representative of this generation.

Tina had always assumed she and her brother, Terrence, were heterozygous (i.e., fraternal or nonidentical) twins. Since she was a girl and he was a boy, it was a pretty natural conclusion! Like many twins, she and Terrence developed a professional as well as a personal interest in things genetic. Terry graduated from medical school and specialized in genetic diseases. Tina finished a medical technology program and took a position with a fertility clinic. In the course of her work, she was asked to prepare a chromotog chart, a picture of the separated human chromosomes, which the doctors would use in their role of educators to prospective parents.

Not a particularly difficult task, it was well within Tina's capabilities. She began doubting her technique, however, when she lined up her own separated chromosomes, which she was using as the model of the photograph, and discovered that instead of a pair of XX sex chromosomes, the usual for females, she had an X and a Y! A hasty repeat of the procedure left her in no doubt.

Despite all appearances to the contrary, Tina was a man!

Sometime during the double circumcision shortly after the twins' birth, there'd been a terrible slip of the knife, and in order to help her readjust to her new gender orientation, no one had ever told Tina she wasn't born a girl.

On the face of it, this legend simply doesn't fly. It would take numerous, progressive bouts of surgery to effect a total gender change. Hormone therapy would be a lifelong requirement. Psychologists and pediatricians, concerned with the mental and emotional side of such gender reassignments, would follow the case closely. It would have been impossible for Tina not to have been aware of all this activity.

As it happens, actual cases of accidental castration and sexual reassignment are well documented in medical literature. Some reassignments have been successful; others have not. This incident and the legend that preceded it are examples of how accurately folk legend reflects current events and fears.

WHEN ONE PLUS ONE EQUALS THREE

For most of human history, pregnancy and sex remained irrevocably linked. The early Chinese tried mercury as an abortifacient. It was efficient, but did little for the *mother's* life expectancy. The Japanese tried designing condoms made from various substances—including turtle shells!—but while useful in the prevention of disease, they didn't make much of a dent in the birth rate. A 1785 publication in Boston suggested regular attendance at church as a trustworthy contraceptive plan!

Before snickering too loudly at such colonial beliefs, read these modern tales of contraceptive woe.

One of the leading folklorists to catalog urban legends, Jan Harold Brunvand, named one of his collections of such tales *The Baby Train,* after one of the most pervasive stories.

A Canadian version is set in Newfoundland, where the only transprovincial engine, ironically called the Newfie Bullet, was reported to travel at a rate "such that passengers wanting some relief from the arduous trip were known to jump off, walk along the track to stretch their legs, then walk *back* to re-board and continue the trip." Needless to say, its eventual arrival in any of the communities along the line was a major event, with lots of people wandering down to meet it, pick up their mail, send parcels on to friends, and maybe greet a relative with sufficient patience to make the journey.

At one stop along the line, the crowd coming to meet the train seemed to be ballooning. Almost every woman in the town seemed to have a babe in arms or one on the way! Eventually—and you must remember how slowly this train traveled—news of the mini-population explosion reached a health official in the capital, St. John's. By the time he reached the tiny outport, another crop of babies had been born and even more were on the way!

Nothing in the immediate surroundings suggested an explanation for the unusual birth rate, but after spending a few days in the community, he did notice that the births followed distinct peaks and valleys. Almost every baby born in the town arrived nine months after the train's last stop! Seems that, with everyone caught in town waiting, and nothing much to do in the meantime, they were doing what came naturally!

Brunvand's version featured a whistle that regularly awoke everyone at an hour just late enough to make it unreasonable to go back to sleep, but too early to encourage people to get up.

The legend surfaces in a number of other event-linked instances as well. In 1966, nine months after the big 1965 blackout in New York City, birth rates peaked for that year. Nine months after the Super Bowl, birth rates plummet to the lowest point of the year. The version that first intrigued me, however, as I happen to live in the area under discussion, was that birth rates in northern regions are cyclical, with peaks nine months after the coldest months and dips nine months after the summer months. While demographics have proven the legends false in the case of the New York City blackout, the Newfie Bullet, and the full string of Super Bowls, a quick check of birth records at Captain William Jackman Memorial Hospital, however, showed distinct jumps and dips, all following the seasonal cycle—a trend continued in dozens of other northern hospitals!

If there ever was a noticeable jump in birth rates, it might well have happened in Toronto in the years 1926 to 1936, the years of "The Baby Race." According to the legend, a Canadian philanthropist set aside a million dollars to be given to the woman who had the most children in the ten-year period following his death.

The Great Depression, the recovery from the First World War, and drought across the United States and Canada all combined to make the late twenties and early thirties a period of scrounging and hunger for many families. The notion that someone was willing to give away a fortune to the couple doing the most efficient job of doing what came naturally anyway must have seemed either the most bizarre circumstance of all time or perhaps a chance—maybe the only chance—of getting out from under.

This may seem nothing more than a fairy-godmother story, the sort where some outside force suddenly arrives to rescue the beleaguered John (or Jane) Q. Public, until you learn that this time there really was a pot of gold at the end of the rainbow!

Charles Millar, a Toronto lawyer, had a lot of fun writing his will. He left scandalous items to upright ministers, made gifts to acknowledged enemies, and gave the "remainder" of his estate, which, while not quite a million, would certainly make life easy for any number of Depression families,

to the woman or women who produced the most children, began the Great Toronto Stork Derby!

In the end, four women, each of whom delivered nine children in the specified ten-year period, claimed $125,000 a piece. Given that an adult man working a full week every week for a year, with no vacation time, might be lucky enough to earn six hundred dollars for the entire year, $125,000 made each woman the equivalent of a multimillionaire!

Unlike Mary MacLean, Kathleen Nagel, Annie Smith, and Lucy Timleck, the winners of the baby lottery, most people, then as now, were more interested in limiting the size of their families rather than figuring out how to fit yet another chair around the table. Folklorists frequently used the words "adolescent fantasy" when discussing urban legends, commenting on how so many of them reflect our most immature dreams and fears. Pregnancy, and its prevention, might well begin as a teenager's worst nightmare, but even adults faced with an unplanned pregnancy can contribute to the growth of baby legends and the introduction of new reproduction technology spurs almost immediate tales of its misuse.

The "Jelly Baby" tale, for example, first hit the streets when the diaphragm became that period's contraceptive choice.

Shortly after being given her new diaphragm and a detailed list of instructions for its proper care and use, a middle-aged

© Peter/Ngaire Genge, 1999

Which one *isn't* a breakfast product?

tion. Like the woman herself, he found the diaphragm firmly lodged against the cervix and, despite his best attempts, impossible to dislodge.

By now the patient was practically hysterical, certainly in no condition to lie back calmly and permit further manipulations. After consulting with another physician, the decision was made to anesthetize the woman for a brief period so they could bring in some equipment and get a better view of the situation. Once she was unconscious, her doctor brought in a light and a speculum, the tool used to expose the cervix during Pap smear testing, hunkered down between her knees, and sized up the situation. Within a few moments he managed to catch the edge of the diaphragm and, still with some resistance, pull it free. An examination of the contraceptive device, however, only deepened the mystery. It was covered with a sticky, dark blue substance that no one on staff had ever seen before!

All was cleared up when the woman awoke. As the instructions said to "use with jelly," which she was out of at the moment, she'd assumed she could substitute the jam she had in the fridge already, blueberry!

Equally popular at the time was the "Jelly on Toast" legend. Once again, a woman is given a perfectly fitted diaphragm and a detailed set of instruction in the use, care, and cleaning of the device. This time she's even given a tube of contraceptive jelly to take home with her. Some time later, of

woman arrived at Mount Sinai Hospital's emergency room in a state of great agitation with "female complaints."

Once behind the cotton curtain, she blurted out, "It's stuck!" For some mysterious reason, the diaphragm, which had been so carefully fitted by her physician, was resisting all attempts to remove it!

Asking the patient to relax as much as possible as she lay back on the examination table, the doctor made a preliminary inspec-

course, she needs to replenish the supply of jelly and heads off to the local pharmacy to do so. The store doesn't carry the brand she's been using, but the pharmacist on duty is very helpful and quickly suggests another brand, which he assures her will be "every bit as effective" as the one she's been using.

Within the month, the pharmacist is shocked to receive papers advising him he's about to be sued! The woman who bought the jelly is pregnant, and blames his advice for her predicament! The whole matter, however, is quickly settled after the preliminary interview during which the woman reveals she'd changed absolutely nothing else in her contraceptive program except the jelly, which, she staunchly declares, she'd continued to take every morning on her toast, even though it tasted much worse than the stuff she'd been given originally!

Given the communications problem evidenced by these two legends, in which, presumably, the doctors, the patients, and their pharmacists all spoke the same language, it's no surprise that health-care workers operating in non-English-speaking countries would run into similar troubles.

Take the case of the innocent CUSO (Canadian University Services Overseas) worker who was dropped off in a small village in Kenya with a supply of condoms to give away and the mission to educate the women of the community in their use.

The women, unlike their North American counterparts, were quite open about their sexual practices and evidently interested in controlling the timing of their pregnancies. As the CUSO worker discussed the various forms of birth control available, she eventually came to the use of condoms. Extolling their value in controlling the spread of disease as well as managing the birth rate, their portability (important in a region where popping into the local drugstore for a supply of birth-control pills isn't an option), and the fact that their men could begin to take some responsibility for having smaller families as well, the health worker soon had a very enthusiastic audience for her demonstration.

Not knowing the local word for penis, she mimed out the process, using her thumb as the handiest replacement. The excited women suddenly began looking a little doubtful, but, with further encouragement from the bubbly CUSO worker, left with a large supply of condoms each.

The women were less enthusiastic when, returning to the village after moving their herds for the summer, three of the fourteen condom recipients were pregnant!

Had they had sufficient condoms to use them every time they had sex?

Yes.

Had they remembered to use them every time?

Yes.

Had they used them properly?

Yes.

Stumped, the CUSO worker contacted her

supervisor to report some failure in the condoms they'd been issued. Since no one else had reported any difficulties, the supervisor hurried out to observe the situation for herself. Shortly after beginning her interviews, the supervisor found the problem.

The women had indeed done exactly as told—right down to rolling the condoms onto their husbands' thumbs!

To further highlight the confusion surrounding sex itself, and contraception in particular, there are the conflicting beliefs illustrated in the "Sex in the Pool" tale.

In the first version, a young man and his girlfriend sneak out to his parents' pool one night, slip into the water, swim about a bit, then, sliding out of their suits, do a little skinny-dipping. When he suggests they take it a step further and try making out in the pool, she's reluctant. After a lot of snuggling and petting, she finally admits she hasn't been on the pill long enough to ensure it would be an effective form of birth control. Waving away her concerns, he tells her that a woman can't get pregnant having sex in a chlorinated swimming pool! Relieved of her concerns, she finally consents.

In the twist to this tale, the girl does indeed find herself pregnant, and because this was the only occasion when they'd engaged in sex without the traditional precautions, she naturally blames him for the whole situation.

Convinced that what he'd told her about chlorine is true, he concludes there wasn't sufficient chlorine in the water, and confronts the pool maintenance man the next time he turns up. Terrified, the attendant reveals that he hasn't put chlorine in the water in months—he's been too busy having sex with the lady of the house!

Some versions of that tale include a caught-in-the-act scenario when the boyfriend, instead of openly confronting the pool guy on his arrival, tapes him in the hopes of proving he isn't doing his job and, in the process, captures the elicit encounter live!

The trophy for Weirdest Sexual Legend Enacted in Water, however, definitely goes to the case of "The Woman Impregnated by an Octopus"!

A young woman accompanied her family to Atlantic City, where they did the usual touristy things before spending an afternoon at the beach, where the water was warm enough to urge them all in for a swim. They're splashing about, enjoying themselves, when the eldest daughter suddenly screams and rushes out!

She claims to have felt something grab her ankle, but when her father and elder brother investigate, all they see are a couple of octopi rolling about, nothing to scare anyone, they assure her. Mollified, she returns to the water and, in the excitement of the rest of the vacation, forgets the incident entirely.

Three months later, things aren't well. The daughter, complaining of morning sickness, pain in her abdomen, and swelling in the same area, is, despite all her claims of virginity, showing all the signs of early pregnancy. At first the mother refuses to listen to her claims of innocence, declaring that "time will prove it one way or the other." To the daughter's horror, her stomach continues to swell, and she's feeling increasingly more ill each week! Finally the mother, to end the argument, takes the girl to the family doctor.

Mom seems vindicated when the first assessment concludes that "uterine enlargement is pronounced, consistent with pregnancy." However, the doctor is more receptive to the girl's claims and allows that other conditions could cause the same symptoms, among them a tumor. With both mother and daughter scared witless, the doctor arranges to admit the girl immediately and perform an ultrasound examination.

The procedure doesn't alleviate anyone's concerns. Though the technician won't say what is revealed, there's definitely something growing in there. The decision to perform exploratory surgery is made. Doctors, mother, and daughter are all equally shocked to discover a small octopus growing inside the girl's uterus!

The notion that the octopi rolling about in the water were mating, and that a free-floating fertilized egg had managed to make its way up the vagina and implant itself quite comfortably in the uterus, does at first seem rather a bizarre chain of events, even for an urban legend. Certainly there are no documented cases to support this tale, which,

incidently, has been in circulation since at least 1938. What does turn up while leafing through dusty journal clippings for that period are two cases almost as unbelievable.

The first, reported in the office diary of Dr. Spiro Glodipolous of Athens, is of the experience of a young Englishwoman vacationing in Greece in 1928. She'd been swimming in

NEVER AGAIN!

If you think "I love you" or "He looks just like . . ." are the most commonly spoken words after the delivery of a baby, you'd be wrong. According to those who work in maternity wards, the most common response among women to the arrival of their bundle of joy is, "Never again! I'm never doing that again!"

Of course, as the number of second and third children born proves, most women decide that their children are worth the effort.

According to sex researchers Masters and Johnson, however, a small percentage (a *very* small percentage) not only enjoy the experience, but describe it as "not unlike the experience of orgasm!"

the warm waters for nearly a month without any noticeable ill effects when, while toweling off, she felt something sharp dig into her back, immediately between her shoulder blades. Unable to reach the spot, she swung her towel around and swished it back and forth until the sensation went away, then dressed and went about the rest of her vacation. Some days later she began running a fever and developed a rash and some localized swelling around her mouth and eyes. She was nauseated on rising, and again just before bedtime. When her hands and feet began to swell and itch, she sought the services of Dr. Glodipolous.

Taking her history, he saw nothing unusual that would account for her condition, and asked his nurse to prepare the patient for a physical examination. It didn't take long to discover a tiny shrimp clinging to a shallow cut on her back! The creature had apparently clipped her with its claws, and her brisk toweling had embedded it in her skin. The rash, fever, swelling, and general malaise were the result of the woman's low-level allergy to seafood!

Even more closely resembling the octopus story, however, is the real-life experience of an elderly Bulgarian woman who also enjoyed an occasional swim.

Despite being a mature woman who'd already completed menopause, she developed sporadic bleeding similar to the spotting that pregnant women sometimes displayed around the dates they would have

been menstruating were they not pregnant. Thinking it just some delayed menopausal response, she put off seeing her physician for some time. It was only the sudden onset of heavy bleeding that sent her to seek medical help. She was hospitalized immediately, though doctors were at a loss to explain why a woman of her years should develop such exotic symptoms. Surely the cessation of her menstrual period couldn't have been due to pregnancy instead of menopause, could it?

The internal examination didn't last long. She certainly wasn't pregnant. There was no sign of any swelling at all. No, the culprit was a leech that, having attached itself to the blood-rich wall of the vagina, had apparently lived there for some time before burrowing through the wall entirely and causing the hemorrhage! Needless to say, several versions of the octopus legend, with leeches taking the starring role, circulated in eastern Europe after the incident was reported in 1968. Snails starred in two different French variations. A barnacle story with similar overtones arose in Italy in 1972. Another, featuring a tadpole that supposedly swam all the way to the uterus, where it set up housekeeping until it became a frog and convinced an elderly woman she was pregnant with all its hopping about, predates the real-life incident in Bulgaria by nearly a century!

While the young woman who brought home a unique souvenir of Atlantic City, the Englishwoman who learned an important lesson on how *not* to serve seafood, and the

Bulgarian matron who probably never swam again, were all cases of mistaken pregnancy, two equally weird tales of actual pregnancy have often been retold in the form of urban legends.

Though neither recent nor actually occurring in anything approaching an urban area, the tale variously known as "Musket Balls" and "Son of a Gun" recounts the tale of a Civil War soldier and how he supposedly fathered a child by a Southern belle miss without ever touching her!

According to the story, the soldier's unit was passing through a plantation when it was pinned down by the enemy, who rained gunfire toward the lawns where the soldiers stood. One shot slammed into a young soldier's leg, and was deflected by the femur and through the scrotum, where it destroyed one testicle, and then sped on. When the scuffle ended and the dust cleared, a call came from the plantation house for the urgent attentions of a surgeon. A young woman in the house had been shot!

The woman was treated for a gunshot wound to the abdomen. Precisely 278 days later, she was delivered of a healthy baby! The woman, unmarried, swore that she'd had no sexual relations of any kind, an assertion that met with understandable skepticism. Only when the physician who treated her recalled his other patient and the through-and-through bullet did he propose another possibility—that the same bullet had injured both, with the trajectory taking it

first through the soldier's testicle and then into the woman's abdomen!

Of course, the whole scenario is pure make-believe. Though the original story is rife with historically accurate detail, including the dates of the sortie, the location, and the names of many present, the medical report, which later appeared in several journals, was, like the *penis captivus* tale, a hoax, an elaborate joke. The legend is therefore a falsehood based on a real article reporting an imaginary situation supposedly occurring during an historical event!

The ultimate legend of virgin birth, however, remains urban in the extreme. Late one night, after heavy partying, a young woman decided to make love with her boyfriend. The woman's private life—made somewhat nontraditional by the fact she had no vagina, a condition known as aplastia—did, however, include enthusiastic manual and oral sex, which had always satisfied her and her partners. On one particular night she was tending bar when her latest boyfriend showed up. They slipped into a storage room and proceeded to engage in their usual sexual activities. When a former boyfriend appeared and caught the couple in the act, knives appeared and all three were eventually admitted to the hospital with a variety of wounds.

The young woman suffered a gash to her palm and a single stab wound to the upper abdomen, which, surgeons quickly learned, had punctured her stomach in two locations. Thankfully, there were no stomach contents noted at the time and, after rinsing the cavity with saline solution, they repaired the wound damage and released her several days later.

Everyone associated with the night's events was astonished when, nine months later, the same woman was admitted with severe abdominal pain. Two things became immediately apparent. First of all, she was in labor. Second, this woman had no vagina! An emergency cesarean section was performed and surgeons were able to confirm—from the inside, no less—that there was absolutely no physical connection between her uterus and the outside world. Which raised the obvious question: How had she become pregnant in the first place?

Careful questioning began bringing the story together. The sperm responsible for this pregnancy had evidently spilled from her pierced stomach into her abdominal cavity. The saline rinse may well have forced them

even deeper. Eventually the sperm reached the open end of the fallopian tube and zipped right along to encounter their natural target and—*voilà!*—the first medically documented virgin birth!

The legend, easier reading than the case written up in the *British Journal of Obstetrics and Gynaecology* in September 1988, is an example of just how fast an oral account can travel. It crossed two continents (the original incident taking place in Africa, and being reported back in Europe) and leaped over an ocean to begin circulating in America in January of 1990! It actually took longer to identify its point of origin than it did to evolve into a legend!

Women, as curious as men about what the opposite sex is hiding under their clothes, have long associated the size of various body parts with the size of a man's penis. Long fingers, a long nose, big ears, big feet, or long toes could all hint at a man's actual sexual endowment, or prowess.

One urban legend out of Korea, "The Baby Factory," combines these old chestnuts with the fearful tale of baby-breeders then circulating. The dark story begins with the sorry prospects of prostitutes too old to attract clients and pimps who saw one more way to make a few bucks. Pregnancy, a serious career hitch for most hookers, became these women's last-ditch attempt to accumulate a retirement nest egg when Westerners provided a lucrative market for all those previously unwanted babies. Two or three babies, "adopted" for 25,000 American dollars each, could buy a lot of rice!

Of course, anyone "lucky" enough to produce twins could basically double her income for relatively little extra effort. It became a matter of economics, then, to screen for the men most likely to produce twins. (Though twinning is often the result of multiple ovulation and is therefore, in Western tradition, attributed to some female aspect, Asian traditions have long suggested that men were the determining factor. Remember that as the tale unfolds.)

Eventually, through "extensive testing," the women decide that, ears, noses, and toes aside, it's the size of a man's testes that indicates how likely he is to father children. The working girls, as a service to those who went before them, did the screening, determining which of the clients were likely candidates and sending them along to the older women. The "freebie" was usually more than enough to persuade them to donate their sperm to the retirement-fund project, and before long the retirees were enjoying a plethora of twin births!

(The whole twin scenario plays out again in one of the many legends surrounding the adoption issue when these twins, separated at birth, discover one another or fall in love with one another or try to locate one another.)

That Asian babies were adopted into the United States in large numbers, especially during the early 1990s, is fact. That some of those babies were deliberately conceived for sale is also well documented. The only part left to legend is whether Korean women had discovered the secret to twins on demand. Oddly enough, an article in the August 1988 *Discover* magazine addresses just that issue!

If the results of investigations by Dr. Jared Diamond of UCLA are correct, the girls might have had it right. His preliminary studies discovered, first of all, that testis size varies significantly among ethnic groups. For example, in ascending order of size are Asians, Caucasians, a non-Yoruba African group, and Yorubas. Not surprisingly—to Korean prostitutes, anyway—the rate of twins in each group is, in ascending order, Asians, Caucasians, non-Yoruba Africans, and Yorubas!

Are other factors at work as well? Possibly, but for the moment it seems the Korean prostitutes are the acknowledged leaders in this field of inquiry!

PAYING FOR IT

In the tales retold so far, all the victims eventually pay for violating sexual "norms" in the currency of humiliation, another set of tales revolves around those who pay for their sexual encounters with both embarrassment and cash!

Considering the frightening nature of much modern folklore, cathouse tales and their kissing cousins are remarkably innocent.

> A woman on vacation in San Francisco was unlucky enough to be involved in a Hyde Street cable car accident. According to the suit brought on her behalf against the Municipal Railway when she sued them for half a million dollars, she incurred bruises and emotional damage, and became a nymphomaniac as a result of the accident. Citing one occasion when she was incapable of preventing herself from engaging in fifty sexual encounters in five days, she aroused the sympathy of judge and jury, who awarded her $50,000 in damages in April of 1970.

A favorite tale, "Madam Social Butterfly," juxtaposes the highest realms of society with the lowest:

A society debutante who went on to an Ivy League school before marrying a well-placed member of the diplomatic corps accompanied her new husband to his next posting in Hong Kong. There she fluttered from social event to social event and delighted in the shopping areas where her American dollars were welcomed, but she merely dabbled in the culture surrounding her.

On her return to the United States, she easily impressed her equally flighty friends with her knowledge of things oriental. That she couldn't keep her facts straight, frequently misrepresented traditions intrinsic to the region, and often mixed up important dates and names made no impact on her usual circle of friends—they simply didn't know any better.

Some years later, while the couple was stationed in Washington, they were invited to a dinner party with the Chinese ambassador and his staff as the guests of honor. Deciding to go all out, displaying her familiarity with all things Asian, she decked herself out in dressy kimono and elaborate hairdo. As the finishing touch, she slipped a medallion decorated with Chinese characters around her neck. In this over-the-top ensemble, she flounced into the middle of the event and immediately began regaling everyone who would listen with tales of her own sojourn to the East.

At some point in the evening, she glimpsed one of the ambassador's secretaries staring at the pendant. Stroking a finger over it, she exclaimed, "Oh, you like it? I suppose you know what it says?"

The woman flushed and looked toward the floor. "Oh, ma'am, I'm sure I couldn't say."

Laughing with delight, the society lady winked at those who'd been listening to her remembrances. "Isn't that something, I know more of the lingo than the ambassador's own people!" With that, she reached out and quickly slipped her arm through that of the passing ambassador. "Maybe you'd care to tell me if you can read this. It seems your aide there is having trouble."

The aide flushed brilliantly and continued to stare at the floor. Evidently surprised, the ambassador turned to eye the jewelry himself. He stared for a moment in silence.

Preening under his gaze, the diplomat's wife gave him her most charming grin. "So, sir, can *you* read my pendant?"

"Of course. It says, 'Licensed Prostitute, City of Shanghai.'"

Clutching her kimono to her and clattering along on her wooden sandals, the horrified society dame raced away from the gales of laughter erupting around her.

There are, of course, many stories revolving around this general theme. One has a young woman using Chinese characters for a needlepoint project without checking their meaning. A friend's giggles alert her to her error and leave her blushing when she discovers the tapestry she's hung in her foyer reads, "For Lots of Fun, Enter Here"! Another woman decorated the paper panels in her room divider with a variety of symbols copied, without concern for their actual meanings, from a Chinatown newspaper. The screen, which separated her living and dining rooms, included the characters for "cooked" and "dog," "greed" and "gluttony," and "burnt" and "straw"! A young man fascinated with the martial arts, though completely untrained at any dojo, bought a brilliant white *gi* and had his girlfriend embroider it with authentic Chinese symbols in flashy red thread. Having no clue what they meant, she picked those that looked best to her from a bunch of the martial arts magazines lying about the apartment. Imagine the young man's embarrassment when he later learned that the pretty characters, read in order, basically said, "Bad Fighter, Bad Lover, Hopeless"!

Of course, it doesn't take a foreign language to confuse some people.

In Wisconsin, a certain group of college girls supplemented their income by accepting cash presents in exchange for their sexual favors. Naturally nervous about actually having to discuss prices and services with men who could easily be undercover vice officers, the girls devised a code system that they shared only with those who'd already paid for some service in the past. Each girl had a series of four brooches. Each brooch was set with a ruby, an emerald, a diamond, or a sapphire. The customers were aware that a ruby was manual sex, emeralds indicated oral sex, diamonds symbolized traditional genital sex, and sapphires stood for "something kinky."

When a young man called up, he told her where he'd like to pick her up, what time, and would throw in a statement along the lines of, "Oh, and can you wear that diamond pin I'm so fond of."

Wearing a particular pin out in public indicated the girl was available for that service and could be approached by anyone up on the system.

Needless to say, these young women frequently had young men hovering about, and

Kathy, a new girl on campus, began noticing that women wearing the pins appeared to be the in group. Deciding that this was some sort of local fashion trend, she, too, began sporting brooches of various types. Soon she was getting all the male attention she could handle! It took two botched dates for her to discover she'd been wandering about her new school advertising herself as the girl to see if you wanted something kinky!

Not everybody looking to purchase a little pleasure actually calls up the local cathouse. Most people, especially young men, take a lonelier, not to mention cheaper, option and pick up a handful of adult magazines instead. Perhaps the next urban legend illustrates just how much time is spent poring over these under-mattress-stuffers.

According to the legend, the stars surrounding, or decorating, the *P* on a *Playboy* cover were an inside joke perpetuated by the sales director at the expense of that month's centerfold and the ultimate playboy, the magazine's owner, Hugh Hefner. If the tale of tail-chasing was believed, then the number of stars indicated either the number of times the woman slept with the mag owner, how good the woman was on a scale of one to five, or, if the stars were outside the *P* rather than printed over it, the number of times Mr. Hefner tried, without luck, to seduce that Playmate of the Month!

Of course, despite the numerous tales told of Hugh Hefner and the Playboy Mansion, business is business, infinitely more prosaic than the imaginings of teenaged boys, and the stars served a considerably more boring purpose—they were routing codes for shipping! The placement of the stars, inside or outside the *P,* resulted solely from the cover designer's desire to make them as visible as possible.

Another American myth shot down.

OH, SCARE ME!

 or most people, their introduction to urban legends begins around a campfire or huddled under their blankets. With night sounds whispering from the darkness, their voices just low enough not to wake the adults, children pass the best urban legends from older siblings to younger ones, to their cousins, and then on to their best friends as ghost stories.

All urban legends contain elements of the horrific. (The two-timed girlfriend with her curling iron, recounted in the preceding chapter, isn't exactly traditional bedtime fare for young children.) Some, however, seem to exist solely for the purpose of reminding us that we live in a dangerous world. These next tales strike from darkness, from the spaces under our cars and beds, from the safety of our homes, the places where we live and play. It's in these tales that our fears, phobias, and prejudices are given free rein.

SAFE AT HOME? OR ANY-WHERE?

Dead bodies don't belong in hotel beds, bathtubs, armoires, or trees. The freedom to picnic, neck, and enjoy the local funhouse isn't enshrined in any bill of rights; we assume them. So we're affronted, not to mention scared witless, when death and dead things, especially *parts* of dead things, invade our secure worlds.

Even camera crews who literally walk through buckets of blood daily, who regularly assess the "freak factor" of this dismembered arm versus that legless-foot-in-a-shoe, and who turn nightmares into 3D specials, have the right to lose it when confronted with the reality of death. And, according to legend, they've had plenty of opportunity to do just that!

Around 1998, vampires made a big comeback. *From Dusk to Dawn* was a hit for Clooney and company. John Carpenter's horrific talents brought *Vampires* to life in distinctly contemporary settings. *Buffy the Vampire Slayer* turned up the heat, and teen hormones, on television. The vampire mistress herself, Anne Rice, was penning her tale of *Armand.* It took *Blade,* however, a comic-turned-movie, to generate urban legends outside theaters across the country.

"Watch the rave where the vamps are showering in the blood! There's one that doesn't move! It's the dead guy! Some lunatic murdered him right on screen, but in all that blood, no one knew until they were cleaning up! The cops are looking at every frame of film trying to find the killer!"

According to the legends, a vampire, a *human* vampire who slit his victims' throats for blood, was stalking the film. If all the rumored deaths were added together, at least half the cast and crew left the lot in body bags!

"Yeah, the special-effects guy, he sent his assistant for coffee, turned around later, saw her sitting in the corner of the trailer, covered in blood, and thought she was joking! That guy killed her right there, right behind him, and he didn't know it! Just wanted to know where the coffee was!"

"*I* heard it was the caterer. Some Italian guy who was really into the vampire thing, big Lugosi fan. He begged to have a bit part, you know, just a stand-in so he could point to it and show his kids, right? Well, the director said it was okay, they shot the scene, and everyone went to lunch. Everyone but the guy who was supposed to be *serving* it! See, they'd told him to stay really still. He was supposed to be a dead body, right? So he did. It was only when they suggested he get up and start serving lunch, and he didn't, that someone discovered he was dead! Throat cut!"

Of course, from time to time, people do die on movie and television sets. It's tragic, but seldom suspicious. What's infinitely more rare is for film crews to stumble accidentally across preexisting dead bodies! So, when the crew of *The Six Million Dollar Man* discovered that a dummy covered in fluorescent spray paint in a Long Beach amusement park was real—really well preserved!—they screamed as loud as anyone else!

It began when the crew moved into the funhouse and shifted the dummy out of their way. In a twist unseen in any film anywhere, an arm fell off, revealing an obviously real human bone sticking out!

The "dummy," actually the very well preserved body of one Elmer McCurdy, began

© Peter/Ngaire Genge, 1999

As metal grilles give way to plastic-coated foam, will the "Girl in the Grille" legend disappear as well?

his life-after-death as an example of the funeral director's art when no one claimed his body following a robbery-gone-bad shootout. He was bought by carnival operators, appeared in the film *She Freak* (a non-speaking part, of course), was shown in at least one wax museum, where it was assumed he was a wax figure, and finally ended up as an amusement-park prop. He probably saw more of the country dead than he had alive, and by the time he ended up in the Long Beach funhouse, everyone had forgotten he was ever alive! He's now buried next to Outlaw Bill Doolin, another bank rob-

ber, under several feet of concrete—just to make sure this "travelin' man" don't travel no more.

The star of "Grilled to Death," a man who stumbled into his house after a raunchy, drunken bachelor party given for a co-worker, certainly wasn't thinking about dead bodies. His immediate problem, finding the garage door opener, took nearly ten minutes to resolve! Inside, he stumbled upstairs and fell into bed with his wife, mumbling "great time" in response to her inquiries about the evening.

The next morning, over cups of black coffee and a tall glass of tomato juice, he confessed to not remembering much past the arrival of a large cake and his next round of drinks.

His wife is still laughing at his sore head when she trails along behind to kiss him good-bye outside. When he backs the car from its crooked position inside the garage, her laughter quickly turns to screams. Pulling up short, he stumbles out and looks behind him but sees nothing. She screams louder, pointing at the *front* of his car.

Looking around the front fender, he staggers backward, grabbing the house for support. There, embedded in the radiator grille of his car, is the body of a young woman!

In addition to the implicit warning of this tale, don't drink and drive, there's the less obvious life lesson: Don't drink tomato juice and black coffee just before discovering a dead woman splattered over your car!

Variations on this one are few. In a rendition from France, where some regions are apparently notorious for their tiny garages, it's the wife who's killed when the drunken husband fails to see her inside the garage. Her body, stuck in the grille, is discovered the next morning when, after griping about the fact that she's not around to make him any breakfast, he backs out of the garage in full view of his neighbors.

It's a real-life Canadian tale, however, that came closest to re-creating the well-known legend when a cyclist, struck by a speeding truck, flew off the bike, over the cab of the truck, and into the bed. The driver fled the scene, apparently unaware of the fatally injured person he was carrying away. Widely reported on a *Year's Dumbest Crooks* segment, it was remembered less for the death than for the fact that police tracked the truck by the license plate left at the scene!

Real horror, though, begins when it invades places close to us. The front of cars, the back of pickups, some little-known funhouse—who really expects to be safe in those places? Safety and comfort, the building blocks of real security, begin with warm blankets, deep pillows, and nothing more dangerous than your cat curled around you toes.

"There Really Is Something Under the Bed!" takes direct aim at our fear of that brooding space under our mattress. It juxtaposes the scene of our earliest childhood fear and the center of our spiritual solace. A psychological study suggests we never actually put away those fears. Of nine thousand people surveyed, roughly 55%:45% male:female, a full 82 percent admitted they were "uncomfortable to very uncomfortable" with the thought of letting their hand hang over the side of the bed with the lights off. Nearly half would refuse to look under the bed at night, lights or no lights! Thirty-two percent had actually purchased beds with pedestal bases so they'd never have to worry about the "monsters under the bed" ever again—or so they thought!

Dead-person-under-the-bed legends vary

in location, but are surprisingly similar in other details.

Typically, a German couple takes center stage in "The Monster Under the Bed" when they arrive late and check into a hotel, usually not their first choice. The room looks fine, and because they're really tired, they quickly shower and tumble into bed. The next morning they both notice an odd, decidedly unpleasant smell clinging to everything in the room. On their way to breakfast, they report the scent to the concierge and ask for housekeeping to give the room a thorough cleaning. Returning a few hours later, they find the scent has grown from merely unpleasant to downright pungent!

Again the concierge is notified. A flustered manager arrives to defend his staff, but instead quickly agrees that the room stinks. The cleaning staff comes back and, under the watchful eyes of tourists and manager, opens all the windows and scours the entire room with powerful disinfectants. For a short time the room seems perfectly normal, and the couple eventually falls into bed for their second night.

Long before morning, the couple is awakened by the returning stench. This time they demand a new room. The night manager

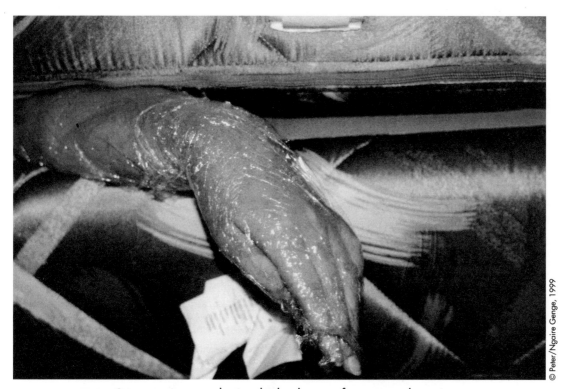

© Peter/Ngaire Genge, 1999

Some tourists must have a high tolerance for mattress lumps!

arrives to supervise the change in accommodations, and to apologize profusely for the difficulty. By then the woman's nose assures her the smell is coming from the bed itself. Her husband, apparently in the fifty percent of men who *aren't* afraid to peer under beds, hunkers down, but, other than dust bunnies, he finds absolutely nothing. The wife remains convinced the scent originates in the bed and insists that the staff flip the mattress. Proving the superiority of the noses of German matrons, they find a body in the advanced stages of decomposition!

The crime scene's location varies, embracing nearly every well-known hotel chain from Ho-Jo's to Doubletree, though Travelodge, EconoLodge, and other midrange hotels bear the brunt of this legend. The couple always spends at least one night actually sleeping with their unwanted bedmate. The tourists are nearly always a German couple—though that may simply reflect a strange reality. The Hoteliers Association doesn't keep statistics on the number of bodies found in and about their hotels, the nationalities of those who find them, or the frequency with which they break down and thoroughly clean a room, but bodies *do* turn up, and in an amazing number of cases, it's a *German* tourist who does the finding!

In south Florida, in a single year, three bodies were found in popular midrange hotels. In all three cases a pervasive odor was the first hint of trouble, and in two of those a German couple was in residence when the bodies were found. All three corpses were concealed under the bed.

One murderer, Jerry Lee Dunbar, made a habit of hiding his victims' corpses, including those of Deirdre Smith and Marilyn Graham, in hotel rooms. He shoved Graham under his bed; Smith spent some time there, too, but was eventually consigned to the crawl space beneath the floor itself. Like the rest, scent gave away the locations.

Even the quickest search of just three news archives reveals over thirty individual cases of bodies-under-the-bed being discovered by tourists in recent years. Those corpses shoved willy-nilly under any convenient box spring, just out of reach of the vacuum, obviously weren't intended for long-term storage. One body, discovered by a German couple in Fort Lauderdale, Florida, *was* wrapped in plastic when it was found by police, but that probably only delayed the discovery by "a few days, certainly not weeks."

Samuel Cornelius Walls, who was sentenced to fifty-two years in jail for the kidnap-rape-murder of Mary Jean DeOliviera, evidently gave some thought to disposal of the body. Perhaps taking the victim's history into consideration—the woman was once arrested for stealing a bottle of vodka—Walls washed the body and the room with vodka before secreting her under a platform bed and sleeping above her for several nights.

Murderers with long-term plans prefer these platform-supported beds, which, according to a Howard Johnson's house-keeper, are typically moved only once, "maybe twice," a year. Failing that, though, at least half a dozen bodies get stuffed into cutout spaces in the box spring and covered with the mattress. So, when it comes right down to it, it's not enough to look *under* the bed—even if you could work up the nerve!

Bedrooms, creepy enough places to find dead bodies, aren't the only places where people have stumbled over, into, even through, corpses.

Among emergency personnel and wreck-ing crews, the daily possibility of having to extricate bodies from crushed wrecks weighs heavy. That fear spread to ordinary folk in Great Britain when a simple slowdown on a major highway created a chain-reaction acci-dent that involved dozens of cars and trucks, even pedestrians. Injuries and deaths piled up as quickly as cars. Flames leaped along gas leaks. People died horribly. One man burned the skin from both palms in a futile effort to rescue passengers from a small car.

Urban legends in the months that fol-lowed included caught-in-fire tales, buried-alive tales, and, going to the heart of the traveling public's fear, a revival of stories like "The Lost Bug."

A young couple and their two children piled into their VW Bug and took off to holi-day at the seashore for the weekend. It was a clear day, so, not expecting any trouble, they zipped along, thinking that coming up with games to amuse the children would be their biggest problem.

Coming out of a sharp on-ramp, their view was temporarily blocked by concrete barriers installed to prevent cars from sliding off and falling to the highway below. Gunning the lit-tle engine to get up to the usual speed of traf-fic on a major highway, they burst out and, instead of slipping smoothly into the flow, found themselves racing toward a jackknifed semi! It only took one glance in the rearview mirror to realize that another problem— another big rig!—was barreling toward them.

The aftermath of the accident, which would eventually involve nearly twenty vehi-cles, took days to clear. The bigger wrecks, eighteen-wheelers and articulated trailers, were simply dragged to the side, their man-gled and entangled shapes more like bizarre modern sculpture than prosaic transport trucks. They certainly couldn't be taken away by a standard tow truck!

During the long cleanup procedure, which included extensive environmental efforts to capture lost gasoline and diesel fuels, an all-points bulletin on a missing family was circu-lated, but no sign was found of them. They never reached their hotel on the coast, and they didn't turn up back home. They simply disappeared.

Weeks later, after the site was made available to the wrecking crews that would cut the trucks apart and ship the scrap off to the wrecking yards, the mystery was solved when the bright red bug, and the dead family squashed inside, was discovered *between* two crumpled trucks.

Some variants actually link this story to the real crash; others mention Germany's Autobahn. In North America, the scene of carnage moves to "one of the big turnpikes" or a similarly busy locale. In some cases the family would have remained undiscovered indefinitely if not for the smell of decomposition that led wreckers to the hidden car. To date, no such incident has been reported anywhere.

"The Lost Bug" appears to be a direct descendent of other lost-car tales, though, some of which may trace their roots even farther back, to lost-wagon or lost-buggy tales!

"The Missing Studebaker," reported by several legend collectors in New York State, relates the story of a construction crew working on the upper links of a massive aquifer and aqueduct system that when complete, would funnel millions of gallons of water to the boroughs of New York City. In the process of dumping rubble away from the site of a new concrete pour, one of the workers heard a distinct *ting* where there should have been nothing but dirt sliding over dirt.

Calling to the dump-truck driver to stop, the worker scrambled down the bank and discovered they'd been dumping over an old woods road. The worker is horrified to discover a car, apparently passing by at the

time, now buried beneath the rocks and dirt, with nothing but the left rear fender sticking out! The worker yells for help and frantically digs into the pile, desperately trying to rescue the car's passengers, who he can imagine inside dying of suffocation!

Half a dozen men rally around and swiftly remove the loose dirt until one of them can jerk open a door. The family inside isn't in any hurry to leave; the skeletonized remains of a couple and their three children have clearly been sitting there for several decades. At a much less frenzied pace, the rest of the car is slowly uncovered to reveal a 1939 Studebaker caught in a rockslide some thirty years earlier!

A Canadian tale, "Collect-a-Wreck," incorporates all the main elements of lost-car stories, but sets them in a rather unusual venue.

In the early 1980s a local Canadian Broadcasting Company news station challenged residents to locate as many wrecks as they could and have the eyesores, environmental time bombs, dragged away to proper disposal sites. The program, Collect-a-Wreck, wildly successful on a local scale, pulled rusted heaps from backyards, woods, even bogs, and was quickly expanded to cover the entire province.

The legends arose when rumors that the program was actually a ruse to locate a particular vehicle, missing for years and suspected of harboring a large amount of lost, hidden, or stolen money, began circulating.

Various descriptions of the vehicle ran through high schools where students were actively involved in searching out and removing the wrecks. A gray sedan with a broken right front headlight, or with a bullet hole in the driver's door, or with the trunk locking mechanism jammed with a piece of metal (to keep anyone from getting in and finding the money) proved most popular. All over the province, students weren't just looking for cars, but were tearing them apart in search of the hidden money.

One group of car hunters, in true legend style, found a little more than the money— they found the thieves, dead for over twenty-five years, sitting in the car after killing each other!

Tales mixing truth and fantasy remain the most difficult to nail down. This time the program was real; the whole dead-bodies-and-stolen-money-in-the-car part was the fiction.

What makes these tales persist is simply that occasionally they are true, in every detail.

A piece of Arkansas folklore, "A Man, a Worm, and a Car," relates the story of an elderly man who wanders out to his favorite fishing hole one morning, only to snag an unsuspected wreck instead of breakfast. He reports the drowned vehicle, but since it's local custom to toss old junkers in the nearest pond instead of paying to have them dumped legally, there's no rush to get it out. Looks like it's been down there awhile, anyway. No one thinks much of it until the car

has been pulled from the shallow pond and loaded aboard a tow truck. Something glinting on the ground beside the truck catches the old fisherman's eye, and with help from the toe of his shoe, he turns up a finger bone still encircled by a gold wedding band!

The mystery of a supposedly runaway wife is solved, leaving her out-of-county husband, who has suffered these many years, still alone but knowing he hadn't been deliberately deserted.

Tragically, this old tale came true for five families in Palm Beach and surrounding areas last year. A man fishing in the canals just outside Boca Raton was looking for the bright reflections of some local fish. What he hooked instead was a van that had once sported brilliant yellow stripes and outrageous painted palms on its side panels. A strange catch indeed.

Because it could prove an obstruction to water traffic in the shallow water, it was quickly pulled out and slated for crushing at a local yard.

In the Lake Park impound, years of accumulated mud and guck exerted considerable strain on the body of a rusted van that no longer had the support of its watery environment. Eventually the back doors of the battered vehicle burst open, and a human shin bone slid out on the pavement. On closer examination, five skulls and enough bones to reconstruct the accompanying bodies were found inside.

Five young people, Kimberly Marie

WHAT TO WEAR?

Everyone's heard stories of people being buried in their favorite suit, or with a treasured object tucked inside the coffin. On the next level, the level of legends, are stories of eccentrics buried in their four-poster beds, or in their best canoe, or in hip waders, or . . . well, you get the idea.

Sandra West, heiress to an oil fortune, died in 1977 and put all the legends to shame by being buried in a baby-blue '64 Ferrari. For this important event, she sat behind the wheel in a lace negligee.

Barnes, William R. Briscoe, Matthew G. Henrich, Phillip Joseph Pompi, and John Paul Simmons, had been located eighteen years after supposedly leaving on a road trip to California that didn't even take them as far as the state line.

They'd died in their own backyard and no one had realized it.

Declare any location "safe," and, without fail, there's a legend to destroy such naïveté.

In our rural past, barn dances and church socials provided places to meet, greet, and do a little necking out behind the shed. Today it's the mall, and urban legends are ready to open our eyes to the dangers lurking somewhere between Wal-Mart and the A & P!

"The Commercial" is perhaps the most complex.

"Hey, you like pizza?" A guy with a clipboard and a tray of miniature pizza samples jumps in front of a pretty girl. "Try this, tell me what you honestly think, okay?" Giggling, the girl tries to move off, but the guy is insistent. "Oh, come on, just one bite?"

Eventually she tries a steaming morsel, and, much to her surprise, it's delicious! He offers her a different combination. Likewise, marvelous! Her enthusiastic comments leave him smiling.

"Great, glad you like it. Now, can I let you in on a secret? We're testing this product, but we're also looking for people to appear in our commercial." He points to a camera up in the ceiling. "See that? We've got you on tape!"

"No! Oh, my God, I look awful!"

"You look great, really natural, which is what we were looking for. Actresses are fine, but we want real people, you know?" He rummages through the clipboard. "Oh, great, I'm out of release forms."

"Release forms?"

"Yeah, we need your permission to use you in our commercial and the release is a sort of contract. You let us use your tape and we pay you $250 dollars for a fifteen-second spot! Not bad, eh? Think of the shoes you can buy with that tonight."

"Two hundred and fifty dollars? Tonight?"

"Yeah, if I can just find that stupid form." He lays down his tray and rummages through a bunch of identical forms. "These are all filled in." He pauses for a minute. "Look, I've got to get some more hot samples from the van outside, and I know I've got some extra forms there. You want to come along, sign the forms, see our setup, get your money?"

She hesitates but the thought of that money in her hand eventually has her following him. Outside, he leads her to a panel van and opens the door for her to step inside. There's nothing in there!

Before she can back out, she's struck from behind, hustled deep inside, and tied up. She's never seen again—not alive anyway.

To the best of any police department's knowledge, this scenario has never been enacted anywhere, though warnings about just such a setup have burned their way across dozens of large cities and actually been investigated in a few despite the lack of any real, tangible evidence.

Constable Geoff Canning of the RCMP can see why people would believe in just such a situation. "Here in Edmonton, we have a huge mall. Thousands of young women and girls wander through here, alone, every day. If a sexual predator was hunting, he could do worse than choose a large mall for his predations.

"That particular scenario, while not real just yet, includes some pretty savvy ideas. In one sense, it's a reassuring story because it indi-cates that people, on some level, *are* aware of the strategies these people might use.

"The whole thing with the camera, for example, makes him look legitimate—even if the camera is nothing more than a standard security camera. The stack of forms already filled out gives the impression that others have signed on. Even the lure, the cash, isn't dangled too obviously. It's actually a pretty good setup, if you're a criminal."

Other twists in the tale suggest the pizza contains a sedative that'll make the woman easier to take, that the man has buddies in the parking lot, or that the "tester" tells the woman his crew is waiting outside to shoot the commercial. Each of these variations certainly makes the woman that much more vulnerable, and the execution that much more complicated.

Much simpler setups can be equally effective. Another legend that's been linked to the Edmonton Mall, as well as most other large shopping centers, including the Mall of America, is "The Lurker Beneath the Cars."

A woman leaves the mall with her keys gripped firmly in her hand to return to the car she's left parked under a bright sodium vapor lamp. Keeping a close eye on her surroundings, she walks with purpose, never lingering near any pools of shadow. There's no one in sight when she quickly slips the key in the lock. Suddenly, pain lances through her ankle. Her leg crumples. As she gropes at her bloody leg, she realizes her hamstring has been cut and that her assailant is crawl-

The Killer-Cam view?

ing out from under her car with the knife still in his hand!

Helpless to run, the woman is shoved into her own car and taken off, never to be seen again. Another remarkably consistent tale, which really has only one variation. Perhaps in response to the outbreak of Rohypnol-induced rapes reported in the past few years, or as an adjunct to the used-needle scares that have been raging for nearly a decade now, some larger centers have substituted a syringe full of Mickey Finn Oil for the knife. This version was included in an episode of *The X-Files,* "Unruhe," and made Special Agent Dana Scully, usually the antithesis of the helpless female, a victim.

Again, the moral is simple: Never assume your precautions are enough, or your mall parking lot safe enough!

Even in broad daylight, with people aplenty about, urban legends can still remind us how vulnerable we appear to the serious predator.

A bit of a modern-day Red Riding Hood tale, "The Ride" is always set in the shimmering heat of a parking lot at high noon. People bustle back and forth. There's no immediate sign of danger. In fact, on the face of it, there's nothing to worry anyone. A woman arrives back at her car, which, having nothing important in it, she hasn't bothered to lock. An elderly woman is sitting on the backseat, the door open, with her feet rest-ing outside on the pavement, looking perfectly harmless.

Asked what she's doing in the car, she claims to have been overcome by heat, or to have simply become too tired to get all the way to the mall. Seeing this car unlocked, she'd just paused for a moment. The woman stows her packages in the trunk while waiting for the woman to leave—but she doesn't. Eventually she asks the woman when she'll feel ready to go on her way. Now, panting heavily, the woman claims to be feeling quite ill and asks for a ride to the nearest hospital.

The car's owner quickly agrees, but, claiming to have left a friend inside, says she'll have to let her know she's leaving. Back at the mall, where there's no friend, she finds the nearest security guard and quickly explains that she has a stranger in her car who refuses to leave. Outside again, the security guard, a modernized version of the woodsman, manages to pin down what seemed "odd" to the driver: the woman sitting in her car has hairy arms. It's a man impersonating a woman! The wolf!

Occasionally the woman does offer her wolf a ride, only noticing that the "woman" has hairy arms when she's far away from help. For these stories to have any shot at the "happily ever after" ending, the woman must use some ingenuity, similar to the nonviolent revenge scenarios, to survive her own stupidity. For example, she may stop for a windshield wash at a gas station (where she finds a new woodsman in the form of the atten-

dant); stop to check the rear brake lights (the old woman is asked to have a quick peek while the driver applies the brake, but the driver applies the accelerator instead); or she may drive to the nearest police station (where she finds lots of woodsmen).

A true classic of the fear-and-invasion variety begins, once again, with a young woman traveling along in the supposed safety of her own car. It's late in the evening, but not unusually so. It's dark out, but certainly not the "dark and stormy night" of gothic horror tales. Nor does she have far to travel, probably no farther than the distance from her local mall to her suburban home. Still, suburbia isn't the busiest place in the world, and when she notices a car behind her, hanging on her bumper, she begins to get nervous.

Putting her foot to the gas doesn't help, but merely spurs the driver behind her to speed up as well. When he starts flashing his lights at her, she grips the wheel in both hands and races toward home. When she's just a few miles from her driveway, blaring horns erupt behind her and continue even as she pulls up in front of her house, stumbles out, and runs, screaming, across the lawn.

Her husband, not to mention dozens of neighbors, pour out of their homes in response to the racket. Fully expecting the second car to shoot on by with all these witnesses about, the woman is shocked when it screeches to a halt immediately behind her car and the driver jumps out with a tire iron in his hand! They're even more startled when, instead of pursuing the woman, he yanks open her rear door and drags a rough-looking man from her backseat!

A heavy-bladed knife is found, half-hidden under the driver's seat.

All the horn-blowing and light-flashing had been the second driver's response to seeing the man with the knife popping up in the backseat. By drawing her attention to her rearview mirror each time the man attempted to attack, the "woodsman" of this tale had given the woman a chance to glimpse the man behind her or, as it turned out, delay the attack long enough for the woman to reach the safety of her home.

Again, a tale with a clear message: Check the inside of your car before getting in it!

Moving the action from cars to the heart of our hopes for security, our homes, is the basic premise of yet another classic, "The Choking Doberman."

A young woman arrives home and is immediately confronted with the sight of her Doberman pinscher sprawled on the floor, gasping, clearly in serious distress. Without wasting a moment, she drags him back out to her car, hefts him into the backseat, and races for the nearest veterinary clinic!

Once there, they whisk her canine friend into the operating room, and since she isn't allowed in while they're treating the animal, they advise her to go on home. They'll call her when they have something to pass along, good or bad.

The phone is ringing when she arrives

home and, fearing the worst, she sprints to answer it. It's the vet, but his message seems to have nothing to do with her dog.

"Get out of the house! Now! I've called the police! Run!"

Scared and confused, she does as she's told and is standing in her front yard when several police cars race up. As half a dozen officers run past her and into the house, one stops to explain the situation. The vet had quickly identified the dog's problem when, on examination, he found two human fingers lodged in the dog's throat!

Since the dog couldn't have survived long in that condition, the vet knew the attack must have occurred just moments before she arrived to find her dog is such distress—the fingers' owner could still be in the house!

Sure enough, they find the bleeding man, short two fingers and showing advanced signs of shock, still crouched in the closet where he hid to escape the protective dog. A large knife found in the closet with him makes it clear he intended to do more than rob her!

"The Mexican Pet," perhaps the best known of all urban legends (Brunvand made it the title of one of his collections of urban legends), takes "The Choking Doberman" (also the title of one of Brunvand's books) and turns it on its ear.

In this popular tale, a woman and her family pop across the California/Mexico border for a day's shopping and perhaps a little cultural education. While there, the kids share their picnic lunch with a stray dog wandering along the edge of a parking lot. The little thing follows them about for most of the day, continuing to be fed by the kids and eventually by Mom as well. When the time arrives to go back, the kids start the "He's a stray, Mom, can we take him home?" song and dance. Mom, a softy, gives in after deciding they can probably hide the critter in the spare-tire well in the trunk just long enough to get over the border.

With all their shopping receipts and forms in order, the border guard is satisfied with a cursory check of the trunk and the mother, breathing a quick sigh of relief, boogies back into California. The kids play with their new dog all the way home, plying it with food until Mom, afraid for the upholstery, suggests they just let it sleep for a bit.

Back home, it's accepted by the family's other canine companion, a toy poodle, and the last hurdle seems to have been crossed.

Several days later, however, the family is awakened by bizarre squeals coming from the basement. Telling the children to stay upstairs, the mother rushes downstairs. The bloody remains of Fifi the poodle, recognizable by the tufts of white fur left in the trail of gore leading to a new hole in the wall, send Mom back up the stairs in a rush.

The father doesn't need to go down before deciding to call pest control, the exterminator, and local animal control. In the meantime, neither Mom nor the kids can find the new dog, either, and they begin to fear the worst.

Armed with tanks of gas, the long noose on a stick, and several nets, the assembled experts head down to the basement. When they emerge an hour later, the family is horrified to see their new dog dangling from the end of the pole, clearly quite dead. The animal control officer, confused, dumps the dog in a bag.

"Look, I'm sorry about your poodle, but your other dog must be around here somewhere—probably smart enough to hide—and now that we've killed this Mexican sewer rat, it should be safe!"

The variations on this one are numerous. Some change the person who kills the rat, others the breed of dog that gets killed or the length of time before the rat reverts to type. Some even change the identity of the "new dog" to a Guatemalan rat, a Honduran rat, or whatever. In one divergent version, the rat is exposed when the woman takes it to the vet for routine shots.

The underlying theme remains unchanged, warning us against allowing virtual strangers into our lives without a thorough vetting! Though none of the tales related in this section has included an ethnic slant, many are easily adapted to xenophobic fears in addition to our basic fear of invasion. In "The Choking Doberman," the fingers are sometimes identified as belonging to a black man or a Latino. The woman who races home with a killer in the backseat, in some versions, notes that the second driver is black and this heightens her fears.

Gives a whole new meaning to "What did you give up for Lent?"

Taking our fear of invasion, of strangers, of different cultures, and of dead bodies to the ultimate extreme is "The Care Package."

A family in Austria often received packages of clothes and such luxurious food items as spices, dried fruit and meats, and other nonperishable items from an elderly aunt who'd moved to America, but had never forgotten those at home in the Old World. Her parcels were always a treat, often including chocolates and candies for the children and a long, newsy letter that was read over supper.

When the next package arrived, however, it contained only a single large jar and a letter in English! Putting the letter aside until the weekend, when a niece who could read English would be home, the hausfrau eyed the contents of the jar and decided it must be a seasoning of some type and proceeded to sprinkle it over a variety of foods, without much result, in an effort to discover just what it might best be served with. Her family simply shrugged as dish after dish appeared basically unchanged except for a slightly gritty texture added to some foods.

When the niece appeared, the frustrated and impatient housewife had a small snack waiting, but as soon as hospitality was satisfied, she handed the niece the letter and asked what sort of meal this condiment was intended to season.

The niece's eyes widened as she read, and she sank into a chair before asking, "You haven't eaten any of it, have you?"

"Yes, I've tried it in everything I can think of, even that muffin you just had. Nothing!"

The matron was shocked when her niece, gagging, raced to the washroom and, according to the sounds emanating from inside, proceeded to throw up the muffin and anything else she might have eaten for the rest of the day.

Back in the kitchen, the shaken girl made sure the cover was on the jar, then took it out and stood it on the mantel.

"The letter is from your aunt's companion. She says Aunt Ingrid wanted to be buried in Austria, and, since the estate didn't leave enough to ship a coffin in good time for burial, she authorized a cremation and has sent you the ashes in the hope that you'll carry out Aunt Ingrid's last wish."

Unbelievably, there are worse invasion stories—discovering something *missing* from your body!

INVASION OF THE BODY-PART SNATCHERS

In the early nineties, a new invasion story circulating around North America, Europe, the Indian subcontinent, and large parts of Africa quickly made all the old legends seem, well, almost unimportant.

An American example begins in Baton Rouge, Louisiana, during the famous Mardi Gras celebrations. William Rowe, a single guy, came to town on business but soon found himself caught up in the party spirit. When a group in his hotel's bar spilled out onto the street, he staggered right along. The parades, the dancing, the food, the half-naked women, and especially the bourbon, swirled into a single experience—then nothing!

Rowe awoke the next morning, not on his bed or curled up on his coat in one of the city's parks, but back in his own hotel room, in the bathtub! A tub full of ice water, the cubes floating all around his shivering body! Before he could pull himself out, he noticed that someone had been rearranging his furniture. A desk chair dragged into the bathroom held a phone and a note. Still in a state of shock, Rowe picked up the note.

Dear Sir,

Reach behind you and feel your back. You need to see a doctor immediately. Do not move. Do not leave the tub. Louisiana is on the Emergency Response Network. Call 911. You have been warned!

On feeling his way across his back, Rowe quickly discovered a tube running from a surgical incision! When he could finally get his shaking fingers to tap out 911, the operator who answered his call repeated the warning: "Do not get out of the tub, sir! I have emergency personnel on the way. Don't leave the tub!"

The EMS team that arrived, far from being surprised by his predicament, seemed all too familiar with the situation and rushed him to a local hospital where the emergency staff there, too, appeared to know more about what had happened to him than he did.

After being pushed through a battery of tests, he was tucked in bed to await the doctor's verdict: Someone had stolen his kidney!

In addition to the poorly investigated "news reports" that typically turn up when any urban legend first sweeps into a new region, this legend became the plot for a widely seen prime-time series. Despite its usual disclaimer, "The people and situations depicted herein are fictitious," *Law & Order* is well known for its ripped-from-the-headlines stories, so, when two New York City cops discover a blood-soaked man—alive, but minus a kidney—on a Central Park bench in "Sonata for Solo Organ," it would be surprising if the audience *didn't* assume the entire scenario was reality-based.

Fortunately, marauding gangs of organ thieves aren't yet lurking at Mardi Gras celebrations, picking up likely candidates in bars, or casing the dormitories of America. Anyone waking up in a bathtub full of ice cubes is undoubtedly the butt of a practical joke, but nothing more.

So prevalent did the stories of stolen organs, kidneys in particular, become during the middle nineties, however, that the National Kidney Foundation in the United States and Transplant Ontario in Canada both established permanent Web sites to deal with the multitude of inquiries flooding their switchboards daily.

The location of choice for "The Phone in the Bathroom" might be the United States, but the Land of Opportunity probably isn't the point of origin for this tale. Selling organs is illegal here; other countries consider body parts property that can be freely bought and sold—so freely, in fact, that Ahmet Koc, a citizen of Turkey, took out an ad announcing he had a spare kidney for sale! He ended up in Great Britain and was shortly relieved of his kidney. A simple business transaction concluded to everyone's satisfaction, right? Sort of. Almost as soon as Koc's kidney hit the ice chips, he started screaming "Theft!"

The story took up its share of headlines, was even reported in the United States via BBC's *World Service* newscast. It's a sad fact that wild claims get air time while court decisions, like the one proving Koc had willingly given up his kidney, are lucky to find their way into the footnotes.

Even if there are unscrupulous surgeons willing to sneak out an extra organ from time to time (three Indian doctors face such charges as this book goes to press), even if Third World poverty ensures an endless supply of those desperate enough to give up parts of themselves for cash, the basis of the current version of "The Phone in the Bathroom"—the unwary traveler invaded while innocently involved in some social activity—has absolutely no basis in fact.

BURIED ALIVE!

Urban legends race from person to person, changing and evolving with each telling. A sort of folkloric State of the Union address, they reflect our modern fears—especially those so-called modern fears that actually have been with us for millennia, like death.

Stumbling over a dead body is spooky, and provides fodder for dozens of modern myths; being *mistaken* for a corpse, however, makes for truly personal nightmares—and great legends!

It was 1943. The war was at its height. The bodies of soldiers were being shipped home by the hundreds. Their stacked coffins filled the holds of ships designed to carry less precious cargoes. Long, dark aisles between rows of identical boxes discouraged crewmen from lingering below decks. When a stormy crossing forced the captain of HMS *Pansy* to post a watch below, the assignment was less popular than cleaning the heads or the bilges. Seamen Charles Veitch and Malcolm Campbell, the two unlucky enough to draw the assignment, spent much of their shift huddled close to one another, playing a desultory round of poker.

The first low moan was ignored. Ships creak. Heavy seas cause ropes to groan against the strain. It could've been anything, anything at all. Maybe a seasick rat! Except rats don't call "Help!" in the middle of the night, don't pound on the inside of coffins, don't scream out their terror!

Finding one box amid hundreds took time. Freeing it from the ones over, under, and to either side of it gave Veitch and Campbell plenty of time to memorize the sound of absolute horror. Forcing the lid from a military coffin with just two pocket knives and a short crowbar took the better part of a half hour, but neither man, listening to the whimpering pleas for freedom, could bear to leave, not even to bring assistance.

When the cover finally gave way, a white-haired specter, hands bloody from clawing at the lid, rose up to wrap itself around them. It clung to them. As the two men held the sobbing man, all three realized that, except for an accident of weather, no one would have heard the screams of Private Albert Cooghan—and, but for the grace of God, it could have been any one of them screaming away the last of his oxygen inside that box!

Mary Baker Eddy, founder of the Christian Science Church, was, according to legend, going to make sure she didn't get buried before the Good Lord called her home. As she'd recovered from near-fatal injuries before, in a fashion she claimed bordered on the miraculous, it made sense that she'd need some extra insurance, right? To facilitate her swift removal from the vault, or just in case she needed to contact any of her followers with breaking news from the world beyond, Eddy reportedly had a telephone installed in her crypt.

Or maybe she was calling Mr. Ball, of canning-industry fame, who also had a phone installed in the family vault against the possibility of being accidentally sealed inside a little early. To the best of anyone's knowledge, however, neither was burning up the wires, at least not for the two years immediately after Mr. Ball's death. When his widow

THE BIG "D"

Not surprisingly, death is the most commonly reported fear. What is surprising is that, when pressed, a significant number of people confess it isn't pain or suffering or fear of the unknown that generates all that dread—it's embarrassment!

Considering the irony of the following deaths, actual incidents that have mutated into regional legends, embarrassment is a real issue!

A young man in Texas returned home after a night on the town, tripped on his garden hose, fell, became further entangled as he struggled, and eventually strangled himself!

An angry golfer threw his club at a golf cart. The club broke in half, and one piece ricocheted back at him and sliced open his jugular vein, killing him.

A good old boy in Arizona stopped to fire a few rounds into a saguaro cactus—which promptly toppled over and crushed him to death.

A hospital worker in Massachusetts was dragged into an industrial dryer. He didn't survive the six-minute tumble at 120 degrees.

An armored car guard died when $50,000 worth of quarters landed atop him as his partner braked to avoid an accident.

An Iranian man attempting to pin a snake to the ground with his shotgun was shot himself when the snake coiled around the trigger and the gun discharged. The snake escaped, but the hunter died of his injuries.

was found dead of a heart attack in her kitchen, a look of terror across her face and a phone receiver clasped in her cold hand, everyone assumed she'd died while trying to call for help. It was only as she was being slipped into the crypt next to her husband that anyone discovered *his* phone was also off the hook!

Dr. Fantas, a medical examiner with the state of New York, couldn't reach anyone by phone when six bodies arrived in his morgue for autopsy just moments before he was due to leave for the day. The bodies, victims of a bank robbery gone bad, needed immediate attention, but, without more staff, Dr. Fantas could only tag and wash the bodies, complete the paperwork for bagging the victims' personal belongings and clothes, and store the corpses in the body safe before calling his wife to see if she needed anything picked up on the way home. She didn't, so he locked up and left for the night. Imagine his surprise an hour later when, as he was about to sit down to supper, his phone rang and his caller ID identified the caller at his empty morgue!

The young woman on the other end of the line seemed as confused as the good doctor. She had no idea where she was, where her clothes were, or why she'd been left amid five dead bodies!

By the time Fantas and security arrived at the morgue, Glenda Pasquez was past her initial disorientation. She knew exactly where she'd woken up, exactly where the through-and-through hole at the base of her neck came from, exactly why she was stark naked on a cold slab, and exactly how close she'd come to having her insides displayed! Ms. Pasquez wasn't asking questions anymore, she was screaming her head off in an effort to attract help!

Why had she called Fantas? How had she known his number?

She didn't.

The phone in the morgue, part of a larger switchboard, wouldn't let her dial outside without pressing "9" first. Desperate and unable to understand why the phone wouldn't work, she'd simply hit Redial. The last person called was Dr. Fantas's wife, just before he left!

A separate direct line was installed in the morgue the next day.

Or it would have been if there really was a Dr. Fantas or a Glenda Pasquez!

This tale and the three preceding stories illustrate our common fear not only of death, but of finding ourselves supremely powerless. Similar stories featuring patients who, for one reason or another, awaken under the scalpel in mid-procedure, or find themselves physically unconscious while mentally alert, are careful to present situations that seem not only possible but perfectly plausible.

One of the most heartrending *M*A*S*H* episodes featured a soldier who'd already been zipped into his body bag before a single tear sliding across his cheek finally alerted Hawkeye that the "body" they'd been stepping around all show long was alive!

The Victorians created dozens of remarkable gadgets to give interred victims time and the ability to alert those aboveground to their predicament. Breathing tubes, bells activated by the movement of glass spheres laid on the decedent's chest, flags designed to spring from their concealed position inside funeral-poles once a string inside the coffin was pulled, and, of course, speaking horns to let the trapped victim bellow for help were all available to those afraid the legends would come true.

The Germans created a whole new business, the "waiting mortuary," whose sole purpose was to provide a place where bodies could sit around and begin to rot—the only sure sign that a person was actually dead. Elaborate strings, bells, and pulleys attached to each finger would bring the attendants running should any of the bodies so much as twitch. To stifle the scent of putrefaction and hide the zinc trays and antiseptic vats under the bodies, banks of flowers surrounded the corpse. It's unclear whether anyone actually benefited from the elaborate setups, but urban legends had attached themselves to the process even back in 1785. According to one in Munich, a child was actually saved by the procedure, but on seeing her revived child, the mother was so overcome by emotion that she died on the spot!

Medically documented cases of supposedly dead persons suddenly coming to life *do* exist, though less often now than in previous years as we develop more accurate means of detecting life.

Oh, and, for the record, Mary Baker Eddy never asked to have a phone installed in her crypt. There is no phone in her crypt. A line *was* connected to the cemetery for the convenience of the very-much-alive security officer who watched over her body at Mount Auburn Cemetery's general vault until her crypt was prepared a few days later.

". . . PASSED PEACEFULLY AWAY"—NOT!

Perhaps the only thing worse than "waking up dead" is dying unnaturally in the first place! Legends of maniacal killers, deadly spirits, and the shades of those killed brutally or young (usually both!) make up the scariest tales of all and are, for many, the essence of urban legends—the real classics.

In "The Dead Roommate," two young women (though later versions sometimes include two young men, an example of equal opportunity in action) find themselves alone on a Friday afternoon, the last to leave their dormitory at the College of William and Mary in Williamsburg, Virginia, for the much-anticipated Christmas vacation. One, Tracy, is the only child of divorced parents. Because she can't spend the holiday with both of her folks, she stays in town to meet up with her dad before leaving to visit her mom. Her father is due to arrive the next morning, but has sent word that if he got off early, he'd try to catch an earlier flight and pick her up that night to go to his hotel. So, as Tracy and Pat, the dormitory supervisor, sit down to supper together, both girls are hoping to spend Friday night somewhere else, Tracy with her dad, Pat with her boyfriend, before likewise taking off for the holiday.

When the doorbell sounds below, Tracy grabs up her bag. "That must be for me! I'll see you in the New Year!"

Pat smiles and tucks the extra plate in the fridge. "Have a great time. I'm sure Phil will take care of that when he arrives."

About an hour later, Pat hears the bell again and goes downstairs to let in her own visitor. The two spend the evening exchanging their gifts, polishing off the food and a large bottle of wine, and engaging in a little petting. When Phil suggests he stay the night, especially since Pat is in the dorm alone until she catches her train in the morning, Pat is seriously tempted. However, the supervisor is a paid position and one of the rules is that no men stay overnight, no exceptions. Phil points out that there's no one left in the building to set a good example for, but Pat, despite Phil's best efforts, sends him on his way at a decent hour.

Later that night, she wishes she hadn't!

A heavy thumping startles her awake and sends her racing across her room to make sure she has really locked the door. As she waits to see if the thumping is repeated, a low moan, just barely audible, seems to float through the heavy door. When she crouches closer, however, she hears nothing! Eventually she manages to convince herself it was just pipes or the wind or whatever else encourages old dormitories to produce weird sounds, and leaving her door locked and the lights on, she goes back to bed.

On leaving the next morning, she finds the butchered body of Tracy, who never did meet her father, lying across the doorway!

If she'd opened the door when she heard the first groan, she might have saved her friend's life. Then again, if the maniac was still in the building, she might have ended up dead as well!

Two more roomies star in "Don't Turn On the Lights!" One girl, Lindsey, has been feeling unwell for several days, and when the rest of her floor descends on the common room for a pre-final crash session, she decides she'd be better off with an early night and skips the pizza-and-physics cram. Her roommate, Gayle, realizing she's left one of her notebooks upstairs, creeps in quietly and, without turning on the lights, gropes her way over her desk until she finds her backpack. Not bothering to search out the individual book here, she grabs the whole thing and slips out again. She's equally considerate when, hours later, she sneaks in and crawls into bed.

The next morning, Lindsey is still curled in her bed when Gayle awakes, obviously not intent on getting up just yet. Secretly glad to have first crack at the shower, Gayle slips into the bathroom. She's just started the tub and put paste on her toothbrush when she sees "Aren't you glad you didn't turn on the lights?" written across the mirror in lipstick! Suddenly scared, Gayle races back into the room to shake Lindsey awake and demand an explanation.

When Lindsey rolls over at Gayle's first touch, it's obvious she won't be answering questions at all—not with her throat slit!

"The Dog Under the Bed" assumes the two women are living in one of the student-run apartments instead of a traditional dormitory, but like the two prior stories, this one is set on Any Campus, U.S.A.

Sarah and Tiffany share their apartment with Tiffany's happy-go-lucky Irish setter, Red. The dog, given its choice, would spend every night lolling about on Tif's bed, but, as the bed is only a small twin (about all you could fit in such cramped quarters), Red has adjusted to being pushed off the bed in mid-snooze by simply crawling under whichever bed he's closest to when he hits the floor!

So, when Sarah returns to their place after a late date and falls into bed without turning on the lights, she isn't in the least surprised to hear something move under her bed, or to have a wet tongue stroke across her palm when her hand happens to dangle over the side of the bed.

Sometime later that night, she's awakened by a steady drip-drip coming from the bathroom, but instead of getting up, she buries her head under the covers and goes back to sleep.

The dripping is gone when she wakes at nearly lunchtime the following day, as are her roommate and Red. Enjoying this rare bit of privacy, she goes to the bathroom, where she uses the toilet and splashes water over her face before brushing her teeth. She doesn't bother to shower or change yet, deciding to have a leisurely brunch before getting ready for the rest of her day. A bagel and a cup of coffee later, she's just pinning up her hair and reaching for the taps when her fingers brush something furry beyond the curtain!

Yanking back the curtain, she's horrified to find her roommate and Red hanging from the shower head, their throats cut, their blood—which had dripped all night—pooled in the tub below. Scrawled across the shower enclosure, in that same blood, is the message, "Humans can lick, too!"

Dormitory-invasion stories, prevalent during the early 1960s, when women first began moving out of the house in large numbers, return to prominence whenever real-life tragedies leap into the headlines. Both "The Dead Roommate" and "Don't Turn On the Lights!" became popular again in Canada when a madman slaughtered nine women at Montreal's Polytechnical Institute in 1996. All three tales circulate in a more limited way at the beginning of fall semesters and have been attributed to almost every major campus.

Young girls do three things really well: They watch TV, they babysit every chance they get, and they're always the first to get to a ringing phone. "On the Phone" plays into all three activities.

A couple ask a neighbor's daughter, fifteen-year-old Jennifer, to watch their three children while they go out for a well-earned evening alone. The girl is perfectly capable, the kids are asleep, and the parents have left all the numbers where they can be reached. Despite living in a rather out-of-the-way location, the couple leaves without a care in the world.

Jennifer is deep into the network premier of *While You Were Sleeping* when the phone rings the first time. A deep voice cackles at her, then intones, "I've got the children. I've got the children. I've got the kids!"

Convinced it's someone playing a bad joke on her, she slams down the phone. A few moments later the phone rings again. "I've got the children. I've got the children!" She slams the phone down again.

When it rings again, she turns up the TV and tries to ignore it. It keeps ringing!

Turning the sound down, she considers calling the parents for instructions. Afraid it's actually someone she knows, maybe someone who called her own home earlier and was given this number, she hesitates for a second, then decides to call the phone company instead.

The operator takes the complaint and tells her they'll try to trace the calls. Mollified, she curls up to wait. This time there's no laughter, just the voice: "I'm going to kill the children. I'm going to kill the children. I'm going to kill the children."

Jennifer listens for as long as the operator suggested, then hangs up. She's about to go check the kids and the door locks when the phone rings yet again. This time it's the operator.

"Look, we can't trace this to an outside line. It must be coming from an extension inside the house! I've called the police! Get out!"

"The kids?!"

"Get out!"

She's barely reached the front lawn when a heavy man bowls her over. Her struggles gain her nothing. She can smell his breath, feel the handle of a heavy knife protruding from the fist pulling her hair. Jennifer knows she's about to die!

Suddenly, all around them, headlights blind her, sirens scream, and the flickering red and blue of police lights paint the scene

SCARY THINGS

The best horror flicks, the best thrillers, and the best urban legends all play into our most common fears. Here are a few of the least common. Though they're legitimate phobias, most sound like the plots for comedies instead of tragedies!

PELADOPHOBIA: fear of bald people

GENIOPHOBIA: fear of chins

COPRASTASOPHOBIA: fear of constipation

PEDIOPHOBIA: fear of dolls

AULOPHOBIA: fear of flutes

APEIROPHOBIA: fear of infinity

GENUPHOBIA: fear of knees

PENTHERAPHOBIA: fear of a mother-in-law

EPISTAXIOPHOBIA: fear of nosebleeds

LUTRAPHOBIA: fear of otters

ARACHIBUTYROPHIA: fear of peanut butter sticking to the roof of the mouth

METROPHOBIA: fear of poetry

PUPAPHOBIA: fear of puppets

OMBROPHOBIA: fear of rain

HOMILIOPHOBIA: fear of sermons

LINONOPHOBIA: fear of string

PTERNONOPHOBIA: fear of being tickled with feathers

PARTHENOPHOBIA: fear of virgins

PLUTOPHOBIA: fear of wealth

RHYTIPHOBIA: fear of getting wrinkles

in macabre colors. She's saved, but just by seconds. As two police officers drag off the maniac, others swarm through the house and find the children bound and gagged, but alive, in their beds.

(Some versions, especially the earlier ones, don't end quite this happily. In those variations, the parents arrive just as the police do, and while the cops are handling the invader, the parents discover their slaughtered children inside.)

Though this tale, like the other maniacal tales, seems apocryphal, not based on any single incident, it's been immortalized in any number of films, among them *When a Stranger Calls* and *Urban Legends,* as well as any number of television episodes.

An invader of a different sort lurks as close to us as our mirrors. In a true classic, perhaps more than a thousand years old, "Bloody Mary" waits, vampire-like, to be invited into our sanctum sanctorums, our bedrooms and bathrooms, places where we expect the most privacy, the most security.

Every girl who's ever attended a slumber party knows her by name, and knows that she was once beautiful and young, that she was horribly disfigured by a jealous friend who wanted Mary's boyfriend for herself (or that her face was cut to ribbons when her drunken boyfriend ran them off the road and Mary flew through the windshield, or that her boyfriend went crazy and slashed her face to pieces, or that she bled to death when the same boyfriend slammed her face through a

mirror). They also know how to call her forth from the other side.

Whispers and squeals seem integral to the setting, as important as the darkened room, the mirror, and the single candle placed before it. The chant, "Bloody Mary, come to us!" repeated thirteen times, gradually drowns out the whispers as those gathered about the mirror peer into it for the first sign of her hideous face. It's a love-hate relationship, though. Not a single girl around the mirror *really* wants to be the first to see her. According to the legend, the first to discern her misty shape will be her first victim, the one to have her own face slashed to bloody strips! Why would anyone hazard such a fate?

To belong.

In addition to providing the scare factor necessary for the success of any good slumber party, it's been the initiation rite imposed on younger sisters and friends for at least half a dozen generations!

If the story sounds familiar, but you've never heard of Bloody Mary, perhaps you've seen the film *Candyman*?

In a much less terrifying tradition, some Chinese girls make magic mirrors of their own by pouring spring water into a bowl, which is carried outside during the Moon Festival. When the moon can be seen clearly reflected in the water, young girls stare into the depth of the bowl in hopes of seeing the face of their future husband. Presumably, *he* doesn't rip them to shreds.

Vengeance plays into most supernatural

tales of horror, and what more natural setting could there be for a spooky story than a cemetery where a beautiful but badly abused young woman is buried under an awe-inspiring monument sculpted in her likeness?

As in the best-known versions of Bloody Mary, Black Aggie, the girl under the statue, died horribly at the hands of her lover, and, not surprisingly, Aggie's story is also the basis of an initiation ritual. Almost every cemetery sports at least one sizable angel, or a crypt with an appropriately spooky history. Imagine those towering stone guardians as they appear at night, especially on a foggy night with the moon casting just enough light to confuse, but not enough to illuminate. Imagine how loud every night sound becomes without the voices of friends to cover them. Imagine spending the night in the darkest spot in the whole cemetery, that statue's shadow. Now imagine that a single glance into her eyes will strip your screaming soul from your body!

If you can't grasp the difficulty in sitting alone in a cemetery for an entire night with a massive statue looming above you *without* looking into its face, try this: For the next ten minutes, *don't* think about pink elephants.

In one of the few instances of a legend becoming *less* dangerous over time, those who put themselves under Black Aggie's grace don't actually expect to be burned to death by her demon eyes. Being the brunt of their friends' laughter and taunts after sneaking back home could, of course, be considered a worse fate in some circles.

What makes Black Aggie tales intriguing is that occasionally real life intrudes, and aspects of the basic legend become entwined with actual events and people. This next variation is well established in eastern Canada.

In St. John's, Newfoundland, a young woman was killed and the man she'd agreed to marry, one John Breen, was charged with the murder. He protested his innocence throughout, but was nonetheless convicted of the crime in 1926.

It was a violent death, and perhaps to mitigate their awful last memories, the girl's parents erected a beautiful statue above her grave, an angel with their daughter's face, her arms reaching out. The statue required some maintenance, a task the family was happy to undertake.

In 1939, John Breen was released from jail, still claiming his innocence. During that time, he reportedly gave considerable thought to the particulars of the incident, and on regaining his freedom, he immediately accused his older brother of killing his fiancée.

Of course, there was no way to prove or disprove either brother's claims. John Breen and his family, however, were of Welsh descent, and the Welsh have folklore of their own, tales of the dead finding ways to accuse those who've done wrong by them. He proposed that if each of them spent a night above the grave, his bride-to-be might find her own way to tell them all the truth.

The older brother, Brian, wasn't having any of this until pressure from the community, everything from snide comments to outright shunning, left him with little choice if he wanted to live in his own home.

John and he, accompanied by half the neighbors, went off to the graveyard, where John immediately curled up on the base of the statue, between its arms and in the shade of its wings, to await morning. The same crowd arrived the next morning to find him still sound asleep and perfectly well.

Brian decided to spend his night on the ground—as far from the statue as he could get without leaving the confines of the grave site. The next morning, when the neighbors arrived, they found Brian curled in a ball at the foot of the statue, quite dead, with a look of stark terror frozen on his face. Needless to say, John was vindicated in the eyes of his community if not in the courts.

As the years passed and members of the fiancée's family died off, the statue began to fall into disrepair. A concerned community took it upon themselves to move the statue to a local park, where it could be cared for by public funds, and erected a smaller headstone on the original graves. To this day, some believe that a person guilty of any crime spending the night in the statue's shadow will die.

Separating the legend from local history is, in this case, made more difficult by a number of unusual circumstances. The Second World War turned the city into a staging area for thousands of units, the ideal condition for importing legends from other regions, thereby muddying the folkloric waters. In 1949, the then-country of Newfoundland became Canada's tenth province, creating as chaotic a paper trail as any detective would like to unravel. Municipal records were warehoused, submitted to new government agencies, or simply lost. Amazingly enough, it's remained possible to trace some key events. John Breen was convicted of the murder of Eileen Winter in the second half of 1926. A statue similar to the one described was a fixture at a local cemetery for nineteen years. Many people who grew up in the area around Victoria Park remember the statue clearly—two photos actually show a figure that could conceivably be the grave marker—being there until a drought shut down the city's numerous fountains. Many fountain figures and other statues were removed during this period to reduce maintenance costs; most were never replaced.

Interestingly, a short story titled "Silent Justice," by Maureen Jansen, which appeared in the fourteenth volume of a collection of speculative fiction, *Writers of the Future,* re-creates all these regional details while adding a *second* vengeance motif!

The best known of spook tales is undoubtedly "The Vanishing Hitchhiker," a story that's been well documented since at least 1944, and has been claimed by all fifty American states as well as several countries overseas.

The generic, nonregional version begins on an anonymous highway outside a large population center. The stretch, completely flat and straight, encouraged tired drivers to drift off as they floated through the darkness—just in time to slam into cars crossing the highway at the only intersection in a fifty-seven-mile section. A plan to put in an overpass keeps coming up in council, but because the intersection includes state as well as county roads, arguments over funding have left it on the back burner.

Our driver, a traveling salesman named Charles Best, while more careful than most, is still startled to see a young woman walking along the empty highway and swerves quickly to avoid her when she appears to lurch toward the pavement. Thinking this is no place for anyone to be alone, much less on foot, he throws the car into reverse and leans out the passenger window to ask her if she'd like a ride to the nearest gas station.

The front seat, covered with his orders, briefcase, samples, and lunch, would take ages to clear, so he suggests she hop in back. The young woman, clad in nothing more than a party dress, jumps at the chance to get off the road. Seeing her shiver as he pulls back onto the highway, he shrugs out of his jacket and hands it back to her. "Put this on until you get where you're going, okay?"

"Thanks, sir!"

"And where exactly were you headed out here all by yourself?"

"It's a long story. Thanks for the ride, though. You can let me off in the next town, if that's not too much trouble."

"Sure, where?"

The young woman tells him her parents live at 1616 Oak. He can drop her off there. Best has no problem with the short detour, and the two chat on and off for the next ten miles. When they reach town, Best turns his attention to the street signs, but in the dark, in an unfamiliar town, he's having a hard time locating Oak. When he turns to ask her for further directions, he finds himself staring into an empty backseat!

When he pulls over, there's absolutely no sign of her—or his coat!

Too spooked to continue, and anxious to report the incident to someone, Best decides to hold off on the next leg of his route and sleeps in his car until morning. When the local coffee shop opens, he makes inquiries about Oak Street and the location of the nearest police station. The waitress hands him coffee and a napkin on which she's drawn a rough map that should get him to Oak. The police station is actually half an hour down the road, in the next community. Thanking her, he hurries off to 1616 Oak.

There he knocks on the door and is relieved to have it opened by a woman who, though older, bears a family resemblance to the girl. Best assumes the woman is her mother. When he begins to explain about picking her daughter up the previous night, and how worried he was over her odd disappearance, the woman bursts into tears and runs back in the house. Since she's left the door swinging open, he follows after only a few moment's hesitation.

He's met halfway back through the main hallway by a gentleman who hustles him back out onto the porch.

"This is all very hard on my wife, especially with people showing up out of the blue lately."

"I'm sorry?"

"She says you tried to bring our girl home last night?"

"Yes, I did. I—"

"I know. Look, why don't you come with me? There's something you should probably see."

Mystified, but anxious to get to the bottom of it, Best follows the girl's father to his pickup truck and climbs inside. All his attempts to initiate further conversation are waved off until they pull up next to a cemetery. There the man climbs out and walks to a particular grave.

"This is my daughter's."

Stunned, Best leans in and reads the dates, which tell him the woman he'd picked up the previous evening had died over a year ago. There, next to the stone, is the coat he'd loaned her!

To give some idea of the scope of the tale's travel, the same plot not only appears in a Washington Irving novel, *The Lady with the Velvet Collar,* printed in 1824, but a modern comedic film, *Mr. Wrong,* released in 1985. One hundred twenty-one years old and still going strong!

While these supernatural twists intrigue us, the majority of classic horror legends center on physical threats, with "The Swinging Man" and "The Hook" being exceptional examples of the type.

"The Swinging Man" begins, for an *urban* legend, in a decidedly rural location when a young man, who's spent part of the evening joking with his date about "running out of gas" so they could neck, actually finds himself puttering to a stop some distance from the last gas station!

For the first little bit, they do indeed indulge in a little petting, but when the boyfriend suggests they take things further, the girl quickly backs off. For a time they sit quietly, listening to the radio and hoping someone will happen by and offer to assist with a lift back down the road. When an hour goes by without any traffic passing, the boyfriend finally kisses his date, lets the car roll off onto the shoulder under a tree, cautions her to stay in the locked car until he comes back, and, gas can in hand, heads back toward the distant gas station.

The wait grows boring in short order, so, to pass the time without wearing down the battery, she curls up under her coat on the front seat to nap. She snoozes for some time, eventually awakening to the sound of something scratching against the roof of the car. *Skritch-skritch.* It sounds like a branch of the tree rubbing over the vehicle in the wind.

It's annoying, and she's tempted to get out and crack off the offending branch. Remembering her boyfriend's admonition, however, she sighs, stays inside, and turns the radio back on, in hopes of drowning out the repetitive noise. When her young man still hasn't turned up an hour later, she assumes the gas stations in this rural area must close for the night and, deciding to put up with the noise rather than run out of light and sound later, curls up again. The noise continues, no better, no worse, but she eventually manages to drift off to sleep once more.

The sun is just coming up when a car goes by. Again, she's tempted to get out in the hopes of flagging someone down. Before she can make up her mind one way or another, she's startled by three police cars, lights flashing, pulling up around her. One officer quickly opens the door and leads her directly away from the car.

"Just come with me, miss, and, please, don't look back."

With that simple line he guarantees that, no matter what, the startled girl will somehow twist her head far enough around to see what she was leaving behind.

Dangling upside down above the car, his fingernails just brushing the roof, her boyfriend, who she'd thought was safe and sound on some gas station porch, hangs lifelessly.

As the screams rise in the back of her throat, the officer drags her away from the scene while attempting to explain about a killer who's been operating in the area.

"The Hook" also starts with a couple of young lovers out for an evening of simple necking on Lovers' Lane. Things are pro-

gressing well, at least from the young man's point of view! The girl responds to his advances; the radio plays slow, sleepy love songs; and for the first time in weeks they've got the whole place to themselves!

He's about to press his attentions when an announcer interrupts the programming to bring them a special announcement. An escapee from a hospital for the criminally insane is on the loose! The man, described as gaunt, dark, limping, and with a hook instead of a left hand, was last seen just minutes outside of town.

The mood is dead.

Regardless of his inducements, his young lady is having nothing further to do with him. Even when he turns angry instead of ardent, she demands to be taken home immediately. Frustrated, he burns out of the narrow lane and heads straight for his date's house. Despite her attempts to at least engage him in conversation, he ignores her. By the time he pulls up in front of her house, she's more than ready to leave, and jumps out before he can even come around and open the door. Just as she's about to slam it, she shrieks.

Dangling from the door handle is a prosthetic forearm with a gleaming steel hook!

These classic tales, like those that began this chapter, share one obvious element. Whether it's an entirely human maniac, a lonely ghost, or even a supernatural fiend, they all force their way into those places their victims find most secure, proving that no one is safe anywhere!

HAPPY HOLIDAYS

he special occasions of our lives, rare moments outside our daily grind, spawn a picturesque subset of urban legends often called proto-tales. The modern myths we've examined so far all defy borders. Like "The Hook," they spring up across broad geographic and ethnic regions, essentially unchanged except for the substitution of local place and family names that make each story more personal, more immediate, to the listener.

Special-event legends, however, while adhering to the definition of an urban legend, frequently exhibit a different flavor and, initially, pervade a distinctly localized area. Some eventually break out, gaining prominence among the general population, but most remain isolated, though unusually well accepted, within a particular area.

Many folklorists view these proto-tales as local gossip that, if heard at a moment when a specific fear is rampant, can rapidly escalate, grow, and evolve into full-blown legends reflecting the emotional landscape of the larger population.

"Flashpoints," the moments when territorial stories abruptly find their audience, may well be inspired by factual events. Grisly murders, natural disasters, wars, and epidemic diseases create highly charged emotional responses in literally millions of people within abnormally short periods of time. The bombing of the Federal Building in Oklahoma City shocked, revolted, and stunned an entire

> Medieval English marriages came in two types: church and private. Church weddings transferred property. Private weddings allowed for easy dissolution if the couple discovered they just weren't suited. The rich got land, and the landless probably had happier family lives!

country in less than two hours. In short order, even before rescuers began digging for bodies instead of survivors, entombment proto-tales, which had previously circulated in sequestered pockets as small as a single town, raced from person to person, erupting hundreds, sometimes thousands, of miles from their long-established point of origin.

Considering that most proto-tales feature special events like weddings and birthdays, occurrences affecting entire populations, at some point in their lives, special-event tales would seem likely candidates for broad audience appeal, capable of engaging the imagination of nearly everyone. Why, then, would it require an incident on the level of a national disaster to bring them to prominence? One theory, that proto-legends are based on factual events and therefore are originally circulated only among those who participated in the events, their immediate circle of friends and family, suggests that they aren't handed on as legends because the originators *knew* they weren't legends.

If that theory proves true, then the evolution of some widespread urban legends may require either a major initiating incident, like the Oklahoma City bombing or the AIDS epidemic, or a period of distancing during which residents in the area where the proto-legends arise can forget the factual specifics of the actual original incident. Or perhaps both.

A third factor involved in these special-event tales is, of course, that they are resurrected just once a year, maybe only once in a generation. Who tells Valentine tales over Thanksgiving turkey? If the "flashpoint" theory is one of the mechanisms by which holiday proto-legends become full-fledged legends, then it seems likely that the real-life event, be it a natural disaster or a media sensation, might have to occur *during* a holiday when the proto-legend was active! Quite a progression of coincidence and circumstance.

Another characteristic that separates special-event legends from those that circulate year-round is simply their laugh factor. Most urban legends depend on stomach-turning or terror-inducing elements for their punch; special-event legends poke fun at us. They remind us of our essential natures, the tomboys behind wedding veils and the calluses inside the velvet gloves.

WEDDINGS

Of all the events that define lives and bring families together, weddings rank number one on the list of stress-inducers and events most likely to generate proto-legends. Young

The heel of choice at churches with floor-mounted air vents.

women spend hours dreaming of "their" day, planning every detail, imbuing each choreographed second with as many levels of meaning as possible. The Jewish faith proclaims every woman a queen on her wedding day; other brides simply do everything in their power (and budget) to make themselves *look* like queens! Pearl-beaded satins and silks, towering pillar candles, soaring church spires, a full greenhouse's worth of exotic blooms, and, over it all, the building fanfares of organ and cello.

Not the time or place to envision Cinderella in her rags, to find a epi-pen, or to suspect that ecologists might lurk among the cut flowers, right? Wrong!

"Cinderella's Slipper" typifies the special-event legend's impish humor with it's sense of the farcically inevitable.

Jeanne Dyson-Smith and her intimate coterie of debutante friends spent hours preparing the oldest church in traditional Hartford, Connecticut, for her wedding to Charles Mason-Doyle. Creamy roses, twined through swags of English ivy and draped from tall candle stands, lent a heady fragrance to the rarefied air of the historic chapel. Banks of beeswax tapers cast the most complimentary light for the bride's delicate peaches-and-cream complexion. A quartet of musicians from the state symphony orchestra played the recessional. Six bridesmaids, in rich brocade gowns that rustled as they moved, and slippers of the same fabric dyed to an exact match, took the arms of six handsome young ushers and stepped lightly over the rose petals scattered by an adorable four-year-old.

Everything was perfect.

Until one bridesmaid discovered that historic old chapels have special peculiarities, such as heating ducts that emerge in the center of the aisle, ducts covered with brass grates perforated with holes the perfect diameter to capture the heels of hand-dyed slippers!

Without a break in the step-glide-step procession toward the outer door, the unlucky bridesmaid stepped out of the shoe and continues down the aisle on tiptoe. Behind her, the usher escorting the next bridesmaid, seeing the shoe left behind, stooped just long enough to make a grab for it before continuing to step-glide-step his partner down the aisle. Unfortunately, the shoe in his hand hadn't come free cleanly, and he's just realized the grating is still dangling from the heel when, from behind him, a hysterical scream announces that the bride, one leg firmly jammed in the open duct, has just found the resulting hole in the floor!

The new Mrs. Dyson-Smith-Mason-Doyle gets plenty of practice writing that ostentatious moniker as she signs stacks of admission and insurance forms at the hospital instead of throwing her bouquet at the reception.

Of course, fate may have been saving her from an even more embarrassing destiny.

It's said that in Helsinki, Finland, there are more flowers than food on a well-set table. Flowers, especially in Nordic countries, remain synonymous with formal, dignified occasions. They're pressed as keepsakes, thrown with joy, and collected into potpourri pillows to provide pleasant dreams for nights to come. One hospital in Norway actually brings bouquets of the flowers their patients chose for their weddings into the delivery room in the belief that the scent will arouse pleasant memories capable of mitigating some of the pain associated with childbirth!

So when Marjle Heinki dreamed of marrying her childhood sweetheart, Tor Johannson, her fantasies naturally included sprays of delicate baby's breath twined into her hair, lush arrangements on every reception table, and a bouquet of blooms that reached nearly to the floor. Her doting father raided every florist's shop to make that vision a reality, and Marjle's wedding took place amid a sea of flowers.

When the time finally came to throw her bouquet into the massed arms of the brides-maids screaming on the steps below her, Marjle pulled a single thornless rose from the bunch and tucked it into her hair before sending the rest arcing out high enough that no one could later claim she'd deliberately thrown it to any particular girl.

The rose was still tangled in her hair when Marjle and Tor finally escaped from the milling guests to their honeymoon suite. Nature took its course, as it usually will with two healthy young people who've waited until now to consummate their vows, but, as Marjle's pleasure peaked, Tor was startled by her sudden loud screams! Trying to hush his new bride, reminding her that all their friends were just a thin wall or two away in the hotel's other rooms, only brought on louder wails!

Tor was every bit the blushing bridegroom as, wrapped in a sheet, he raced down the hall yelling for a doctor to attend his bride. It's hard to say whether his reputation went

A side note in a funeral-industry magazine once noted: "While women's wedding bands must frequently be removed by special means, those on male clients are generally sized repeatedly during the client's life and seldom present any difficulty." Think that has anything to do with how often men take their wedding bands off?

© Peter/Ngaire Genge, 1999

Instruction on a bridal bouquet: "Check for bees before throwing"!

up or down when the remainder of the guests learned that the passionate cries they'd heard echoing from the bridal suite weren't the result of any particular proficiency on Tor's part, but had been brought on by the sting of a bee that, until it was rolled about on their bed, had been hiding in the rose from the bridal bouquet!

Some versions of the tale skip the bloom from the bouquet and simply suggest that the bee came with the flowers holding her veil in place. Others say that it lurked in the groom's corsage and stung his wife's breast when he crushed her to him at the "you may now kiss the bride" instruction. The most

risqué version also has the bee hiding in the groom's corsage, but the bride is stung on her bottom. I'll leave you to figure out how she was stung *there.*

Though flowers are clearly more available in the south, this story tends to circulate in northern areas where even common blossoms seem exotic. As flowers are associated with the upper classes in Finland, even this simple tale pokes gentle fun at the families who perhaps overspend on luxury items to "keep up with the Johannsons."

Considering the diversity of wedding trappings and traditions—can you think of even one other occasion when it would be acceptable for a husband to remove his wife's underwear in public?—and the imagination evident in most legends, it's hardly surprising that almost every wedding accoutrement is associated with a least one wedding legend.

"The Wearing o' the Garter" actually combines two wedding traditions, though not in the usual way.

Kelly Doyle's wedding wasn't particularly posh. A Galway girl, Kelly viewed the ceremony as a blessed sacrament in God's house and figured that, as a guest visiting that house, she'd be showing poor form to suggest that her wedding required it to be decked in any extra ornamentation. Still, even salt-of-the-earth types have favorite little traditions and, just before she'd finished dressing, her da came up to press a shiny silver dollar in her hand. "For your shoe, to make sure you and your young fella walk in plenty when I'm not there to watch over you."

With tears in her eyes, the young bride slipped the coin in her shoe, kissed her da, and followed him downstairs to be escorted to the church. Before they arrived at the church, Kelly discovered how damned uncomfortable walking around with a heavy coin under her heel might prove. Careful not to let her da see what she was up to, she eased it out. But where to put it? Wedding gowns are short on pockets, and she could hardly shove it down her bodice while sitting next to her father! Pretending to rearrange the heavy folds of her gown, Kelly slipped the coin under the skirt and under the band of that other wedding accessory, her garter.

The wedding, even without the elegant props that delighted other brides, proceeded without a hitch. Quietly elegant and sincere, it was everything Kelly dreamed. When she walked out on the arm of Michael Patrick Doherty, the happy bride was more than ready for the less awe-inspiring part of her day—the rousing Irish reception!

Without playing into any stereotypes, the Irish know how to have fun. No party with Irish guests lets the band play for an hour while the attendees huddle around their table instead of putting shoes to the floor. In the midst of that natural exuberance, Kelly and Michael danced, kissed, laughed, and danced some more and, when the time came to throw the bouquet and garter to the waiting crowd, they entered into the old tradition

with the same enthusiasm they'd brought to all the other reception activities. Still, even a salt-of-the-earth type of girl from Galway can be forgiven for blushing when her bridegroom, in the process of collecting that garter, instead pulls out—and holds up to public view!—the silver dollar she'd totally forgotten!

Weddings, while some of the most precious moments of our lives, frequently act as lightning rods for all the emotional baggage any two families can lug. Seating plans become battle strategies. Guest lists burgeon like runaway infections. Emotions run high and skins grow thinner than usual. While not attaining the level of urban legends, stories of wedding plans wrecked on the immovable rocks of family prejudice are certainly part of the backdrop against which these events are played out. Two such tales that crop up at bridal parties in pockets of the eastern United States and Canada are "On the Wing" and "Uncle Al's Little Problem."

It used to be that when a couple decided to get married, Dad got out the checkbook, the bride and groom eyeballed the menu at their reception site, picked the chicken or the roast, figured out if they'd serve white or red wine, and asked Mom to ask if Dad was springing for a liquor tab. Since then, things have gotten complicated.

There are vegetarians who aren't going to eat roast *or* chicken.

The allergy-aware need detailed recipe plans before deciding whether they can even sit in the same room with your chosen dish, much less *eat* it.

Then there's "Uncle Al" and his "little problem."

Everyone has an Uncle Al, that slightly embarrassing member of the family whom you'd rather leave off the guest list, but since he's married to your favorite aunt, you're stuck with him whether you like it or not.

The Uncle Al in this tale, however, is a problem for lovers in the eighties and nineties. Affable drunks, once just ignored, now merit "interventions" and exceptional consideration. How could any young couple with a smidgin of compassion expect poor Uncle Al to sit in a room full of people enjoying that red or white wine, partaking of the liquor tickets Dad finally agreed to supply, or sneaking a nip from the flask they brought along so they wouldn't have to pay the outrageous bar prices? How could they think of tempting him with the sherry sauce slathered over the chicken? How could they be so *cruel*?

Easily—according to the groom, at least.

When the family starts dividing itself into the pro-Al and anti-Al camps, and the bride and groom suddenly find themselves on opposite sides of the contentious issue, it doesn't take long for someone to suggest that if this couple can't work out such a simple problem, well, obviously they simply aren't ready for marriage in the first place!

Two days before the wedding, Uncle Al and Aunt Belle arrive, with the booze/no booze decision still up in the air. Uncle Al sits

like some modern Buddha in the midst of the tempest his "little problem" has created, while Aunt Belle cries on the couch. The bride and groom argue, both sets of parents get in on the act, and finally the minister is called in to mediate. As the fighting intensifies, our good man of the cloth wades in and sends the combatants to their corners—all but Uncle Al, who continues to sit on the couch as if none of this concerns him at all!

Hoping to arrive at some reconciliation by speaking to the source of the dispute, Uncle Al himself, the minister pulls up a chair and launches into a lengthy discussion of how it might be better if Al were to take this decision out of the young couple's lap? Could Al just forgo this particular event? Through the impromptu sermon, Al keeps his silence, except for a heavy sigh when the minister's hand comes to rest on his shoulder. Getting nothing more from Al, the minister gives up and goes to counsel the bride and groom.

Things go badly, harsh words fly, and a distraught bride races into the living room to throw herself at Uncle Al's feet. With her head in his lap, she begs him to go home before she and her fiancé come to blows! Her sobs turn to screams when, looking up through her tears, she realizes Uncle Al is staring off into space, thoroughly dead!

Though saddened by her uncle's passing, the bride eventually gives a sigh of relief. Without Uncle Al's "little problem" to deal with, they can hold the wedding they've planned for these many months, right?

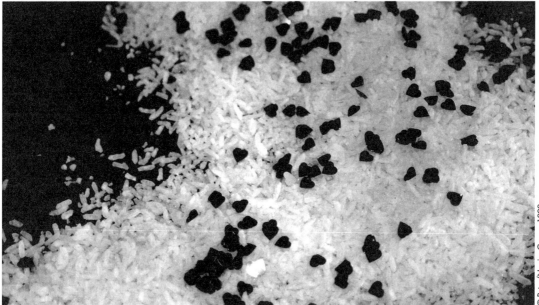

Go ahead—feed the birds!

So it seems—until Aunt Belle's voice carries through the house. "Surely they wouldn't go ahead with the wedding, with poor Al laid out down at that funeral home? How could they be so *cruel*?"

And the silliest thing families have taken up as a bone of contention at some poor unfortunate's wedding? How about a first cousin to the paper-or-plastic-bag controversy raging at an A & P near you? "On the Wing," a humorous tale of a family divided against itself over the issue of confetti or rice as the most politically correct projectile with which to pelt your favorite couple, pits proponents of renewable resources (like rice) against bird-hugging ecologists who claim it's better to use scrap paper (confetti is actually a planned product for many com-

panies, but let's not make it any more complicated!) than endanger the lives of their feathered friends.

Yeah, really.

According to one version of this mini-tale, a pair of yuppies from Toronto nearly decided to "live in sin" when the bride's sister, a dedicated environmentalist, went into hysterics while picturing all the birds who'd surely die after pecking up the hard rice kernels negligently tossed about by wedding revelers.

"They eat the rice, it blows up in their stomachs, and they burst! Do you really want to leave on your honeymoon with the bloodied bodies of dozens of beautiful birds scattered all over the church steps?"

Apparently the girl must have read one of Ann Landers's columns, where, in all seriousness, that good lady warned all prospective brides and grooms of the environmental hazards of rice: "Please encourage the guests to throw rose petals instead of rice. Rice is not good for the birds."

Unfortunately, Ms. Landers's background in ornithology is sadly lacking. Birds eat grains, all types, as part of their natural diets! In Ms. Landers's defense, however, she didn't actually *say* the birds blew up—that's the evolution of urban legends in action.

Though none of the previous tales can be authenticated, and are probably all apocryphal, there's at least one recent wedding tale circulating with a definite source.

According to the Boston version of "The Rising Cake," a young couple had actually managed to get through all the wedding preparations, the ceremony, and the receiving line without incident and, thinking themselves safe from wedding disasters, sat down to enjoy their reception dinner. Tempers flared when, in the midst of the traditional exchange of wedding cake, the groom tripped and slammed his piece of cake into his new wife's face à la the Three Stooges! Enraged at this humiliating end to her perfect day, the bride responded by lifting the entire top tier off the cake and throwing it at the groom!

The groom ducked.

The minister's wife turned to see what the excitement was all about—just in time to catch a faceful of royal icing and miniature wedding figures! Obviously a woman lacking in humor, she plucked a handful of dessert from her face and threw it straight back at the bride.

Figuring he wouldn't survive long should his bride be covered in a second layer of cake, the groom jumped in front of her, sacrificing his dignity, only to deflect the gooey blob into the lap of his own mother!

In a farcical string of interrelated throws and misses, it wasn't long before the entire assembly was covered in the remains of a seven-tier wedding cake.

The final humiliation in this version occurs when the bride's father, viewing his daughter's cake-encrusted form, has no sympathy for her misery, but instead wails, "The rental shop'll never take that dress back now!"

John and Tracey O'Donnell, the real couple who distinguished their wedding from all others by starting a cake fight, didn't actually drag all their guests into the fray, but their eventual ignominy was even more humiliating when the local police force of Westport, Connecticut, responded to the scene and arrested both for disturbing the peace! It's not every couple that can include a pair of mug shots in their wedding albums!

Degradation and photographs combined again in "Smile! You're on Candid Camera!" As a relatively uneventful wedding was slowly coming to a close in the small community of Garden City, Missouri, the father of the bride reached into his back pocket to retrieve his wallet and pay the band that was about to play the last waltz. He was shocked to discover that someone, evidently someone so close to the family that he or she had received an invitation to this memorable event, had lifted his billfold sometime during the evening! Revealing the situation to the band and asking their indulgence while he sends his wife on an emergency run to the nearest ATM was mortifying enough, but imagine the look on the face of the father of the *groom* when the family later got together to sort through the wedding photos and discovered a picture of the groom's father stealing the missing wallet!

Again, this widespread fable can't be proven true or false, but that's not to say there are no criminal tales associated with weddings. A well-reported case from Pasadena, California, relates the true tale of two sisters who developed a real liking for the society pages of their local papers. Jean Kolentik and Helen Eposto spent hours poring over wedding notices, paying particular attention to those that mentioned that the new couple would be honeymooning at some distant location. Then, while the couple was away, blissfully unconcerned with events back home, the sneaky sisters would break into their homes and remove everything of value at their own leisurely pace!

It's not that they had anything against young lovers, though; the women were also fans of the obituaries, and would just as happily steal from the recently deceased as from the recently married in their attempts to raise the funds necessary to indulge in little luxuries like trips to Las Vegas.

Wonder how many toasters and blenders they fenced. . . .

A Canadian incident that gained almost as much publicity as "The Obituary Burglars" was, happily, proven false. Since wedding photos are meant to last a lifetime, it's hardly surprising that couples carefully choose classically beautiful locations for their formal sittings. Summer weddings naturally lend themselves to outdoor settings like parks and botanical gardens. One of the most beautiful and popular retreats in Quebec, the Montreal Botanical Gardens, hosted hundreds of couples every summer—until an urban legend swept the city in 1982.

For no apparent reason, radio talk shows suddenly found themselves fielding questions on "the bride who'd died in the Gardens, you know, the one who got bitten by the snake?" The Horticulture Department, baffled by the calls they received, called both the local hospitals and the Sureté, Quebec's provincial police force, in an attempt to track down the mysterious woman everyone believed had died from a venomous snake bite while surrounded by bridesmaids and blossoms in the public gardens. The Parks Department, inundated with requests for descriptions of indigenous poisonous snakes (there are only two, one of which only inhabits waterways and their close environs; the other, the eastern timber rattler, a naturalized resident, could hardly go unnoticed in any setting), finally found it necessary to issue a public statement that no snakebites, certainly no deaths, had been reported anywhere in southern Quebec!

Urban legends, faced with incontrovertible truths, like a lack of poisonous snakes to have bitten this mysterious bride, don't just fade away—they mutate. Okay, so maybe the woman wasn't bitten by a snake. Maybe it was a tarantula? Or a scorpion? Of course, neither tarantulas nor scorpions are native to Quebec, either, but it *was* a botanical garden, and they *did* import exotic plants from remote locations, where it was *possible* the plants came in contact with spiders or scorpions, right?

Not according to any hospitals—or morgues—in the area.

The tale, however, continued circulating briskly for two years in the early eighties before major articles in *La Presse* and the *Montreal Gazette* identified the story as an urban legend and brides flocked back to the exquisite setting.

"The Snake in the Garden" is one of only two wedding tales that involve a death; the other, "The Stolen Gown," leans heavily on the horrific tradition common to other year-round urban tales.

It all begins calmly enough with a happy couple tying the knot in an ordinary service in Small Town, U.S.A. Some versions place the story in Virginia, others in Arkansas. The bride and groom withdraw to the local Kiwanis Club, rented for the reception and dance, and spend most of the meal staring deeply into each other's eyes. When they lead their friends onto the dance floor, everything is perfect—except for the odd odor that begins rising from the fabric of the bride's gown. Dismissing it as the remnant of dry-cleaning solution being activated by her rising body heat, the bride in her antique dress steps outside with her groom for a few minutes to air out the numerous folds.

On the wide veranda, the scent fades away but the bride begins feeling nauseated and soon complains of vertigo as well. Her concerned groom leaves her on a bench and darts inside to find Uncle Harold, the town's doctor. By the time he leads the way back to her side, his bubbly young wife is dead!

Even the autopsy mightn't have turned up the correct cause of death if the desolate widower hadn't recalled the peculiar odor permeating the antique fabric of the gown. Careful backtracking revealed that the odor came from formaldehyde and to the discovery of the local mortician's interesting sideline as a purveyor of expensive period clothing! The mortician, to save on overhead, simply "recycled" the clothes that would otherwise have been buried with clients who had no further use for them!

According to the story, dancing opened the unfortunate bride's pores and warmed the formaldehyde impregnating the cloth. The fumes, absorbed through the skin and carried throughout her system, poisoned her as surely as ingestion could have done.

Another, more convoluted version of this story circulated through the United States as early as the 1930s. The bride of that variation also ended up with a corpse's death dress, but not via the machinations of a greedy mortician. Rather, the corpse's family, anxious to present the best-looking cadaver they could, bought a dress from a chic department store. However, since the dress was a luxury they couldn't really afford, they switched it for one of the deceased's own plain dresses before the funeral home closed the coffin for the last time, and *returned* the fancy dress to the store. The store then unwittingly resold the gown to the young bride.

Considerably more humorous is the tale of "The Busted Bridegroom," a story that likely originated in England—they have better train service—but that circulates in the United States as a "local" story and usually transposes the key event from train travel to car travel.

It begins in Manchester when a group of blokes from Blackpool—up for the football, of course—wander into a local pub in a family hotel and order some drinks to help drown their sorrow over the Blackpool loss. Before long, they discover the chap at the end of the bar is also a Blackpudlian, and they all fall in together, consoling each other that the home side couldn't possibly have won if not for the blind officials who'd spent the afternoon looking the wrong way. Before long, they're all three sheets to the wind.

When the time comes for the group to return to Blackpool, the considerate drinking buddies lug their new companion along with them. A quick rummage through his pocket had turned up the guy's return ticket and a wallet that yielded his home address. They all sleep until the conductor yells, "Blackpool!" in their ears, then stumble into a van belonging to one of the football fans. When they arrive at the chap's home, the lady who answers the door is horrified to see him hanging off the shoulders of two drunken men with their faces painted in Blackpool's colors!

"Well, missus, don't he live here?"

"Well, yes, he does! But where's his bride? He was in Manchester on his honeymoon!"

Oops.

HALLOWEEN

Of all holidays, Halloween, perhaps not surprisingly, is the lone event to inspire nothing *but* tales of the morbid. Though this first one is less well known than those that follow, "The Rising" is one of my favorites because it still retains a certain naïveté, the horror arising more in the imagination than in any actual physical harm.

It begins in the tiny community of Cupids, in the Canadian province of Newfoundland and Labrador, a province folklorists universally agree is an amazing microcosm of Old World tradition. In fact, historians, linguists, and folklorists from all over Europe regularly trek across the ocean to trace the origins of *their own tales*! It's a land of mummers and ribals, where snatches of language still carry the listener to tiny vales in Cornwall and Wales. Needless to say, people that cling to their roots so tenaciously also remember their tales and songs.

The Rising, a trial for murderers, traces its lineage back to early Welsh custom. It's believed that a corpse, touched by its murderer, wells blood from wounds if they were the cause of death, from the mouth if death was by poisoning, from the eyes like tears if magic was the cause. You may recall elements of this story in the "Black Aggie" tales of cemetery statues that condemn killers and take revenge for their owners. Like other trials and ordeals, the results aren't open to debate.

Children imitate their elders, even to copying their fears, beliefs, and superstitions—

with variation. In Cupids and neighboring Brigus, tales of the Rising mutated into a Halloween trial of courage almost as important as the amount of tooth-rotting junk food that could be collected. First, the grave of a murderer or, failing that, a victim must be located. Though the cemeteries of these tiny communities aren't exactly stocked with either killers or their prey, they're overflowing with headstones so old it's nearly impossible to read anything on their faces—which means any one of those old stones could mark a killer's grave, right?

Having located the "right" grave, those aspirants to peer-worship produce the next element of the ritual, the knife. As they huddle in the darkness on Halloween night, the knife flashes down, impaling the corner of a coat in the dirt! Pinned in place, the candidate is left behind under orders not, under any circumstances, to pull the knife free! If they're brave enough, nothing will happen; if not, if they even think of getting away, the blood of the corpse, regardless of how long deceased, will bubble up through the ground around the knife, marking the coward's clothes in the process!

Though few parents were washing blood from their children's coats on November 1, an amazing number of "accidents" required small holes in the corners of jackets to be mended.

It wasn't cemeteries that were outlawed during the next Halloween, but pocket knives!

Less innocent is "The Hung Hayman." In the United States, Thanksgiving and Halloween often merge into a single long harvest-time celebration, with decorations for one holiday being altered only slightly for the other. Scarecrows, corn wreaths, and pumpkins sit happily alongside each other on porches everywhere. Even events like hayrides, which, in Canada and Great Britain, are reserved for Thanksgiving, have become popular Halloween treats—with a few extra touches.

In Chicago, a "haunted hayride" carried riders past dozens of locations, each one sporting some spectacular decoration or performance. At one house, a hanging appeared to take place when Brian Jewell, standing atop a homemade gallows, said his last words and then stepped off into space! Of course, the scene was carefully set and Jewell had no intention of hanging himself. The driver became seriously concerned when, on his next round, there was no speech, no jump, nothing, just the guy dangling there! Saying nothing to his passengers, he continued on, becoming more and more anxious. His apprehension proved well founded. Something had gone terribly wrong: the noose, which was designed not to tighten, failed, leaving Jewell dead by hanging.

Tragically, that tale is true. Equally tragically, it's not a lone incident. At least three other people, Carlos Ametzco, Bill Odom, and Frank Calliwell, are known to have died while acting out similar scenarios for Halloween.

Urban legends, resilient under the worst of conditions, thrive amid high-tech gizmos like fax machines and e-mail, which allow modern myths to travel faster than ever, and pop up over and over like super chain letters.

The following warning flew across the Internet, in dozens of different forms (all specific to the local conditions, of course), in October of '94, '95, '97, and '98. (Wonder what happened in '96? A massive, early, pre-emptive debunking throughout the media and university system.)

One Halloween hoax was aimed at parents, not kids. A faxed message claiming that some face paint was poisonous, and easily absorbed through the skin, sent parents racing to check labels for a fake ingredient, methadigitactylasine. Unfortunately, when a real warning circulated three days later, almost no one heeded recall notices for "6000 vinyl Vampire capes with a paper insert that reads 'Child's Vinyl Vampire Cape, No. 50282. Made in China.'" The capes were so flammable they could burst into flames even when several feet from a lit jack-o-lantern!

WARNING***WARNING***WARNING

Students at Michigan State University, please take note that noted psychic Yvonne Debournier, while appearing on the Oprah *program on October 11, made the following prediction.*

"I have seen this so clearly. A madman, a mass murderer, will assault the very cream of this country's youth. A bomb, something in the food, I can't tell, but it will kill dozens, maybe hundreds, on Halloween, this Halloween. It's at a university, in a public building, shaped like an 'H' or maybe a 'T.' A lot of students congregate there. . . . Yes, I see it, fire and noise. A bomb! It'll kill them all!"

Please, warn everyone you know on campus, call their parents, notify university administrators and staff to the urgent danger facing them! Ms. Debournier is a certified psychical researcher whose predictions have been heard by presidents and major CEOs. Her accuracy rating, published in major newspapers, is over 95 percent! This is no joke. Please add your voice to those currently contacting Michigan State University and local law enforcement. Ensure the safety of our students.

Despite repeated debunkings between outbursts, this story proved mushroomlike in its ability to appear full-grown just before Halloween, causing panic at numerous locations and tying up the resources of police, university staff, and, incidentally, the public-relations personnel at *The Oprah Winfrey Show,* who regularly issue statements to the effect that no such person ever appeared on her program, that no such prediction was made, and that no one was threatened.

Of course, the most pervasive Halloween legend rests firmly on factual occurrences. The short version, that nasty people all over the country are putting sharp, pointy things in Halloween treats given out to innocent children, is absolutely true. However, even truth isn't always what it seems.

Dozens of cases get reported—and investigated—every year. The results of those investigations paint a picture quite different from that of the psychopath sitting in his darkened room, staring into his TV screen, waiting for news of the innocent lives he's snuffed out to hit the media. In most incidents, the objects, pins and needles, occasionally bits of broken razor blades, are found by parents, *not children.* Of the objects found by children, a significant number were put into the treats by *parents!* There appear to be at least as many parents anxious for some form of media attention as there are actual nut cases in search of their moment

In 1995, Los Altos, California, schools banned Halloween parties, citing the holiday's pagan nature. In one U.S. county, witch and Indian costumes have been banned—too politically incorrect.

of fame. And, odd as this may sound, in some cases, it's the children *themselves* who've doctored their bag of goodies!

Comprehensive studies in the New York and New Jersey region reveal that even in those cases legitimately attributed to random insanity, actual injury is rare. A couple of stitches seems the upper limits of medical intervention needed. While it's impossible to condone even that level of violence and disregard for human welfare, it's important to note that nowhere are there waves of serious injuries, certainly not *deaths,* attached to trick-or-treating.

It's significant to realize that Halloween, which, from a pedophile's predatory point of view, presents a smorgasbord of opportunity, has no statistical relevance to the number of kidnaps, assaults, or murders perpetrated against children. Apparently, Halloween just isn't a big deal for most criminals.

CHRISTMAS

One of the most widely celebrated of all holidays—even in Japan, where less than one percent of the country is Christian, throws great department store sales—Christmas legends run the gamut of horrid to hilarious.

My all-time favorite, reported everywhere from *The Economist* to *The Christian Science Monitor,* is actually set in Japan and, to date, has generated more completely inconclusive research than any other holiday tale.

The story goes that in 1945, when Japan was working hard on post–World War II

> Bobbing for apples, a traditional Halloween and Christmas game, began as a form of divination by which young women might discover whom they should marry. Initials carved on the bottom were believed to be portents.

appeasement, one of the major department stores in Tokyo's Ginza district decided this might be an opportune time (they *were* under Western occupation, after all) to celebrate (and sell) a Western-style Christmas. Of course, with the exception of some not-too-successful missionaries, few Japanese recognized the distinction between the religious iconography and the commercial ornamentation. Imagine their surprise when, on unveiling their brand-new Christmas display windows, Westerners stormed off instead of flocking inside! It took some time for the ad people to figure out what might be offensive in displaying a two-story-tall Santa Claus spread-eagled on a cross!

Though the story appears to be set some time ago, independent record of this farcical juxtaposition doesn't appear to go much farther back than the mid-eighties, when, incidentally, movies like *Gung-ho,* which helped American audiences mitigate their fear of Japan's growing industrial strength, began to appear.

Christmas tales frequently exhibit some bizarre juxtapositions. Take, for example, the story told by the female interest in *Gremlins* of how she's never been able to enjoy Christmas, not since her father, the traveling salesman, returned early for Christmas and decided to surprise his kids by actually coming down the chimney instead of in the front door as usual. In the ironic twist, no one knows he came home and no one discovers it until several days after a very lonely Christmas when a strange odor causes the lady of the house to call a chimney sweep (they think some bird or squirrel might have died up there) and the father's corpse, arms full of their presents, is discovered dead and wedged in the flue.

Immediately after the movie aired, claims that the story line was based on an actual Christmas tragedy began making the rounds. Comments from some crew members quizzed on the topic implied that even during filming, "someone in the cast" had wondered if the writers hadn't taken these events from real life. Of course, as with most friend-of-a-friend tales, the trail of the true story behind

the film version fizzled out—until the film's general video release overseas.

Almost immediately—or as soon as pirated copies made it into Bulgaria—local viewers there jumped on this subplot as being a reference to a real-life incident in, believe it or not, Bulgaria! It appears that during the filming of *Gremlins,* a young Bulgarian had indeed managed to get himself stuck in a chimney, where he remained for several weeks while police searched vainly for any trace of him. He was found on Christmas Eve when his family attempted to light the Yule fire.

That such a bizarre little story, from a relatively remote village, could cross not only the Atlantic but a wide language barrier swiftly enough to make its way into a film being shot halfway around the world would be an incredible coincidence, but it's retold as fact over and over again in at least one village!

Before any North Americans start feeling in the least superior to their Bulgarian friends, or start wondering how anyone could possibly believe such a patently outrageous coincidence, it might be worthwhile to recall some of the *other* urban legends already firmly entrenched in the American mind.

Take poinsettias as a case in point. Would you feed them to your cat, or your little boy? Probably not. In fact, at least 67 percent of Americans can tell you, without a moment's hesitation, that poinsettias, the Christmas Miracle Flowers, are poisonous.

> **Rudolph the Red-Nosed Reindeer has nothing to do with Clement Moore's "The Night Before Christmas." He's the invention of copywriter Robert May, who wrote the poem as a promotional scheme for Montgomery Ward department stores.**

It's not true. In fact, a group of nursery grow- ers in Pennsylvania have, for the past twenty- three years, eaten poinsettia salads in their outlets just to prove the point, and they're all alive and well!

In 1919 a two-year-old Hawaiian child died and the doctor erroneously attributed the death to the ingestion of a poinsettia leaf. The doctor himself widely admitted his error, but the warning had already entrenched itself. It's now known, and recorded in the national Poisondex database, that a fifty- pound child could safely eat *five hundred* leaves and suffer no ill effects beyond the stomachache anyone would endure after stuffing themselves with the equivalent of *sixty* salads in one sitting.

Didn't fall for that one?

Okay.

Are you among the 92 percent of the pub- lic who *knows* that suicide rates are highest between Christmas Eve and New Year's Day? Well, you've been hoodwinked by yet another urban legend.

A thirty-five-year study in Minnesota dis- covered absolutely no correlation between suicides and holidays!

A study by the New York State Association of Mental Health also rebuts the commonly held belief. In fact, suicides and psychiatric admissions are at their *lowest* point about two weeks before Christmas, Thanksgiving, and Easter. Suicide rates for those same holidays are at, or often below, norms estab- lished for the rest of the year.

> Mistletoe, that romantic stuff that every- one wants to kiss under, means, according to one expert, "dung on a twig."

Studies in Great Britain, Sweden, South Africa, and Israel all confirm that general trend.

In Ireland, where suicides are seldom recorded for religious reasons (a Catholic who commits suicide cannot be given a requiem mass or be buried in consecrated ground), no official data was available, but trends there, at least according to the Medical Association, suggest that the rate of "unexplained acci- dents" rises as the unemployment statistics rise, following that pattern on about a three- week delay. Early reports on statistical analy- sis addressing this theory in the United States are also showing significant results. According to Dr. Mazil Bay, the head of the American Society of Practicing Practical Psychologists, "Christmas is a busy time for businesses. The rate of unemployment actu- ally drops for about a month before the holi- days, and stays down until the new year. If these early numbers hold up, we can expect to see peak suicide rates in mid-February." Bay's theory is upheld by Mental Health Association findings in their 1998 report titled "Depression and Suicide in the Under- and Unemployed Male."

The irony often found in urban legends depends heavily on setting seemingly oppo-

> **"I didn't like the turkey, but I loved the bread he ate!"**
> **—Anonymous young girl on her Christmas dinner**

site images and beliefs in close proximity, and Christmas legends take this to the limit.

As Christmas 1998 approached, broadcasters and writers across the United States, as well as some in Great Britain, were cautioning parents about participating in the special supplements, usually extra newspaper pages filled with pictures of hopeful children and their letters to Santa, commonly prepared about a month prior to the holidays.

One announcer warned, "It's just now becoming clear that pedophiles are using these Christmas supplements as their version of the Christmas Wish Catalog, circling the pictures of those children they find most attractive and, in too many cases, tracking down their victims from hints included in the letters themselves." Hometowns are often listed, along with the child's full name and age. Sometimes particular schools are mentioned if the letters to Santa were written as part of a classroom project. Brothers and sisters are frequently mentioned by name, as are other family members. Together, the public-service announcements contended, these were enough clues for a determined monster to track down your child! Further, the stories

asserted, not only was it possible, it had already happened! To "hundreds of unsuspecting and innocent children."

Luckily for the "hundreds" of families who would have been torn apart by such occurrences, the messages, though timely, aren't supported by actual cases.

The Center for Missing and Exploited Children has responded to these warnings several times, indicating that neither they nor the law-enforcement agencies that regularly report to them have ever made a connection between a Christmas supplement and an abduction, assault, or murder. They're quick to add that just because it hasn't happened is no reason to assume it *couldn't* happen—especially as the legend circulates and is heard by more and more pedophiles.

Which is why the legend persists. Even when the media become well aware that there aren't "hundreds" of missing children out there, they take a better-safe-than-sorry approach and will often run the story despite a lack of factual cases to back it up. Of course, the dramatic contrast of images, the innocence of children still naïve enough to write letters to Santa and the loathsome malignancy that spurs pedophiles to prey on children, also makes for great copy.

Another dramatic pairing of opposites provides the imagery for "The Stolen Kettle." According to local gossip in cities as widely separated as Houston, Texas, and Anchorage, Alaska, local Christmas revelers were looking at the Salvation Army "kettles," the hallmark of that generous organization's Red Shield Appeal, in a whole new light.

As you may know, a considerable portion of the Salvation Army's efforts are devoted to the rehabilitation of those whose alcoholism left them nothing. Employing a little irony of their own, then, the Salvation Army seems particularly fond of placing their kettles directly in front of liquor stores. That strategy failed, however, when a man desperate for his Christmas cheer raced by the front of one liquor store, snatching up the kettle, which he then carried to another liquor store, where he used the proceeds of his theft to buy booze. Not content yet, he snagged a second kettle on the way out, along with a hand bell used to attract attention to the display, and headed for yet a third store downtown!

Too much irony at work here? Sure this is another urban legend? Nope, this one is the real thing. Additionally, the thefts became so widespread in the Midwest that a representative for the Salvation Army admitted they had to "ship in a new load of hand bells from a different district—we didn't have one left!"

VALENTINE'S DAY

Valentine's Day begins with confusion. A day for lovers named after not one, but *two*, saints who died *single*! Both Valentines are said to have performed miraculous cures—for which they were rewarded with death,

> **Valentine's Day was a little misunderstood in Japan. There, where it's known as Red Day, it's women who are expected to give flowers and candy to the men! This was later "fixed" by adding a second holiday, White Day, to March, when gentlemen could bestow gifts aplenty on their ladies.**

really horrid death. The second Valentine was beheaded, eventually. It took seventeen whacks to completely decapitate him. Doesn't exactly inspire romance, does it?

So how did these guys become associated with Valentine's Day? It's all a matter of dates. The feast days for both Valentines (along with Saint Antoninus and Saint Maro, though almost no one has even heard of them) was set for February 14, the same date when, according to medieval belief, birds began to pair off for the season. Of course, that might just possibly be the oldest urban legend of all!

In the intervening 1,200 years, Valentine's Day legends have popped up from time to time. Poisoned-candy tales, close kin to similar Halloween legends, arose, but in general the public doesn't seem to *want* to sully its sweetly romantic holiday with such things.

"A Card Too Far," circulated around Valentine's Day, 1997, is one of the few horrific "sweetheart" stories to gain broad exposure.

An unappreciated, indeed abused, housewife, believing in marriage for life, had silently accepted her fate. When she picked up the extension to find her husband engaged in phone sex with one of his mistresses, she accepted it. When she discovered a video of him having sex with another woman, she accepted it. When she arrived home just in time to meet one of his many liaisons rushing out the front door, she accepted it.

When Valentine's Day arrived, along with a huge red envelope tucked under her front door, she even managed to think, for at least a few moments, that her loyalty and devotion were actually appreciated! Until she opened the card.

Instead of the sentimental note she'd been hoping for, she discovered the card was for her husband, and instead of the mushy Valentine one might expect, this one was a veritable photo album of all the kinky sex her husband and this latest woman had enjoyed—at least half of it in the wife's bed!

It was too much, the proverbial last straw.

When he breezed in after work, without so much as a "Happy Valentine's Day!" his wife met him with a .38 instead of a pot roast. It was only after he started leaking on the floor that she discovered the dozen roses he'd hidden behind his back, along with the note: "It's been a long time coming, baby, but this time's for real—To My One and Only Valentine!"

Despite a very active year, this tale quickly died off and will likely be one of the many faddish stories that simply get lost from the oral tradition. Why? First of all, because it's simply not what people want to think about on Valentine's Day. More important, in 1998, a truth-is-stranger-than-fiction angle was added to the tale when Helen Cummings stood trial for the Valentine's Day slaying of her husband, Tyler. A *Fort Lauderdale Sun-Sentinel* article relates part of the trial:

Helen Cummings said she stayed with her husband, Tyler Cummings, even after she saw a videotape of him having sex with another woman in her bedroom. She said she often overheard early-morning phone calls to other women while he thought she slept nearby. But it was a Valentine's Day surprise that caused the confrontation that ended in his death: a card to him from another woman, complete with nude pictures.

Tyler didn't bring his wife roses and apologies that Valentine's Day, so the ironic ending of the myth remained unfulfilled, but, the coincidence of details was so eerie, and so tragic, that telling the original story now left a bad taste in the storyteller's mouth. Who wants to get laughs from someone else's misery?

Instead, more humorous and naughty tales typify this particular holiday, like this one, "Glove Love."

Barton Tully, of Little Hampton, England, was enamored of Darlene Clarke, also of Little Hampton, and when Valentine's Day came around in 1949, he began a search for the perfect gift. Back then, of course, gentlemen didn't give their girlfriends edible underwear, and Barton was vacillating among several ideas, hoping to find something that expressed his respect and admiration, but wouldn't appear too personal. (Not an easy task in 1949, when even perfume was considered too intimate a present, as it conjured up visions of female fingers stroking the liquid over female skin.)

At a bit of a loss, he eventually asked his girlfriend's younger sister to accompany him on his shopping trip. Because she needed to pick up things for herself, and was always in need of a lift, she came along quite willingly. While she picked out panties for herself, she also agreed that the white gloves he'd been considering would be just the perfect thing.

Neither of them watched the clerk wrapping the purchases, Barton because he flushed every time he even considered the notion that he might inadvertently see his girlfriend's sister's underwear, the younger sister because she was too busy browsing all the impulse-buy items scattered across the counter! And so the packages were switched. As if the mixup wouldn't have been embarrassing enough on its own, his gift was accompanied by the following note:

My Dearest Darlene,

I chose these because I noticed that you are not in the habit of wearing any when we go out in the evening. Your sister assures me you would prefer these to the long ones with buttons as those are old-fashioned now and altogether too hard to remove. She tells me the latest fashion is to wear them folded down so as to show a little fur.

I wasn't sure if I should purchase them in such a light color, but, after viewing the clerk's own, which she said she'd been wearing about three weeks, and seeing no sign of soiling, I believe you'll have similar results.

I wish I could slip them on you for the first time, but, failing that, I hope no other hands will hold them before mine. I know I shall enjoy kissing the backs of them until next Valentine's Day.

All my love,

Barton

P.S. The clerk said to remind you to blow into them lightly whenever you remove them as, naturally, they'll be a little damp from wear.

SAINT PATRICK'S DAY

Everyone knows the story of Saint Patrick, the fifth-century patron saint of Ireland, who was actually named Maewyn and was born in Wales. He was a pagan until he turned sixteen and was kidnapped by Irish raiders. He escaped eventually, became a Christian, and decided to return and preach the gospel to the Irish. But he didn't do well in his studies, and didn't even get to go to Ireland until the guy who was chosen to go, Saint Palladius, decided he'd rather go to Scotland. Not familiar with that version? Then you're probably thinking of the Patrick who drove all the snakes out of Ireland. Funny, isn't it, how, even with fifteen hundred years to debunk Saint Patrick, reality constantly comes second to a "really good story"?

That being the case, though, we'll skip the Irish history lessons about shamrocks and leprechauns and snakes and turn our examination of Saint Patrick's Day legends to the American side of the Atlantic and a delightful tale now lost to even the most dedicated Saint Paddy's fans outside Newfoundland.

As if to prove the old saw that "behind every good man, there's a better woman," Newfoundlanders watch carefully for snow on Saint Patrick's Day. According to their legends, Saint Patrick was accompanied on his travels by Sheila, a learned woman who helped ease his way through the many pagan communities he visited. Some believe she was his sister, others say his mother, his housekeeper—or even his wife! Please remember that the Irish clergy up into the eighth century, five hundred years after Patrick's ministry, was not only permitted to marry, but included as many women as men!

In any case, the legend of Patrick's helpmate remains strong around the Avalon Peninsula and the South Coast, and if snows should happen to fall on Saint Patrick's Day, local custom calls this "Sheila's Gown" in remembrance of the white linen shift she wore (a symbol of both law and spirituality in Irish custom), and the following day is "Sheila's Day" in her honor.

Sheila leads in a long, white gown
As Paddy walks the shores around.
—"Irish Tides"

Saint Patrick's Day is a popular celebration even without any religious overtones. One of the traditions, an urban legend in New York City schools, states that, in order for you to remain lucky all year, you must pinch any classmate who *doesn't* wear something green on Saint Patrick's Day.

GROUNDHOG DAY

How does a Jewish ritual become a weather prognostication? By forgetting that Mary's life continued after the birth of Jesus and substituting a groundhog for a badger.

Most modern Christmas stories end with the birth of the babe in the stable, but considerable ritual is associated with births in the Jewish faith and Mary was, after all, a Jew. Accordingly, forty days after the birth of Jesus, Mary would have undertaken a ritual cleansing, a purification. That date, February 2, if you take Christmas Day to fall on December 25, was known in the Christian faith as Candlemas.

Beginning in the seventh century, Candlemas represented a significant series of events. It was the last day of the Christmas season, the day when candles used for the following year were blessed. During Imbolc, the pagan festival between the winter solstice and the spring equinox, which Candlemas replaced, priests distributed candles to illuminate the depths of winter. On Candlemas Day, all decorations were stored until next year. The greenery and other plants, such as mistletoe, that had been used on the altars and in homes during the season were burnt to ashes, and the ashes were scattered over the fields to ensure a good harvest. Even then, there was a connection to the weather. If it was sunny, tradition said winter would continue for another forty days; if it was overcast or snowing, spring would come early that year.

If Candlemas be fair and bright,
Winter has another flight.
If Candlemas brings clouds and rain,
Winter will not come again.

A Scottish couplet concurs:
If Candlemas Day is bright and clear,
There'll be two winters in the year.

And, from Germany:
For as the sun shines on Candlemas Day,
So far will the snow swirl until May.
For as the snow blows on Candlemas Day,
So far will the sun shine before May.

The American version illustrates the New World shift in focus:
If the sun shine on Groundhog Day,
Half the fuel and half the hay.

The intermediary step is found in Germany, where locals watched for the appearance of badgers on February 2. The manifestation of shadow behind the animal indicated there was enough sunshine to declare the day sunny. If not, the day was considered overcast.

When the Germans settled the rich land of Pennsylvania in the United States, and regions of western Ontario in Canada, there were no badgers, but there were *plenty* of other critters, especially woodchucks, also called groundhogs—which, coincidentally, the Delaware Indians held in high regard.

In modern times, particular sites and particular groundhogs gained a certain reputation. In the United States, Punxsutawney, Pennsylvania, became so closely associated with the weather legend that its designated groundhog, Punxsutawney Phil, and the town itself, were the subject of the film *Groundhog Day*. Nearly thirty thousand people arrive there each year to see if they can see a shadow behind the big rodent. Up north in Canada, an albino groundhog named for his hometown, "Wiarton Willie," drew crowds from 1956 until his death on Groundhog Day 1999. Going back to Imbolc, when the positions of stars and the relative placement of human sites upon the ground, Wiarton Willie's home, at precisely 45 degrees north, balanced between the Equator and the North Pole geographically, and between the winter solstice and the spring equinox chronologically, it's still possible to draw symbolic lines between the first weather prognosticators and the next generation of albino groundhogs.

CHRISTENINGS AND BAPTISMS

Baptisms and christenings epitomize innocence, presenting an unlikely venue for tales that depend on revenge, irony, or horror for their resolution. Only two legends fall into this category and, like innocence and depravity, they're at opposite ends of the urban-legend spectrum.

The basic ingredients of any baptism or christening are a minister, parents, and, of course, a child. "The Reprehensible Parson,"

set deep in the Bible Belt, where full immersion is a common form of baptism, begins by inserting the seed of sin into what would normally be a pristine, tranquil tableau.

Charles Golden, the man standing hip-deep in the local creek with a beautiful baby boy in his arms, is completely unaware that his pretty wife, Amanda, is anything other than his devoted wife and the mother of his first child. He's certainly completely ignorant of her affair with the man standing across from them, his robes floating lightly in the current, Pastor Milt Roberts! Or that little Charlie junior is about to be baptized by his real father!

Smiling in the sunshine, Charles Golden hands the beautiful child across to the pastor, confident that his son is about to be welcomed into the church community. Amanda Golden, however, with her child about to be submerged by its resentful father, has sudden doubts about the whole situation and reaches out for him just as, with a smug grin, the pastor plunges the boy deep into the water.

Charles, mistaking her concern for a mother's natural protectiveness, gathers her into the circle of his arms and whispers reassurances into her ear as the pastor slowly, ever so slowly, intones the last words of the service. Even he's getting nervous, however, by the time the boy is finally lifted, dripping and squalling, from the water. No one on shore notices anything unusual, and if Amanda is a bit quick to snatch her boy back, well, she's just being a mother, right?

Following the immersion in water with the traditional anointing with oil and a sprinkle of salt on the tongue (easy to accomplish with the boy at full wail), the four emerge from the water with no one, including Charles, aware of the hidden tension between the pastor and his former lover. Everything seems perfectly normal as the family hurries home to change into dry clothes and wait for the usual parade of friends and relatives to stop by. The baptismal lunch has barely started, however, when a wail of fear and terror cuts through the happy chatter. Looking up from where she's been attempting to tickle the boy's chin, a woman sobs, "He's dead, ma'am, he's dead!"

Despite the minister's absence—he also had to change clothes before following them home—Amanda, completely undone by grief, instantly accuses him of murdering the child. As police and EMT teams arrive, the young wife breaks down, admitting her guilt and pointing the finger at the absent pastor. Before the boy is taken away, she kisses him lightly on the lips, then sits quietly under the heavy cloud of horror and censure.

Charles, insane with grief, slams out of the house, away from his wife, and soon encounters the minister on his way to the baptismal reception. When the Goldens' station wagon slams into the pastor's sedan, neither man survives.

Police officers racing back to the Golden house with news of the tragedy are appalled to discover there's no widow to give the bad

> Some cultures believe that telling some-
> one your true name gives that person
> power over you, so every person has
> two names, one public and one private.
> Before you assume this applies to some
> tribe deep in a jungle somewhere, con-
> sider this English (and later American)
> nursery rhyme:
>
> *What's your name?*
> *Pudding and tame.*
> *If you ask me again,*
> *I'll tell you the same!*

news to! Though it takes several days for the autopsies to be completed, it's discovered that Amanda Golden died as a result of contact with the poison her lover hid in the baptismal salt. The last kiss given her son had sealed her own fate.

The final irony? In examining all four bodies, something the minister would never have allowed in life, the coroner easily concluded that the beautiful child had been Charles Golden's son after all.

Needless to say, this isn't one that gets passed around at too many christenings. It's actually been traced to the numerous charges laid against the clergy of all faiths in the last decade, a revelationary tale of the corruption behind even the most innocent rites of faith.

Fortunately, the most common tale told at christenings is considerably more upbeat.

Many parents spend the entire nine months of pregnancy debating what to name their precious child. The modern trend of discovering the baby's sex before it's born hasn't made the task one bit easier either. What with family tradition, theories on how names affect behavior, unflattering combinations of initials, and the unisex solution to take into consideration, not to mention personal preference to satisfy, it's a miracle anyone gets named anymore! Small wonder, then, that desperate parents might choose some unusual means to name their children.

First there's the woman who misread the sign outside the delivery-room door—it split down the middle as her bed was pushed through it—and decided to name her gorgeous new son Nosmo King (No Smoking). The name doesn't actually appear in the population or voter registration lists for the period, but a comedian once adopted this moniker as his stage name and became well known on the vaudeville circuit.

Then there are those parents who adopted names from a medical dictionary based solely on what they believed they would sound like, or from mispronouncing words on their children's charts in the mistaken belief the hospital had named the baby already, or from the card on the crib or the ID bracelet on their child's arm, or . . . well, you get the idea.

From these *faux pas* come names like Famallee spelled F-e-m-a-l-e, Sue-Phyllis spelled S-y-p-h-i-l-i-s, Colleen or Colin spelled C-o-l-o-n, Testacleas spelled T-e-s-t-i-c-l-e-s, V'jeania spelled V-a-g-i-n-a, Xema spelled E-c-z-e-m-a, Beulah spelled B-o-w-e-l, Uriah spelled U-r-e-a, and Placencia spelled P-l-a-c-e-n-t-a!

Other pleasant sounds taken out of context: LaMongelo spelled L-e-m-o-n J-e-l-l-o, his cousin Orangelo spelled O-r-a-n-g-e J-e-l-l-o; and LaTrene or LaTrena spelled L-a-t-r-i-n-e, Mabel spelled M-a B-e-l-l, Daisy spelled D-i-z-z-y, Adrienne spelled A D-r-a-i-n-O, and Arnette spelled H-a-i-r-n-e-t.

A few others are simply the result of unfortunate combinations of first names, surnames, or initials. The Lears that lent their name to the Learjet were blessed with a beautiful daughter to whom they gave the equally lovely name Shanda, which means "serene" and "peaceful." What could be wrong with that? Well, nothing until you add the surname: Shanda Lear. Chandelier.

Ima, a relatively common name in the 1880s when the then-governor of Texas bestowed it on his daughter, is, in itself, pretty innocuous. Guess her father, James Steven Hogg, simply hadn't considered the combination: Ima Hogg!

Sometimes it's the meanings behind a combination of names that threaten to leave some unwary minister giggling mid-service. Take Cecil B. DeMille as an example. How ironic that the literal translation of his name means "the miller's dim-sighted son!" Calvin Klein, a name parlayed into a multimillion-dollar industry based solely on appearance and style, means "small bald man."

Another name tale explains how Mr. Jackson Ezekiel David James Nathaniel Sylvester Willis Edward Demosthenes Henderson ended up with a name so long he was thirteen before he could answer reliably when asked his name. His mother, the poorest member of a Charlotte, North Carolina, family, had high hopes that by naming her son after all his rich uncles, at least one of them would remember her boy in their will. Not one of them did.

Resurrecting old family names isn't always the safest answer, either. Mr. Henderson got off easy. Other *popular* names of the period include Feather, Dozer, Babberley, Bugless, Abishag, Salmon, and Murder! As one young man discovered, history isn't all it's cracked up to be. When his parents, Muriel and Paul Baker of Knottsville, couldn't decide what to call their son and left it up to his paternal grandfather, he simply pulled out the family album and began rattling off names. The boy's eventual moniker? Clapham Despair Strongitharm Baker.

Can you blame modern pastors for practicing the names of infants in private before trying to say them with a straight face at a christening?

ON THE ROAD

According to the American Travel Industry Association, in 1750 the average thirty-five-year-old man traveled 212 miles in his lifetime; in 1950 he traveled 214 miles *each week*! Some travel legends actually date back to 1750, but it's in this century, particularly the latter half, that this subgroup have come into their own.

PLANES
Preflight Check

Long before anyone boards anything, be it plane, train, or automobile, someone somewhere has tested everything from the Scotchgard on the seats to the little plastic O-ring that ensures the chemical toilets don't leak. Some tests, however, like the one related in "Bird Bombs," just don't leave us with that firm sense of reassurance.

The U.S. Federal Aviation Administration, in agreement with the American Standards Council, recently engineered a device to test the windshield strength of airplanes. Inspired by the devastating effect of a midair collision with birds, this device, affectionately known as the "Chicken Cannon," fires chicken carcasses at windshields, engines, and undercarriage at the amazing rate of eight birds per second!

When the United Kingdom came up with a new high-speed locomotive, they realized that even though they hoped their trains would stay on the ground, bird collisions at the speeds they hoped to attain could still be a serious concern. Therefore, once the industrial architects finished their calculations, they borrowed the cannon to field-test their windshield strength. The results were spectacular.

The first bird not only broke through the windshield but destroyed the engineer's seat before burying itself in the rear wall!

After checking their calculations once again, and resetting the device in careful accordance with FAA instructions, they promptly destroyed the cabin of yet another locomotive!

Completely flabbergasted, they quickly sent off a description of the test scenario to the States with a request for suggestions. The return response was swift and to the point:

"Thaw chickens first."

The message in this tale is a subtle but deliberate poke at a favorite American target: non-Americans! Several variations on this one do exist, set in numerous foreign locales, none of these foreigners ever seem capable of figuring out that frozen birds aren't too likely to be flying around in the natural world!

On the side of the Americans, however, is the fact that there really *is* a "Chicken Cannon," and it really was developed by Americans. Still, this seems nothing more than a funny story with no basis in fact.

Boarding!

"Orville and Wilbur's first flight was delayed," said Charles Lindbergh, "and it sort of set the standard for every flight thereafter!"

Actually, 91 percent of North American flights depart within ten minutes of their scheduled times, and 90 percent arrive within ten minutes of their ETA. Not bad, really. Which makes the next travel tale, "Home Is Where the Heart Is," all the more incredible.

In 1977, Merhan Karimi Nasseri disagreed vocally with the Shah of Iran. He was quickly deported—so quickly that he found himself outside Iran's borders, with no passport!

Over the next four years he desperately sought refugee status in seven European capitals. No one, it appeared, wanted a cast-off Iranian of questionable political stripe. It wasn't until 1981 that he was finally declared a political refugee by Belgium's United Nations High Commission. Official status at last! But what could he do with it? Get to Britain, he hoped.

A long journey later, he arrived in Paris by train where, before he could say "Parlez-vous anglais?" his briefcase, containing his precious papers, was stolen in the station!

Not to be deterred, he boarded a plane for England. Staff at Heathrow, where the guards carry automatic weapons at the ready, showed no sympathy for this "man without a country," and shoved him on the next flight back to Paris—where he was promptly arrested for illegal entry! His only saving grace? France had nowhere to deport him to. Without a passport, they couldn't even send him back to Iran!

It took until 1992 for a French court to

Home away from home?

decide that Nasseri had arrived at Charles de Gaulle Airport, specifically Terminal One, legally. He was a refugee. They couldn't evict him from the premises. Of course, they didn't have to let him out of Terminal One, to roam the French countryside at will, either! French government practices, like most, remain slow, contradictory, and swamped with forms in quadruplicate. They admitted he was a refugee, but refused to allow him citizenship in France, or to provide the transit visa that would let him leave!

Nasseri's world collapsed to the size of a tiny concourse.

Attempts to return to Belgium, where he'd been given his original documents, were prevented by the lack of transit documents, and Belgium refused to send the refugee-status and travel documents to France. Though they were completely cognizant of Nasseri's situation, Belgium demanded that Nasseri claim his papers in person!

Eventually, Belgium agreed they'd allow the "displaced person" to return—if, and only if, he'd agree to reside there for a full year under the supervision of a government-assigned social worker. Nasseri politely declined to trade one prison for another.

And so he sits, making use of what facilities are available at the airport while the rest of the traveling population moves on to homes and holidays.

Fortunately, stories like Nasseri's are rare. Perhaps the star of the following tale, "What He Said!," should have read it before moving into the limelight.

During the wee hours of January 11, 1986, in the midst of one of the worst storms ever to hit Chicago—and it's been hit by some doozies—United Airlines was forced to cancel a flight already delayed by five hours. The same lousy weather prevented replacement staff from getting in, and Gloria Best, the lone agent still working the United counter, faced just over two hundred tired, disgruntled passengers who'd probably end up sleeping in the airport, since even the hotel shuttles had stopped running hours ago.

Taking a deep breath, Ms. Best put on her smile and started working through the passengers as quickly as she could, offering sympathy and advice along with the complimentary toothbrush. She'd gotten through a dozen passengers, pulling the families with small children and the elderly to the front of the line, when a man in a business suit pushed his way to the counter and slammed his ticket down.

"Look, I paid for a first-class ticket on this flight, and you're going to get me there!"

"I'll be happy to see if there's alternate transportation available, sir—as soon as I've dealt with your fellow passengers here."

Not impressed by the elderly auntie with her walker, or the young mother juggling her three small children, the businessman stuck his chin out and planted his feet before asking, at the top of his voice, "Do you have any idea who I am?"

Without missing a beat, Gloria Best picked up her PA microphone and, staring at the rude passenger, said in her most polite voice, "Could I have your attention, please? We have a passenger here who has no idea who he is. If there is anyone who can help him establish his identity, please come to Gate One."

Passengers on all sides broke out in laughter, delighted at the beautiful putdown.

The businessman showed none of their humor. Instead, he snatched up his ticket with a snarled, "Fuck you!"

As calmly as ever, Gloria smiled. "I'm sorry, sir, I'm afraid you'll have to stand in line for that, too!"

Though apocryphal, the above story gives listeners too deep a sense of satisfaction for it to fade away anytime soon.

As this next myth, "They Can't Get Us All!," proves, though, getting *on* the plane provides no assurance that you will actually reach your destination.

A USAir employee, Bill Gay, assigned to a new route, was traveling under an employee voucher to his departure airport, Miami, when he boarded flight 1002. Since there was someone in his assigned seat, he simply took the one across the aisle and waited for the cabin crew to make any changes they deemed necessary.

As it turned out, the flight was overbooked, and a member of the ground crew hurried on board to give Mr. Gay a pass for another flight that would also get him to Miami, just a few hours later. Going straight to Gay's assigned seat, she tapped the man there on the shoulder.

"Are you Gay?"

The man looked uncomfortable for a moment, then nodded. "Yes, I'm gay."

"I'm afraid the flight is overbooked, sir, so you'll have to get off."

Overhearing this, and realizing the woman had been looking for him, Bill Gay stood up. "Excuse me, I'm Gay."

"Oh, okay, well, as I said, you'll have to get off."

A third passenger, seated nearby, surged to his feet, his face flushed. "Hey, I'm gay, too, you can't throw us all off!"

Needless to say, had these events actually taken place, that flight wouldn't have been among the 91 percent that depart on time.

In Flight

Many air-travel legends highlight our fears. Boats *could* sink, but few people have the leisure to travel by sea regularly anymore, so, with the exception of a few months when *Titanic* dominated theater screens, no one really has reason to pass along boat legends. Car accidents happen regularly, but, to equal the body count of a plane crash, nearly one hundred vehicles would have to collide with one another at the same time! Trains carry as many passengers as planes, but, at least

It's a commonly held belief, if not quite an urban legend, that better than 90 percent of flight recorder tapes recovered after crashes include at least one of the following phrases:

"Oh shit!"
"Uh-oh."
"Jesus Christ!"
"Oh fuck!"

until recently, trains remained free of terrorist activity and hijacking, and simple accidents rarely seem to befall trains. Falling isn't such a big deal, either, most rails being inches off the ground as opposed to 32,000 feet.

To deal with the extra stress associated with air travel, some passengers spend their preflight time in the airport bar; others plan on immersing themselves in the latest Grisham novel; and some, like the lady in "Sweet Dreams," down a few sleeping tablets before boarding in the hope of passing the entire trip in sweet oblivion.

Mary Carter hated to fly. The security checks reminded her of hijackings. The belts, low ceilings, and cramped quarters nudged her claustrophobia into high gear. On top of all that, her feet always ended up two shoe sizes larger before she got where she was going.

Only the christening of her first grandchild could have persuaded her to board Air

Canada flight 2026 from St. John's to Halifax. Knowing that they would have to cross the Cabot Strait, a wide expanse of open water, did nothing to calm her fears. Though she wasn't in the habit of relying on chemicals to alter her state of awareness, she did take one of the two sleeping pills her sister had pressed on her that morning. She drifted off almost immediately, and all appeared well, right up to the point where she awoke to see a flight attendant pulling a life preserver over his head!

Thinking she'd been asleep for hours, Mary's visions of the open Cabot Strait rushed before her eyes, and almost before she was aware of what she was doing, she slammed her palm against the emergency door release, and shoved.

Imagine her embarrassment when she immediately heard the door thud onto the ground outside!

Instead of being halfway through the trip as she'd thought, they were still taxiing out to the runway as the flight attendant worked through the safety demonstration in both official languages!

Though no one at Air Canada can remember such an incident actually taking place, one pilot and three flight attendants are sure it happened—on Canadian Airlines!

The staff at Canadian Airlines hasn't heard that one, but they're sure the events of "One on the Aisle" happened over at Air Canada.

Unlike Mary Baker, Pierre Martin thought flying beat boats, trains, and automobiles anytime. He settled back into his tiny seat, tucked the tinier pillow behind him, and decided to nap until the beverage cart reached his seat, back in the twenty-third row.

All went smoothly until a mixup with the public address system suddenly sent the soundtrack of the in-flight movie booming through the cabin! Martin's eyes flew open. He gasped once, gripped the arms of the seat that he'd kept in its "full upright position," then died of a heart attack right there in 23B! All attempts at resuscitation failed.

What was showing that afternoon?

Airport '77.

With fears that pronounced to deal with, the next legend, "Something in the Air," becomes that much more plausible.

Grandchildren, Mary Meade always believed, were the reward given to parents for surviving their own children. She just wished hers didn't decide to live in Australia, of all places. It severely limited the occasions she could share with them as she, herself, lived in Aberdeen, Scotland. Still, she loved the young ones, and when they begged her to come for Christmas, and sent her a plane ticket, she just couldn't say no.

It was well into the trip, the plane had landed in Fiji, and the crew had just opened the doors to allow some passengers to deplane, when Margaret noticed a faint mist spraying from the overhead air vents.

"What's that?" she asked the gentleman in the next seat.

"Something to keep the natives from pan-icking, some sort of sleeping gas."

Startled, Margaret quickly twisted her vent closed, but just after the door closed again, she watched as the cabin crew passed up and down the aisle with atomizer bottles. Without any comment, they calmly sprayed a fine mist to either side as they walked.

"Now what are they doing?"

"More of the same stuff, in case anyone turned off their vent."

Margaret held her breath as the flight attendant in economy passed by.

Noticing his companion sitting there with her face turning a shade of dark plum, the gentleman laid a finger to the side of his nose and winked. "If you'd rather keep your wits about you, make sure you ask them to hold the ice in your drinks, too!"

When the attendant had passed well by, Margaret took a shallow breath and gasped out, "Why?"

"They put a sedative in the water they use for the ice! See how yellow it is!" Holding up his own glass of water to the window, in front of the startling white clouds outside, he showed her just how off-color the ice and water were. "In fact, you'd be better off to get the canned juice, it's in the water, too!"

On finally arriving, the first thing Margaret did, after kissing the grandkids, was write an angry letter to the airline protesting their "drug policy." She was turning that same shade of dark plum when she read their reply, if for different reasons.

Dear Mrs. Meade:

We are so sorry to hear of your dissatisfaction with our service. However, please allow us this opportunity to offer another explanation for your observations.

1. As you know, we keep our cabins at a steady 68 degrees for the comfort of our passengers. We do this through the use of individual, overhead air-conditioning units. In locations such as Fiji, where the outside temperature hovers around 85 degrees for much of the year, the cooler air coming from our vents causes condensation, like fog, to appear where it encounters the hotter air entering through the open doorways.

2. This rapid condensation and the natural reduction of moisture due to the air-conditioning vents severely reduces the humidity of our cabins. Most passengers dislike the dryness of mouth and skin this causes. To alleviate this, we ask our attendants to mist the cabins as they deem necessary.

3. Any discoloration in the ice accompanying your drinks is a result of our decision to use the fresh water of your homeland, Scotland. As many people prefer not to drink the water when they travel, we choose to make all our ice from water at our departure points. The discoloration results from the peat surrounding so many Scottish lakes.

We hope this alleviates your concerns and that you will fly with us again soon.

She'd been had by *three* common air-travel legends!

This tale sums up nearly every unfounded rumor about the sneaky ways the airlines have of calming their passengers. The only one missed, one that gets run out more frequently in Europe than in North America, is that major airlines like SwissAir and Cathay Pacific deliberately keep the cabin pressure lower than at sea level to induce sleepiness. It's true that cabin pressure is kept low, but lower pressure typically keeps people alert!

Considering an airplane's elegant complexity, you'd think passengers would have plenty of novel things to ponder during their flight, right? The next two tales, "Hail to the Chief!" and "Sit on It," however, illustrate our obsession with the mundane, even in the most exotic of locations.

And what could be more mundane than a toilet?

Police Chief Herbert Halley of Maple Grove, Indiana, was enjoying a well-deserved day off. The football game was a close one, keeping him and his buddies on the edge of their seats through the first half. The beer was cold. The dip was homemade, his favorite, and the party-sized hero sandwich still occupied half of the dining-room table. Life was good.

Then, with a roar that witnesses would later describe as somewhere between a lion and a runaway locomotive, the roof fell in—literally—on this convivial gathering of men.

The ceiling exploded, plaster rained down,

bits and pieces of the roofing trusses flew through the room, and shingles fluttered through an overhead hole big enough to accommodate a small car!

For a moment nobody moved. Then, taking charge of the scene, Chief Halley waited just long enough to ascertain that despite a variety of injuries, everyone was capable of crawling, limping, or hobbling outside. Just in time, too. As the last few men got out to the backyard deck, massive sections of the roof, unstable without the heavy roof braces, tumbled inside. Before emergency crews could arrive, most of the roof was inside instead of over the family room!

Naturally, the first order of business was attending to the cuts, bruises, sprains, and strains, but before long, Halley and his deputy, along with several members of the fire department and the town engineer, were climbing cautiously over the rubble. Despite their thorough investigation, no one was able to find anything that could possibly have smashed through the roof. Their only clue was a large damp spot beneath the debris, just in front of the spot once occupied by a wide-screen television.

The mystery was solved by, of all people, a local crop duster who, just moments before, had watched "this monster hailstone" sail past the nose of his little plane before slamming into the residence below. When it was pointed out that no hail was reported anywhere in the area, the crop duster nodded sagely, unconcerned with this apparent contradiction of his eyewitness testimony.

"Well," he drawled, "then I suggest you find out what airliner was flying overhead."

"What?"

"We see it all the time. They flush them toilets at that height and the water freezes into a big ball of ice!"

Of course, this folksy explanation doesn't hold up. Airline waste is stored on board and pumped out on arrival at the next airport. Still, it makes for an interesting story—which is the point of most urban legends. One variant on this tale is set in France, where outbreaks of cholera are found to occur in villages under airline flight paths. Part of the story's endurance may be a holdover from the days of train travel, when anyone walking along the tracks could prove that train waste fell where it was flushed!

That loud swoosh as the vacuum toilet bowl's contents disappear from view has startled more than one first-time passenger. "Sit on It" articulates a what-if scenario that could easily pass through any passenger's mind in the brief four seconds or less that it takes to complete the waste-disposal cycle.

Obese passengers aren't fond of airplane travel. The seats pinch. Attendants always speak at the top of their voices when asking, "Do you need an extender for that seat belt?" Worst of all, the bathrooms, tight squeezes for the tiniest person, simply don't readily accommodate persons of even moderate girth!

What if a passenger with a little extra flesh on his bones were to hit the flush button while his bottom formed a tight seal around that tiny toilet seat?

Every air-disaster movie ever made includes a scene where a cabinful of loose objects is sucked through a tiny hole in the side of the plane, through a broken window, or through an open doorway. The notion of that sort of vacuum pressure being applied to a bare bottom leads naturally to visions of intestinal evisceration, yards of precious internal organ dragged into the waste system, the mother of all hemorrhoids!

No such incident has been reported by any airline.

Nor has the second scenario, where a child slips through the seat and into the bowl, where an equally tight air seal is formed, with similar results.

What have been reported in the medical journals of both North America and Europe are several cases of children inadvertently sitting on the intake lines of swimming pool pumps! That danger is apparently all too real.

Another tale, "Citizen of the Skies," is considerably quainter than those featuring unstrung intestines, and is perhaps one of the best circulated of the travel stories.

Marie Tremblett, in her eighth month of a blessedly normal pregnancy, decided she'd like to deliver her baby in her hometown of Anjou, back in France. Her husband, a trucker in Quebec, couldn't guarantee he'd be home the day she went in labor, and they'd agreed Marie would be happier close to her own mother.

She boarded an Air Canada flight from Montreal, and settled in with a good book for the eight-hour flight. Needless to say, with all that baby pressing down on her bladder and up into her lungs, the trip wasn't entirely comfortable. It wasn't long, however, before she became aware that her "discomfort" was rapidly escalating. She was in labor!

Out over the Atlantic, there was no opportunity for a landing anywhere, and in any case the delivery went so quickly it was doubtful she'd have made it to a hospital anywhere before her new daughter, Annette, arrived. All things considered, the delivery, attended by a flight attendant and a passenger who'd been a nurse, went well. By the time the plane touched down, mother and daughter were curled up in a first-class seat and doing fine.

The immediate problem as they stepped off the plane was that young Annette, who hadn't legally existed at the beginning of the trip, had no passport!

Though the customs and immigration staff at the airport had no experience on which to draw, they did arrive at an innovative solution. Declaring Annette a citizen of "France, Canada, and the Skies," they decided she had the right to travel anywhere her home airline, Air Canada, traveled. Air Canada, joining in the spirit of the moment, which would allow Annette to avoid miles of red tape, announced that Annette would never have to pay for air travel as long as Air Canada flew!

Air Canada, of course, has no record of these events, and it seems this tale is another instance of an earlier story being updated, made more relevant, for a modern audience. A nearly identical tale, set aboard one of the Cunard ocean liners some fifty years previous to these events, resulted in the new arrival being given a lifetime pass on any ship Cunard owned. Though neither Air Canada nor Cunard can confirm any actual incidents aboard their equipment, the legend developed a life of its own when three airlines voluntarily extended the privileges of the myth to actual children born on their flights. Not to be outdone, so have two railways and a cruise-ship line!

Of course, in-flight births aren't the only hazards flight crews face. Common events, such as unexpected turbulence, affect all their passengers to one degree or another. Whether it's irritation that they can't read with all the jiggling, or outright fear of falling from the sky, passengers demand high levels of emotional support as well as technical excellence from their crews, as "The Blowhard" illustrates.

A United flight to the Caribbean in 1965 attempted a detour around the edges of a tropical storm, but for nearly an hour the battered plane endured turbulence heavy enough to force even the most experienced flight attendants to buckle up. Throughout the shaking, the pilot's voice over the PA system reassured his passengers that this wouldn't last long, and generally kept them from panicking.

When the flight smoothed out again, the copilot appeared from the flight deck to smile and walk back through each section while the flight attendants hastily got the beverage cart in gear and handed out complimentary drinks.

Eventually the pilot's voice, noticeably tight and weary, sounded again. "Say, sweetie, I could *really* use a coffee and a little tender lovin' care."

One attendant, realizing the pilot had intended this message to go only to the galley, and not out over the public address channel, raced up through the aisle to the flight deck door.

Behind her, a passenger who'd complained bitterly throughout the ordeal shouted, "Hey, *sweetie,* you forgot the coffee!"

A modern, more risqué tale repeats the key events but substitutes the pilot's line with "I could really handle a blow job and a coffee, in either order, about now!" This lewder version, it should be noticed, doesn't even mention the inevitable nasty passenger ready to turn a tired man's private thoughts into ribald humor.

Some tales are more closely tied to particular events than others. "The Blowhard," for example, pops up whenever a hurricane runs ashore in the United States. An interesting side note to this tale is geographic: The milder form of "The Blowhard" still circu-

lates regularly in the southeastern states; the cruder version, however, has almost entirely supplanted the original on the West Coast!

Sometimes stories are resurrected, or reworked, in response to a particular incident. This next travel tale definitely falls into the oldie-but-goodie category, but, for whatever reason, has fallen out of favor in the eastern States and Canada. "Occupied!" begins on a major airline, on one of its larger aircraft, on a long-distance nonstop flight between two major cities on opposite coasts. In the States, the cities are usually New York and Los Angeles; in Canada, Halifax and Vancouver provide the necessary distance.

Leaving New York, Serima Klein glanced around the first-class section and smiled to herself. This was the only way to travel. No children. No pets in little cages under the seats. No getting squished between two cigar-smoking businessmen who assumed one was terribly interested in whatever the heck they sold. The footrest was a nice touch, too. She even had a view of the flight deck whenever the door opened, and from time to time she could actually see out the cockpit windows!

And hadn't that handsome blond pilot just smiled at her as he went to the washroom?

Yup, this was the way to go!

The beverage cart hadn't negotiated its short trip through first class before yet another handsome young man, this one brunette, stepped through from the flight deck. Serima smiled widely when he caught her watching him and touched his fingertips to the brim of his pilot's cap.

Her smile faded when the door to the lavatory nudged the door to the cockpit, urging it closed and blocking that glorious view.

Oh, well, no doubt when one or the other returned, they'd open the door again. She settled into her seat to wait, then giggled when the two doors, on opposite sides of the short aisle ahead, opened together. The pilots' simultaneous apologies first left Serima giggling behind her hand, then, as she saw horror cross both handsome faces, and saw them stare at the closed cockpit door, all humor fled.

Both pilots were on *this* side of the door!

If nothing else, Serima Klein learned a lot about the safety precautions airlines used to keep terrorists out of the cockpit. Just moments before the autopilot would have pushed them past their fuel limit, the door was breached and the disaster averted.

Perhaps because this tale simply doesn't work—the majority of major airlines have a cockpit crew of three, and even in first class there are only two lavatories, so it would be impossible for the entire crew to be in the head—it gradually faded from the collection of air-travel legends. It cropped up again in Ontario and both the northeastern states and the eastern provinces in the latter half of 1998—right after Air Nova and Air Ontario, which service those areas, announced they were reducing their crews from three to two!

Thank You for Flying!

Considering that one of the acknowledged functions of urban legends is to let us play with and express our fears in a relatively harmless setting, you'd expect to find dozens of legends surrounding the most common air-travel anxiety, a crash. It makes sense, but it's not borne out by the mass of legends circulating. It seems some fears aren't even safe to play with at the arm's distance that oral folklore allows.

Instead, the folklore ignores the most dangerous part of the trip—the landing—and skips right along to tales set firmly on the ground.

"The Free Wives Club," for example, doesn't even take place until months *after* a group of executives complete several long business trips without any untoward incidents at all!

With new airlines biting into the business-travel pie every year, the bright boys in one firm's marketing department devised a scheme they hoped would lure their customers back permanently. In this incentive program, business travelers could rack up points for each flight they took. After three trips, they could bring their spouses along free of charge on the fourth outing. It didn't even have to be a business trip.

The program seemed popular, as many men submitted their points for air tickets. The promotions team, anxious to know if they were also building a nonbusiness client base that could be tapped later, decided to survey all the wives who benefited from the program.

The survey provided all the information they could have wanted—though not what they expected. Of the two hundred women surveyed, more than half responded, "*What free travel?*"

The clever style of this tale, similar to "The Case of the Missing Clock," marks this as an early legend. *Reader's Digest Books, The Big Book of Jokes for Public Speakers,* and *Lewd Jokes for All Occasions,* which date from 1958, 1941, and 1937 respectively, all present this as a joke, with no pretense that the events ever occurred anywhere. While it was reported in one of Brunvand's books in 1993, it had faded from the scene for the nearly forty years in between.

What brought it back to prominence?

Perhaps it was the introduction, in the early nineties, of new "point programs" such as Aeroplan, Frequent Flyer Miles, and Air Miles Rewards?

Some tales, such as "Back from the Dead," are clearly as old but adapted to new circumstances, like air travel.

The modern version of "Back from the Dead" begins in New York, where a woman tries to buy a ticket for her pet dog. The airline refuses her request, but assures her the dog will be perfectly safe in the cargo area. Against her better judgment, she agrees and lets the pet carrier be checked.

Arriving in Jerusalem, her destination, she's left waiting at the cargo counter for so long that she suspects something is seriously wrong. The staff continues reassuring her that all is well; it simply takes longer to offload cargo as the priority is always to reunite passengers with their luggage first. She waits.

Behind the scenes, panic reigns. A single glance inside the pet carrier assures everyone that the woman's dog, a miniature schnauzer, is very dead!

Two cargo handlers receive a blank check, a list of nearby pet stores, and instructions to return ASAP with another dog, one as close as possible in appearance to the corpse. The woman at the cargo desk receives more assurances that her dog will be along in a few moments.

Eventually the baggage handlers race in with a miniature schnauzer, tuck the live animal in the cage, and send it along on the little rubber track to the front counter.

The animal's owner takes one look in the cage and swiftly gets hysterical!

"That's not my dog! What have you done with my dog?"

Attempts by the staff to convince her this is her dog fail miserably.

"That can't be my dog! My dog *died*! I brought it here to bury in my own yard! What have you done with my dog?"

As early as 1910, this tale was told in England, but the animal was an exotic bird and the means of travel a boat. A 1980s version ignored the travel altogether. Instead, a man's neighbor buries her dead rabbit in her yard. The man's dog digs it up. The man assumes the dog attacked the rabbit. He quickly washes and dries the body, then props it up in its hutch in the hope the owners will assume it has died naturally. The neighbor, naturally, thinks some crazy person has been in her yard! Who else would dig up a dead animal and put it back in its cage? What air travel added to the legend, of course, was speed of transport. Clearly, a dead dog couldn't travel in the cargo hold of anything else for very long before revealing itself through its stench alone!

Occasionally, it's simply the technology that appears to catch human imagination. "The Firefighting Diver" is a case in point. Almost as soon as water bombers and helicopter buckets became part of the forest-fire-fighting arsenal, stories of strange things scooped up by the craft that skimmed the lakes came into vogue. The *London Times,* the *Toronto Star,* and even *Tass* carried reports of fish being dropped over forest fires! In France, the story grew, eventually spawning the tale of a Côte d'Azur diver who was scooped up by a water bomber, then dumped into a raging fire! The pilot knew nothing of his extra passenger until ground firefighters discovered the diver's charred remains dangling in the charred limbs of a blackened tree!

The macabre image stuck.

It migrated to California, where the diver went aloft in a helicopter bucket, to British Columbia, where he wasn't discovered after the fact but struck the ground with a decisive *splat* in front of a startled line of axe- or shovel-toting ground crews, and to Spain, where the diver turns out to be a missing American tourist who's been bobbing innocently about in the Med!

Even here, however, traces of older folkloric lineages do exist. In a firefighter's guidebook circulated to volunteer fire squads around the London docks in 1890, there's a warning to "avoid schools of fish or other creatures which might foul the mechanism" of the fireboat pumps!

It appears all things old are made new again—at least in folklore and urban legend.

TRAINS

With so many travel tales translated into modern forms featuring planes, finding *modern* stories about railroads is rare. "The Phone-y" defies any attempt to set it aboard a plane by depending on the one technology that planes can't yet accommodate—the cellular phone!

We've all seen them in airport terminals, of course, men (and occasionally women) wandering about with their cellular phones to their ears, turning an activity normally considered private into an opportunity to show off their new toys. While those in phone booths huddled with their backs to the press of the airport, stuck fingers in their ears, and spoke just loudly enough to be heard at the

Of planes, trains, and automobiles, the one with the fewest active legends.

far end of the connection, cellular callers wandered through the center of the terminal and spoke at the tops of their voices! Like the men who stared deeply into the monitors of their laptop computers—only to be discovered playing solitaire, or involved in the obviously taxing job of changing the colors on their screen savers—these cellular customers quickly became pathetic stereotypes.

Luckily for air travelers, those phones had to be shut off once passengers actually boarded the plane. Train passengers unfortunately weren't granted such blessed reprieves, and they continued to be subjected to loud, disjointed, and one-sided conversations of absolutely no interest to anyone but the speaker!

"The Phone-y" begins when a Via (or Amtrak) train loses its own communication signal and a coach conductor hurries back through each car asking if anyone aboard has a phone he can borrow to notify the next station of their problem. An elderly woman quickly points to a young man who's been berating someone at top volume for the past half hour—much to the annoyance of the coach's other passengers.

"He's got one!"

Secretly, everyone in the car hopes this emergency will last long enough to completely drain the uncouth young man's battery!

When the conductor politely asks to borrow the phone, however, the owner refuses!

"Sir, it's an emergency."

"Find someone else's phone, I'm on a very important call!"

"Sir, there *is* no other phone. I really must insist—"

"No!"

Eventually, more train personnel arrive, passengers begin to get restless, almost panicky, and the young man is forced to admit that his phone won't do them any good—it's a fake he's been using in an attempt to look like some kind of power broker!

A female passenger returning from a trip to the lavatory quietly pulls the conductor aside and volunteers the use of her own cellular phone.

The underlying morals don't require much explanation, do they?

AUTOMOBILES

When Henry Ford decided Americans should have a car in every driveway, he probably didn't realize he was producing something that would soon kill as many people as guns. Coming from a culture used to moving at the speed of a horse and buggy, he certainly couldn't have anticipated "road rage"!

Nor is it likely that Ford conceived of our modern relationship with our cars. Who, in Ford's time, would have considered taking on a monthly car payment higher than the mortgage payment on the family farm? Who would have believed that dwellers in some large Asian cities would start their cars at four-thirty in the morning and not park them again until eight o'clock in the evening, and

that these same families would adapt to a lifestyle in which homework was done, meals were taken, and even social engagements were conducted in a car?

That the auto would earn a reputation as a death machine simply wouldn't have crossed the mind of an American used to plodding along in a wagon behind a horse!

Yet automobiles and death coexist in modern societies. How else to explain the multitude of urban legends linking the two?

The "Suicide Car" tale pops up in every garage. Some mechanic or body-shop worker, while checking on a wreck that probably should be written off, will recall hearing, from some friend of a friend, about this really terrific car that no one would buy. The car, often a Porsche or other foreign muscle car, was in primo condition, not a scratch on her, low mileage, a truly great car.

So why wouldn't it sell?

Seems someone committed suicide in it, blew blood and gray matter so far into the interior materials that no matter what cleaning solutions or methods were used, a strong reek emanated from the upholstery and carpeting. At first people bought the car for its ridiculously low price, perhaps believing they'd find something to eliminate the odor. Each time, though, it was returned, still stinking.

One drawn-out version finally sees the car sold to a man who, even weeks later, hasn't noticed anything wrong with his purchase. Surprised, the salesman eventually asks him how he stands the smell.

It's the buyer's turn to be surprised; he'd never smelled anything. Of course, come to think of it, he hasn't even smelled his morning coffee for some months . . .

Less than a week later, the car is returned to the lot—covered in blood and brain tissue!

The salesman is horrified to learn that, alerted to his diminished sense of smell by the salesman's inquiry, the man had made an appointment to see his physician. The diagnosis was that the loss of smell was caused by an inoperable brain tumor that would soon leave the man blind and incontinent. In despair, he'd committed suicide just as the car's previous owner had done.

Variants on this tale include suicides by other means, as well as murders and deaths by accident. Suicides generally include deliberate carbon monoxide poisoning in a remote location. The distance is the factor that allows the body to go undetected long enough to decompose and impart its horrid scent to the interior. Murders run the gamut of methods. Again, the important factors are time and distance. If the death isn't sufficiently messy on its own to account for the smell, then decomposition must have time to work its black magic. Oddly, all the accidents encountered to date are by carbon monoxide poisoning. In direct opposition to real-world observations, accidental death in this legend is a gentle, tidy process!

Some folklorists attribute widely divergent versions of the same tale to simple age. The longer a tale has been around, and the more

To accommodate emergency vehicles, many automated traffic lights incorporate a special sensor that picks up the frequency of light flashes used by emergency lights and automatically changes the lights to allow these vehicles to proceed unimpeded.

When this feature became common knowledge, drivers at traffic lights across the country tried flashing their headlights in order to fool the lights into letting them go.

Turns out the lights were more discriminating than the drivers. Not one was fooled.

people have retold it, the more opportunity exists for minor differences to sneak in. Since "The Suicide Car" is trackable at least as far back as 1956, age is one plausible explanation.

Another theory contends that when numerous variants appear to arise concurrently, it's possible that several true tales are converging. Each teller gets the story a little different because the actual cases varied in detail. As the stories butt up against one another, an "official" version eventually emerges that combines the diverse details into one story. Of course, because the "official" version in one town may differ from another, the variants remain, but tracing them becomes exponentially more difficult. Stirring in fictional depictions, like those elements of "The Suicide Car" also found in the films *Christine* and *Mr. Wrong,* frequently sway popular memory toward one regional story or the other.

"The Suicide Car" may be an example of the second theory at work. To date, four different researchers, in four different locations, have all managed to unearth a true tale that conforms to at least one interpretation of this legend.

At the opposite end of the research spectrum is the "Flashing Headlights Initiation" legend.

According to this modern gangster legend, young men trying to join a gang cruise the streets with their headlights off. The first person who flashes his own headlights at the wannabe gangbangers, to alert them to the problem, becomes that night's target. All that's left to complete the ritual is for the initiate to kill the target. Some legends insist this is done up close and personal with a single shot to the head; others, especially in California, suggest the murder is accomplished by simply pushing the target, along with the car, off the road.

Despite dozens of reported instances, however, this one defies authentication as anything other than an urban legend!

The reports sprang up everywhere, nearly convincing local law-enforcement officers that they'd missed something by the sheer number of queries pouring in!

Several investigations and computer analysis of the standardized violent crime survey failed to turn up any trend. Specific inquiries netted not one actual incident, much less a gang "rampage."

People do sometimes make unusual connections based more on emotion than on fact; it's part of what we call intuition and ingenuity. The one widely reported incident of gang violence actually to erupt during the time frame when this legend grew fastest could fall into that "emotional" category.

KTLA television in Los Angeles, as well as several national news organizations, all car-

AIRBAG FACTS

Airbags can cause facial burns when deployed.

Next to stereos and phones, airbags are the item most likely to be stolen from cars.

A car thief once attempted to sue the owners of a car he'd stolen. The reason? They'd failed to replace their airbag after a minor fender-bender. When the thief was later involved in a crash, he received severe facial injuries from slamming into the steering wheel!

ried the story of a family of tourists who made a wrong turn while visiting the City of Angels. A gang, interpreting this as a turf invasion, shot and killed three of them, including a two-year-old girl.

The emotional-content theory suggests that, on hearing this horrific account, especially accompanied by full-color images of the child limp in a policeman's arms, sets up a chain of thoughts that conclude, "If a gang could do this—with no provocation—why not target some innocent driver just for the hell of it?"

Incidentally, Los Angeles also appears in an old legend attached to earthquakes. "The Flat Thief" begins simply. A young man, intent on impressing his date with a car he's often described but doesn't actually own, finds himself stalking the big parking lots. He's looking for a car he can "borrow" for the duration of his date, after which he'll just dump the car somewhere convenient to the original lot and later tell his girl he sold the thing for a great price. No real harm to anyone, right?

Finally he finds the right make, model, and color, and before he can explain how he does it, he's inside with the car thrumming under his hands.

The owner never does find the car dumped nearby, but after the chaos surrounding the Northridge earthquake, which strikes that night, that's no surprise. He *is* surprised to find a policeman on his doorstep a week later, asking him if he can explain how his car managed to end up

crushed between two layers of a highway, miles from where he last saw it?

No.

Then he'd have no idea *who* was found inside the car, either?

No!

It takes a missing-person report filed by the girlfriend, including a description of the stolen car, to solve the mystery.

Not the most intriguing tale ever, but persistent, especially in areas like Los Angeles, San Francisco, and other seismic hot spots. What is surprising is that this particular tale is common all over North America! In fact, if asked, people from coast to coast can actually *picture* the collapsed two-tier highway, with the cars squished like icing between them! Amazing considering no such story ever aired, on any network!

A similarly well-believed legend continues to pair cars and death scenarios. The scene is a typical suburban home, complete with white picket fences, which need painting, and cedar shingles, which need repair. The man of the house decides to start at the top and tackle the shingles first, while his wife runs off for paint and brushes.

Eyeing the steep roof, he concedes that extra precautions are in order. A rope seat comes together under his able fingers, and before long he tosses the free end of the rope over the roof peak, securing it to a nice, solid object on the opposite side from the damaged shingles.

He's just working his way up the roof, congratulating himself on thinking ahead and perhaps saving himself a nasty fall, when the rope jerks tight around him! The *upward* motion isn't noticeable at first, concerned as he is with being castrated by his own knot-work. It isn't until he's dragged up and over the roof that he remembers *what* he tied his rope to. The car his wife is obviously using to go for the painting supplies!

Before he can yell "Geronimo!" he's pulled up and over the house to plummet two and a half stories and die.

The moral of the story? Don't forget your wife has her own set of car keys? Or maybe, more simply, carelessness and cars don't mix.

A lot of the folklorically important tales, the ones with survival messages, are short and to the point. As cars and death seem such a match made in heaven, many automobile legends are little more than a single sentence, the transportation equivalent of "Frogs give you warts!"

How many times did your parents tell you to keep your hands inside the car? As many times as you were told that sitting too close to the TV could leave you sterile? More times than you were reminded that sitting on cold concrete could cause hemorrhoids?

Tragically, while piles and sterility shouldn't be a problem—those really are urban legends—dozens of injuries per year do result from allowing body parts to dangle irresponsibly out of moving vehicles.

One man from Sacramento died when his hat, a custom cowboy model, blew out the open window. Witnesses say he opened his door, leaned out far enough to spot the hat on the pavement, began backing up, leaned out farther to retrieve it, fell out, landed on his head while the car continued to roll, and died.

A teenager from New York State hung out the window of a bus on the way home. He never actually reached home because of a utility pole between him and his destination. He died instantly.

An Alabama man, much too drunk to be driving at all, held his beer out at arm's length in the belief that the breeze would keep it nice and cold. He didn't notice the stop sign that took his arm off just above the elbow. (See what unthinking belief in urban legends can cause? Holding his beer outside actually *warmed* it up!) He did notice that his beer was missing, and incidentally his forearm—which prompted him to go to the hospital. According to the reports filed at the time, including a statement from the victim, he "felt no pain at all during or after the amputation."

Modernization doesn't help. Almost as soon as power windows became common options, stories of amputation, asphyxiation, and death, all attributed to power windows, became the urban-legend vogue. Unlike the actual deaths attributed to indiscriminate dangling, this legend existed, completely unfounded and repeatedly debunked, for nearly a decade in the United States. A case eventually did appear, reported in the United Kingdom, involving the death of a young girl through asphyxiation when her neck was trapped in a power window. This naturally set off new rounds of the tale and lent authority—albeit false authority, as the tale predated the event—to all previous rumors of injury.

Clearly, not every encounter with a car is fatal. The surgeon general hasn't slapped big warning signs on their bumpers. Still, even among those tales where cars aren't the immediate tool responsible for the featured death, death lurks close by.

Car owners tend to think of their vehicles as extensions of their homes, mobile spare rooms where they can leave half of their CD collection instead of lugging it on and off public transportation day after day. American law acknowledges the inside of a car as a private space that can't be searched without a warrant covered by the same strict guidelines that would apply to a residence.

Carter Brown, the car owner of "In the Trunk," evidently agreed with that assessment. Everything from his first illegal dozen beers to this year's Christmas presents spent time in his trunk.

So, when a night of hard drinking and harder fighting left one man dead in the shadows of a parking lot, the body found its way into the trunk! And after a thing like that, well, Carter *really* needed another drink for the road.

He locked the trunk, but, suspecting his keys might be harder to manipulate when he came back out, he left the doors open. Who was going to steal the collection of empties in his backseat anyway?

© Peter/Ngaire Genge, 1999

Recessed designs ensure that no little knees hit these controls by accident.

When closing time finally forced him out of the bar, Carter stared around the lot with his keys dangling from his fingers. He wouldn't have to worry about locks or inconvenient encounters with cops though, his car was gone, stolen! And with a corpse in the trunk, he couldn't even report the darned thing missing! At a loss, Carter tucked his keys in his pocket and started walking.

He hadn't gotten more than a quarter of the way home when he found the car abandoned in the middle of the road, with the trunk wide open. Whoever had decided to jimmy the lock evidently didn't like what they found. As Carter closed the trunk and fumbled the key into the ignition for the remainder of the trip home, he wondered how long it would be before the body started to smell. He couldn't afford a fancy-schmancy alarm system, but if all he needed was a body to run off thieves . . . well, bodies couldn't be that hard to come by . . . And you could hide a lot of six-packs under a body.

Simple economics play an important role in "Road Trip," too. A young man, unable to afford all the expenses of his grandmother's funeral, decided to cut what costs he could by using his own car as a hearse. He had a panel van big enough to accommodate the coffin, and late one evening he pulled up to the rear of the funeral home, slid the box inside, and headed for the church where the service was to take place the following morning.

Coffins being heavy things, he brought along a friend to help. As the favor he'd asked of his friend might be considered above and beyond the call of duty, he could hardly refuse his friend's request that they stop at the off-track betting shop on the way.

Imagine their shock when, on returning to their parking spot, they discover the van missing!

They'd just run back inside to call the police when a screeching of tires and a slamming of doors indicated something unusual was happening outside. As they burst out through the betting shop doors, one fellow was just turning the nearest corner at full speed. His partner in crime, a bit slower, glanced back over his shoulder long enough to shout, "We're just bagmen! You keep to your thing, we'll keep to ours!"

The two car thieves had mistaken the corpse for a victim of professional hit men and quickly decided the better part of valor was simply to return the van!

Another version of this chestnut begins when the grandson discovers the casket won't fit in the back of his van and he's forced to tie Granny's box, suitably concealed under an old blanket and some plastic tarpaulins, to the roof rack! Again, he and the friend dragged along for this job stop at a betting shop. Again, the van is stolen. The denouement this time comes when the two men, standing on the curb and trying to figure out just how they'll describe their "cargo" to the police about to arrive, hear muffled cursing and one panicky shout from a nearby alley.

Racing into the dark lane, they're almost run down by the two men coming the other way! One keeps going, while the other shakes his head and slows long enough to shout, "And you call *us* crooks!"

Proving once again that life can be at least as strange as legend is the true story of Peter Bashucky and his father, Nick. When Nick died in Los Angeles, Peter realized that despite the distance, his father would want to be buried at home in Toronto. The trick would be getting him there. Needless to say, flying a casket home was an expensive venture, especially since the two had been vacationing, and if Peter were to fly back with his father, he'd have to make yet more arrange-

That's "cruise control," folks, not "autopilot"!

ments for his father's Winnebago to be shipped home as well.

Being of a more practical bent, Peter laid his father out in the back of the camper van and packed him around with ice, which he could replenish easily at gas stations along the way. The four-thousand-kilometer trip was accomplished in good time and, thanks to Peter's foresight in keeping the heat off the whole way, the body was in good condition when it was finally handed over to the firm with whom Nicholas Bashucky had a pre-arranged funeral plan.

Asked how he negotiated the border crossing at Niagara Falls with a corpse in the back, Peter replied that the border guards had only asked about liquor and cigarettes. "They didn't ask about bodies and I didn't volunteer."

Motor homes feature in another legend, "Cruise Control." It seems that salesmen may have hyped this new convenience, especially popular on RVs, which were typically driven long distances, just a little too much. Some people actually believed the claim that their new vehicle would "practically drive itself," and dozens of tales recount the misadventures of those who expected driving miracles.

The first version, circulating in British Columbia, starred a frazzled mother and her three children who were heading into the interior to meet the kids' father for a camping holiday. She'd never tried this newfangled option before, but with one baby in need of changing and another squalling for something to eat, she flipped the switch and headed into the rear of the vehicle in search of diapers and food. The camper, naturally, headed for the nearest ditch, and the poor woman was the butt of many a joke in the time it took to deal with tow trucks and police reports.

Locations change in the telling, but the one constant is that the driver is always a woman, a "foreigner," or an elderly person, the implication being that no one in any of these groups is up to the challenges regularly handled by WASP men in their thirties!

Of course, that theory is shot down by "The JATO Engine," a tale of a boy, his car, and a cliff.

In this classic, a young WASP man had about reached the limit of his car's ability to be further "souped up," but, being an aircraft mechanic, he happened to spot a JATO rocket (the acronym means jet-assisted take-off!) sitting under canvas in a seldom-used corner of the hangar.

As he progressed through the afternoon's routine, that unit filled his mind. With a couple of customized couplings and a little nudging here and there, that baby, which no one was using anyway, sure would give his 1992 Chevy Impala one hell of a boost!

It'd take a bit of work, but when your car is your life, work becomes worship. After sneaking the solid-fuel rocket out of the hangar, he spent weeks considering all the possible

problems. First he'd need to secure the unit to the frame of the car. Just strapping it to the back could be a problem if the darned thing tore loose and blasted *through* the car instead of pushing the car ahead of it. And he'd need protection from the noise, which meant insulating the entire interior of the Impala, another week's work. Not to mention that he needed some way to conceal the addition! He could hardly drive down the middle of town with a bloody great rocket sitting up there for everyone to see, could he?

In all, it was nearly two months before our intrepid driver finally headed onto the highway in search of a long, straight stretch of road near Far-From-Anywhere, Arizona. Sitting there, eyeing the expanse of pavement ahead of him, he felt a deep sense of satisfaction—and impatience. He'd waited long enough.

It took only a few minutes to strip off the tarp he'd used to conceal the JATO unit and assure himself he had the entire road to himself for as far as he could see.

> The trees along one French avenue cause serious problems for some individuals. The setting and rising sun casts shadows over the road that, when driven through at the posted speed limit, create a strobe effect that can trigger epileptic seizures.

Slowly he eased his foot down on the accelerator and watched the needle climb. Soon he was flying down the highway, using every RPM to his advantage. When he couldn't squeeze one more ounce of speed from the Impala, he set off the JATO unit.

Some hours later a highway patrol officer leaned back against the fender of his own car and scratched his head. Embedded in the cliff ahead of him were what appeared at first glance to be the remains of a small plane! Black soot surrounded the impact site. Scraps of metal and some odd insulating material rocked gently in the breeze on the ground nearby. The officer's only question—other than what fool slammed a plane into a cliff in the first place—was where were the wings?

Eventually the investigators realized they were dealing with a car, not a plane, that the car's brakes were completely burned away, and that whoever was driving this thing should have realized that things that throw you through the air at nearly 400 mph don't come with an "off" switch!

As neat as this story sounds, it's yet another urban legend. The Arizona Department of Public Safety takes inquiries into the incident with good humor, but, as they published a major denial in both the print media and in cyberspace, they can also be forgiven for the heavy sigh that usually begins each conversation.

Of course, not every car tale ends in a death. Some just end in extreme agony . . .

The "Bachelor Party" reminds us that although cars are sometimes referred to as modern-day horses, they were never meant to be ridden like horses.

Apparently, Todd Eldridge, who was feeling pretty good after a boisterous bachelor party in his honor, didn't realize that all passengers are supposed to remain *inside* the vehicle. When he and his buddies staggered out into the parking lot of the local bar, they discovered they had eleven guys and only one car! Everyone piled in as best they could, but when it came down to it, they were short space for one more. Both seats and the trunk were already full.

Eventually, Todd, the odd man out, crawled on the hood and leaned back against the windshield.

"Hey, man, you can't ride up there!"

"Sure I can! It's only until we get to Pappy's place, then I can get back inside. It's not that far."

"What if you fall off?"

"I'm not going to fall off. See, the air pushing against the car will keep me flat against the windshield. Don't worry, just drive."

Impressed with Todd's knowledge of physics (which doesn't say a lot for his buddies, does it?), the driver nodded and started the car.

The trip to Pappy's wasn't bad, considering. The driver remembered to swerve gently around the bumps and to signal the turns so that Todd could lean in the right direction. Unfortunately, both he and Todd forgot that

"Hey, Donald! You in there?"

wind pressure wasn't going to keep Todd in place when the brakes were applied! As soon as the driver's foot touched the brake, Todd began sliding toward the nose of the car!

Still, things mightn't have turned out too badly. The driver, spotting Todd sliding ahead, braked quickly enough to avoid running over him, and he wasted no time hopping out to look for his missing friend. In fact, *everyone* piled out to see where Todd had gone!

With considerable relief, they found him curled in a ball just under the bumper. What didn't make sense were the low, mewling sounds that rose eerily from his throat. He

couldn't have hurt himself falling less than three feet! Pappy solved the mystery, though, pointing out that the car used to have a hood ornament until Todd slid, crotch foremost, down over it!

Bet his wedding night wasn't quite what he was expecting.

All the car legends thus far have featured people of average means, but the rich and famous drive, too, and occasionally they turn up in legends.

The most notorious star of "The Flat" has recently been no less a celebrity than Donald Trump.

A city worker is peering through a lashing rainstorm on his way home after a long day, when, on a particularly tricky section of rural road, he spots a long white blur off on the shoulder. Coming closer, he realizes there's a stretch limo with a flat off the road!

Outside the elegant car, a chauffeur struggles in the mud to find enough solid ground to get the jack in place. The city worker pulls over, rummages in the trunk, and brings a piece of plywood to the scene, giving the jack firm purchase. In just a few moments the tire is changed and the worker is shoving his piece of plywood back in his own trunk. He lifts a hand to wave, but pauses when the chauffeur calls him back.

"The folks inside wanted to thank you."

Much to his surprise, it's Ivana and Donald Trump inside!

Is there any way they can thank him?

"Well, as a matter of fact, this is my anniversary." He looks down at his mud-spattered clothes. "I was going to pick up a bunch of roses for my wife on the way home, but the shop'll be closed by now. How about you send her some flowers?"

They take down his address and both cars pull back onto the street.

Needless to say, his wife is skeptical of the whole tale, so, a few days later, when a massive bouquet of roses arrives at the door and, after reading the card, his wife sort of sinks into the nearest chair, our Good Samaritan is feeling pretty smug.

"See? I told you!"

"No, you don't understand . . ."

With a shaking hand, she gives him the card.

> *Thanks so much for all your help. The flowers didn't seem like much, so we've paid off your mortgage as well!*
> *Ivana and Donald*

Everyone loves a fairy-godmother story, but this one is probably too good to be true. Despite some coy responses by Trump's people, the city worker who got all muddy on his anniversary has never been identified—and who wouldn't tell everyone he knew that some guardian angel had paid off his mortgage?

Add in the fact that this tale, with other celebrities in the rear seat, has circulated since 1958, and it starts to sound apocryphal. How likely is it that Buddy Holly, Phil Collins, the Trumps, Bill Cosby, Nat King Cole, Mrs. Nat King Cole, Patty LaBelle, and Aretha Franklin would *all* find themselves stranded in middle-class neighborhoods where they had no reason to be, in white cars, with drivers who couldn't change a flat?

If all the versions of this one are to be believed, then an awful lot of mortgage bankers are giving out private information about their clients!

Without a little humor to brighten the picture, this would be one of the more dismal categories of urban legend. But these last car tales continue to bring on the grins, despite their evident age.

"Blast Off" seems totally modern at first glance. A group of good ol' boys decide to do a little duck-hunting deep in the woods of Michigan. Since it's January, and all the lakes are likely to be frozen, they add some dynamite to the usual gear: guns, beer, ammo, decoys, and, of course, beer. That takes up most of the room in the back of Bobby's Jeep Grand Cherokee. What little room is left after the six hunting buddies take up the seats is quickly filled by sixty pounds of Labrador retriever named Gump.

When they reach the lake, it's clear that the best shooting will be from the other side, but there's no road on that side, and the close-set trees prevent even these hardy souls from seriously contemplating any cross-country activities. Instead, in the long-established tradition of northern hunting parties, they simply drive the truck across the frozen lake!

Don't panic, it's perfectly safe.

At least, it's usually safe.

Anyway, as they thought, the ice that's solid enough to hold up a heavy vehicle is just a tad too thick to yield to their hatchets. While one of the guys pulls out the insulated seats and beer coolers, Bobby tackles the more delicate task of preparing the dynamite. Gump and the rest of the boys basically chase their tails.

Bobby passes on the beer while choosing the perfect location to create his artificial opening in the ice. Not too close to shore; the decoys foul up in old weeds. Not too

deep; ducks like calm water. Eventually he picks the ideal spot, away from the bank but sheltered by a stand of trees. Nothing worse than having to interrupt a shooting session to chase windblown decoys around the opening, right?

With meticulous care, he lights the fuse, judges the distance, calculates the breeze's speed, and hurls the stick out in a perfect arc over the ice. He's just about to congratulate himself on his aim when sixty pounds of Labrador retriever flies by his shins, intent on doing precisely what he's been trained to do—retrieve!

Gump is therefore terribly confused when all six men yell and scream at him for doing his job. Scared and baffled by the curses and shouts hurled at him, he slinks under the nearest cover, Bobby's brand-new Jeep! When the chaos immediately doubles, poor Gump drops the stick he's retrieved so well and heads for the greater cover of the woods.

His tail just clears the first line of brush when a low boom sounds behind him. The horribly slow creaking that follows seems to chase him even deeper into the underbrush.

It's a long time before he comes back out.

It's a long time before Bobby and the gang can tear their eyes away from the gaping hole where the beautiful Jeep—not to mention the beer coolers—used to be!

Modern as this urban legend appears to be, it's probably based on one of the many cruelties that were part of the events of

World War II. For months, Nazi dog handlers trained their loyal animals to eat under tanks captured from Russian units. The plan, elegant yet simple, was to create an association in the dogs' minds between Russian tanks and food, warmth, and safety. Before going into battle, the dogs were given little food and marched hard. At the last moment, just before the dogs would encounter the tanks, sticks of dynamite were tied to their collars and lit.

It's a not-so-subtle irony that the dogs, even treated so badly, refused to leave their masters—even for food. Instead, they ran for their own tanks. Dozens were slaughtered by the Nazis in an attempt to protect their equipment; scores more simply blew up. All died horribly.

Even that may not be the beginning of the traditional tale, however. At least a dozen stories, some going back to the late 1800s, include elements of "Blast Off." If stories with similar plots, but animals as different as squirrels and rabbits are included, almost thirty fictional pieces could provide the underlying structure for this particular story.

That probably says more about our love of seeing the stupid suffer than about the limitations of twentieth-century writers!

"The Drunk Decoy" also appears more modern than its roots suggest.

Private citizens aren't supposed to be privy to the plans police officers make, or the drunk driving traps they set up, but in the real world, certain truths can be held sacred.

Doughnut shops attract cops.

Cops aren't any more motivated than the general public.

A fair chunk of the general public likes to dance and have a few drinks on the weekend, usually at the local watering hole.

The local watering hole will be under observation by cops at closing time.

Any portion of the general public who wavers, staggers, or trips on leaving the local tavern can expect to be hauled over to blow in a bag or walk the center line.

The general public knows these facts as well as the cops do.

So, when a group of young people emerge from the bar after an evening out, they're well aware the dark car across the street is an unmarked police car. Still, they proceed to their own vehicles and, after some adjusting so that couples can sit together, they all pile in.

At that moment another patron, ushered out by the bartender, stumbles into the bright light of the arc lamps around the parking lot. As the first carload of kids pulls away, this last one trips over the painted lines separating parking spaces! Some minutes later he actually manages to get his key in his door lock and tumble inside. It takes him a while to find the ignition. Still, just as his engine turns over and the headlights pop on, sirens and flashing lights suddenly stream across the lot. The poor chap doesn't even have time to find his accelerator before one of the cops taps on his window.

"Sir, could you get out of the car, please?"

"Why?"

"Come on now, sir, let's not make this difficult. Come out of the car."

"All right, just a second." The unfortunate object of police attention looks around. "I've just got to get my seatbelt off."

"You aren't wearing your seatbelt, sir."

"Oops!" A long giggle. "Well, then I guess I won't undo *that* belt, will I?"

Eventually they get him outside the car. Much to their surprise, though he's slow to comply, he does manage to pass all their sobriety tests. Suspecting something is up, the two officers eventually drag him back to the station, where they administer a standard Breathalyzer test.

He passes!

But he now has two irate cops wondering what the act was all about.

"Well, my buddy wasn't sure he'd pass the test, so he left in the other car while you were watching me find my keys!"

Want to bet that stunt doesn't work twice?

And what does this bit of tomfoolery have to do with "Blast Off"? Like that story, "The Drunk Decoy" traces its historical roots to World War II. According to *The Great Big Book of Yiddish Humor*:

Klein and Rosenburg were late ariving from their factory jobs at a time when the ghetto was under close scrutiny. Just when Klein spotted an SS officer strolling down the street, he also recalled that he'd left his identity papers at home that morning!

Being caught without his papers would, at best, rate him a long interrogation at the SS office. At worst, he could receive a prison sentence! Confessing his predicament to Rosenburg, Klein was already considering just giving up and throwing himself on the mercy of the officer.

Rosenburg brushed that off right away. "Just keep walking, I'll take care of him."

With that, Rosenburg briefly met the officer's eyes, then picked up his heels and raced back the way he'd come!

Confused, Klein kept his head down and kept walking.

The officer blew a whistle as he ran past Klein and began shouting at Rosenburg, "Stop! Stop! I order you!"

Rosenburg kept running.

The SS officer picked up the pace and soon turned a corner still chasing Rosenburg—at which point Klein took off for home!

Eventually, Rosenburg calmly slowed his pace and allowed the SS officer to catch up with him.

"Didn't you hear me shouting at you?"

"I heard you shouting, yes. Were you shouting at me?"

"Let me see your papers!"

Rosenburg handed over his papers without comment, and proceeded to stretch out his cooling muscles.

"Why, these papers are in perfect order!"

"Yes, I know."

"Then why did you run?"

"My doctor suggested I could benefit from a brisk run each evening."

"But didn't you see me running after you?"

"Yes, I thought maybe you had the same doctor."

> **Bill Gates and some Microsoft employees were seriously dismayed when their $600,000 cars, Porsche 959's, were confiscated at the dock in 1990. Reason? The vehicles weren't proven to conform to federal safety, not to mention environmental, standards! Guess you get what you pay for!**

Unlike "Blast Off," this tale is never told as anything but a joke, a joke that has mutated into a number of authority-snubbing tales, but a joke nonetheless.

These last two stories play into our secret desire to put down those who spend a fortune on what for the rest of us is mere transportation.

Even the folks who build luxury cars like the Cadillac sometimes find themselves resenting those who can afford to drive what they can only build. In "The Rattle," a gentleman who'd just bought a brand new Caddy keeps bringing it back to the shop, complaining of an annoying sound when the car reaches higher speeds. The mechanics pore over the engine but can't find anything wrong with it. They don't charge their customer, but they don't fix his problem, either.

By the time he's brought the car back for the third time, the car owner is ready to ask for a refund. The rattle is driving him crazy! When they can't fix it this time, either, he storms out to find the salesman who sold him this "heap of junk"!

Eventually the car is returned to the factory, where a better-informed team of workers ignores the engine completely. Instead they remove the dashboard. As anticipated, from behind it they pull out a rough stone wrapped in a note that reads, "You get what you pay for!" Apparently, during a labor dispute, this was a common form of protesting the salary reductions management was suggesting *might* save worker jobs.

Another factory tale, immortalized in a Johnny Cash song, paints a different picture of Cadillac employees, but once again illustrates the differences in life situation between those who buy the opulent cars and those who just build them. According to both song and legend, an auto plant worker spent nine years stealing an entire car piece by piece!

What we won't do to get a great car.

ALL THE REST

Economists love trends. Forty-three years ago, Perkin Williams, noting the burgeoning numbers of drive-in movie theaters and drive-through restaurants, forecast an era when we'd bank, receive health care, and get married at drive-through windows. He was also a collector of rare vehicles. He owned the only bicycle built for five in Nebraska, a baby carriage for sextuplets, fourteen motorcycles (three with sidecars), an ice boat, a thirty-two-foot-long toboggan, a prototypical skateboard almost as long as the surfboards this new toy was based on (it could easily carry eight), two air balloons (one in the shape of a teapot), and nine pairs of roller skates. Believe it or not, he never owned a car! Not one.

These next few tales would likely tickle his fancy.

"There's Gas and Then There's Gas," which began circulating in the late seventies, presents an intriguing scenario—without ever describing the center of action!

An RV owner had been taking relatively short trips with his wife each summer, but when he finally retired, he suggested it was time for the two of them to play gypsy for a full year. The romance of going wherever they wanted, for as long as they chose, certainly appealed to his wife, and while she began closing up their house, he took the RV to the nearest garage for some special outfitting.

In all their years of traveling, they'd never run short on gas, but they'd often found it was a long way between waste-dumping stations. To alleviate this problem, the husband suggested they convert one of the double gas tanks to a spare waste-disposal tank. The boys eyed the setup and agreed it wouldn't take too much effort to have the modifications ready by the date of their client's retirement.

The couple stuck around just long enough to collect the company watch and stock the RV, then hit the open road. For several weeks they just wandered, delighting in their newfound freedom. Then, one dark and

stormy night, they were startled awake by a choking sound immediately outside their door! The husband picked up a fire extinguisher, ready to bean anyone coming inside, but to their surprise, the hacking sound faded into the distance.

Things became clear the following morning when they emerged to find a siphon hose hanging from the modified disposal tank and a pool of vomit just a few feet away!

Over the next two decades, this tale was passed around trailer parks everywhere, and in 1989, a wit living outside Banff, Alberta, did a brisk business selling "Siphon at Your Own Risk!" stickers to RV owners using the park.

Believe it or not, that's not the only body-waste joke making the rounds of transportation legends. "The Warm Stream" probably appeared just after "There's Gas and Then There's Gas," and, surprisingly, *doesn't* seem to have arisen in the United States, as most transportation legends usually do.

A sudden cold snap closed down around Alberta, Canada, startling residents who'd been enjoying an Indian summer. Robert Byrd, the owner of a small delivery van, was looking forward to a warm supper as he headed down a rural road. He'd zipped right past a motorcyclist on the shoulder before he'd even realized anyone was there, but, catching a glimpse of waving arms in his rearview, he quickly pulled to the side and backed up.

A young rider, well bundled up but clearly

chilled, was in a rather unique predicament. A spare can of gas was neatly tied to the back of the bike, but, in the cold, the gas cap was frozen onto the tank! Both drivers stared at the situation for a moment, then, with a shrug and the mumbled comment, "Well, it's not like you've never seen one, right?" Robert unzipped his fly, pulled it out, and proceeded to urinate over the cap. Steam rose and, when Robert tried the cap again, with a gloved hand, it opened without a hitch!

The rider quickly filled the tank, shook hands (not the gloved one), muttered a hasty "thank you," and headed off down the road.

Thinking this was rather brusque, even if his solution had proven unconventional, Robert shrugged the incident off and climbed into his van and hurried on home.

Several days later a note arrived in the mail, and Robert suddenly understood the rider's hasty retreat.

> *Dear Sir,*
> *Just a quick note to thank you for the generous assistance you lent to my* **daughter.** *Good Samaritans are rare these days.*
> *Thank you,*
> *Reverend Charles Goel*

Insurance companies get lots of unusual calls. One woman once rang up Crosbie-Reed Stenhouse to ask if her car insurance covered collisions with flamingoes. The agent was about to say "Sure!" when she stopped and thought about it once more.

"Flamingoes?"

"Right, big pink birds."

"Ma'am, are you on vacation?"

"No, why?"

"Well, ma'am, according to the address on your policy, you live in the *Arctic!*"

"Yes, well, that's true." There was a brief pause. "Maybe I asked the wrong question. Does my policy cover collision with a zoo?"

That agent would surely have sympathized with whoever handled the claim of an Oregonian, Walter Umenhofer, who, in 1970, was traveling along the coastal highway when his Buick was crushed by a fifteen-square-foot piece of *whale!*

It seems a whale that had washed up on the beach below some time ago was now in mid-rot, and residents were becoming a little dissatisfied with the aroma associated with this wholly natural process. Thinking to speed things along, the Oregon Department of Highways concluded that blowing the carcass into smaller pieces with dynamite would allow easier predation by crabs, gulls, and whatever else ate dead whales.

Unfortunately, no one warned those traveling nearby or those standing about watching that blowing up whales isn't exactly an exact science. The attempt didn't go as planned. Instead of raining dead whale back into the sea, it flew *inland.*

Umenhofer's assessment of the situation: "My insurance company is never going to believe this!"

Though this story is absolutely true, and reported in sources as widely available as

> A cruise director for the Carnival Line tells the story of a frazzled passenger who stopped him in the passageway to ask, "Excuse me, can you tell me when the Midnight Buffet starts?"

The New York Times, it's achieved a sort of life after death as the urban legends most often titled "Thar She Blew!"

The police of Hiawatha, Ontario, were also scratching their heads when they came upon a nine-car pileup surrounding a skateboarder at a four-way stop. All nine drivers readily confessed to crossing lane markers—they'd all been desperately attempting to avoid hitting the skateboarder, who was variously described as "erratic" and "demented" as he flew through the intersection *four* times with absolutely no regard for oncoming traffic!

Deciding to let their superiors sort it all out, they dragged everyone back to the station, where a routine round of Breathalyzer tests began. No one actually expected these drivers to test in excess of the legal limit. The accident had occurred in broad daylight well before anyone might have indulged in a liquid lunch. Much to their dismay, one driver failed the test: the skateboard driver!

It took several days for a prosecutor to determine whether a skateboard constituted a vehicle in the sense of the laws covering driving under the influence.

It didn't.

Despite doing 112,000 dollars' worth of damage to nine cars, and causing two cases of whiplash, the drunken skateboarder couldn't be charged with anything except being drunk in public!

Before anyone decides to storm Capitol Hill to correct this miscarriage of justice, however, they might want to discuss the case with Preston Taig, a law-school attorney who used to use this example in one of his case-law classes. Apparently it was so widely discussed by his students that bystanders overhearing their passionate arguments for each side believed the events were real, and another urban legend, "The Drunken Skateboarder," was born!

Perhaps the most widely recognized transportation legend is "Supermom," the tale that recounts a horrendous car crash and a superhuman rescue. In the story, a woman is driving into town to pick up her husband at work, when her car is forced off the road by a drunk driver. Luckily she's thrown clear and not badly injured, and is soon found by a highway patrol officer. He's trying to lead her away when she runs in the opposite direction, yelling, "My baby! My baby! He's in the backseat!"

Sure enough, her eight-month-old son, still secured in his car seat, is dangling upside down in the wreck. His survival so far seems miraculous. The vehicle, also upside down, is nearly flattened. Without metal cutters, the only access is through a window on the far side. They can see the boy, but they can't reach him without moving the car. The officer runs back to his own car to radio for backup and a team with the famous Jaws of Life to come free the boy.

When a strong smell of gasoline begins to spread, however, it seems that help will be too late!

Despite the cop's urging to stay away from a car that could easily explode at any moment, the frantic mother reaches down, grasps the body of the car, and, by some incredible feat of strength, presumably the mother of all adrenaline rushes, jerks the car up long enough for the officer to pull her son through the window on the far side!

In the best legend tradition, they've just made it back to some sort of cover when a spark ignites the gas fumes and the entire vehicle is consumed by flames.

It's a wonderful story, one we've all heard, one we probably believe. Unfortunately, because we'd all like to think we would be capable of something so heroic, there's not a shred of truth to this legend.

Less well known to the general public, but often passed along at naval bases, is the story of "The Stubborn Lighthouse." The tale goes that a U.S. Navy destroyer was approaching Newport News, a massive shipyard. Encountering considerable water traffic, the watch was even more alert than usual to approaching lights and marine call signals. When one light remained steadily ahead of them, failing to move to either star-

board or port as they approached, the watch perked up quickly, and a request for a call sign was sent to the bridge.

"Not registered, sir."

"What?!"

"Not registered."

The executive officer leaned over the radioman's shoulder and snagged the radio. "Light at 223.4. You are in our path. Please heave to."

There was a long pause before a nervous voice answered, "I'm afraid we can't, sir. We're a lighthouse!"

The tale is entirely apocryphal, but the yuk-yuk value is too high for it to disappear any time soon.

Another tale that depends on its bizarre imagery for longevity is "Flying Cows," one of the few legends to come out of Russia and find a home in North America. The odd little tale begins with a Japanese fishing boat bobbing serenely about in the Sea of Japan. A Russian aircraft flying overhead saw nothing unusual and continued on its usual recon course back toward the coast. The situation had changed drastically by their next overflight. Instead of seeing a sizable boat, they spotted a dozen men, clinging to flotsam, scattered across the sea.

Rescuers, who arrived promptly, handed out lots of blankets to the shivering men, but as they listened to their story, they swiftly concluded this event required special investigation. According to all twelve sailors, their boat had been bombed by a cow! The bovine bomb struck them amidships, holed the boat, and then sank into the depths along with their vessel, their catch, and almost everything else they owned!

Needless to say, the Russians found this explanation a little hard to believe and, suspecting some ulterior motive, threw the whole crew in jail!

Red faces reigned when, several weeks later, another branch of the Russian Air Force confessed that the crew of one of its cargo planes, on the Vladivostok route, had encountered a cow wandering at the edge of the airfield. When no one appeared to claim it, and the crew considered the price of fresh beef in the Russian marketplace, they hustled the cow into the hold.

As they reached cruising altitude, however, the cow began clambering about! There aren't any seatbelts for humans in cargo planes, never mind cows. When the animal's antics began endangering the plane itself, they opened the huge rear loading door and shoved it outside.

How were they to know what was floating on the sea below?

The Japanese fisherman, appropriately compensated, were quickly transported home.

Could anything create a more striking mental image than a cow plummeting to earth at thirty-two feet per second per second? How about someone going in the opposite direction, on a lawn chair, three miles up?

That's what two airline pilots reported to the FAA on July 2, 1982, when, glancing out their cockpit windows, they saw Larry Walters, the "Lawn Chair Balloonist," on his way from San Pedro to Long Beach, California. Most people take the expressway, or the local commuter flights. Not Walters. He had a dream.

Walters had planned this flight, in one form or another, for nearly twenty years, but when he finally assembled *Inspiration 1,* it was as simple a craft as he could make it. He started with an aluminum lawn chair, attached forty-two weather balloons, filled them with helium, packed aboard a two-liter bottle of soda, a parachute, a camera (which he forgot to use), a CB radio (to warn air traffic of his presence), and a pellet gun, and, with the assistance of two buddies who cut his tether lines, soared away into the bright blue sky.

Though Walters had absolutely no flight experience, in or out of lawn chairs, he enjoyed a relatively uneventful flight—until he tried to land! For two hours he'd coasted along over beautiful countryside, eventually reaching sixteen thousand feet (a record, if he'd bothered to let anyone know he was taking off). Finding it a bit chilly at that altitude, he used his pellet gun to pop some of his balloons and descend. He was almost back to terra firma in Long Beach when his balloons became entangled in some power lines. He blacked out an entire neighborhood for over twenty minutes!

Still, despite the inconvenience, and the fines imposed by the Federal Aviation Administration, Walters personally declared his flight a success, a dream come true.

Unlike those images generated by the cow story, the bizarre visions inspired by "The Lawn Chair Balloonist" have the added advantage of being true.

Perkin Williams would, of course, have enjoyed them all.

CRIME JUST DOESN'T PAY, DOES IT?

rime titillates us. Serial killers, monsters who neighbors swear seemed "just like regular folks," intrigue us. We stare into their newspaper photos, vainly attempting to see the animal lurking behind the smile.

Crime scares us. We firmly believe violent crime is on the rise—despite evidence to the contrary. The "good old days" gleam a little more golden as our kids pass through metal detectors on their way to school.

Crime awes us. Lawyers, courts, and cops intimidate us. We *know* simple innocence isn't enough to carry the judicial day. Cops plant evidence, crooks get off on technicalities, juries are whatever the lawyers want them to be—but definitely not a panel of one's peers, and the judge who decides your fate today could be jailed himself tomorrow! And even if John Q. Public isn't found guilty of whatever frivolous suit dragged him into the slow machinations of the legal system in the first place, well, he can rest assured his own lawyer will soon put him in the poorhouse.

True or not, the common perception, that the little guy doesn't have a chance against the criminals or the cops, stands firm. Which explains the multitude of legends that inject a little humor into the morass of all things legal.

TALES OF THE CRIMINALLY STUPID

Despite assuring us that violent crime is down 12 percent in urban areas, there's not one law-enforcement agency out there *encouraging* women to hang around parking lots, or to let children roam the neighborhoods, or take up hitchhiking again. Being scared is one of humanity's few adaptive behaviors, but existing in a state of constant terror would incapacitate us, leave us all quivering behind locked doors. We don't really need to be reminded of our vulnerability to crime, so, instead of the usual tales of horror, legal legends tend to belittle our criminal foes, allowing us a moment's reprieve from our daily vigilance.

Even the best-laid plans occasionally go awry, but these next few tales leave us wondering if there was ever a plan to start with! If there was, they assure us that even criminals with plans seldom think out the full repercussions.

"Where There's Smoke, There's Fire," set in a dozen American cities, but most frequently related to that haven of cigar aficionados, Miami, begins with a rather average guy who, after years of paying insurance on this, that, and the other thing, finally thinks he's found a way to beat the system.

For years he's been collecting the finest stogies, storing them in hermetically sealed humidors until he graduated to building his own climatically controlled cigar room. He was discussing this new addition with his insurance agent when the agent suggested that an investment like that should be insured separately from the rest of his property. Before long, our smoker had his new policy covering the collection against theft, failure of the environmental controls, fire, and water damage.

As he sat there in his collection room, he was feeling pretty satisfied with himself. The policy somehow seemed to give his habit, which until now his wife had declared "filthy," a certain something, a certain . . . status! Not surprisingly, he read the entire document several times, delighting in it, paying close attention to the fine print. It was then that our previously honest collector was suddenly struck by a brainstorm!

Fire!

His collection, some 2,100 cigars, was insured against destruction by fire!

As he chose that evening's cigar, he rolled his plan around in his mind and read the policy once more.

Nearly a year later, he presented his claim to his insurance agent. The entire collection of cigars had been destroyed by fire.

The agent shook his head, puzzled. "But there's no claim on your homeowner's policy for a fire. How did your cigar room burn down without damaging the house?"

"The cigar room didn't burn down. Just the cigars." To support his contention that every single stogie had been reduced to ash, he produced the ashes—bags of ashes.

Naturally the company wasn't going to stand for this. Smoking the cigars didn't, in their mind, constitute "destruction by fire." A judge, however, on reviewing the policy, could find no exception clauses and was forced to rule in the policyholder's favor. He suggested the company rethink the language in their forms, and ordered them to pay up.

Delighted, the man accepted the company's check.

He was less pleased when they had him arrested for arson!

This tale, while clearly nothing more than a legend, is typical of the category. Even when the law seemed to be on our petty criminal's side, the big company managed to eke out a win.

More often, though, the criminals of urban legend fail, not because of the efforts of law enforcement, but simply because they were too limited, too stupid, to see the big picture.

"An Order of Onion Rings" begins in Ypsilanti, Michigan, just before eight in the morning. Perhaps figuring he'd get the night deposit before it could be taken to the bank, a would-be thief wandered into his local Burger King, pulled out a handgun, pointed it at the cashier, and demanded all the cash in the register for starters.

The cashier stared at the gun, then at the register, then back at the gun before shrugging helplessly. "I can't open it unless you order something!"

It's at this point that the holdup man's plan began to go awry. He hadn't considered the technical aspects of opening a cash register—they don't cover that part in most movies—and improvisation clearly wasn't his strong point. After shifting from foot to foot for a minute, glancing at the menu overhead, and perhaps trying to figure out how much money he might have in his pockets, he ordered the cheapest thing on the menu. "Give me an order of onion rings."

"That's not on the breakfast menu, and we don't start serving lunch until ten-thirty, sir."

Completely derailed now, the crook stared at the cashier for a moment, then simply walked out!

Evidently he needed to work on that plan.

The real beauty of this tale, however, rests in the fact that it's true! Readers of the *Ann Arbor News* must have felt considerably safer after that story ran. A lot of their neighbors must also have found comfort in that tale, as it now pops up all over the country, always set locally, of course, as a legend.

Tales like the next one, "A Real Education," prove several "facts" held dear by the general population.

1. Children should never be given enough time or resources to get themselves into this much trouble.
2. People with money should keep a better eye on it.
3. It's possible for even the youngest criminals to keep the police hopping—for at least seven months.

This tale rightfully begins in Egypt, though it's since been adopted by dozens of locales in America and elsewhere. Two young men taking a computer science course happened to run into an online pornography site and immediately realized the financial implications of their situation. Not all students were enrolled in the expensive computer courses, but most of their fellow male students shared their interest in sex. By downloading the pictures and videos, then selling them to their friends, they could easily finance not only their computer science classes, but any number of other amusements as well!

The only hitch was that in order to download the images from this and other sites, they needed a credit card!

Well, once the decision to embark on a life of crime had been made, they evidently took the "as well hung for a sheep as a lamb" philosophy and promptly stole a credit card number with which to access the various pornography sites.

Over the next seven months they downloaded pictures and films worth $147,000!

They were eventually caught when the real cardholder reported the purchases to police, who turned the case over to Egypt's new Internet fraud division, who then contacted the Internet provider and traced the downloads back to the eager entrepreneurs!

A case of crime investigation gone right, right?

Sure. But it does sort of beg the question: Who has a credit card limit that could accommodate $147,000 in charges *and not be noticed for seven months*!

The moral here is obvious: Stupid crimi-

nals are only aided and abetted by stupid *victims*!

TALES OF THE CRIMINALLY WEIRD

Along with the tales of the criminally stupid, there also exists another subset of tales that leave us feeling safer simply because we can't imagine anyone we know ever coming up with these crimes in the first place!

In early 1994, the "The Tale of the Un-Handmaid" began circulating by fax machine and Internet e-mail. It outlined the tragedy of William Gump, who married a woman with no hands. The tragedy wasn't the woman's handicap; he could live with that easily. The tragedy was that it wasn't until after the wedding that Bill discovered the new Mrs. Gump hated sex!

No matter how romantic his efforts, she simply wouldn't let him anywhere near the marriage bed.

As the marriage had never been consummated, Bill probably wouldn't have had much difficulty obtaining an annulment, but somehow he saw it as degrading to admit publicly that his wife of less than two weeks found him physically repugnant.

After considerable debate, he decided it would be less embarrassing for all concerned—especially himself—if he simply killed her.

Of course, he didn't want to spend the rest of his days in jail, so he set out to find the perfect "accident." He considered several options before deciding it would be poetically just to kill her in that honeymoon capital, Niagara Falls. It was well known—at least to Bill—that handicapped people were frequently depressed, even suicidal. If his wife were to throw herself into the falls, he felt sure he could convince local authorities that she'd been depressed and that the trip, meant to cheer her up, had only exacerbated the situation—much to his dismay, of course.

To enhance the illusion, Bill took his bride to that most romantic of spots, the overlook at Table Rock, to watch the nightly light display. With everyone's eyes fixed on the flashing lights, he figured it would be a simple matter to heave her over the rail under cover of darkness. The roar of the water should drown any stray shouts for help as easily as the torrents would drown his wife. He'd been promising himself his freedom for so long that when the moment to toss her over the falls came, adrenaline pounded through his body and, except for a momentary pause while she tried to struggle free, the whole incident took just a few seconds!

One minute he was married to a frigid wife; the next he was a happy widower!

It wasn't until he returned to his hotel that he discovered his wife hadn't gone over as easily as it appeared at the time. As he'd lifted her shoulder high to dump her over, she'd bitten off a piece of his earlobe! It had bled rather profusely, but he simply disposed of his bloody shirt, showered, and then calmly called the police to report his wife

missing. He even managed to sound concerned and to work in a few references to how moody she'd been since they arrived.

In time the body was found downstream, the police assumed a suicide, and the whole affair appeared about to be wrapped up. Then the coroner discovered something odd lodged in the woman's throat—the severed piece of her husband's earlobe! Police became suspicious when they were assured the woman couldn't possibly have bitten her husband, choked on the earlobe, walked all the way to the falls, climbed over the rail, and thrown herself into the maelstrom.

If you find it difficult to believe this one, that anyone would conceive of such a convoluted scenario, remember that truth truly is weirder than fiction.

Just after that tale made its rounds, Christina Mack, a woman from Peoria, Illinois, was arrested and charged with aggravated domestic battery against her one-legged husband. Her modus operandi? She covered the linoleum floor of her kitchen with cooking oil. Her downfall? She slipped on the floor herself and was still unconscious when taken into custody!

Clearly a woman with too much time to think.

Equally unusual was "The Tale of the Hungry Stripper," which hit e-mail boxes everywhere at about the same time. It seems this particular male stripper figured that he could work as many parties as he liked, even advertise in the local papers, as long as he didn't ask for money. Guess he'd seen all those movies where the hooker couldn't be arrested until she'd actually taken the john's money. In any case, he, too, appeared to have too much time on his hands and eventually came up with a plan. Instead of money, he'd strip for food stamps!

It wasn't that he was starving; he simply thought he'd come up with a plan to outwit the system. So, he was more than a little surprised to find himself caught up in a sting operation. What could they charge him with? Indoor nudity wasn't illegal, and he hadn't accepted any money.

All true, the police assured him, but because he was receiving groceries purchased with food stamps issued to an individual other than himself, the use of the food stamps constituted *fraud*!

While some tales come out of nowhere and can therefore be put down to someone's overactive imagination, it seems that, as unlikely a set of circumstances as this appears, this tale is also based on a real incident!

Benford Clay, a part-time teacher in Dayton, Ohio, did indeed agree to dance at showers and parties for food stamps. He was even charged with misusing food stamps to the tune of three hundred dollars. He, unlike the fictional star of the urban legend, however, was cleared of all charges.

Tales like "The Smoking Jesus" typify this subset of weird crimes, leaving us wondering what would possess a person to contem-

plate, much less carry out, acts the rest of us can't comprehend even after the fact.

According to the tale, which surfaced about the same time that garden gnomes and granite frogs were being stolen from gardens in the UK, a statue of the infant Jesus was kidnapped from a small church in the Texas panhandle. A note left behind gave some clues to the identity of the thieves, but certainly not enough to track anyone down: He looked like he needed a break from being the center of the universe, so we've decided to let him relax for a while. Police questioned every fraternity and sorority member in a fifty-mile radius of the church, figuring this for pledge humor or something, but found nothing.

Eventually the incident was put aside while more pressing problems took up investigators' time. Imagine their surprise when, nearly three years later, the church called to report the statue returned, but vandalized! At the scene once again, they photographed a large hole in the Christ Child's head, about as big around as a fist, and took samples of what appeared to be common dirt from inside the hollowed-out space. Lab results confirmed the presence of dirt, along with 20-20-20 fertilizer! It seems Jesus had become a plant holder at some point in his travels.

Other than as a variant of the stolen garden gnome tales, this legend would, at first glance, show little signs of staying power. There's no big twist at the end, no lesson to be learned, really—unless you have statuary kicking about that you hadn't thought about securing. There's nothing to keep it in the public's mind at all except the nagging question: What sort of mind could look at a nativity scene and think "planters"!

Yet, despite its lack of dramatic elements, this tale made the rounds again in 1995 and 1997.

In 1995, a statue of Jesus as an infant was stolen from the Shrine of Our Lady of the Island, a church of no particular note in Eastport, New York. No note suggested God was in need of a vacation, no one was ever charged with the theft, the statue simply disappeared. Equally inexplicable was its return two years later—converted to a marijuana pipe! This time, investigators managed to track the theft back to a resident of Eastport, who was charged with possession of stolen property. As in the legends of roaming statues, however, there's still no explanation that even begins to explain the need not only to steal and vandalize bizarre items of no value, but to *return* them!

Maybe the moral of some stories is simply that you can never really know what your neighbors are thinking—or stealing!

Legends of obsessed shoppers going to outlandish lengths, even risking jail, to obtain the latest fad toy have been common since the Cabbage Patch Doll, but it took Beanie Babies to spark one woman's rise to the rarefied atmosphere of urban legendhood.

In 1998 a story began circulating that a woman had been put under house arrest for treatment of her "Beanie Baby addiction."

Fellow Beanians, horrified at the thought they too could be legally prevented from fulfilling their God-given right to amass stuffed toys, immediately began a petition to have the woman freed—or at least given access to her Babies!

Several judges in Connecticut and Arkansas, whose names were inexplicably linked to the growing legend, found themselves on the receiving end of thousand-name petitions and, in one case, a death threat!

In Alabama, one Beanian was so shocked by this tale of cruelty that she organized a drive to collect spare Beanie Babies and mail them to the suffering collector. The plan fell rather flat when she couldn't discover the woman's name or address. Before long, even the most dedicated collectors began doubting the existence of the incarcerated fan, and the tale began fading in popularity.

Then the *Monterey Herald* broke the story wide open.

Tamara Dean Maldonado, twenty-five, wasn't under house arrest, but Judge Jonathan Price had given police and probation officers some unusually wide authority to make sure she stayed clear of Beanie Babies. For starters, Tamara was forbidden to own, handle, or seek out Beanie Babies for five years. To make sure she stayed "clean," officers of the court could make spot inspections of her home at any time—well, at any time *after* she'd served her six-month jail term. Once again, Beanians were horrified. What terrible crime could Maldonado have committed to warrant such extreme measures?

None, other than stealing credit card numbers for the express purpose of obtaining eight thousand dollars' worth of the stuffed critters to satisfy her self-admitted addiction.

While that might have meant something to Beanie Baby collectors, the rest of the population can be forgiven if they're still shaking their heads and wondering what possessed an otherwise apparently normal young woman to begin a life of crime.

Tales abound of criminals planning elaborate scenarios for their crimes, only to be tripped up by the obvious. Such is the case in "What Goes Up," but this tale has the added value of being true—though most listeners would swear *no one* could possibly do anything this weird.

Early one morning in Bowling Green, Kentucky, employees of a Mid-Am Bank were shocked to find themselves being held up by a very ordinary-looking woman, probably a local housewife. She didn't yell or shout as she demanded money from the tellers. As there was nobody else present except the woman, the three tellers, and one bank officer out back, all of whom had evidently been caught flat-footed by this unassuming robber, there didn't even appear to be much cause for alarm, as there might have been if the bank was busy.

Perhaps that's why they didn't hop to it as fast as this robber expected. Things rapidly spiraled out of control when the woman reached into her pocket and then held a small box above her head. Claiming it was a detonator that would set off a car bomb outside, killing them all, she once again demanded they bring on the money. As expected, this got the staff's attention.

What wasn't expected was that one of the tellers would simply stride around the counter, refuse to participate in the robbery any further, and attack the woman! Just a few moments later the other tellers joined in the act and quickly subdued the woman until police arrived.

What had inspired this sudden upsurge in bravery?

One of the tellers had spotted the word "Sears" written across the bottom of what she then recognized as a garage door opener!

Karen Lee Joachimi didn't find the Lake City, Florida, staff at Howard Johnson's any more amenable to being held up. Then again, why she thought anyone would feel threatened by an electric chainsaw that evidently wasn't plugged in remains something of a mystery.

An old cliché contends that necessity is the mother of invention, and perhaps, at least in "The Tale of the Terrified Turtle," that maxim explains some of the seemingly inexplicable choices made by criminals.

Most love stories begin the same way, so we can skip that part of the story. Unfortunately, the endings of love stories seem restricted to "They lived happily ever after," or "She/He left sawdust on the floor of my heart!"

There wasn't ever going to be a happily-ever-after for one young man in Wisconsin; his soon-to-be-ex-girlfriend told him so in no uncertain terms. As far as she was concerned, it was already over, so why didn't he just mosey on home so she could get ready for her date—with someone else—that evening?

The young man left, but not happily or willingly, and thoughts of revenge, not love, danced in his head as he trod the dirt road toward home. If he'd found a bat or a tire iron or even a big stick along the way, he wouldn't be a legend at all, so you know that wasn't what his eyes lit upon as he kicked rocks into a muddy ditch.

No, when he stormed back into her lonely trailer, and chased his ex around the bedroom, this disgruntled boyfriend threatened her with . . . a snapping turtle!

Luckily for the ex—snapping turtles can deliver nasty, powerful bites—the turtle obviously didn't actually understand the role he'd been given to play and, like most actors who don't have the script beforehand, did nothing. Eventually police were summoned, and the boyfriend became the first man charged with assault with a reptile!

This tale, around since at least 1983, remained widely held as apocryphal until an officer interviewed for the TV program *America's Dumbest Criminals* revealed that the events, essentially as described in the legend—right down to the snapping turtle—

occurred in Illinois! He was the one who eventually found a happily-ever-after to the tale. Apparently the ex-girlfriend was so grateful to the turtle that she adopted him, and they certainly lived happily ever after—without the boyfriend!

WHAT A WAY TO GET CAUGHT!

You've no doubt gathered, even from this first set of tales, that "crook" doesn't necessarily equal "criminal genius." Even the cops freely admit that while some cases require serious investigation, a high percentage of criminals basically *catch themselves* through their own carelessness.

As you read the remainder of this section, imagine yourself as a criminal sitting in your cell and trying to explain to your huge cellmate, Earl, *exactly* how you came to be stuck inside. Bet you wouldn't admit to any of these scenarios!

Too Stupid For Words

"Charge It!" is the sorry tale of Johnny Maxwell of California. He wasn't what you'd term a "high risk" sort of crook. While some criminals really get off on the high of scoring a major crime, Johnny seemed content to tackle the low-risk end of the burglary trade. No well-guarded museum treasures for him. His modus operandi was simple. He'd wait until someone went on vacation, jimmy their door with his favorite credit card (one with a slightly beveled edge worked best, but he could always smooth one out a bit if he didn't have a naturally beveled card on him at the time), then rob them at leisure. He even stayed the weekend at a few of the nicer places he knocked over.

Johnny had been doing just fine for himself for several years, which might explain why he got a bit careless one night. He'd heard the Bakers would be out of town until Monday, and decided to make a long weekend of it away from his wife. Unfortunately, he hadn't double-checked his information and was still loading up the car out back when the Bakers pulled up out front!

Not able to go out the front door, and too far from the back door, Johnny resolved his problem by pulling out a credit card and springing the lock on the side door! He figured he was away clean—until he tripped over the family dog, which raced into the house between his legs!

Still, Johnny was a strong, healthy young man, and he quickly picked himself up, shut the dog inside, and sprinted for his car. He was grinning as he pulled out of the back driveway. He'd made it, and probably had minutes to spare, too, as the family was still out front, hauling out luggage, when he drove sedately around the block on his way home.

That pleasant feeling of having escaped by the strength of his thighs and the wit of his brain faded quickly when, on stopping for gas on the way home, he discovered that he had not only used his *own* Visa card to pop that side door, but he'd dropped it during his collision with the dog! He might as well have left his calling card!

Perhaps our legendary housebreaker got lucky up at the Big House though; he might have gotten Jack Wright for a cellmate. And how would that be lucky? Well, Wright left his Sears credit card at the last place he robbed.

"Don't Forget to Write" proves that stickup men aren't much brighter than their housebreaking kin.

A local scalawag decided to enliven his Saturday night, and fill his wallet, by sticking up the nearest liquor store. Of course, Saturday night is a busy time at liquor stores, so, when he walked in and realized the place was more densely populated than was wise for a stickup, he wandered about for a few minutes, waiting to see if the place would clear out soon and be a little more easily handled. It didn't, and he didn't have all night to wait around, so, rummaging in his pocket, he pulled out an old piece of paper and quickly wrote a stickup note on the back.

The cashier eyed the note, nodded, and prudently decided to do as she was told. The $536.24 in the register wasn't anywhere near as important to her as her life.

The stickup man nodded back, smiled, and left with the cash.

Her boss was furious. Couldn't she have signaled him or something? Hadn't the silent alarm been installed for just these sorts of occasions? What was she thinking?

His anger cooled quickly when she

handed him the note and, turning it over, pointed out that it was written on an appointment letter from a probation officer. There, in black and white, were the robber's name, address, and telephone number!

Don't laugh. Almost every police department can produce evidence to prove that crooks will write on almost anything: appointment slips, pay stubs, love letters, draft notices, and, in at least one case, a marriage certificate!

Of course, there's always the possibility that even cops like to spread an urban legend or two. This next tale, "That's Her!," has been publicly claimed by the upright officers of justice in four municipalities in four different states. While coincidences do happen, having these events play themselves out that often could stretch anyone's ability to believe.

The story always begins the same way. A patrol car near a large shopping mall is alerted to a recent purse-snatching. For once, the victim has a clear description, and the description can't fit that many people. (Of course, this is where the stories diverge, but my favorite description wins out here.)

"A white youth, about eighteen, six feet, hair dyed white, scrawny, almost losing his army pants off his hips, white T-shirt, black vest, lime underwear."

Lime underwear?

Well, the witness did say the kid was losing his pants.

Sure enough, dodging through the mall parking lot, scattering the contents of the purse behind him, is the kid from the description. They quickly tuck him into the backseat, where he can't help hearing the conversation between the patrol car and the cop inside with the victim. They'll just drive around to the main entrance, get the kid to stand outside for a positive ID, and go on. As they pull up, the driver warns the kid, "Nothing funny now, you hear? This'll go a lot easier for you if you cooperate."

The lad is apparently overflowing with cooperation on this particular day. (This is the part where the stories all converge again.) As he steps out and the victim comes to look at him, the youth nods quickly. "Oh yeah, I can ID her. That's the woman I robbed, all right!"

I don't care where you get sent up, nowhere is the aforementioned Earl *not* going to think he's got the dumbest cellmate on the block! Though the star of "Un-hand Me!" should challenge for the title.

Seems Dimmy Crane needed cash fast. He'd decided that of the criminal options available to him, bank robbery might be the easiest way to get lots of money with little risk. He knew about the silent alarms and all that, but he also knew that most employees, including bank employees, were instructed to simply give up the money when faced with a gun. He was willing to take his chances on a getaway after he had the cash.

The fact that he didn't actually own a gun wasn't, in his mind, an impediment. He'd just use his thumb and finger to convince someone he satisfied that part of the plan.

All went well. His clothes were nondescript enough to provide no clues to his identity. He was wearing gloves. His ski mask covered everything except his eyes, and he even squinted so as to make identification even more difficult, should it come to that some day. His note, which was written on a plain deposit slip, contained no unintended information, and in any case he remembered to take it back from the teller to avoid leaving even handwriting evidence behind.

Unfortunately, the hand that reached for the note was the hand that until now had been the "gun"!

Maybe this guy will get lucky, too, and have Californian Steven Richard King share his cell instead of Earl. King would understand that plight. He committed the same booboo, in a Bank of America, years after the original legend arose. Guess he never heard the legend.

They Turned Themselves In?

Those unlucky enough to find themselves entangled in criminal activities, whether as perpetrator or victim, seldom find the experience in the least romantic. Fear-induced body odor, lice treatments, and accidental urination don't figure nearly as often in Hallmark commercials as they do in crimes or arrests. Still, for whatever reason, the public not treated to the real thing seems determined to turn bad guys into folk heroes, glamorize organized crime with the trappings of honor, and turn criminal careers into movies-of-the-week.

One of the most enduring cinematic images ever, Jimmy Cagney screaming out, "Top of the world, Ma!" before being shot down, has nothing to do with reality. Still, we apparently find it hard not to identify with even the worst criminals so long as they're doing something we understand at gut level—like trying to put one past the cops. Given a decent enough actor, and a high willingness to put aside facts, we can cast the fugitive criminal as David and the massed cops as Goliath.

What we apparently can't relate to, even viewed through Hollywood's deceptive filter, are crooks who *give themselves up* instead of going out in a blaze of glory and gunfire.

Can you, in thirty seconds or less, name even one film, one book, that ends with the hero, or antihero in this case, turning himself in?

Didn't think so.

Of all legal legends, those few featuring criminal capitulation are the rarest. These next three, while presented in the legend form they're most commonly known for, can all be traced back to real events. Of note to those trying to put these tales into context, as a means for us to play with our fears, or warn one another of danger, is that the original incidents, while factually represented in the tales, weren't nearly as funny as dozens of retellings eventually made them. Once again, we don't understand and don't want to relate to those who simply give up. If we have to include stories of crooks who gave themselves up, we demand comedy.

"Take Me, Please" begins in a small rural police station late in the graveyard shift. The deputy, a native of the town, knew all the residents pretty well, the good, the bad, and the ugly. He knew Mrs. Potton would call to report her husband missing on Saturday night; he'd go retrieve him from Spanky's Bar and get him home halfway sober. He knew Herman Collins would die a grisly death before telling a lie; his wife had once blacked his eye after asking for his opinion of her new dress. And he knew Jack Benson would be arrested once a year—if he wasn't in jail already.

In fact, he had the latest warrant for Jack Benson, on a petty burglary charge, sitting on his desk right now. Figuring to round him up in the morning—the deputy knew his usual haunts and Benson wasn't much of a runner—he was surprised to receive a predawn call from Benson!

"Hey, Deputy, that you?"

"Yeah, Jack, it's me. You know I got a warrant here for you, don't you?"

"I thought you might."

About this time, the deputy noticed that Jack's voice was getting lower and lower. "Can you speak up, I can't hardly hear you."

"Can't do that right now, Deputy."

"Well, what do you want?"

A steady *bang, bang, bang* carried over the phone line, almost as loud as the now-whispering criminal. "I want to turn myself in."

"Right, tell me another one, Jack. Now, what are you up to?"

"Nothing. I want to turn myself in. I'll give you the address, you just come pick me up, okay?"

"And what'll you be doing while I'm out in the patrol car? Going back for what you missed at the diner?"

"No, man, I'm serious here. I want to turn myself in!" The *bang, bang, bang* was now louder than Jack's voice.

Sighing, the deputy stood up. "Okay, give me the address, but I'm warning you, Jack, you screw me and I'll make life very unhappy for you."

"Don't worry, just get over here."

When the deputy arrived, he took in the situation at a glance. The address was the home of Clar Reisman, his eighteen-year-old son, Lar, and his fifteen-year-old daughter, Clarisa. Jack wasn't there to visit Clar, or Lar. The burglar had snuck into Clarisa's room, not an isolated incident, apparently, but this time her father and brother had discovered the dalliance! As the deputy pulled up, the father, inside the dwelling, was banging a fencepost against the door while, outside, the brother stood under the bedroom window to thwart any attempts at escape.

Compared with this familiar riot, the jail was an oasis of quiet solitude!

"The Sewer Rat," however, had no intention of turning himself in as *his* tale began. Clyde Demos, hiding from several layers of law enforcement, had six excellent reasons to avoid legal entanglements: three charges of petty larceny, one charge of telephone solicitation for illegal purposes, one charge of harassment, one charge of petty theft.

Despite a roving lifestyle that saw him bunking down at a different address almost every night, the law eventually tracked him down. (They had some help from a disgruntled girlfriend who was rather suspicious of his traveling-man ways, but Clyde didn't know that at the time.)

Still, Clyde wasn't caught completely flat-footed. Like his gangster heroes of old, he'd scoped out an escape route and, of all the locations he'd used, this one provided one hell of a back door!

In seconds, Clyde scampered up through an old air-conditioning vent that gave him access to the roof. On the roof, he clambered up a short ladder and threw himself into a water tank. Most water tanks feed into domestic water supplies. This one fed directly into the sewer system through an open chute that emptied into an underground water cistern. The cistern, in turn, emptied via a wide pipe into the new city sewers. Knowing the new service to be extensive, something like eight hundred miles in total, Clyde assumed he'd easily find a convenient outlet and enter the city at some location remote from his entry point.

The problem, of course, lay in Clyde's assumption.

He'd never actually gone farther than the big cistern on his scouting foray. Still, grin-ning at his own cleverness in eluding the police so far, and in anticipation of his imminent escape, he hurried ahead. For the first fifty feet, all was well. The older lines, made of large clay pipes and joints, let him scoot along quickly on his hands and knees. It was the new tunnels that presented difficulties. Far from "bigger and better," the new tunnels were smaller pipes, of galvanized steel. Soon he was reduced to pulling himself along on his stomach. Then, when he had no hope of turning around or even backing out, the pipes dipped and shrank. Before he knew what was happening, he was tightly enclosed by eighteen-inch pipe!

From time to time he'd passed beneath openings to street-level grates and, seeing slightly brighter light ahead, he determined to squirm his way forward until he could perhaps haul himself up through the larger rain shafts. Leaving a lot of skin behind, he inched ahead, cursing the rippled surface of the pipes, which alternately pinched and released him as he slid forward. Hours later, he nearly tore his ear off in an attempt to twist around the ninety-degree turn that led upward to freedom.

At least he hoped it did. He certainly couldn't continue through the pipes. Even if he didn't mind losing more skin, this new pipe, unlike the old clay pipes, had sagged when it was backfilled. Even his skinny frame couldn't move through the damaged areas.

Looking up, he was at once delighted to see azure skies float across the opening, and dismayed to see the unmistakable outline of a trooper's hat silhouetted against the sky!

"Come on, Clyde. Let's call it a day, eh?"

Like Cagney, Clyde wasn't about to give in. "Screw you!"

"Have it your own way."

Squished in the elbow of the pipe, Clyde considered his predicament. Back wasn't possible, up wasn't happening, which left onwards. Struggling in the rain shaft, he gradually shucked all his clothes except his BVDs. A thin trickle of green, slimy water flowed into the flattened pipe, and, thinking it might help lubricate the route, Clyde smeared himself with the sludge before easing himself, feet first, into the next section of pipes.

Immediately he realized it wouldn't be easy. The pipe had been squished into an oval, which ought to have made passage of a basically oval human body that much easier. Instead, while he could move his hands a little more freely, Clyde couldn't catch a full breath! He could pant, shallowly, but a single deep breath was out of the question. Hoping, praying that the flattened section wouldn't last long, he squirmed deeper.

Mistake.

With just his head left to go into the pipe, he stuck. No amount of twisting, exhaling, or scratching with his toenails could shift him!

Above him, the hat shadow returned. "Looks like you're in a little trouble there, Clyde."

"Screw you!"

"Good enough."

The shadow pulled back, but, frankly, Clyde hadn't developed any new plans during that discussion and he was still stuck.

No matter where you go, everyone has the same thing to say about their part of the country. "If you don't like the weather, wait five minutes." As Clyde lay in his galvanized pipe, six hours passed and the weather did indeed change. The clear skies clouded over and a light rain began. It was then that he first stopped to consider the purpose of the rain shaft . . .

With water running through the pipe he'd already traversed, falling down the shaft into his face, and with him blocking the lower end of the pipe—well, it didn't take a rocket scientist to realize he was in serious danger of drowning.

Again the hat shadow fell across his face. This time he was grateful for the respite it gave him from falling rain.

"So, Clyde, what do you figure now? Ready to come out?"

Even facing certain death, the stuck criminal rebelled at the smug assurance in the trooper's voice. He'd have given a lot to tell him, once again, to screw off. However, with water rising around his head, he finally capitulated. "All right, you pig, get me out of here!"

Now Clyde's biggest worry was that, having given in, his rescue would be too slow to prevent him from drowning.

It was with mixed feelings then that, only a few short moments later, a great weight was lifted off Clyde's chest and, with a mighty roar, the pipe itself was tugged forward, carrying Clyde into the fresh air!

After all that soul-searching, Clyde discovered he'd worked his way into an end tunnel. The sag in the pipe was caused by a piece of heavy equipment sitting atop the end of the run, waiting to continue laying pipe the next day! Tugging the pipe free had been accomplished by simply removing the last section of pipe laid! Clyde had been less than a pipe-length—some twenty feet—from freedom!

Sometimes life doesn't seem worth living.

Two men from Alabama had a different view of the world. (*They* hadn't spent eight hours in a slimy pipe.) When an opportunity presented itself, these two convicts quickly checked out of their state-owned accommodations, "liberated" a pickup truck, and headed north.

Along the way, they also "liberated" as much gas as they could from parked cars. Eventually they entered the sweeping prairie of Indiana and discovered two things: First, when your nearest neighbor is hours away, folks don't tend to leave cars parked along the road. Second, winter is cold in Indiana! They ran out of gas and soon agreed that the shorts and T-shirts they'd been wearing back in Alabama just weren't cutting it here in the twenty-degree chill of a farmer's field.

By the time they'd shivered for half the day—learning in the process how rare it was for *any* car to pass by—they were happy enough to throw themselves into the warm, handle-less backseat of the first patrol car to come along. Their only request? "Extradite us!"

The Botched Getaway

Clearly, most criminals don't want to be captured, but although crimes themselves may be carefully planned, the getaway schemes intended to top off the infractions frequently prove the weak link in the whole strategy.

"Cover Up" proves that even the simplest robberies need careful thought.

Art Penney, a sometime thief, hadn't been planning to score when he set out from home for a stroll to his buddy's poker party, but the sight of an entire window of jewelry soon caught his eye. Merchants had long ago discovered that the safest place to leave their wares overnight was locked up in a safe, so, seeing an entire display sitting just inches from the plate-glass windows long after the street's businessmen had retired for the night, Art decided this was an omen.

All he had to do was smash the glass and run!

First, not wanting to leave blood about anywhere, he looked for something with which to break the glass, something besides his bare hands. Until now, Art hadn't realized how few mobile objects there were on night streets. Mailboxes, garbage cans, newspaper machines, everything was bolted to something else. The only movable—and let's use that definition loosely here—item he found was a manhole cover!

Well, he could be sure the glass would break, right?

It did, and within minutes he'd filled his pockets with thousands of dollars' worth of gold and gemstones. He'd have come up with even more if he hadn't been interrupted by a strolling couple coming around the corner.

Oh, well, omens didn't happen every day, and he'd already scored more than he might have in a half-dozen smaller jobs, so, content to get away unidentified, he left the rest of the booty and raced toward a conveniently dark alleyway across the street.

Then, in mid-getaway, he remembered the manhole cover. It was still in the display window—not atop the manhole he'd just fallen through.

The moral here seems easy enough to pick out: Even if fate seems to be holding out her hand, you've still got to keep watching for the foot that's about to trip you up.

Jasper Dean, a young man from Kansas, gave his escape route a little more thought, but, like Art, decided to stick to foot power. When you're only eighteen, fleet of foot, and know the area around your target like you were born there (mostly because you *were* born there), there's no need to complicate your getaway plans with things like cars that might not start, that might be described by witnesses, and that can't go cross-country!

"Take to Your Heels" begins, appropriately enough, with Jasper making sure his laces were neatly tied and tucked inside his running shoes. Satisfied, he pulled a paper

bag with eye holes in it over his head, pulled a gun from his back pocket, sauntered into the corner convenience store, and demanded all the money. He then shoved the money in a back pocket, slipped outside, and raced down the street.

Coincidence plays a part in every crime, and Jasper was just unfortunate enough to be spotted by a roving patrol car before he could ditch the bag and resume a normal walking pace. As the cops turned on the siren, Jasper cut hard right and headed straight for a nearby wilderness park. He knew it well, had run its trails since he was a youngster, and figured to ditch the cops quickly in the darkness.

The patrol car pulled to a stop, and while one cop called for backup, the younger of the two, who looked capable of running nearly as long as Jasper, immediately took up the chase.

Under the dense leaf cover, Jasper remembered to keep his breathing quiet. He tossed the pale bag aside and ducked into the darkest shadows. He fully expected to lose this cop within yards. When he slowed to listen, though, loud footsteps sounded just behind him, and he sprinted ahead again without even looking back.

Using some of his best duck-and-dodge, Jasper threaded his way through a thicker stand of trees. Though the trailing footsteps fell back marginally, it was by no means enough to allow Jasper to stop and hide. Then he heard the sound of approaching sirens, and before long, the cop behind started yelling out to all his buddies, "I'm on him! I'm on him!"

How, Jasper couldn't figure. Taking a deep second breath, he wheeled to the left and headed up a steeper incline, still running hard. To his horror, a second voice soon chimed in!

"Hey, I see him! Heading north!"

As cop after cop joined the race, Jasper began wondering if these guys could see in the dark or what. No matter how he spun and ran, he could hear them—more of them every minute—closing in on him. He'd just about concluded that the local police department must have started issuing night-vision gear when, out of the blackness to his right, the first cop tackled him. He hit the ground hard and came up swinging. All to no avail. Before long he was trussed up and being quick-marched back to the patrol car.

"Not fair, you guys, not fair!"

"What are you talking about?"

"Using that spy gear to see in the dark!"

"What spy gear?"

About then, Jasper realized that no one was wearing anything unusual.

"You ain't got no night-vision gear?" They shook their heads. "Then how'd you see me?" the frustrated youth demanded.

The first cop shook his head and had to stop while he laughed—which only aggravated the already irate crook. After finally catching his breath, the cop pointed to Jasper's feet.

Jasper groaned.

He'd put on his best runners for this gig, forgetting that those shoes had light-emitting elements in their heels that lit up at every step. They'd been following his shoes!

Even for crooks, technology occasionally runs ahead of full understanding.

"The Vegas Vacation" features a special sort of criminal, the sort that views life as one long holiday, the amount of fun dependent only on the amount of money that can be begged, borrowed, or, more often, stolen along the way. Never settling in one place, Mickey Conway figured, was one way to keep a healthy gap between him and the police.

Mostly he practiced small-time holdups at corner stores, along with a little residential break-and-entry when things got slow. In each case he'd move into a new town, play a bit, then pull a holdup to get him settled in the next town. When he decided he'd like to go to Vegas, though, he realized he'd need a bigger score than usual, and rolled into a midsized town with a selection of targets to choose from.

The heist went off as easily as all the rest. Most tellers and cashiers, having long since decided that discretion is the better part of valor, don't put up much of a fight anymore. By avoiding the mom-and-pop stores, the ones run by families who took his little "withdrawals" personally, Mickey managed to avoid most entanglements.

As he discovered when he attempted this latest robbery, however, not all the small-town habits transferred to this new location equally well. None of the cashiers presented a problem, and, in his role of tourist, his RV made for such an unusual getaway car that most cops passed over it without thought. Not so this time.

Drivers outside small-town U.S.A. aren't friendly to thirty-two-foot-long recreational vehicles attempting to pull out into midday traffic! It took him so long to move away from the curb that police called to the scene had plenty of time to check *everyone* in the area. The cashier, accompanying the officers up and down the street, pointed him out, and patrolmen on foot soon caught up to him in the gridlock.

While any tale that casts the crook as a clown is likely to linger in public memory, stories of criminals hoist by their own petard, caught up in their own crimes, hold a special place in the public's heart. When the tale, like "You Light Up My Life," proves to have a basis in fact, well, the poetic justice imagined to be at work behind the scenes almost guarantees a legend's place in history.

The tale begins in Florida, and like many crimes that sweep seemingly normal people up in bizarre situations, this story begins with two neighbors. Whoever said that "Good fences make good neighbors" obviously had Eldon Green and Joseph Carnesi in mind.

It seems Carnesi had, by design or the sheer force of his personality, gotten so far up his neighbor's nose that, instead of taking his complaints to his lawyer or the local city

council—or even Carnesi himself—Green felt driven to take matters into his own hands.

Loading up his car with bottles, gas, a bunch of rags, and his lighter, Green drove the short distance to Carnesi's house and proceeded to manufacture, light, and lob Molotov cocktails onto his neighbor's roof! When he was finished, he got back into his car and drove away—completely unaware of the bottle that had rolled off the roof and back into his car!

He'd just pulled away when the gas bomb exploded. The car burst into flames, lurched forward, and only stopped rolling when it ran into a nearby tree!

The legend that arose from this incident ends there, satisfied to see a criminal suffer at his own hand, but in reality, Eldon Green was pulled from his car by firefighters and died of his burns at Tampa General Hospital. Where many tales that are later proven to be based in fact, or that become self-fulfilling after the fact, fade from popularity, this one continues to spread even when its factual nature becomes known. It seems Eldon Green fulfills our need for vengeance without arousing enough of our sympathy to let him rest in peace.

"I Shouldn't Have Left Them Alone!," also based on real-life events, isn't likely to arouse a lot of sympathy, either—if for different reasons.

Michael Gilbert, his girlfriend, and their willing accomplice pulled up in front of a Raleigh, North Carolina, convenience store that Gilbert had decided looked ripe for the plucking. Giving some thought to the technicalities, it was decided that Gilbert would be the inside man, the girlfriend would watch the street from the passenger seat, and their male companion would sit behind the wheel in case a quick escape was required.

Everything inside went fine, but when he raced back to the car, he discovered his girlfriend and his best buddy making out in the car! (Makes you wonder how long this robbery took, doesn't it?) Just to make sure they weren't disturbed, they'd locked the doors and rolled up the windows. A very upset Gilbert was still pounding on the car when police arrived in response to the clerk's summons!

Of all the botched getaway tales, both those that began as real events and those that seemed only the product of an active imagination until someone came along and proved crooks really could be that pathetic, "The Barbed-Wire Mall" paints the most vivid picture of a getaway gone wrong. It's also one of the few tales to go interstate.

Vincent McKenzie was in Agawam, Maine, when he allegedly held up the town's largest bank. The robbery went fine, except for the police pursuit that followed almost immediately, putting a serious crimp in McKenzie's getaway plans. He raced through Windsor Locks and Suffield, crossing into Connecticut in the process. With cops from four states on his tail, he suddenly pulled off the highway, screeched to a halt in a parking lot, and, on foot, sprinted for the entrance of

the MacDougall Correctional Institution, a high-security state prison! As soon as the doors closed behind him, he was trapped! Both the inside and outside door bolts slammed home as confused guards looked on. Needless to say, police had no difficulty apprehending their suspect at that point.

Just why did McKenzie throw himself into the arms of prison guards? Did he figure he might as well skip the trial and go straight to jail?

Not at all.

According to officers on the scene, McKenzie didn't notice the miles of razor wire surrounding the huge building. He thought it was a mall, and hoped to lose himself in the crowd!

JUST WHEN THEY THOUGHT THEY GOT AWAY CLEAN

Despite all the bungles and blunders criminals regularly invent on their own, some few crooks do, by accident or intent, actually get away clean! Having dodged the legal bullet once, you'd imagine this lucky scattering of outlaws would be extra careful to stay out of trouble. How wrong you'd be! The following tales, like the previous ones, are more often than not based on real-life events, and prove that luck and brains don't always go together.

Computers Have Long Memories

The first thing fugitive miscreants evidently forget is that everyone leaves a paper trail, or, in modern times, a digital trail. Prints, numbers, and cash touch everyone. From our first breath, someone somewhere is assigning numbers to our performance. Apgar scores, birth registrations, school IDs, driver's licenses, social security, job applications—the list of information sources on a single individual staggers the imagination. And it's worse if you've ever been charged with anything, or have even been a material witness in some legal action. Which only makes these next tales the more difficult to believe.

Take "The Case of a Working Joe" who just couldn't make it from payday to payday on his blue-collar salary. He could've moonlit, could've persuaded the wife to get a job, could've hit the boss up for a raise. Instead, Joe walked into a local bank in Grand Forks, North Dakota, handed over a holdup note, collected $34,000 from the startled cashier, and walked out, to all appearances a free man.

That illusion shattered when police picked him up just a short time later. His note, written on the back of an envelope, also contained his pay stub, complete with name, address, and social security number!

When our next Joe Average, the star of "Heading North!," robbed an Arkansas pharmacy while waving a knife at the frightened clerk, his luck immediately after the holdup wasn't so good. Apparently distinctive enough for even a terrified person to recall, he was quickly picked out of a mug book and duly charged.

Taking this as a sign of more bad things to come, the knife-toting stickup man decided to skip his trial and simply disappear! Did an admirable job of it, too, eluding police not only in Arkansas, but in New York City, which was alerted to his possible reappearance there as the folks down South weren't feeling too friendly toward him, since he'd ducked out on the big shindig they'd planned.

Though it remained an open case, officials readily acknowledged that, without some clue, they had no way to track him, in Arkansas or anywhere else. As it happened, despite having slipped successfully out of the net once, this criminal appeared destined by his own lack of wit to fall right back into the arms of justice. Arkansas investigators were startled, then delighted, when an FBI agent with the unglamorous job of completing the routine background checks done on state and federal job applicants rang them up one sunny afternoon. It seems their robber had voluntarily submitted his prints back up in New York when he'd applied for a job with the NYPD!

Guess he didn't realize the background check was being done by *that* FBI.

When police arrived to serve a warrant for receiving and cashing a stolen check in "I'll Need Two Pieces of ID, Sir," they weren't surprised when the alleged thief strenuously denied any involvement in the whole affair. After all, almost nobody actually *admits* to anything anymore—these days the police don't find too many suspects like those that used to haunt the drawing rooms of Agatha Christie novels or the final scenes of *Columbo.*

They were ready for the inevitable "What makes you think it was me, anyway?"

Handing over the check, they pointed to the forged endorsement on the back.

"Yeah, I see it, but isn't that the name on the front of the check?"

"Yes, sir, it is. It's the name and ID below that, the ones you used to identify yourself to the teller when you *cashed* the check, that gave you away."

The man stopped, stared, then groaned. "I didn't!"

"Yes, sir, you did."

Falling into the habit of a lifetime, the forger had, when asked, produced the requisite two pieces of signed ID, *his own ID.*

While that man can probably learn from his mistake, the jewel thief in the next tale, "It Only Takes One," won't get a second chance.

The heist was going beautifully! He'd turned off the alarms, including the silent one the store owner evidently thought couldn't be breached, and had the entire store all to himself until staff would arrive the next morning. Still, recognizing the dangers of getting too complacent, he decided to whip through this scene with the same vigor he'd have used if the alarms had gone off.

The adrenaline flew through his system as, with methodical precision, he broke and emptied case after case into a physician's black bag. Time to empty fourteen cases, two display cabinets, and the owner's office? Seven minutes, twelve seconds. His best ever. Patting himself on the back, he took care of the last item of business, namely stealing the surveillance camera tapes, before stepping back outside, resetting the alarms, and walking away.

Even police later admitted the robbery was perfect.

So how did this thief get caught?

In the excitement, he failed to notice how neatly he'd cut the tip from his little finger with a piece of shattered cabinet glass. Despite these events occurring pre–DNA testing, the cops quickly tracked their man. They simply printed the fingertip and ran it through the system!

Our next rogue, a real scalawag from Lafayette, Louisiana, was convinced he could "Talk His Way Out of Anything," even the rather extraordinary circumstances that found him standing in the middle of someone else's kitchen, with the back door jimmied, when the owner arrived.

Following the old maxim that "a good offense is the best defense," our housebreaker immediately took the lead, suggesting that since nothing had actually been taken, they just forget the whole thing. The homeowner, naturally, wasn't altogether sure that was the approach *he* wanted to take; he favored the call-the-cops plan.

Anxious to defuse the situation, but not of a naturally violent bent, our young rascal protested that, as no crime had been committed, calling the police would only waste valuable police time.

What about the break and entry, the broken door?

Well, he'd only broken in because it was so hot outside!

What?

Hadn't the homeowner noticed it was over one hundred degrees outside?

Sure . . .

Well, it was the heat, or more precisely, a powerful thirst brought on by the heat, that had left him so desperate for a drink of cool water that he'd taken the extraordinary step of forcing the back door—all he'd really wanted was a glass of cold water. Couldn't he just get the water and leave, with no hard feelings?

Surprisingly, the homeowner agreed! He filled a tall glass with spring water, added a scoop of ice chips, wiped off the condensation covering the outside, and handed it across while passing a genial comment on the unusual length of this latest heat wave.

The rascal downed the water and, delighted to have talked himself out of a tight situation, took off!

The homeowner, for his part, called the cops.

Within minutes they arrived and promptly began castigating the homeowner for letting the man, clearly not a dangerous threat, get away. Instead of an easy collar, they now had to locate a man with nothing more than a physical description to go on!

The homeowner smiled.

What was so funny?

"Well now, it seems to me that a boy smooth enough, with enough native gall to even attempt talking his way out of that situation, *must* have been at this for a while, probably got a record somewhere, right?"

"Yeah, so?"

He handed over the glass. "Then I imagine you'll find all the prints you need right there."

Sure enough, the courteous crook was back in custody within two hours.

The next tale, "Hit and Run," is as memorable for its victim as for its unique irony. Let's face it, most hit-and-run incidents feature a car and a pedestrian, occasionally a cyclist, skateboarder, or roller skater. Whatever the car hits, it's undoubtedly going to be *smaller* than the car, right?

Not in Rochester, New York, where a drunk driver slid off the road and eventually crashed into a *house*! Miraculously, when everything stopped shaking, the car's engine was still running and, faced with the choice of sticking around to face the homeowner and the cops, or running like hell, the driver threw the car in reverse, crunched back over the debris until he found the road, and quickly raced off into the night.

Given the lack of witnesses, the rough debris that wouldn't hold a tire print, and the impossibility of matching paint chips from a batch that had probably been sprayed on thousands of cars, the police couldn't offer much assurance of ever finding the reckless driver—until a search of the debris turned up one startling piece of evidence.

While reversing away from the impact site, the car's license plate had hooked a piece of loose wood or masonry, had fallen off, and was just sitting there waiting for the computer at the Department of Motor Vehicles to point its accusing finger at a driver who might otherwise have gotten off with nothing but a bill from his body shop!

What could be more convenient? How about a criminal who walked up to the nearest cop and, without any provocation, calmly handed over his ID? That's exactly what happens in "How Does That Work?"

A Detroit cop, perhaps a little bored with his latest assignment, attending a Career Day at a local school where his part of the demonstration was to show how computers had been carried from the office into the patrol car by letting the kids crawl inside and play with the keyboard, looked up in surprise when an adult stuck his head in the opposite side of the car and asked an intelligent question.

"Does this system just access the local databases or is it hooked into the national system?"

"Oh, it's jacked into everything!"

"Really?"

"Sure Is!"

After some more discussion, the cop suggested he demonstrate the speed with which he could get a response, and the gen-

tleman, delighted with the offer, volunteered his own driver's license for the experiment.

Imagine the gent's surprise when the terminal spilled out his life history in a little less than twenty seconds!

Imagine the cop's surprise when that printout included outstanding warrants for a two-year-old armed robbery back in St. Louis, Missouri!

He was probably disappointed to lose such an avid audience, but it was undoubtedly the easiest collar of his career!

The opposite situation appeared to be developing for officers in "The Double" when an ordinary sort of fellow appeared at the station in company with an older woman. It seemed the Las Vegas police had, for the past two weeks, been circulating a sketch and description that so eerily resembled this poor fellow that, eventually tiring of the strange glances he was getting at work, he invited one of his colleagues to accompany him to the station to prove, once and for all, that he wasn't guilty of the much-publicized assault!

His companion, clearly uncomfortable, nevertheless leaned over the terminal as the man presented his license to the officer. Sure enough, it quickly proved that this man and the Nevada assailant couldn't be the same person. The woman, about to give a sigh of relief, soon, however, had an entirely different story to take back to the office the following morning.

Though innocent of the Nevada assault, he was all too guilty of the same crime back in California over a year ago. If he'd just sat tight, he'd never have been caught!

The Personal Touch

Before you come to the conclusion that it was computers that doomed the modern criminal, you'd be wise to remember that the vast majority of cases are solved by human ingenuity and basic observation skills. If you can remember that, you'll be ahead of at least seven legendary criminals. And, yes, all these legends grew out of the real-life experiences of cops and crooks.

"All in the Family" proves there may well be considerably fewer than six degrees of separation between any two strangers. Officer Pierson was patrolling the most burglarized neighborhood in all of Georgia when he spotted a pickup truck suspiciously like one reported at the precinct meeting as the getaway car in a robbery. Notifying the station that he was going to stop the truck at his earliest opportunity, Pierson was told to hang on to the driver, even if he didn't spot anything unusual right away. Another car had just brought in the inside man on the robbery and they had high hopes of playing the criminal conspirators off against one another. If he could keep the suspect talking, a second officer would be along shortly to help take him into custody.

Keeping a relatively low profile, Pierson pulled up behind the truck and flipped on his lights, but didn't use the siren. (Sirens figure prominently in most high-speed chases.) As

he hoped, the driver pulled over calmly and Pierson did his best not to look threatening as he glanced at the license plate and walked forward to speak to the driver.

"I think you might have a faulty signal light back there."

"Really?"

"Yeah, it flashes on and off whenever you go over bumps."

"Oh, well, I'll check into it as soon as the garage opens in the morning."

"Great. Listen, just put your foot on your brake for me, will you?"

"No problem."

Pierson wandered back and pretended to watch closely, then sighed and returned to the window. "I hate to do this, but I'm going to have to write you up."

"Why? I said I'd take care of it first thing."

"I know, and if you had just the one violation, that'd be fine. Unfortunately, it looks like you've got a bigger electrical problem. Not only is your signal indicator doing the hula back here, your left brake light isn't working at all. Two violations, I got no choice, I got to write you up."

"Yeah, well, I suppose it could be worse. At least it's not a moving violation."

"Right, there's that. Give me your license and we'll get the dirty deed done as quickly as possible, okay? Get you back on your way."

Pierson was so busy stealing a glance back down the highway, he had the ticket half written up before noticing something odd.

"Are you sure this is your license?"

The man glanced at it and shrugged. "Yeah, it's mine. Why, something wrong?"

"No, just procedure. Can you repeat the information on this license for me?"

"What for?"

"The department likes to make sure we ticket the right guy. Had a few cases of fellows giving us their buddy's license. They were pissed, we had a lot of paperwork, you know how it goes. So now they make us do this. Can you tell me the address on this license?"

"Sure, 1320 Maple, Oak Park, Atlanta."

"Date of birth?"

"May 2, 1954."

"Full name?"

"Mark Peter Pierson."

When the second patrol car pulled up, the man who called himself Mark Peter Pierson suddenly got nervous. "Hey, you want to give me that ticket now? I got places to be."

"Sure, just a minute."

Holding on to the license and waving the second car into a position just ahead of the pickup, Pierson waited only until his colleague opened his door before asking the pickup driver to step out of his vehicle.

Pierson was slapping on the cuffs when the second officer whispered, "I thought we were just supposed to bring him in. What's with the cuffs?"

"That was before he handed me *my brother's* license. I can't prove he was involved in that robbery this afternoon, but I can guarantee he was involved in one at 1320 Maple, Oak Park, Atlanta, last week!"

A dope dealer in "Home Sweet Home," incriminated by one of his buyers, decided he'd do well to get off the street for a bit, and arranged to stay at his girlfriend's place until his picture in the post office was covered by something bigger and better. Not a bad plan, really—if your girlfriend isn't the sheriff's housekeeper, and the sheriff's housekeeper doesn't live in! The dealer was arrested; the housekeeper ended up looking for a new place to live and a new job.

A thief in "Just a Little Pink in the Center," who lit upon the brilliant notion that the doctors' staff room of a Salisbury, England, hospital might be a terrific spot to score some pagers, thus raising some quick cash, ran into a bit of trouble when a security guard saw him ducking back into the hallway.

He took off, quickly losing the chubby guard, but was left with the problem of how to escape the hospital. Even if the guard hadn't physically tracked him down, the thief was sure a description had been passed along to all entrances. He could wander around the hospital, which would likely lead to his immediate capture, or he could find somewhere to hole up until the uproar died down, and then sneak out with the visiting-hours crew.

He'd decided on finding himself an empty bed for a few hours when, sneaking along the hallway, he spotted a vertical tanning bed! Here was a way to hide out and get himself a free solarium session at the same time! Stripping off, he hid his clothes and the pagers, set the timer for forty-five minutes, then hopped inside and got comfortable.

Sadly, the pager thief hadn't realized this was no ordinary tanning bed. Designed to treat a variety of skin conditions, including burns, it emitted radiation on an unusual wavelength, and was used only in ten-second bursts! He'd taken three hundred times the normal dosage, was covered in blisters, and, on finally escaping this hospital by pulling surgical greens to pass as a doctor, immediately drove himself to the emergency entrance of Southampton General, twenty minutes away.

He still might have pulled the scheme off, having traded large sections of his hide for a half-dozen pagers, if the observant doctors at Southampton hadn't noticed this "doctor's" greens were stamped with the laundry mark for Salisbury! Why would any physician in this sorry state *not* get treated at his own hospital?

It's not just cops and doctors who can spot the oddities that lead to arrests. In "What's Under the Hood?," a mechanic from Texas was swift to report the presence of eighteen packets of marijuana found wedged around the engine compartment of a customer's car.

When asked why she'd left the evidence in plain view to anyone lifting the hood, the woman replied that she wasn't aware you had to lift the hood to change the oil!

A bunch of drug traffickers were a little more mechanically savvy. When the crooks in "I've Got Gas!" decided to bring 6,240 pounds of marijuana over the border into El Paso, Texas, from Mexico, they knew they'd have to be technically perfect to get away clean. Realizing that their transport vehicle of choice, a propane tanker, would have to be functional when it was inspected at the border crossing, they carefully packed their dope into a central package, then flooded the remaining space with real gas. No matter which of the six nozzles the border guards checked, propane would whistle out.

It was with considerable confidence, then, that this bunch of crooks approached their interview with the border crossing personnel. Sure enough, they checked the gas outlets and, finding everything in order, proceeded with the usual questions.

"Business or pleasure?"

"Business."

"Purpose of visit?"

"Taking the truck to the garage. Can't get parts for it across the border."

"Duration of stay?"

"Hoping to go home tomorrow."

The interviewer was about to pass the truck on through when his partner eyed the logo on the side and lifted an eyebrow. The crooks might have been technically perfect, but they certainly weren't *letter* perfect—they'd misspelled the name of the gas company!

Considering the role that luck, good and bad, plays in most crimes, it's not surprising that some crooks develop their own little superstitions, or that they might look for a little extra insight from time to time.

In "1-900-PSY-CHIC," a sly house thief might well have gotten away with everything, the break and entry, the theft, even the use of the homeowner's Magic Fingers bed, if not for the call he made to his favorite psychic hotline. After managing to leave nothing of himself behind, he gave his real name when he requested his "personal psychic reading"! When the homeowner discovered the 900 number on his bill, on the same night as the robbery, he faxed the bill to the police and let the wheels of justice turn until the hot line produced the name that eventually brought the thief to his day in court!

And they say psychic hot lines don't help anyone!

"Beauty and the Thief" is the ultimate caught-by-close-observation tale. While a Pennsylvania purse snatcher's victim was carefully committing her assailant's face to memory, her mugger was taking in every detail of the woman's striking features. Even with his gun hiding one whole side of her face, she remained the most beautiful woman he'd ever seen!

In the weeks following the robbery, our mugger simply couldn't get the woman out of his mind. Remembering that he had, after all, stolen her wallet, with all her identification inside, he rummaged through it for more than money and, with her address in hand, penned his very first love letter.

It wasn't the usual love letter, of course— more like a cautious negotiation. He'd give her his pager number. If she called him back, he'd meet her for drinks, return the wallet and money (which, on reflection, he was terribly sorry for having stolen from the woman he loved), and start over again.

She called the pager.

He agreed to meet her at her favorite bar.

She identified him.

He got arrested.

She got her wallet and never looked back.

ANYTHING TO AVOID CAPTURE

Unlike the crooks who turn themselves in, a different segment of the crime club entertains us by going to extremes, stupid extremes, to avoid their stint in the clink.

In "The Lost Boot," a simple drunk-driving checkpoint sparked a cross-country chase when one driver decided to protest this inconvenience by shooting at the officer signaling him to one side with the big flashlight, running the barricade, and attempting to run over two more officers before streaking toward the open road.

By the time our rebel ran out of gas, four police cars and a volunteer fireman in the station's tanker (who joined the procession just to see what was going on) had joined the chase. Undeterred, the fugitive jumped from the sputtering car and made for the nearest field and a thick stand of woods beyond it.

If not for the cold autumn rains, the

escape might have proven much easier. As it was, the rebel found himself trudging through knee-deep mud, thick, sticky, and freezing cold. It slowed his pursuers, but left him at the far end of the field without his boots! Still undaunted, he plunged into the thick underbrush.

He might have made it, too, if not for an elderly woman who saw the search parties, noticed that the door to her outhouse hadn't swung in the breeze all afternoon, and put two and two together. Following the woman's pointing finger, they cornered their prey in the outhouse, where the driver, still dreaming of escape, was wrapping whole rolls of toilet paper around his nearly frozen feet, preparatory to continuing his mad dash through the wilds, in temperatures approaching 15 degrees Fahrenheit!

A drunk driver wished he had a clear line of flight when he failed "The Sobriety Test" given at roadside and was tossed in the back of a patrol car for a trip downtown. Compared to the chaos a drunk-driving charge would rain down on him, frostbite seemed mild punishment.

At the station, he asked to visit the bathroom before taking the test. The cops agreed, but when he failed to come out after a reasonable time, they burst in. Their DUI suspect did not look well. Curled into a ball on the floor, the man was clearly unconscious—with blue foam oozing from his mouth!

A few hours after rushing the perp to the

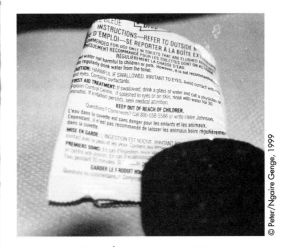

© Peter/Ngaire Genge, 1999

"Breath mint, anyone?"

hospital, the situation cleared up for everyone. The cops discovered that the popular DUI urban legend, that a Breathalyzer test can be fooled by breath mints, lives on, that their driver believed it, and that, desperate and caught without his breath mints, he'd substituted the sanitation disk from the urinal!

The driver discovered that, far from escaping his fate by half killing himself and putting an extra few hours between his last beer and the Breathalyzer, his arrival at the hospital had effectively frozen time. The breath test couldn't deliver reliable results now, but, the blood drawn on his arrival in the emergency room could be tested at the lab's leisure!

The moral here, of course, is that even the most daring antics can't turn back time or give criminals a second chance. The tales are meant to reassure us, but the sheer desperation behind them—eating a urinal tablet?—only makes these fugitives appear that much more alien.

TALES OF INVESTIGATIONS AND COMMONLY HELD CRIMINAL BELIEFS

For good or ill, popular films and police procedural novels are as close as most people ever get to observing law enforcement in action. Occasionally a spectacular crime so shocks the public that media correspondents actually report the entire proceedings from the first news break to the bitter dregs of a verdict, but, on the whole, we remain wonderfully isolated from judicial reality. Even those films and books lauded for their cutting-edge realism propagate as many myths as they attempt to debunk.

A case in point arose when the film *Seven* debuted in theaters. Amid the dozens of factual insights into police procedure presented, one event, one incident, one "fact" sank deep into the psyches of American audiences—and that one fact was the most misrepresented, the most horribly inaccurate, of all the methodology portrayed!

Anyone who's seen the film knows how Morgan Freeman's character tracked the bad guy by tracing the names of people who'd checked out certain "subversive" books from public libraries. Perhaps it was the image of law-enforcement agencies conspiring with all those little old ladies who hiss "Quiet!" at you while you work that captured public imagination. Or perhaps the thought of Big Brother invading the halls of academia and the repositories of knowledge and free speech actually managed to shake even our blasé attitude to government intervention in our private lives. In any case, the belief that libraries kept secret lists of select books and records of everyone using them quickly gained acceptance.

It's simply not true.

On the contrary, laws in place nearly a decade before *Seven* strictly prohibit libraries from attempting to assemble "profiles" of their clients, and those same laws prevent the government from even suggesting such schemes.

According to staff at the New York Public Library, "We don't even sell our client list to the ad agencies! And that could probably bring us in millions!"

Nor do airport officials, border guards, or customs and excise officials have a set profile of the "typical" drug smuggler. "Strip Search," set in an airport security area, is nearly unique among legends. Instead of spreading a common belief, it actively attacks a misconception, proving that anyone *could* fit the smuggling mold.

The original legend, "The Missing Remote," is a thoroughly nasty piece of work, detailing a husband's exhaustive search for the television remote control that he'd normally find in his obese wife's hand. When all else fails, he eventually searches the woman herself, then delights in telling anyone who'll listen that the remote, along with a half-decayed pork-chop bone, was found among her many rolls of fat!

"The Strip Search" also features an overweight person, but this time it's a man who, from the description of two security guards, manages to come across as genial enough, even if hefty—a far cry from the woman, who's portrayed as not only fat, but slovenly, unclean, and lazy.

The man of this tale, we're given to understand, wouldn't even have attracted undue notice if not for the suspicious activities of the drug-sniffing dog. Despite having searched the overweight man's pockets and carry-on bags, the dog continued to act as if it'd keyed on one of its target drugs!

Eventually, with much reluctance (certainly more than the husband showed his wife) the guards pull the man aside and insist that he retire to a side room to be strip-searched. They attempt to proceed with respect, but, well, a strip-search just isn't a cordial procedure, and when they discover a long, thin bag containing eleven ounces of cocaine concealed between two rolls of fat, they're forced to concede that the dog was a better judge of character than they were!

That this tale began as a story with little purpose other than to degrade, and finishes as a cautionary tale against judging by appearances, is one of the nicer ironies of the world of urban legend.

Another irony shows up in "Three Times, You're Safe." While several dramatic buildups have accompanied this tale, the *Reader's Digest* version goes something like this: If a hooker asks her john "Are you a cop?" three times, and is told "No" each time, she can't be arrested for solicitation.

Again, wrong.

Police officers—justice's first line of defense—are exempt from any requirement to answer a citizen's question honestly! While a criminal can be charged for lying to elude capture, cops can legally lie to anyone they like, even for the purpose of entrapping citizens who are supposedly innocent until *proven* guilty.

An even older legend contends that anyone who survives the state's attempt to carry out a capital-punishment sentence can't be subjected to their tender ministrations again. In effect, you can't kill the same person twice for the same crime.

Again, not true.

While some pardons have been issued to survivors, there's no legal requirement to let the "lucky" ones go. You may not be able to kill a man twice, but the state can't stop you from *half-*killing him twice!

With execution methods becoming more efficient, and better technology making it more difficult to fool physicians into declaring a severely traumatized body dead, fewer and fewer criminals survive to question their legal status. But this doesn't stop popular culture from returning to the perceived conundrum's dramatic potential again and again.

A tale that plays directly into two common beliefs about police investigations—that no doughnut or piece of cake is safe around a cop, and that evidence is frequently mishandled—"The Evidence" is a short story, even by urban-legend standards. A piece of wed-

© Peter/Ngaire Genge, 1999

"Does that look like a lunch bag to you?"

ding cake is bagged as evidence. The bag gets left on the lunchroom counter by a careless cop. The cake gets eaten. Only afterward does the careless cop realize the cake was bagged as evidence in a poisoning case wherein the new bride was anxious to become a new widow!

In an eerie coincidence, the British newspaper *The Guardian* reported the following: "Sign seen in Christchurch, New Zealand, police canteen: 'Will the person who took a slice of cake from the Commissioner's Office return it immediately. It is needed as evidence in a poisoning case.'"

Weird.

WHEN LAWS ARE STUPID, TOO

Did you know that it's illegal in Canada to board a plane while it's in flight?

No?

And you probably can't think of one good reason for anyone to ever enact such legislation either, right?

How about this one: It is against the law for a monster to enter the corporate limits of Urbana, Illinois?

Monsters?

Planes, at least, exist, and factoring in bizarre stunts or even terrorist activity, the inventive mind could *eventually* construct some scenario that might possibly explain why it would be illegal to board a Canadian plane in flight, but monsters?

Well, if you were looking for entertainment in 1890s America, you would probably find it in a traveling show, a circus, or a minstrel troupe. Minstrel troupes or theater companies performed plays, gave dramatic readings, sang selections from operettas, and danced—but basically kept their clothes on. A circus wasn't the wide-ranging show of today, and was generally defined as an animal show. Lion tamers, equestrian acts (including trick riding and shooting, though these later became thematic Wild West shows), boxing bears, and the like made up the majority of acts. A traveling show, on the other hand, featured human beings, many naked to better display their peculiarities, as the main attraction. There were vaudevillian side shows, haunted houses with real people popping out of the woodwork, and the human freak show: the bearded lady, the two-headed boy, the alligator man, giants, dwarves, and, yes, monsters, those acts that didn't fit any other categories. One famous monster had Proteus syndrome, the disorder from which John Merrick, the "Elephant Man," suffered; another was an unrecognized victim of leprosy!

As it turns out, the monster actually could enter the corporate limits, if it had a license to do so. Such licenses could, of course, be obtained from the town hall for a fee.

With all their "heretofores" and "sobeits" and "wherewithals," the average Joe could spend hours reading legal documents and, at the end, be not one whit wiser than when he began, so it's no surprise that lists of apparently incomprehensible laws are one of the most popular of the faxlore group of urban legends. The following sampling of laws that are or have been on the books has only one purpose: to illustrate how pompous or foolish we can appear when given the opportunity to sound profound.

- **In Brewton, Alabama, it's illegal to operate a motorboat on city streets.**

- **In Tennessee, it is illegal to drive a car while you are asleep.**

- **In Baldwin Park, California, nobody may ride a bike in a swimming pool.**

- **In Memphis, Tennessee, no woman shall operate a car unless a man is running or walking in front of the car waving a red flag to warn approaching pedestrians and motorists.**

- **In Connecticut, bicyclists traveling in excess of 65 miles per hour can be stopped by the police.**

- **In Devon, Connecticut, walking backward after sunset is unlawful.**

- **In Minnesota, it's illegal to stand in front of a moving train.**

- **In Belvedere, California, one municipal ordinance reads, "No dog shall be in a public place without its master on a leash."**

- **In France, you cannot park or land flying saucers in any vineyard.**

- **In Florida, you cannot hunt or kill deer while swimming.**

- **In Norfolk, Virginia, hens can't lay after 4:00 P.M. or before 8:00 A.M.**

- **In Memphis, Tennessee, it's illegal for frogs to croak after 11:00 P.M.**

- In Maine, it's against the law to molest an alligator.

- In Greece, kissing a woman in public can lead to the death sentence.

- In Kentucky, women between the weights of ninety and two hundred pounds, appearing in a bathing suit on a public highway, must be escorted by at least two officers or armed with a club.

- In Los Angeles, infants are forbidden to dance in public halls.

- In West Virginia, a man can only legally marry his first cousin if she's under the age of fifty-five.

- In Kentucky, you may remarry the same man four times, but not five.

- In Dyersburg, Tennessee, it is unlawful for a woman to call a man and ask him out.

- In Idaho, it is illegal for a man to give his sweetheart a box of candy weighing less than fifty pounds.

- In Newcastle, Wyoming, the law specifically bans couples from having sex while standing inside a store's walk-in meat freezer.

- In New Mexico, females are forbidden to appear unshaven in public.

- In Joliet, Illinois, a woman can be arrested for trying on more than six dresses in one store.

- In Florida, it is illegal for a housewife to break more than three dishes in one day.

- In Denver, it is against the law to lend your vacuum cleaner to your next-door neighbor.

- In Chicago, it is illegal to eat in a place that is on fire.

- In Xenia, Ohio, spitting in salad bars is unlawful.

- In Lexington, Kentucky, it's unlawful to carry an ice cream cone in your pocket.

- In Pueblo, Colorado, growing dandelions is illegal.

- In Natoma, Kansas, it's illegal to practice knife-throwing at men wearing striped suits.

- In Louisiana, it is illegal to rob a bank and shoot the bank teller with a water squirter.

- In Hawaii, it is against the law to insert pennies in your ear.

- In South Carolina, if you inadvertently kill someone while attempting suicide, you have committed a capital offense punishable by death.

- In Maine, a law calls for a legal hunting season on all attorneys.

- In New York, it's illegal to do anything illegal.

IN THE HALLOWED HALLS

Although popularly depicted as arenas of high justice, the battlegrounds of truth, the last stand of the innocent man, courts are, more often than the legal profession would like to admit, the places where people in suits (or robes) get together to make public their glaring humanity.

A case in point, "The Bulge"—which, incidently, couldn't have happened at all if not for the firm belief that defendants were required to wear a suit to court—left the judge in stitches and the defendant wishing he'd sewn his lips shut instead of demanding his day in court.

Still, our defendant, accused of minor drug-possession charges, began his appearance in court with what he honestly believed was a legitimate argument: he'd been searched without a warrant.

The judge's eyebrows rose as he looked at the arresting officer. "Is that true?"

"Yes, Your Honor. But we didn't feel we needed a warrant in this particular case."

"Really?"

"Yes, Your Honor. The defendant had a suspicious bulge in his coat and we had an honest fear that he was carrying a gun."

"A gun? A bulge?" The defendant jumped to his feet and appealed to the bench. "Your Honor, this suit I'm wearing is the exact same suit I was wearing that day. Do you see a 'bulge'?"

"Well, no, I can't say I do."

With a triumphant smile, the defendant handed the jacket up to the judge. "Now, sir, if you'll put your hand in the pockets, you'll see that it was impossible for these officers to see any 'bulge,' either!" The startled judge pulled his hand out and found himself staring at a packet of marijuana. "See, that's the same amount I was carrying that night! If you didn't see no 'bulge,' sir, then neither did they and they had no right to search me without a warrant!"

Only when the judge burst into laughter did the defendant appear to realize he'd just proven, in court and on the record, that he was carrying two bags of marijuana on two different occasions!

Suits feature rather prominently in "The Green Double-Breasted" as well. A Michigan youth was told by his probation officer that he needed to make a really good impression on the judge at his preliminary hearing if he had any hope of being tried in youth court for his most recent break-and-enter.

The young man took this advice seriously. He had no desire to do hard time in an adult institution. So, on the morning of the hearing, he made sure that his hair was neatly trimmed, that his shoes gleamed, and that he was wearing the nicest suit in his closet, a green double-breasted model of watered silk!

His lawyer looked pleased with his appearance, the judge even nodded at him as he settled into his seat, and his probation officer gave him a quick high sign from the back of the courtroom. The victim, the homeowner, however, was outraged!

"Your Honor, I protest! That's *my* suit he's wearing!"

A quick check of the designer label confirmed the claim.

The next time the youth stood before the bench, he was wearing a bright orange jumpsuit and cuffs!

There's no record of what a Texan convicted of sexual assault, who stars in "I Didn't Say Nothing!," wore to court the day he decided to launch an appeal against a piece of information he felt was wrongly admitted at his trial.

During his original trial, one officer had stated that upon being arrested, the defendant had immediately "defecated in his pants."

The defendant, quite rightly, thought this information portrayed him in a bad light and prejudiced the jury against him.

The prosecutor, however, won the day with the unusual argument that the state of the defendant's pants should come under the section of the law that allowed a suspect's "excited utterances" to be admitted in court!

No wonder the public refers to legal arguments as "verbal diarrhea"!

"The Man Who Represents Himself Has a Fool for a Client," the tale of an armed robber who fired his own lawyer midway through his trial, serves only to prove the adage.

Although he appeared to handle the first six witnesses against him with the same grace that any overworked and underpaid public defender might have managed, he sort of lost it when the store owner, in whose face he'd once waved his gun, pointed at him across the courtroom and

declared in a loud, clear voice, "I'd know his ugly face anywhere."

The defendant surged to his feet, his face flushed and his tie looking decidedly tight as he shouted, "You bitch! I shoulda blown your &$#)! head off!" As gasps went up around the room, the man suddenly caught himself in mid-roar and calmly added, "If I'd been the one in your store that night."

The jury convicted him to thirty years in less than twenty minutes.

"The *Star Trek* Fan" had a completely different reaction as his trial on the charge of drunk driving continued and the evidence against him became overwhelming. Instead of yelling at and threatening the many witnesses called to testify to his state of intoxication, this defendant squirmed lower and lower in his chair.

His lawyer, the judge, and the gallery eyed the man out of the corners of their eyes, but since he wasn't doing anything threatening, they said nothing.

The next witness was the physician who'd examined all those involved in the accident. His testimony, that the defendant was so drunk on admission that he "hadn't been able to find the arms in his sweater after his exam," left the gallery laughing—which explains why it was several minutes before they noticed the defendant's latest antics.

Scrunched even farther down in the chair, the about-to-be-convicted driver had pulled out his wallet, flipped it open, and, accompanied by a series of clicks and whistles, was now talking to it in a hoarse whisper. "It's getting bad down here, Scotty, how much longer?"

Weird, yes, but, as he still wasn't actually disrupting the trial, the prosecutor simply called his last witness, the lab chemist who'd analyzed the defendant's blood sample. His conclusion: "The defendant's blood alcohol level was *three times* the legal limit!"

At that moment the defendant dove under the table, flipped open his wallet once more, and yelled, "Now, Scotty! Now! Beam me up!"

He must have been terribly disappointed not to dissolve in a wash of glittery special effects.

However strange these legends may seem, however inexplicable the actions of those involved (and remember, these legends grew from partially remembered or partially understood reports of real cases), courts have an equally strange effect on those who earn their living inside them day after day. For nearly twenty years, stupid courtroom quotes have made popular faxlore topics. Here's a sampling, all from actual case transcripts, to prove that lawyers can look just as foolish as their clients. The moral? Lawyers are people too. They can, occasionally, even laugh at themselves.

"Now, doctor, isn't it true that when a person dies in his sleep, he doesn't know about it until the next morning?"

"The youngest son, the twenty-year-old, how old is he?"

"Were you present when your picture was taken?"

"Were you alone or by yourself?"

"Was it you or your brother who was killed in the war?"

"Did he kill you?"

"How far apart were the vehicles at the time of the collision?"

"You were there until the time you left, correct?"

"How many times have you committed suicide?"

Q.—*So the date of conception (of the baby) was August 8th?*
A.—*Yes.*
Q.—*And what were you doing at that time?*

Q.—*She had three children, right?*
A.—*Yes.*
Q.—*How many were boys?*
A.—*None.*
Q.—*Were there any girls?*

Q.—*You say the stairs went down to the basement?*
A.—*Yes.*
Q.—*And these stairs, did they go up also?*

Q.—*You went on a rather elaborate honeymoon, didn't you?"*
A.—*I went to Europe, sir.*
Q.—*And you took your wife?*

Q.—How was your first marriage terminated?

A.—By death.

Q.—And by whose death was it terminated?

Q.—Can you describe the individual?

A.—He was about medium height and had a beard.

Q.—Was this a male, or a female?

Q.—Is your appearance here this morning pursuant to a deposition notice which I sent to your attorney?

A.—No, this is how I always dress when I go to work.

Q.—Doctor, how many autopsies have you performed on dead people?

A.—All of them, I hope!

Q.—All your responses must be oral, okay? . . . What school did you go to?

A.—Oral.

Q.—Do you recall the time that you examined the body?

A.—The autopsy started around 4:30 P.M.

Q.—And Mr. Dennington was dead at the time?

A.—No, he was sitting on the table wondering why I was doing an autopsy!

Q.—You were not shot in the fracas?

A.—No, I was shot midway between the fracas and the navel.

Q.—Are you qualified to give a urine sample?

A.—Yup, have been since early childhood.

"How long have you been French Canadian?"

"Do you have any children, or anything of that kind?"

"Were you present in court this morning when you were sworn in?"

"Was that the same nose you broke as a child?"

All of which go to prove another old adage drummed into all law students: "Never ask a question you don't already know the answer to!"

THE THINGS LAWYERS WILL DO!

Urban legends love setting up authority figures just to tear them down again a few lines later, which gives us average folks a nice, warm, fuzzy feeling inside, so no collection of legal legends would be complete without a few (of the many!) tales of lawyers clearly out of their element. And what makes the following four tales so deliciously sinful is, of course, that though they've now become generically legendary, they all began life as honest-to-goodness truths!

Horace Greeley once said, "I'd trust my life to my lawyer, but I wouldn't let him bandage a scuffed knee," meaning that while no one lawyers better than a lawyer, they probably shouldn't dabble in other, more prosaic aspects of life. Take the lawyer in "Here, Kitty, Kitty!" He'd worked a long day, driven a long way home, and was ready to get at least half drunk before falling into bed. He was working toward that goal when he went to the kitchen for some extra ice. Balance wasn't really his forte by that point, and his staggering steps weren't aided by the Persian kitten hopping around his feet and trying to rub its fur all over his black trouser legs!

Despite a strong desire to kick it aside, he forced himself to step around it each time. The cat belonged to his wife, and for reasons he couldn't understand, she was quite fond of it. Still, it persisted in purring and twining its tail around first one shin, then the other, while he filled his glass and the ice bucket. He'd just picked up a new bottle to carry back to the living room when disaster struck.

His shoe landed on the cat's tail, the cat yowled, the lawyer tripped, and the cat was doused in a fine single-malt Scotch! Having thus far managed to keep his little bender to himself and not wake his wife upstairs, he certainly didn't want some cat, soaked and stinking of booze, to race to the bedroom and jump on the bed next to her!

Glancing about the kitchen, he didn't see a towel, but he did see the microwave oven . . . or at least that's what he told his lawyer and the judge when he was charged with the death of one Persian cat.

A Toronto tale, "The Long Fall," proves that lawyers shouldn't attempt to upstage tour guides. One lawyer, who worked in the Toronto Dominion Bank Tower, a state-of-the-art complex with dozens of then-innovative features, frequently played host to visiting colleagues and law students, showing them around the firm's offices on the twenty-fourth floor, and demonstrating some of the building's new gizmos.

His favorite demo involved an explanation of how the windows themselves contributed to the structural strength of the tower and how even a full-grown man couldn't break one of the huge panes. To illustrate his point, he habitually backed up a few paces from one window, took a short run at it, and bounced off.

You can see this coming, can't you?

One morning, while leading a bunch of students about, he did his usual routine, but instead of bouncing back, he broke through the window, plummeting to the courtyard below.

Lawyers should stick to lawyering.

Perhaps the most famous lawyer legend is "The Heart Attack." Like the others, it's based on fact; unlike the others, the legend itself completely contradicts the facts it's based on.

A group of recently graduated lawyers had gathered for one of the examinations required by the bar association of the state of California. Needless to say, people were anxious and edgy. After all those years of education, this was the test that would determine whether or not they could actually practice law and start paying off those student loans!

When the examiners said, "You may now begin," a hush fell over the room and only the sound of pencils scribbling could be heard—at least for the first three-quarters of the exam. In the last half hour, one hopeful, an elderly man, suddenly grabbed his chest and tumbled to the floor! All around him, other would-be lawyers continued to scribble, ignoring the man's pleas for help! Of the hundred or so gathered for the exam, only two felt moved to leave their seats and begin CPR.

After the ambulance arrived and took the still-gasping man away, the two Samaritans returned to their seats just as the timer indicating the end of the test period sounded. The two continued to scribble madly, but were told to hand in their papers. They could not have extra time!

Their fellows looked on sympathetically, but made no comment when the two handed in their papers.

Word of the event spread quickly, of course, and, before long someone called the bar association offices demanding to know if these two saints wouldn't receive some sort of adjustment to their scores based on their willingness to assist their fellow hopeful. The association's response: "We weren't testing their CPR skills, just their knowledge of law. We have no comment at this time."

There's a part of everyone that believes goodness, selflessness, and charity should be rewarded, and in the face of this display of callousness, great indignation arose in response to the story of the two Samaritans who were punished for saving a life! Eventually, the legend continues, the two flunked and couldn't repeat the test for another six months!

In the way of legends, other little bits gradually associated themselves with this story. One of the students, about to declare bankruptcy, committed suicide instead. The other, struck by a car driven by a lawyer, died in the street when no one would stop to help her.

As with all legends, separating the truth from the fiction of this story isn't easy, especially when casting lawyers in the worst possible light seems to satisfy so many listeners and storytellers! However, in this case, the truth isn't that well hidden—especially as the two Good Samaritans, both quite alive, actually appeared in several public forums to debunk the wilder aspects of the legend.

Yes, they did take the bar exam. Yes, a man fell over with an apparent heart attack. Yes, they were the only ones administering CPR—but CPR is a *two-person* task. Anyone else joining in the effort would have had *nothing* to do. The situation was under control, trained help was on the way, there was no need for further assistance! As to whether or not anyone else *would* have helped had the need arisen, they had no doubt any help necessary would have been forthcoming.

Okay, what about the exam supervisors? Weren't they coldhearted in demanding these two hand in their exams? Couldn't they have given them another half hour?

No. To do so would have *invalidated* the exam! In other words, the three-quarters of the test they had completed would have been thrown out as well—eliminating any hope they had of passing. (And, as noted by others taking this exam, the last half hour of the exam may have consisted of nothing more than a spelling and grammar check. Many people finish their bar exams with a half hour to spare. It's entirely possible that with only a half hour left in the exam period, these two would have been nearly finished anyway. They certainly would not have wanted to chance invalidation of a *completed* examination!) In any case, the examiners had no authority to permit extra time. Any irregularities that might merit special consideration would have to be addressed by the bar association itself.

Right, the same people who refused to give them special consideration because they "weren't testing their CPR skills"?

That's not what was actually said. The Association's decision on whether or not to make adjustments for special circumstances would only have been made *after* the pair actually flunked. If they passed, there was no reason to consider special circumstances and mark adjustment. As it happens, both first-aiders passed their entrance exam *without* any mark adjustments whatsoever!

But, still, surely they could have done better if they'd been given the extra time?

It's irrelevant. This is an all-or-nothing situation. They were either allowed to practice law in California or they weren't. They wouldn't be allowed to practice *more* law if they got higher scores.

So, broken down to its component pieces, it seems this tale proves nothing at all about lawyers!

The tale's final form does, however, reveal something about the audience: Though we all protest the callous treatment we believed the lawyers to have received from their peers, *not one version of this tale tells us if the heart attack victim lived or died, and no one ever asks!*

Lawyers study other lawyers the way actors study old movies, always hoping for a new trick, a new tactic they can use in their own cases, some little thing that will catch the jury's or the judge's eye. Often these ploys are quite visual. An American example, the image of O.J. Simpson trying to squeeze his hands into those bloody gloves proved the turning point for many observers who'd remained undecided of his guilt or innocence. Whether you believe the demonstration actually proved anything is irrelevant. The image stuck, and perception is at least ninety percent of any trial.

In "But It Can't!," an Irish lawyer recognizes the dramatic potential in reenacting a portion of the crime for one of his own cases, and quickly arranges for the suspect's coat and the murder weapon, a long-barreled pistol, to be brought forward. From his own observations he's convinced it's simply not possible for his client to have pulled that weapon from that coat pocket without shooting himself!

When the prosecutor protests that it would be impossible to prove such a contention one way or the other, the defense attorney proposes a demonstration. Perhaps too blinded by their own curiosity, no one seems to see the danger until the lawyer, with the coat on and the gun in place, actually attempts to pull it out.

He shoots himself in the foot and dies that same day!

He'd likely have been pleased to know that his client was acquitted.

AFTER THE CAGE CLOSES

As any lawyer would tell you, a conviction may be only half of the legal story. With appeals and in-prison behavior taken into account, the sentence originally handed down may have little to do with the time a prisoner actually serves—or with his quality of life after becoming a guest of the state.

Take the real case of Allan Kinsella, which so appealed to other inmates that prisoners in Mexico were soon recounting the tale among themselves—though Allan had already become Juan.

When Kinsella, a convicted killer, was brought back into court on charges he'd escaped from his lawful confinement in a medium-security jail, he not only agreed with the charge against him, but had already prepared a countersuit *against the prison.* According to Kinsella, the prison had practically entrapped him into attempting an escape; his suit charged that the jail had "aided and abetted" his escape by allowing a contractor working on the premises to leave a ladder leaning against an outside wall. If the prison was going to leave ladders hanging about, what exactly did they expect prisoners to do? Return them?

While most people would concede that Kinsella had a point there, prison clearly alters a man's thinking in ways no one on the outside can really comprehend, switching priorities into completely new hierarchies that those who've never been to jail wouldn't dream of. That there *are* changes in perspective is made evident, however, by the variety of suits and countersuits convicts dream up, and pursue, while behind bars.

In New York, a prisoner convicted of rape claimed he could no longer sleep and that he'd suffered severe chest and head pains ever since an unqualified barber, permitted onto the premises as part of the barber school's apprenticeship program, gave him a "defective haircut."

Inmates on death row file more appeals and suits than any other group—perhaps they feel they've got nothing to lose—but a San Quentin inmate's suit against the state of California stretched the civil rights statutes to the very limit when he claimed his rights were

Anyone who can see a disguise in a can of whipped cream deserves *A* for effort,
F for common sense!

violated when his packages were shipped via UPS instead of by the U.S. Postal Service.

Though that one might cause raised eyebrows, this next one makes perfect sense to millions: An Oklahoma inmate, serving an extended sentence, sued his prison, his warden, and his state for forcing him to listen to hours and hours of country music!

An Ohio inmate sued because he was denied soap on a rope.

A convict in Colorado sued for early release based on an urban legend! His claim: "Everyone knows a con only serves about three years of a ten-year sentence."

A Utah man escaped and promptly sued the sheriff for negligence!

A different man, but with similar notions, sued the county for the mental and emotional stress he endured while trying to escape custody.

Clifford Olson, a multiple murderer and sexual assailant, who once offered to *sell* the parents of his victims, eight little girls and three little boys, the locations of their children's bodies, isn't suing anyone, though it seems he's still indulging his capitalist dreams. He's recently registered a proposed new video series, *Motivational Sexual Homicide Patterns of Serial Child Killer Clifford Robert Olson,* with Canada's copyright office.

Crime may not pay, but it certainly produces some of the best fodder for urban legends.

The strangest disguise ever used in a bank robbery? One man in Louisiana sprayed his head, from collar to bald spot, in whipped cream!

6
THAT'S ENTERTAINMENT!

If ever an industry generated rumors, and their big cousins, urban legends, it would have to be the entertainment industry. Scandals, real and imagined, plague people, films, even recording studios. Some are true, some contain a hint of truth, some reflect simple misunderstanding of industry practice, and some are outright lies! Our fascination with celebrities keeps these tales spreading; our love of a good story makes us reluctant to give up the best of these legends, even for the truth.

In the next pages, you'll see distinct trends In entertalnment legends.

"They're not what they appear to be!" Whether it's a freckle-faced kid from 1950s programming, or the cartoons that flow into our homes on Saturday mornings, or the performers we perceive as being the most wholesome, legends exist to poke holes in their public personas. Most prove to be nothing more than empty accusations, but some are titillating enough to keep the rest circulating on the "If one, why not others?" ticket.

Other legends concentrate on tragedies, scandals, and deaths. "Didn't he die?" "I heard that show was canceled because the female lead wouldn't sleep with one of the executives!" "Did you know *everyone* to take that role died?" Stunts gone wrong, injuries and deaths from special effects, and films that had to close production when a key actor was murdered on the set make up the bulk of these tales.

Then there are production tales like the episode that was never shown because Company X didn't like the way its products were shown, or because the director refused to endorse a cut made by someone else, or because the actors stormed off the set, or the set exploded and couldn't be rebuilt cheaply enough to make finishing the episode practical. Production tales include anything offscreen that changed the story as we eventually saw it.

The sheer mass of entertainment legends can't be contained in a small section of one book, but these will give you a taste of the styles and types of legends commonly passed along. You'll never know how much of what you thought was true wasn't, until you read on.

FILMS

2001: A Space Odyssey added only one item of real urban folklore to the entertainment category, but it's a contentious one. Movie buffs hotly insist that naming the star computer HAL was a slap at IBM. Alphabetically, the letters H, A, and L immediately precede the letters I, B, and M. The buffs point out that the chances of this being a random coincidence are mathematically as astronomical as artificial life arising spontaneously in your pager, and that Arthur C. Clarke, the book's author, chose them to keep his machine one step "ahead" of Big Blue.

Clarke, for his part, denies it equally vehemently, and since he named the thing, he should know why he called it HAL as opposed to, say, Athena, right? His denial should be the end of it.

Why isn't it?

Because in all the drafts, HAL *is* named Athena. Only in the final copy was the change made, and that, the literary sleuths charge, smacks of anything *but* random chance.

So, if HAL *is* an IBM slap, why wouldn't Clarke admit it?

Perhaps because IBM provided most, if not all, of the technical computer advice for the film?

In *Air Force One,* much was made of the crew's efforts to re-create the presidential airplane—not easy, as the real thing is a high-security item. Still, if legend is to be believed, they must have done a damned good job—good enough to fool two F/A-18 pilots!

The two were dispatched to identify an unknown plane, made visual contact, saw the "bullet holes" along its side (they were stickers that could be removed or used as needed in a particular scene), and quickly radioed in that *Air Force One* was airborne and damaged!

The Los Angeles International Airport control tower sent back a real ID on the mystery plane, identifying it as a movie prop—a confirmation they had to send twice!

Publicity for the film remained coy on the whole topic.

> **For the film *The Abyss*, a not-yet-completed nuclear reactor was flooded to a depth of forty feet, creating the industry's largest underwater set, with a capacity of 7 million gallons! Cast members sometimes referred to it as the "big fish tank."**

• • • • • • •

According to movie legend, one studio executive, on seeing the first rushes of *Aliens*, couldn't quite grasp the whole concept (and obviously hadn't seen *Alien*). When the lights came back up, his first question was "What was that? There's no Mexicans in that!"

He thought the film was about illegal aliens sneaking across the California border!

That bit is actually pure legend, but it's probably based on a real incident featuring actress Jenette Goldstein, who would eventually play Vasquez. On the day of her audition, she arrived wearing heavy makeup and waist-length hair! Not very military—though it certainly made her stand out amid all the other actors who'd arrived in jungle fatigues. She really *did* think the film was about illegal aliens!

Not surprising for a film about farm animals, most of whom are destined for the family dinner table, legends associated with *Babe* all revolve around food.

When nearly every film targeted at the children's market sprouts a series of trading cards, its own line of licensed T-shirts and character figurines, and, of course, product placements for half a dozen food items, the distinct lack of *Babe* memorabilia was remarkable. No fuzzy stuffed pigs. No tradable collectible figurines. No frenzied bidding for a series of fast-food tie-ins.

According to the legend, both McDonald's and Burger King put their brightest minds to developing a marketing strategy that would see a white piglet in every Happy Meal or Kid's Deal, but none of these whiz kids could overcome the basic problem *Babe* presented: How to explain to a three-year-old that there really wasn't any *ham* in *ham*burgers? Wall Street's best were defeated by a childhood misconception.

For a film that didn't receive the hype of, say, *A Bug's Life* or even *Small Soldiers*, *Babe* did manage to attract more than its share of urban tales. In addition to the McDonald's/Burger King dust-up, there were the disturbing rumors, quickly growing to outrage among some populations, that the many piggies, forty-eight in all, that played *Babe* during filming all suffered the same fate, that they became barbecued ribs and pork chops for their human co-workers!

They didn't.

They were retired to farms and petting zoos, where they lived happily ever after.

Though several decades separate *Babe* and *Green Acres*'s porcine star, Arnold Ziffel, it's possible that one piggy legend inspired the other.

Humphrey Bogart, it's often reported, began his public career early as the model for the Gerber baby-food label. The setup is plausible enough. Bogart's mother, Maud Humphrey Bogart, was a well-respected illustrator. Her drawings and sketches, depicting children as rosy-cheeked cherubs, appeared on the cover of *Harper's*. She was the artist behind the Ivory brand promotions, and, yes, she illustrated baby-food products and the ads for those products. Her charming son was a natural model for her, and it's true she used him as her model for a baby-food label, just not the Gerber label. Humphrey Bogart appeared on the label of *Mellin's* baby food!

Dorothy Hope Smith drew the Gerber baby, and the model was Ann Turner, a child from her neighborhood.

Every set differs in temperament and style, usually based on the working habits of the director, the combination of personalities among the cast, and the physical surroundings created by the crew. Some deadly serious comedies become known for the practical jokes pulled on set; some romances come off despite downright antagonism between leads; some comedy sets could put the crew to sleep when the cameras stopped rolling! Other sets seem to take on the character of the film itself. When Dino De Laurentiis suggested his cast in *Conan the Barbarian* wear those leather outfits during rehearsals and

She's been smiling out at us for decades, but she's not Humphrey Bogart.

© Peter/Ngaire Genge, 1999

scene shoots, to give the costumes a more lived-in look, he should have known he'd have a set with a uniquely brawny sort of feel!

A legend that several scenes were shot *Apocalypse Now* style, that is, with the actors half drunk, isn't entirely true; that probably only happened during the outdoor scenes. It seems the fake blood used during the filming was a concentrate that was mixed with water as needed. It worked great inside, but tended to freeze into a slushy mess outdoors. To solve that little problem, the effects crew mixed the concentrate with vodka to keep it fluid. The problem was, several outside scenes required the actors to spit blood after being punched in the mouth. They swallowed the blood instead—necessitating several retakes, with more blood!

The Crow, the film Brandon Lee was making when he died on the set, was, if legend was to be believed, released with scenes of his death still incorporated in the final cut—much against the wishes of his family, who sued. Audiences seeing the "death scene" in theaters found it real enough when the character Eric Draven was knifed, then shot by several people, then tossed out a window, and if those *weren't* the fatal shots, how could Lee, already dead, have come back to shoot that scene?

The truth is that Lee was never in the scene at all.

The original script described the death scene quite differently, with Draven being shot immediately on entering his apartment. A bit of miniaturization on the part of the SFX people would have shown a tiny detonation in a paper bag of groceries to indicate the bullet's trajectory. It was during the shooting of *this* scene that a bit of dummy shell was accidentally fired at Brandon Lee. It was that dummy shell, not the ones fired in the onscreen scene, that caused his death.

So how did Brandon Lee appear in the second scene? The magic of Hollywood. Although digitization was fairly new in 1993, filmmakers added Lee's face to a double's body *after* the scene was shot with the double.

Lee's family did sue the production company for negligence in Lee's death, but not to have specific scenes of Brandon Lee's "death" removed from the film.

Shortly after *Die Hard* hit theaters, a rumor began spreading that some of the actors had slipped some naughty language past the censors by weaving it throughout the lines of the German-speaking terrorists! Apparently the censors don't speak German—or don't care if German-speaking viewers get offended.

Of course, the censors didn't mess up. Everyone knows censors always err on the side of boring, right?

It's true that many viewers couldn't follow all the German dialogue. It's also true that it's the "naughty" words that aren't usually covered in German 101. But that's not why no one could understand what the Germans were saying; the actors were speaking garbled German! Grammar, syntax, even vocabulary were thrown out the window. One line reputedly says, "Race up your back! Upside down!"

One of the most intriguing entertainment legends contends that David Lynch and Raffaella De Laurentiis saw Sean Young, who would later appear as Chani in *Dune,* on an airplane, found out she was an actress, auditioned her in flight from New York to Los Angeles, and hired her before landing!

Sort of a "Lana Turner and the malt shop" thing, yes?

Not exactly, but close. Lynch and De Laurentiis contacted Young's agent to arrange a screen test, but, for whatever reason, Young never got the message and was, in fact, booked on a flight to Los Angeles that evening and away from home all afternoon. Lynch and De Laurentiis were on the same flight, having missed the earlier flight they'd been scheduled to take. Seeing Young, they asked a stewardess to confirm her identity, then asked why they'd been stood up! Once the misunderstanding was cleared away, they spent the trip chatting and looking at the script. She completed the screen test in Los Angeles and the rest was film history.

Buddy Ebsen's entertainment legend, that he was fired from the cast of *The Wizard of Oz* and that his voice would have been eliminated from all the musical pieces already produced if it had been at all feasible, isn't only untrue, it's actually a lot less interesting than what actually happened.

Big productions come with big stress and big decisions—decisions like firing your director in mid-production, which is what happened to Richard Thorpe and resulted in the complete shutdown of the set. When shooting started again, there was no sign of Thorpe or Ebsen, and the two absentees would be connected by rumor. Jack Haley, who came in as the replacement Tin Woodsman, didn't realize Ebsen hadn't been fired for some time. No one tracked Thorpe's movements, but Ebsen's are a matter of record, *medical* record.

Ebsen spent two weeks in the hospital, suffering from a severe reaction to the powdered aluminum dust used to coat any of his skin not covered by costuming! Ebsen wasn't fired, but he nearly *died* from his short stint on the *Wizard of Oz* set!

The Empire Strikes Back, like most Lucas films, was produced to some amazingly high standards. Tales casting Lucas as a control

IN MEMORY OF . . .

Though many legends are about deaths that didn't occur on film sets, some are all too real.

- Ken Steadman died in a dune-buggy crash while filming the *Sliders* episode "Desert Storm" on September 20, 1996.
- Keith Perepelkin died while shooting *Firestorm* when his main parachute failed to open when he jumped from a helicopter onto a ship, the *Stawamus Chief,* in British Columbia, Canada, a stunt prohibited under the filming permit issued in Canada.
- Paolo Rigon died during filming of the bobsled scenes of *For Your Eyes Only.*
- Art Scholl, a veteran stunt pilot, died doing an inverted flat spin for *Top Gun.* The maneuver, always risky, may have gone out of control because the film gear attached to the plane compromised its stability.

freak aren't uncommon, but tales of rebellion against such strict supervision during production certainly are. One such legend is directly tied to production of *The Empire Strikes Back.* After asking the effects people to redo the asteroids of the asteroid storm some six times, they finally came to the conclusion that even Lucas couldn't possibly trace the exact path of each individual asteroid. To prove their point, they tossed a shoe through the scene on their next attempt, printed it, and ran it by Lucas. He approved it, and the shoe still exists in the film version!

Fargo created its entertainment legend—not to mention a really neat publicity angle—by opening with the claim, "This is a true story. The events depicted in this film took place in Minnesota in 1987. At the request of the survivors, the names have been changed. Out of respect for the dead, the rest has been told exactly as it occurred," and then going on to create one of the most twisted tales in modern film, one that includes bodies and wood chippers as major plot points!

Nowhere, however, is there any law or regulation that a movie has to tell the truth—even when it's claiming to tell the truth.

Though many people would try to identify the "innocents" that the film's producers, the Coen brothers, had tried to protect with fake names, there never were any innocents, or victims, to uncover, as *Fargo* was completely the fabrication of that pair of fertile minds.

The X-Files's creator, Chris Carter, pulled a similar stunt when the first episode of his new series began by claiming the events its audience were about to see were based on real events.

Friday the 13th, like most horror films, always attracted certain types of legends: that its cast members died horrible real-life deaths (untrue), that a real body was discovered on the scene (untrue), and that it was inspired by real events—except the real killer had never been caught and still roamed the countryside (also untrue). The unique legend coupled with this film is that, dissatisfied with the quality of "screamers" working on the picture, the director decided he needed more "realism." To achieve that, he sent a research assistant to bribe 911 operators into dubbing tapes of *real* victims giving *real* death-throe screams!

Any tape longer than ten minutes, without pesky voices, brought the operator five hundred dollars—cheap, compared with hiring a professional screamer at guild rates for the duration of the shoot.

The rumor is completely unfounded, but it does have the advantage of presenting a new tale, which means it'll probably be around for quite some time—at least the next several sequels.

Goldfinger created one of Hollywood's most enduring legends when audiences saw Shirley Eaton, apparently covered from head to toe in gold paint, sprawled across the screen. Rumors that the actress had died of asphyxiation, that she was already dead when this scene was filmed, that her death wasn't discovered until the scene was broken down, continue circulating thirty-five years later!

As it happens, humans don't "breathe" through their skins, though they do shed excess heat that way and, through hundreds of sweat glands, keep themselves cool. Overheating was a plausible response to being covered in paint, especially under studio lighting, but not suffocation. None of these things happened to Shirley Eaton, however, and she survived to perform in other films.

Groundhog Day, contrary to popular urban legend, was *not* halted while the Society for the Prevention of Cruelty to Animals investigated a violation against the lead groundhog. Filming was delayed briefly when Bill Murray was violated—*by the groundhog.* Murray was bitten twice by "Phil."

Hedy Lamarr, according to an entire string of legends that date from 1935 onward, shared an intimate relationship with scientists the likes of Albert Einstein and Nils Bohr, was the first woman to appear nude in a major

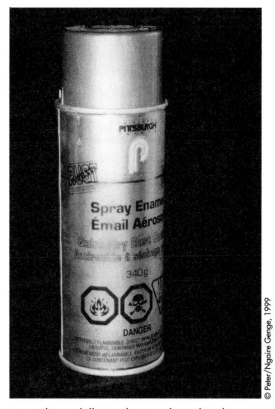

It might not kill you, but it's damn hard to get off after a day's shooting!

motion picture, sat down to supper with both Mussolini and Hitler, then, after sneaking herself and a mysterious package over the Alps and inspiring *The Sound of Music,* was instrumental in winning World War II!

Wow!

And at least half of it is true!

Before coming to Hollywood, Hedy Lamarr was Hedwig Eva Maria Kiesler Mandl, the Austrian wife of weapons manufacturer Fritz Mandl. Mandl sold his product to anyone who'd buy it, including, yes, Hitler and Mussolini. Not surprisingly, he actively wooed those important clients, and sparkling dinners of the rich and famous were a regular part of that effort. Naturally, he brought along his beautiful wife to charm his customers.

Since Lamarr hasn't made any public statements in nearly twenty years, identifying who else might have attended those dinners is difficult, but that the gatherings may have included high-ranking scientists of the time certainly isn't inconceivable. That she was intimate with Einstein or Bohr, however, is almost historically impossible. What might suggest it to the general public is the fact that Lamarr and a famous musician of the time once registered a "Secret Communication System," patent number 2,292,387, with the U.S. Patent Office. Some versions of the mixed-up story even suggest this secret system was what she secreted with her on her trip out of Austria, that she, horrified by what she'd heard around her for years, ran away for the express purpose of bringing this secret system to America.

All of which is actually less incredible than the real story.

Lamarr didn't inspire *The Sound of Music;* she did, however, live in Salzburg Castle, where the film was eventually shot, and she did run away from it. What she was really running from, though, was her husband. Mandl used Hedy. His jealousy kept her a virtual prisoner in her home; she couldn't leave a room without asking his permission! She brought nothing with her on that flight, certainly no secret machinery to win the war. She *was* a brilliant woman, however, and, once free to express herself in America, she finally had the opportunity to pursue intellectual puzzles. Her contribution to the Secret Communication System was substantial; her name on the patent was no honorific. Though she never earned a cent from it, it is now the basis for cellular service, Internet connectivity, and a host of other applications—including the guidance system of American missiles!

Luckily, she *was* paid for her performance in *Ecstasy,* the first feature film to include a nude female star.

Marilyn Monroe was, according to some of the vast number of Disney legends in circulation, the physical model for the animated characters of Cinderella and Tinker Bell in the animated versions of *Cinderella* (1950) and *Peter Pan* (1953).

While Monroe would no doubt have been delighted with either job—her 1949 film *Love Happy* brought in a whopping one hundred dollars!—she has absolutely no connection to either film.

Helene Stanley, who modeled Sleeping Beauty and the young wife in *101 Dalmatians,* a character to which she would later give her voice talents, was also the model for Cinderella. How did Monroe come to be connected with this film? In 1954, reporters became privy to a comment made within the Disney corporation that at least one critic thought Cinderella was altogether too "voluptuous." And who, in 1954, was the most voluptuous? None other than Marilyn Monroe. That Monroe had no connection with Disney Studios, and was unknown in 1949 when *Cinderella* was in production, didn't occur to anyone hearing about the "voluptuous model" after the fact in 1954.

No one is sure how Monroe was linked to *Peter Pan* and the Tinker Bell character. It may simply have been a carryover of the earlier rumor. Though Monroe was unknown in 1950, she was beginning to make a name for herself by 1953, and once the suggestion was planted, it would have been easy to see hints of Monroe in the animated sprite. Of course, it was much *easier* to see Margaret Kerry in those gamine features—if you knew Margaret Kerry. Margaret Kerry, however, despite being the model for Tinker Bell and providing a vocal credit for one of the mermaids in the same film, was, even then, less well known than Monroe.

One Flew Over the Cuckoo's Nest, a film about mental patients, attracted an unusual rumor when Jack Nicholson disappeared for several months before filming. At that time, it was claimed that he was unsettled by the role and needed time away from shooting to work himself into the part. When shooting started, in a real mental hospital, Nicholson simply wandered into the set area and the rumor became legend as it became widely believed that Nicholson had checked himself into the hospital all those weeks ago, just to make sure he had a firm grip on his mentally infirm character!

Further "rumors" that Nicholson went through with the ECT (shock therapy) scenes *for real,* for veracity's sake, seem almost blasé by comparison.

Antz and *A Bug's Life* came out the same year. *Twister* and *Tornado* debuted within months of one another. *Saving Private Ryan* and *The Thin Red Line* stood practically toe-to-toe at the box office. It's sort of a Hollywood thing that what's worth doing once is worth doing twice, and dozens of

> Said Clark Gable on completing filming of *The Misfits,* "Christ, I'm glad this picture's finished! She [his costar Marilyn Monroe] damn near gave me a heart attack!"
>
> Gable collapsed the following day from a heart attack and died eleven days later.

> Remember the touching scene in *City Slickers* where Billy Crystal's character and Jack Palance assist in the birth of Norman the calf? It looked so . . . intimate. Hard to believe that Crystal's half of the scene was filmed in Colorado while Palance's was filmed in New York! For the romantics, Crystal really did help with the delivery, though the delivery seen onscreen was shot using a puppet. The six calves used during filming were all retired to live out their natural lives on a farm.

instances of twinning, studios suddenly finding themselves developing similar ideas at the same time, dot film history.

In 1968, *Planet of the Apes* and *2001: A Space Odyssey,* two seemingly disparate films, found themselves in an interesting situation come Oscar time. Though both films featured apes, and *Planet of the Apes* would eventually win that year's award for best makeup, it was widely rumored that the judges hadn't even considered *2001: A Space Odyssey*'s apes because they believed they were real!

Elvis Presley loved motorcycles. A sampling of his favorites, Harley-Davidsons, remain on display at Graceland, but it's one of those

not on display, the so-called missing bike, that's the basis for one urban legend.

The story usually begins with a guy who's out tooling around when he comes across a garage sale or a driveway with a "Motorcycle for Sale" sign propped up somewhere. Or, in other versions, a young man will inherit or buy a piece of property "as is, where it is," and discover a dusty bike in the back of a garage or propped under a tarpaulin. The bike is always in decent shape, but clearly in need of repair to make it roadworthy. A perfect fixer-up project. In no case does he pay more than five hundred dollars, and in at least one version, the guy gets the bike for nothing just so someone can reclaim the storage space where the bike is sitting.

In the process of working on his new acquisition, the bike fancier runs across some part that can't be obtained locally, and ends up calling the nearest Harley-Davidson dealer to order what he needs.

The first question, of course, is the identification number on the bike. That little piece of info is the only way to really ensure that the part that arrives is the right one. The guy rubs a few likely places and eventually turns up the required number and places his order. The dealer promises to get back to him ASAP.

He does. Much more quickly than the guy expected. The dealer offers him fifty thousand dollars for the bike. The guy says, "Hell, yes!" and waits for the dealer to arrive with the certified check to close the deal. With the money in hand, he finally asks what all the fuss was about. Without a word, the dealer pops the seat, and written beneath it are the words "To Priscilla. Love, Elvis."

This is the missing bike! Identified by its registration number.

The dealer, of course, sells it to Graceland for $250,000.

Alfred Hitchcock's *Psycho* attracted many dark rumors simply by virtue of its grim subject matter, but some of the most intriguing legends relate to the film's production, not to its plot or personalities, either on or off the screen.

Take the old chestnut that when the censors refused to release the film because they believed the shower scene revealed Janet Leigh's nipple—actually that of her body double—and sent it back to Hitchcock, he seemed remarkably unconcerned. To say this puzzled those around him would be an understatement. Without the censors' release, the film would be effectively banned! Hitchcock waited a few days, then, without changing a single frame, sent it right back.

He knew the censors well, and he assumed they would assume he'd made the changes and send it back without checking (which is precisely what happened).

Another legend tells of a frustrated father who sent a ripping letter to Hitchcock. It seems his daughter had stopped bathing when she'd seen *Diabolique*, and now refused to use the shower!

Hitchcock's blasé response?

"Send her to the dry cleaners."

• • • • • • •

Pulp Fiction began attracting a cloudy legend even before it finished filming, when rumors began spreading that there was "something weird" about the scene where Vincent jabbed a syringe into Mia's chest. Of course, "something weird" could mean a lot of things, but before long, another killed-on-the-set legend started rolling. When production staff denied that anything unusual had happened during shooting, this was taken as the early maneuverings of a coverup.

"Something weird" *did* happen, though nothing lethal!

To facilitate the effect of a violent stabbing while keeping the needle in sight almost constantly, the scene was shot backward. Travolta actually pulled the needle *away,* and the film was reversed for the final edit.

Almost everyone recognizes the scene in *Shane* where the villain, Jack Wilson (played by Jack Palance), slowly walks his horse into town; it's classic western imagery. It wasn't, however, planned that way.

> James Dean remains a cult idol, though his fans' methods of showing their devotion tend to the bizarre. His headstone was stolen on two different occasions in 1983, and in 1985, thirty years after his death, it had to be replaced altogether.

At that time, Palance, a New York actor, hadn't learned to ride a horse, and rather than have him rock about in a saddle like a sack of potatoes, the director, George Stevens, found creative ways to film the "horsey" scenes.

The Shawshank Redemption was *not* closed down for cruelty to animals. The only animal appearing in the entire film seems to be the crow kept as a pet by the librarian, Brooks. The American Society for the Prevention of Cruelty to Animals, as usual when animals are involved in filming, was present on the set, but they certainly saw nothing harmful to the crow. Still, they did make one suggestion—on behalf of the grub that was fed to the crow! Citing the scene as traumatic to the maggot, they requested that a maggot that had "died of natural causes" be used. It was.

One of the most publicized of all urban legends claims that a vague outline seen hovering near a window during several scenes is the ghost of a young boy who died, or committed suicide, in the sprawling apartment where *Three Men and a Baby* was filmed. The story further contends that the boy's parents, traumatized by the boy's appearance, begged the film's producers to exclude those scenes, or reshoot them, but the cruel-hearted studio, seeing nothing but dollar signs, refused.

Now for those pesky facts. *Three Men and a Baby,* like most films, wasn't shot on location. The apartment where this mysterious boy died doesn't exist outside the very nice soundstage sets constructed especially for this film. No one ever requested that scenes be reshot. As the boy never existed, there was no one to complain. The vague outline? Early in the film, a cutout of Ted Danson's character, at or near life-size, ended up just outside a window. Owing to an odd lighting effect, the white face and shirt seemed to glow just out of the actual shooting area. There's no ghost haunting *Three Men and a Baby.*

Titanic's producers went out of their way to gain the pre-release thumbs-up for historical accuracy from experts running the gamut of survivors, naval architects, and the Titanic Historical Association, but they were also quick to add, "We're making a movie, not a documentary, so not everything will be perfect."

In fact, several key events were inexplicably turned about, creating modern urban legends about events that happened over eighty years ago! For all those whose knowledge of naval history begins and ends with the film, third-class passengers *weren't* trapped behind gates that would have done a medieval castle proud. The real barriers were quite flimsy, easy to climb or break down. Molly Brown wasn't browbeaten by anyone, least of all a cowardly crewman! The truth? When he refused to turn back, to take on more passengers in the half-empty lifeboat, Molly Brown threatened to toss him into the water and urged the other women in the boat to row back. And, for the record, Captain Smith wasn't trying to beat any crossing records!

None of those discrepancies, however, is the urban legend most associated with this film. That belongs to a nameless young woman from California and is rooted in the unofficial competition among Leonardo diCaprio fans who, to prove their devotion, watched the film over and over, amassing prodigious collections of movie stubs in the process. This girl's devotion wasn't in doubt—she'd seen the film thirteen times in its first week—but her sanity might have been! It seems she discovered *Titanic* was playing at the Rialta Star, a twenty-four-hour playhouse, and, thinking to save herself a few trips to the box office, she pre-purchased a hundred showings and more or less moved into her corner of Cinema 3.

Think about a hundred showings.

With a new showing starting every four hours, that's six showings per day. In order to sit through her hundred showings, this Leomaniac would have to stare at that screen for nearly *seventeen days*. That's if she didn't eat, didn't sleep, didn't do anything except take advantage of the brief period when the screen went dark to dash to the bathroom before grabbing more popcorn and soda!

Needless to say, the ushers got very used to the customer in the last seat of the back row.

When her tickets finally ran out, however, they did expect her to vacate the seat. As she continued to sit there, making no effort to race home to the shower she hadn't seen in weeks, they wondered if they had a real nut case on their hands (as if watching *Titanic* a hundred times weren't evidence enough), and if they'd have to muscle her out or call the police to take her away.

Slowly, edging closer, the security team spoke to her softly, the way you would to a jumper or a lost child—or a guy with a really big gun. "Miss? Miss? It's time to go home now."

No response whatsoever.

Eventually they discovered why she wasn't moving. She was dead. Autopsy results revealed the cause. A steady diet of salted popcorn and soda had so unbalanced her body chemistry that eventually her brain short-circuited!

A diet of nothing but starch, sugar, and salts could go a long way toward frying your brain, but fortunately no ushers have

> One critic commented that the model for *E.T.*'s extraterrestrial must have been "a pile of doggie doo." It was actually based on pictures of scientist Albert Einstein and poet Carl Sandburg.

> **The final scene of *The Full Monty* did, in fact, feature all six leading men performing a full-frontal strip tease—in front of four hundred extras! Even before it began, everyone agreed this would be a "one-take" shoot.**

reported finding any of Lot's wives hovering in the back row of twenty-four-hour theaters.

Marisa Tomei's brush with entertainment legends is the most malicious incident included in this collection. It just may be the most deliberately cruel legend ever, taking what should have been a moment of unmitigated personal and professional success and staining it with hints of scandal and the implications that Tomei not only wasn't deserving of the Oscar she won in 1993 (for her role in *My Cousin Vinny*), but that she'd somehow stolen it from category rival Vanessa Redgrave!

According to a story that circulated widely, Tomei was never meant to win the Best Supporting Actress category, that her name was entered into showbiz history by Jack Palance, the category presenter, misread the card! Tomei's name, they believe, was simply the last thing Palance saw on the TelePrompTer. Redgrave, they contend, couldn't have lost to Tomei unless "the fix," intentional or unintentional, was already in.

That this story was reported in both general-circulation and industry papers, *without being debunked*, is the worst form of incompetence in reporting. The Academy Awards may be subject to political infighting and charges of snobbery during the judging phase of the whole process—and no one could argue that releases from early in the year aren't penalized without reason!—but the compilation of votes and the distribution of the awards is subject to the authority of Price Waterhouse, not the Academy itself. That the tabulation and distribution are supervised, including the presence of Price Waterhouse personnel who stand ready in the wings to correct any mistakes made by the all-too-human presenters, has been common knowledge for decades!

Allowing the rumor to go unchallenged, especially when Price Waterhouse had

> **When Anthony Quinn broke his foot shooting *Zorba the Greek* back in 1964, he knew he couldn't do that big dance scene on the beach as scripted, with all that jumping about. Instead he began the now-famous slow, stately shuffle across the sand. When asked what he was doing by the film's director, Michael Cacoyannis, he replied that this was a traditional number and invented a name for it on the spot!**

promptly denied the charge, was the height of journalistic carelessness.

Marisa Tomei's Best Supporting Actress Oscar for her portrayal of cocky Mona Lisa, who could make an automobile drive train sound sexy, *earned* her award.

Twilight Zone: The Movie was just days away from enjoying a grass-roots boycott when truth triumphed over legend. Right up until the film's general release, it was widely believed that footage of a helicopter crash that killed Vic Morrow and two children appearing in the film had been kept and included in the film.

It wasn't true. In fact, every effort had been made to secure all film shot on the scene that night. Despite the best intentions, however, exposed film was smuggled out and, ten years later, appeared in a lowlife effort titled *Death Scenes 2.*

Twister appeared destined to develop its own bizarre death cult after reports of a real twister bursting through a drive-in movie screen began circulating. According to the legend, patrons of the Moonlight Drive-In were really impressed with the special effects enacted on the huge screen, especially the scene featuring a tornado racing through a drive-in theater—until cars in the front row began flying into the air and they realized a real twister just blew the real screen to Kansas!

As this story, and the superstition that this might be a cursed picture, spread, teens in

> Tula Cossey, a former male, once portrayed a "Bond girl" in *For Your Eyes Only.*

particular began daring one another to take in the film from the supposedly vulnerable position of their car instead of safely tucked inside a steel-and-concrete theater. Some high-school seniors in Baltimore organized mass attendance at a nearby drive-in with the same nervous tension that accompanied "chicken" races back in the 1950s. The hint of possible danger jazzed moviegoers into traveling across state lines so they could say they'd seen *Twister* outside—in Tornado Alley!

The image of a tornado erupting from its image on screen sparks the imagination, which probably accounts for the legend's persistence—that, and an actual incident in Canada that closely mimicked, and probably inspired, the first *Twister* tales. On May 20, 1996, *Twister* was indeed playing at drive-ins across Ontario. A tornado did indeed slam through and destroy one of those screens, at the Can-View 4 Drive-In. It did not, however, happen while the film was playing. It happened in broad daylight when absolutely no one would have been at a drive-in anyway.

Almost every film gets a harsh review from at least one notable critic, but, if legends are true, *Willow* is one of the few films to pan critics on screen!

Viewers will certainly remember the two-headed dragon that grew under a bridge in the frozen castle of the good king and queen. Other than being absolutely evil, it's most obvious trait was that neither of its heads knew what the other one was doing. The dragon's name? Eborsisk. Roger Ebert and Gene Siskel might have given that one two thumbs-down.

Another critic, Pauline Kael, might have noticed something familiar in the evil general. Not in looks or habits. But he too was named Kael.

There's no way to confirm or deny the connection between the two Kaels, but a press kit and a tie-in novel both identify the dragon as Eborsisk.

The Wizard of Oz launched more individual legends than any other film. Some were timely, relating to specific events that no longer have meaning for modern audiences, and have since faded into relative obscurity.

Dozens more, however, are timeless. To this day, many people believe a suicidal Munchkin can be seen swinging from a rope from two different camera angles in the same scene. Certainly, *something* is seen dangling, but whether it's a munchkin or a woman's leg or a wandering stork is often debated. The legend claims this Munchkin, played by a woman, hanged herself, and rather than reshooting the scene to exclude her body, the producers assumed no one would notice her.

In his "Straight Dope" column, Cecil Adams suggests that the large bird, a crane, seen tied to a post near the witch's house in earlier scenes was permitted to wander about as a sort of moving prop, something of a running gag. If so, it fails completely as no one recognizes the bird from its first appearance!

In any case, though more than 120 Munchkins passed through the set, none of them has ever indicated that one of their number died on the set—and isn't that the sort of thing *you'd* mention when your spouse asked, "And how was work today?"

> Arnold Schwarzenegger, while filming *Conan the Barbarian,* was advised to ease off on his exercise schedule—his chest and arms had gotten too thick to allow him to properly swing a sword!

Another Munchkin legend is clearly a holdover of the old studio system. Back when actors signed on with a studio, not to work in a particular picture, studios were known to protect their investment by dictating how performers could conduct their private lives. Bad press wasn't a good thing when *The Wizard of Oz* was being filmed, and a poor offscreen reputation could well doom a young thespian's career. Legend has it that, as the studio intended this to be their family box-office blowout, they severely restricted the activities of many performers, even going so far as to enforce a no-fraternizing rule that banned cast members from dating one another! According to legend, dozens of Munchkins were fired over the course of the long shooting schedule, some for infractions as silly as being seen on the beach in a swimsuit! It wasn't that bad. Really. Yes, Munchkins did get fired, less than a handful in total, but the infractions were much more serious. One of those mischievous little guys held his wife at gunpoint! Simple set security, not an unreasonable moral code, likely resulted in that Munchkin getting turfed!

A final piece of *Oz* folklore is perhaps the most ironic, the one least likely to be believed, yet one of the few true tales associated with this film.

When costume designers were attempting to outfit the various characters, they faced some stiff challenges. The Buddy Ebsen fiasco was definitely the worst; the Professor Marvel costume, in retrospect, seems almost magical. Wardrobe wanted "seedy respectability," and brought in several overcoats that looked the part. The one eventually chosen, a sort of worn velvet with all the nap rubbed off, had once been a custom garment of some value, the sort of thing you find with an owner's label sewn into the lining. Actor Frank Morgan found just such a tag on his costume's inside pocket. It bore the name of the coat's original owner, L. Frank Baum, creator of *The Wizard of Oz.*

TELEVISION

Lucille Ball was a card-carrying Communist! She was even interrogated by Senator Joseph McCarthy and identified as a key celebrity in a propaganda campaign designed to sneak communism into the American home wrapped in the supposedly harmless package of humor—at least so goes the legend.

As usual, a few truths underlie this legend, but even a dedicated conspiracy buff would scoff at the image of Lucille Ball as a Marxist Mata Hari!

Ball *did* register as a Communist in 1936, a fact she freely admits. Fred Hunt, her grandfather and a strong proponent of socialist theory, had urged her to do so and, knowing she could vote as she pleased once behind the voter's box curtain, she'd placated the old man. In 1936, the Cold War was still twenty years in the future, and communism carried about as much political clout as environmentalism!

Still, in 1953, Ball *was* briefly investigated by one of the House Committee on Un-American Activities—though McCarthy was nowhere in sight. A single interview with committee chairman William A. Wheeler seems to have been the extent of Ball's "interrogation." His conclusion: "A review of the subject's file reflects no activity that would warrant her inclusion on the Security Index." In other words, no one was in the least concerned that Ball was sneaking Communist messages out through her public appearances.

Bert and Ernie, who've shared a room in a walk-down apartment for the past thirty-plus years, are finally ready to come out of the closet. They're gay and, in a first for chil-dren's television, *Sesame Street* will integrate an "alternative lifestyle" thread throughout its upcoming season!

And you thought *Ellen*'s outing made a splash?

Unfortunately, though such a plot line might make *Sesame Street* the first daytime show to appeal to that coveted 18–34, gay-puppet-with-disposable-cash demographic, the show's producers have no plans to portray the longtime buddies as anything other than friends. They're well aware of the rumor, and even have a prepared statement to hand out whenever it comes up, but, like most of us, they're baffled by the legend's existence. Bert and Ernie, for their part, have no comment at this time.

Captain Pugwash, a hugely popular kiddie cartoon in the United Kingdom, proves that urban legends are truly borderless, blooming in dozens of locations with remarkable similarity. It also proves that you can fight urban legends and win, sort of.

For years after the program closed in 1967, *Captain Pugwash* was dogged by the belief that clever plays on words had filled the series with sexual innuendo, a claim also attached to numerous shows in the United States. According to rumormongers, the characters included Master Bates (masturbates), Roger the Cabin Boy ("roger" being common British slang for sex), Pirate Bared Ass, Pirate Willy, and Seaman Steines (semen stains). When parents realized what fun the producers and writers were having at the expense of their kiddies, there arose such a heated response that BBC was forced to pull the show. What makes this legend *un*usual was that several reputable papers carried articles indicating the legend was true!

John Ryan, the creator of the *Captain Pugwash* cartoons, had spent years denying the legend, and when *The Guardian* perpetuated the tale without ensuring that its readership also had the other half of the story—the pesky truth—he successfully sued.

The actual names of the cartoon characters? There never was a "Seaman" anyone. Master Bates was actually Master Mate. Roger was Tom. Pirate Willy really was Pirate Willy, short for William and nothing else, and Pirate Bared Ass was Pirate Barnabas. The legend says more for the naughty minds of certain adults than it does about the work of John Ryan.

Ernie, of *Sesame Street* fame, is dying. Over the next season, viewers will watch as the completely huggable Muppet slowly thins out, becomes less active, and finally dies, leaving Bert and the rest of the *Sesame Street* characters to help viewers understand death, a concept producers say children are naturally curious about, and which *Sesame Street* can help them understand in a non-threatening way.

Phone lines lit up across America when this news became public. Jim Henson Productions received hundreds of calls within a few weeks. Articles on Ernie's imminent demise appeared in *The Boston Globe, USA Today,* the *Chicago Tribune,* and dozens of other well-circulated papers. Unfortunately, it seems a high percentage of readers didn't get the point of the articles. Yes, the rumor of Ernie's impending death existed, but it *wasn't going to happen*!

What kept the often-debunked legend afloat? First, the natural human tendency to believe that something dark must exist in the midst of so much goodness and light. It's not that we don't *want* everything to be as wholesome as *Sesame Street,* we just can't seem to believe in it anymore. Second, and more important, this rumor, which reached national proportions in early 1991, was probably ignited by the sudden and unexpected death of Jim Henson the previous May. As Henson provided the voices for dozens of Muppets, including Ernie, some real concern about who would portray those characters in the future did exist. *Sesame Street,* however, had no intention of killing off the affected Muppets. New voice actors picked up where Henson left off. Even the notion that *Sesame Street* felt an obligation to fill this void in the audience's emotional education doesn't hold up to scrutiny; real-life characters have already died "on the show" as well as in real life, and these events were portrayed with the same dedication to compassion and honesty that the show has brought to all its themes.

• • • • • • •

Fred Grandy, famous as both Gopher of the original *Love Boat* cast and as member of Congress, apparently had difficulty integrating his diverse sources of notoriety, and it was widely reported that when a U.S. Capitol page asked, "Promenade or Lido Deck?" as the new congressman stepped onto an elevator, Grandy had the page fired!

Grandy's version of events is considerably different. He admits to a certain "sensitivity" about his acting past when he first arrived on the Hill, and that he likely gave out negative vibes whenever the subject was broached. Later, as he became more comfortable with himself and his new situation, he attempted to ease the tension he'd unwittingly created and, getting into an elevator one morning, *he* asked the elevator operator, "Promenade Deck or Lido Deck?" The turned-about version, of course, makes for a better story and, despite the fact none of the Capitol pages was actually fired, it stuck.

Some of the most interesting entertainment legends are of who didn't appear in a particular role, of actors or actresses turning down roles that later made others famous, or of actors who took on roles they felt sure would launch them into the big time only to have the project fold on its first night, get panned by the critics, or, worst of all, never even make it to full production!

One of these if-only tales suggests that

John Wayne was the first actor offered the role of Matt Dillon in the TV series *Gunsmoke.* He wasn't. He hadn't even been considered for the role—not because of any lack of ability, but simply because, at that time, movie actors were movie actors and television actors were television actors. A TV actor might move up to films, but no one voluntarily went from film to TV.

There *were* John Wayne connections, but they were of a rather different sort. According to Suzanne and Gabor Barabas, who wrote *Gunsmoke: A Complete History,* John Wayne made every reasonable effort to convince the show's future producer, Charles Warren, that taking on the TV project would ruin his career. Wayne's persuasions didn't succeed, mostly because CBS offered Warren huge incentives to do the project. Surprisingly, considering his dislike of TV, Wayne did suggest another actor, James Arness, for the part, and even talked him into auditioning when Arness brought up concerns about *his* career. When the dust settled, Warren directed, Arness starred, and John Wayne introduced the very first episode!

He-Man and the Masters of the Universe, the popular TV cartoon series, wouldn't have existed at all if Mattel, who'd agreed to produce action figures for *Conan the Barbarian,* hadn't seen the early frames and decided the film was too graphically sexy and violent for a kids' toy company to sponsor.

Left with a bunch of brawny figures, they

simply painted the hair yellow and created their own cartoon to go with them!

For many years it's been believed that the ultimate symbol of innocence, the adorable baby on the Ivory Soap box, got more than a little dirty when she began starring in porno flicks as an adult.

Again, the theme of innocence-turned-evil attached itself to an urban legend and, again, there's only the smallest kernel of truth there, just enough to keep the legend alive. It wasn't the baby on the box, but the baby's mother, model and actress Marilyn Chambers, who went on to appear in the "blue" film *Behind the Green Door.* The baby apparently retired from the business before getting out of diapers!

Joni Loves Chachi, one of the successful *Happy Days* spinoffs, appeared set to take Japan by storm when it began its overseas release. Numbers from the first week were huge, especially for an American program. Speculation on what might have caused Japanese viewers to tune in big-time focused mainly on the leads, both of whom had a certain look known to be popular in Japanese markets, and plans to promote the pair extensively took shape. That was all quashed just days later, however, when the second episode to air barely made a blip on the ratings board.

What happened?

It seems that "chachi" is a reasonably good approximation of the Japanese word for "penis." Viewers tuning in to that first show simply didn't get what they expected! Or so goes the legend.

As child actors grow up, one of two things is bound to happen. They continue to act, or

ON BEING BLONDE

When it comes to urban legends, it seems one blonde is much the same as another, and actresses who figure in these modern myths often find themselves cast in a whole different role. Take Susan Olsen (no, not one of the saccharine Olsen twins), who portrayed Cindy on the *Brady Bunch* series, Donna Douglas, the tree-climbing bombshell Elly May Clampett of *The Beverly Hillbillies,* and Anissa Jones, Buffy from *Family Affair.* For nearly twenty years these wonderful actresses have been so confused with one another that many people don't know who's alive and whose not!

- Tragically, Anissa Jones committed suicide, a victim of depression.
- Donna Douglas is a popular speaker with several Christian gospel albums to her credit.
- Susan Olsen is alive and well.

they don't. When they don't, there's always someone to ask, "What ever happened to (fill in the blank)?" And for some reason, there's always someone who responds, with "Isn't he (or she) dead?"

Most aren't. Most live happily ever after. But perhaps because so many people dream of fame and stardom, John and Jane Q. Public can't seem to conceive of anyone *wanting* to live outside the bright lights, or without the wealth assumed to go with early success. If an actor isn't acting, something horrific must be preventing him or her from doing so. Death is pretty horrific in itself, but, urban legends being what they are, even death has to be dressed up a little, and irony plays a marked role in these types of tales. The tale of little Mikey, the Life Cereal kid who'd "eat anything," is a classic.

According to the legend, Mikey died as he'd lived, eating anything, and the fatal meal combination proved to be Pop Rocks, the ones that fizz on your tongue, and a six-pack of Coca-Cola. All that gas, expanding rapidly inside the relatively vulnerable confines of his stomach, was simply too much. He exploded and died.

It seems the "eat anything" line played too easily into a host of legends that General Foods, who produced Pop Rocks from 1956 to 1983, had been trying to overcome with strategic advertising and toll-free Information lines for worried parents. In addition to the exploding-stomach tales, there were ones claiming that eating Pop Rocks while holding your nose could result in brain hemorrhage, that pushing Pop Rocks up someone else's nose made it explode, and that Pop Rocks in another location resulted in the mother of all farts, one capable of producing some *really* wild results when combined with a bent-over position and a butane lighter!

The minuscule amount of gas produced by the harmless interaction of spit and carbonated candy couldn't, of course, produce anything remotely similar to the pressure required to rupture the human body from the inside, but facts never get in the way of a good urban legend. Even after the actor who'd played Mikey, John Gilchrist, was interviewed as an adult about his supposed death, an amazing number of people remained convinced that the company had simply hired a guy who looked sort of like the young Mikey "to avoid legal action from parents of kids who also blew up." When General Foods sold the production rights to a second company, who changed the name of the product before marketing it again, and Pop Rocks *appeared* to disappear from the shelves, the rumors actually picked up instead of dying out. In the best conspiracy tradition, this was taken as proof of the initial danger.

Canadians are apparently less likely to believe in urban legends than their neighbors to the south. At least that's one interpretation for the fact that in Canada, Pop Rocks continue to be sold as Pop Rocks, and to the best of General Foods' knowledge, they've never received any hot-line calls from there.

• • • • • • •

The Little Rascals, which once entertained a supposedly more innocent America, was also a product of its times, and regularly used story lines and characterizations that would be racist by today's standards. So offensive do some African Americans find *The Little Rascals* and *Amos 'n' Andy,* and books like *Uncle Tom's Cabin* and even *Huckleberry Finn,* that, led by prominent black celebrities like Bill Cosby, a concerted effort is under way to buy up the rights to these properties in order to ensure that the images and ideas within them aren't passed on to another generation. Cosby already owns the rights to *Amos 'n' Andy* as well as *The Little Rascals,* and is currently negotiating for the film rights to *Huckleberry Finn.*

So goes the legend, anyway.

The facts are somewhat different—and are so ridiculously easy to confirm with a few simple calls to the studios who produced these programs or to the rights department of any large publishing house—that it's difficult to understand how this legend got legs in the first place.

Because the legend is usually most concerned with *The Little Rascals,* we can start there. In early 1998, video releases of a selection of episodes were made available by Cabin Fever Entertainment. They purchased the right to reproduce these episodes from King World Productions. A call to King World Productions reveals two key points: Bill Cosby does *not* own any part of that company, and King World Productions, which has held the rights to *The Little Rascals* since 1965, is not currently negotiating the sale of any rights in the program to Bill Cosby!

In the past few years a number of other prominent African-American men, even those with considerably less strong ties to the entertainment industry, have been attached to this tale, including Tiger Woods and Michael Jordan. Other entertainment celebrities supposedly involved in the buy-out consortium are Morgan Freeman, Denzel Washington, and Samuel L. Jackson.

Jerry Mathers, the Beaver of *Leave It to Beaver,* was killed in Vietnam. This "fact," reported in the popular and supposedly reputable media, served to underscore America's growing disenchantment with its involvement in yet another overseas conflict. Contrasting the horror of war against the nostalgic naïveté of the television world of a rascal like Beaver illustrated, in one dramatic stroke, a nation's loss of innocence.

And how did Jerry Mathers become an anti-Vietnam poster kid? He didn't, not really. While Jerry Mathers served his tour in the Air National Guard, another young man, also named Jerry Mathers, *was* killed. Reporters seeing the name reacted exactly as they would have if the name Elvis Presley had turned up on that day's report sheets; they assumed it was the celebrity who'd died, and passed that information back to the United States.

Though the error was quickly corrected, thousands of people heard the initial reports, and with that juxtaposed image of a freckled face over a body bag firmly set in their minds, many never absorbed the corrected reports. Even when he later appeared in *Still the Beaver,* a large portion of the audience believed the studio had launched a huge campaign to find a double.

Television programs of the 1950s operated on tight budgets. Special effects were reserved for film, extra takes were calculated in dollars per foot of film, and absolutely no one paid regulars overtime! James Garner, the star of the TV series *Maverick,* knew all this and, so the legend goes, as night closed in with an entire complicated fight scene left to film, he began looking for "creative solutions."

When Garner spotted a clump of tall, thick weeds, he came up with the perfect low-cost solution. Instead of shooting the actual fight, the actors stood behind the weeds and shook them while grunting and groaning. From time to time they'd toss someone out, only to have him pick himself up and race back in.

The rushes were hilarious; the footage went to air!

Fred Rogers, who delights children in *Mister Rogers' Neighborhood* while putting their parents to sleep with his soothing voice, for many years was the victim of a rumor that he'd killed someone. When no evidence turned up to verify the truth of this legend, it mutated into claims that the killings (the original single murder wasn't enough, it seems) wouldn't show up on the system because they were government-sanctioned. Mister Rogers was an army sniper!

Again, an urban legend seeks to undermine our belief in the wholesome by tying it to horror, again without any basis in fact. As with many celebrities, much of Fred Rogers's life is a matter of public record. His comings and goings, work history, and personal life have been revealed in hundreds of interviews over a forty-year period. Piecing it together takes less than a day and swiftly provides a life history without any glaring gaps, any stints of military service (the shortest tour would leave a huge hole in any résumé), or any other indication that Fred Rogers is anything other than a children's entertainer and an ordained minister.

The Newlywed Game's whole purpose was to elicit the most embarrassing anecdotes possible from its guests, so, naturally, any legend arising from this popular game show must be a real blusher.

It is.

According to legend, on one episode, the show's host, Bob Eubanks, asked contestants, "Where's the most unusual place you've ever made love?"

Some answers were pretty routine, such as "the in-laws' bedroom" and "at work, after hours." The one that gives this legend its bang? "Ah, that'd be the butt, Bob!"

Despite years of denials by Eubanks, who actually offered a $10,000 prize to anyone who could prove the incident ever happened, the legend refused to die. The money is still unclaimed.

Night Heat, a cop show of the 1970s, took advantage of the favorable exchange rate on the American dollar by filming many scenes in Toronto, Ontario. The setting for the police drama, however, was New York City, and the director was running into a bit of a snag. He couldn't find a street dirty enough to mimic a New York back alley!

Eventually he was forced to truck in some garbage and have his set dressers scatter it about as convincingly as possible. By the time they're finished dirtying up the place, it was about time for the union-mandated lunch hour, and the cast and crew retired to check out the catering wagon. When they returned to start shooting, their street was perfectly clean! The City of Toronto apparently tolerates no mess, even on film sets.

Although this tale has been told of several other shows filming in Canada, especially those working out of the popular North Vancouver lots, only the experience of director Sonny Grosso, who ended up trucking in yet more garbage, has been verified contemporaneously in the printed media.

Ken Osmond, who portrayed Eddie Haskell on *Leave It to Beaver,* is widely believed to have found subsequent fame in numerous porno flicks as Johnny "The Wad" Holmes. Again, the public fills some psychological need to shed its own innocence by cross-casting its Age of Innocence icons as those most likely to fall into the pit of iniquities.

In fact, Ken Osmond served the citizens of Los Angeles for eighteen years while wearing the badge of an LAPD officer!

Adam Rich, the *Eight Is Enough* star, joined the ranks of child actors who supposedly fell for Hollywood's bright lights only to pay for it with their lives when reports flew across the country claiming Rich had died at the hands of a madman! Another disillusioned Hollywood hopeful, now working on and off as a stagehand, cracked late one night as he wandered toward home. Seeing Rich walking alone, he decided to take out his frustrations on those who'd "made it," and proceeded to beat the youth to death with his bare hands, leaving his bloodied body for dogs to pee on until the cops finally arrived.

Hell of a way to go, no?

The miniseries *Crime and Punishment* used so many Hungarian actors during the filming that, instead of trying to rid them all of their Hungarian accent, it was simpler to teach the non-Hungarians to add a little something to their own speech habits.

Sure would be—if it were true. It isn't. Not one single detail. Not even the body found covered in dog urine.

Josh Saviano, best known for his appearances on *The Wonder Years,* a touching coming-of-age drama highlighting the innocence of youth, has, like Jerry Mathers and others, been tied to some of the least innocent acts and events to come down the pike since poodle skirts went out of fashion. Urban legend had the Beaver killed in Vietnam and his buddy, Eddie Haskell, turn to porn flicks to support himself. In the latest lost-innocence tale, Josh Saviano has been identified as none other than Marilyn Manson!

He denies it—and chuckles.

While first-person denials don't always amount to much in the real world (as witness "No new taxes" and "I did not have an affair with Monica Lewinsky"), Saviano would need to have been cloned to appear in all the places he's been seen as himself while also keeping up as demanding a tour schedule as his "alter ego."

Sesame Street, according to the following petition, which has been circulating through fax machines and e-mail boxes for nearly five years, is about to be canceled!

PBS, NPR (National Public Radio), and the arts are facing major funding cutbacks. In spite of the efforts of each individual station to garner further viewer support while decreasing their day-to-day expenses, the government officials responsible for support of the arts have determined that the $1.12/person received as taxes and passed on to funding of these sorts of broadcasting is excessive and not in the public interest.

All of which is true, and was true when students at the University of Northern Colorado began circulating their petition in 1995. Perhaps not fully cognizant of what they'd begun, and certainly not aware of the Internet's ability to mutate information (which is how *Sesame Street* was added to a general petition asking for public support of PBS and NPR), or to keep information circulating ad infinitum (the petition was aimed squarely at the 1996 budgets).

Though they later also circulated a notice that the petition was no longer required, it had developed a life of its own and has made the rounds independently ever since, occasionally landing in the e-mail box or fax basket of someone else who does more than read it (like publishing it in the local paper at their own cost, or contacting the media with this "breaking news") and the whole hue and cry begins anew.

Soupy Sales, through a combination of his own poor judgment and the public's perception of him as being just a tad too naughty for children's programming, attracted dozens of urban legends to himself—even some of which were happily connected to other performers before he came along!

The incident that set him up as the man most likely to pull any television stunt imaginable was the "little green pieces of paper" affair.

It was New Year's Day, 1965, important for the fact that Soupy began the whole scenario by telling his tiny listeners, "Hey, know what last night was? It was New Year's Eve! Bet your mommy and daddy were out having a great time! They're probably still asleep, so what I want you to do is tiptoe into their bedroom and find your mom's purse and your dad's pants. Inside you'll find a whole lot of green bits of paper with pictures of guys in beards on the front. Put them in an envelope and send them to Soupy Sales, Channel 5, New York, New York. And you know what I'll send you? A postcard from Puerto Rico!"

WNEW, the TV station that broadcast the show, was flooded with complaints and pulled the show from the air for a full week.

Yup, true. Which proves that studios were more forgiving then than now!

Following that brouhaha, the American public deemed Soupy capable of almost anything and quickly invented new scenarios that seemed appropriate to his on-screen personality and substituted him for other celebrities in several chestnuts.

Some viewers, who swear they saw it themselves (so it must be true), clearly recall Soupy leaning close to the camera to ask all the kiddies, "What word starts with 'F' and ends in 'K'? . . . That's right! Firetruck!"

On another occasion, Soupy reputedly began a song with the line "If You See Kay . . ." He also supposedly sang songs such as "You Can Squeeze My Plums," "If I Were an Arab with a Camel," and "Playing in the Hayloft."

In a skit with White Fang, a puppet paw, he is trying to teach the unseen dog/wolf the letters of the alphabet. Soupy says, "A." The dog says, "A." Soupy says, "B." The dog says, "B." And so on and so on until Soups says, "F." The dog says, "K." They start over again. Again the dog repeats everything perfectly until he gets to "F." Soupy says, "F." The dog says, "K." And, as all kiddie things come in groups of three, they do the whole thing again until the dog once more says "K" instead of "F." An exasperated Soupy then pops up with, "How is that every time is I say 'F,' you say 'K'!"

But no, even back then the networks wouldn't have forgiven such continuous use of inappropriate subtext. Soupy has admitted the truth of the "green pieces of paper" story, claiming that he never expected to be taken seriously, and the backstage atmosphere of the show was raunchy at times, but he never indulged in sexual innuendo on the air.

Star Trek's theme song had lyrics! Well, sort of. They *were* written by the series' creator, Gene Roddenberry, to the right tune, but they were never performed *as* the theme song. They were sung once, by Nichelle Nichols (Uhura) during an actual episode, but appeared nowhere else until Nichols and Shatner later produced records of their own.

The Tonight Show became an American institution, one of the longest-running programs ever, hosting literally thousands of guests. In all that time, with that many personalities, avoiding a few urban-legend associations would have been quite an achievement. Luckily for lovers of the lewd, *The Tonight Show* figures in some of the funniest moments people honestly believe went out over the airwaves. Luckily for the show, which was always playing with the edges of what the censors deemed "acceptable," none of the following tales actually happened—though thousands will swear they saw these episodes!

Zsa Zsa Gabor, who always does things her own way, really did appear on *The Tonight Show* several times, she really did bring along her pets to several interviews (with Carson and others), and she really did like firing sexually loaded zingers at Johnny. She did not, however, ask him if he'd like to "pet her pussy." Nor did he reply, "I'd love to, but you'll have to move that darn cat!"

Another of the many *Tonight Show* legends stars Mrs. Arnold Palmer as the guest who answered Johnny's question "And does your husband have any little pre-tournament superstitions or funny little habits?" with "Why, yes! I always kiss his balls for luck!" Impressively cute, but impossible, at least in that form, as Mrs. Arnold Palmer was never actually a guest on the show!

Oprah Winfrey's show has attracted great guests and controversy about equally—often because controversial viewpoints are what make guests great, but the urban legends that have attached themselves to *Oprah* guests create controversy for what was never said!

Designers in particular prove real lightning rods. In recent legends, both Liz Claiborne and Tommy Hilfiger have been credited with highly controversial comments.

According to hundreds of viewers who swear they either saw it personally or heard about it from someone who taped or saw the show, Liz Claiborne once claimed that her clothes "weren't designed for black women, their hips are too big!" Oprah, wearing a Claiborne suit at the time, wasn't impressed. An unplanned commercial break ended Claiborne's appearance, and when the show came back from commercial, Oprah appeared in a white terry bathrobe!

At her second appearance, Claiborne reputedly set the entire set ablaze by admitting to her black host and her audience, predominantly black on that particular day, that she supported the KKK, the white government in South Africa, and/or the segregation policy that would have left blacks in the back of the bus!

Another legend has it that Tommy Hilfiger wasn't too impressed with non-Caucasian physiques, either. His comment? "If I'd known blacks and Asians would wear my clothes, I'd never have designed them. They just don't look any good in them."

All false.

In addition to the fact that no tapes are missing from the *Oprah* archive, yet no tapes of any such incidents exist, what could possibly induce two smart designers to cut their own throats, or persuade Oprah to invite Claiborne back for another dig?

Wonder Woman: Legend claims that Maybelline, the cosmetics firm, once had an episode of *Wonder Woman* pulled from the air because it didn't like the way the show's makeup department had handled star Lynda Carter's face!

Actually, the episode in question, "The Velvet Touch," never even made it to production. No doubt the hair and makeup department would have done their usual fine job, but, as the plot of the episode revolved around poisoned cosmetics, which may indeed have elicited funny messages from the Maybelline spokeswoman, it wasn't used at all!

Arnold Ziffel, the charming pig from *Green Acres,* seemed to have it made. He had all he could eat, a popular television show to appear in, and the adoration of thousands. Not bad for a pig. Things were going really swell—right up until the last day of filming.

Arnold probably didn't expect a gold watch, but he certainly didn't expect to get barbecued for the wrap party entree, either!

No, no, no need to throw out your *Green Acres* memorabilia or call PETA. Like the *Babe* rumor that followed, this legend is nothing but hot air. During the course of *Green Acres*'s run, many pigs played Arnold, and all were honorably retired to farms where they continued to roll in the mud until their deaths.

And where did the whole eat-the-pig rumor come from? In 1982 a radio talk show, "Weird Until Morning," aired in several cities in Ohio. It featured the usual late-night stuff: songs from the edge, petty patter, strange statistics on everything from sex to sewage, and, of course, call-in questions. One of the hosts, Brian LePage, clearly remembers fielding one viewer question on the July Fourth weekend in 1984: "What happens to all the farm animals they use in films? Do they get sent to the old actors' home or do they just get sent back to the farm and eaten?"

"I didn't have a clue, and was just about to tell the caller we'd have to check into that one, we had a student who'd run crazy errands like that, when my co-host burst into laughter and said like, 'Oh, my God! Can you imagine *eating* Arnold?!' I could, and I started laughing, too. It was about three in the morning and I was pretty punchy by then. I think we offended the caller because, by the time I spoke to him again, he'd hung up."

RADIO

Captain Midnight's decoder ring—everybody had one, right? For just "fifty Yo-Ho gum wrappers" and the cost of a stamp to the local radio station, every kid in America could count himself among Captain Midnight's junior squad of caped crime fighters, could decode the secret message aired at the end of every episode, and, because girls never got decoder rings, every young man in America could send encoded messages to his buddies without fear of giving anything away to the enemy. Those Captain Midnight decoder rings were about the neatest thing a kid could own, among his most treasured possessions, right?

Wrong.

Not that secret codes weren't the coolest thing, they most certainly were, right up there with disappearing ink and whoopie cushions! But, contrary to the belief of thousands who huddled next to the radio on a Saturday morning with their pencil and paper ready, *there never was a Captain Midnight decoder ring*! Broadcasters from the era, like William Hurt, firmly believed he still had his Captain Midnight decoder ring and, after searching the family attic, even managed to find the decoder ring he'd been so fond of as a kid—but it had nothing to do with Captain Midnight!

"Funny how the mind plays tricks on you!" he exclaimed on discovering that his promotional giveaway was credited to, of all people, Dick Tracy! "I don't remember even liking Dick Tracy, but there's no arguing with facts."

The Green Hornet kept American kids glued to the radio from 1936 to 1952, providing a fantastical hero throughout the war years and beyond. But the war affected everything, even children's programming, and it was only after the bombing of Pearl Harbor on December 7, 1941, that Kato, faithful servant of the Green Hornet's alter ego, Britt Reid, began being identified as "Reid's faithful *Filipino* valet." Since Kato is not a common name outside Japan, certainly not in the Philippines were at least two different dialects translate the name to "coward," it seems an unlikely choice for a superhero's sidekick! Though it is probably impossible to prove at this historical remove, it appears much more likely that Kato was a Japanese character, as his name always implied, until Japan attacked American forces.

STAGE

Charlie Chaplin, a major star of his day despite the modesty of his onscreen persona, lived a fascinating life, one considerably more interesting than many of the films airing at that time! Among the many anecdotes attributed to him are two urban legends that still arise nearly a hundred years later.

It's difficult for us to relate to the manias that periodically erupt around showbiz personalities. Girls who'd faint at the sight of the Beatles, or who'd give up their eyesight if

> Stage actor Antony Wheeler really stayed "in character" for his live performance of Judas in *Jesus Christ Superstar*. In a technical tragedy, Wheeler, who'd performed the role at least twenty times previously, forgot to connect his safety harness just before performing Judas's hanging scene.

it would net them a single drop of sweat from Michael Jackson's face, aren't normal responses to mere human beings. So it may be difficult to imagine the waves of Chaplin-mania that took even Chaplin himself by surprise whenever he ran into evidence of the phenomena. Nonetheless, he attempted to take it all in stride whenever possible, which is how he came to find himself entered in a Chaplin lookalike at a theater in San Francisco—a competition that he lost!

He didn't even make the finals.

He *was* in the thick of things when his coffin was stolen from its grave shortly after his 1977 burial, and for the next three months as his family, Swiss police, and the kidnappers engaged in some hard bargaining over just how much ransom a body, even a celebrity body, was worth. His family had no intention of paying criminals anything, but the bargaining time did allow police to set up several stings, one of which did eventually net them the crooks and the coffin.

• • • • • • •

Harry Houdini, the greatest escape artist of his day, died of appendicitis after inviting a McGill University student to test the strength of his muscles by punching him in the stomach.

Yes, and no.

Yes, Houdini did die of appendicitis (actually acute peritonitis caused by a ruptured appendix that, due completely to Houdini's own stubborn streak, went too long unattended), and the death did occur shortly after the test of strength. The two incidents, however, had nothing in common. The student did not cause Houdini's death; blows to the appendix could conceivably injure the organ, but not cause appendicitis. Given the timing of the incident and the fact that Houdini displayed serious discomfort just a few hours later, it's clear that Houdini already suffered from appendicitis at the time of the punch.

Pia Zadora, while playing the young Anne Frank in the stage version of *The Diary of Anne Frank,* was, according to a spiteful entertainment legend, in the midst of the

> Most actors ignore *Macbeth's* reputation as an "unlucky" play. George Ostroska, however, did everything possible to perpetuate that particular superstition—he died onstage at the beginning of act two!

fateful final scene where the Nazis burst into the safe house, when the audience, as a single voice, yelled, "She's in the attic!"

The implication, of course, is that the audience was so pained by her terrible acting that, in order to hurry the final curtain, they threw her character to the Nazis!

Could she possibly have been that bad?

Not at all. In fact, Zadora never played Anne Frank in any medium, anywhere! This legend, closer to a joke than an actual attempt to convince listeners of its veracity, has attached itself to several other actresses as well, including Vanna White, Shelley Long, and Shannon Doherty, none of whom have played Anne, either.

SONG

The Beatles changed pop music forever. That's no myth. It would actually be surprising, then, if this band didn't create a few legends of another type along the way.

First, and perhaps best known, is the claim that hundreds of people, in an attempt to re-create the *Abbey Road* cover with themselves and their friends crossing that walkway, usually with another friend hanging about with a camera to capture the results, have managed to get themselves killed by playing in the traffic!

It's true that several people doing just that have impeded traffic, and have even been bumped by an impatient driver who didn't put artistic pursuit or Beatlemania high on his priority list. It's not true, though,

that that particular section of roadway is any more prone to pedestrian accidents than any other. Locals claim they drive *more* carefully there, as they're well aware of the spot's touristy attraction.

Following only slightly behind that tale's popularity is the one that claims John Lennon deliberately hid messages in the background of some songs—a claim that's also been attributed to Alice Cooper, Kate Bush, and the band U2, and to almost any recording artist or artists with a reputation for unusual vocals, blurred lyrics, or outright volume. Lennon denied all these claims, including the one in which he supposedly whispers "Paul is dead" and "I buried Paul" on the Italian release of "Strawberry Fields Forever," except for one. He admits to muttering "tit, tit, tit" during the recording of "Girl." Suggestions of different types of hidden messages, like the ones supposedly to be found by playing the albums backward, have been consistently debunked.

Mariah Carey: "The faster they rise, the harder they fall," is a quote often attributed to an agent at the powerful Richard Curtis Agency. A colleague supposedly replied, "And the more determined the public is to haul them back down." What's that got to do with Mariah Carey? For the past three years, Carey's name has been attached to more controversial, stupid quotes than any other single performer—all inaccurately! That one performer could possibly attract such random bad luck is difficult to believe, especially when every quote appears designed to portray her as nothing more than a bubblehead with some pretty weird sensibilities.

Among the spurious quotes:

"When I watch TV and see those poor starving kids all over the world, I can't help but cry. I mean, I'd love to be skinny like that, but not with all those flies and death and stuff."

And, on King Hussein of Jordan's death:

"Jordan was one of the world's finest athletes and a close friend. He'll be terribly missed."

While the first quote can be traced to an online parody, and as such should have been easy for reputable papers with fact-checking staffs to debunk instead of passing along as fact, there's simply no obvious source for the Jordan quote or this particularly nasty one wrongly attributed to Carey during a CNN interview:

"Sure, I resent being treated like a mental lightweight, like I can't tell the difference between something really important, like AIDS research, and something that's not even an issue, like orphan drugs. I mean, everyone knows the state pays for orphans' medical care!"

No one knows how Phil Collins became the target of the incredibly persistent rumor that he'd watched one man deliberately allow another to drown and, years later, filled with remorse for never having reported what he'd seen (or, alternately, determined to let a killer know that someone *had* seen him), wrote "In the Air Tonight" to commemorate the event. Collins himself, in dozens of public appearances, denies he ever saw anyone drown, much less wrote about it!

The scenario comes in many forms, from quite simply suggesting that some line in the song would mean something specific to the killer, to a complicated description of the night Collins debuted "In the Air Tonight." The most elaborate of these has a vengeance-bent Collins spending years tracking the killer, having him observed at a distance, learning secrets about his life, writing the song, ensuring that the man received front-row tickets to the concert, and, while performing "In the Air Tonight" for the very first time, pinning the killer to his seat with the tightest, brightest spotlight in the history of live concerts. Of course, it ends with either the police picking up the killer, who immediately confesses, or with the guy racing out of the stadium and killing himself. Truly ironic twists have him throwing himself into the same body of water where he allowed the other man to die.

It's pure hokum.

Claims that Collins can't read or write a note of music fall into a different category of legend: the truth!

John Denver shares a bizarre connection with Fred Rogers: both have been portrayed as cold, dedicated wartime snipers! In the movies, this would be serious cross-casting, the sort of thing to tip off every member of the audience that something was just left of reality, but because these tales typically play to our deep-seated suspicions of "nice" people, we're willing to let the notion wander through our minds for a few seconds before saying, "Naw, can't be!"

Even after the first denial, another voice will often whisper, "But then, how well do we *really* know these people?"

A willingness to believe that a tree-hugging folksinger could also be a steely-eyed killer who destroyed helpless victims from a distance is merely the flip side of a willingness to believe serial killers have neighbors who'd "never believe" monsters lived next door, so perhaps these tales of evil lurking behind virtue are as cautionary as those warning us against guys hawking pizza in the mall. In both cases, what we see isn't necessarily what we get.

It would be a great theory if the objects of these legends weren't so obviously incapable of fulfilling their roles as evil monsters!

John Denver received his military induction notice, the draft letter, in 1964 and duly made his way to his nearest recruitment center. There, two things became blatantly obvious. First, John Denver was short two toes, the result of a lawn mower accident. He never served in the military, in any capacity! Second, even had he not gotten too close to his garden tools, it's doubtful Denver would have qualified for sniper training, because

those glasses weren't costuming; the man had serious vision problems.

Cass Elliot, "Mama Cass" of The Mamas and the Papas, was dead before attracting an urban legend, and when she finally did, it was a lie. Though nearly every major news service reported that the talented singer died from choking on a ham-and-cheese sandwich, almost no one actually checked the medical examiner's report, which gave her cause of death as heart failure.

Pink Floyd spent years developing a sound dear to the hearts of audiences who also enjoyed experimental drugs. That likely explains why the group's fans have been seen carrying home copies of the newly redigitized *The Wizard of Oz* along with a six-pack. Of course, they already own a copy of *Dark Side of the Moon*.

If legends are to be believed, *Dark Side of the Moon* was written, recorded, and meant to be replayed while Judy Garland gamboled across the screen. Try it for yourself and you'll find some interesting things coming together at 0:03:16, 0:06:18, and 0:12:12—at least so the legend goes. A further millennial sort of reworking of the tale, obviously for the ambidextrous fan, suggests you start your video, get the album spinning, down that first beer, *and* haul out your Book of Revelation. Rev. 3:16, 6:18, and 12:12 supposedly provide "way deeper insights."

Personally, I just don't get the connection

between boils, yellow bricks, and bass guitar riffs, but you may just find something really special.

Debbie Harry, lead singer of the band Blondie, once gave an incredibly detailed account of how she was almost abducted by Ted Bundy to the *St. Petersburg Times*. According to Harry's version of events, she didn't make the connection between Bundy and the man who picked her up in a white car with no interior door or window handles until January of the same year when Bundy was electrocuted, when details of his other crimes were once again prominent in the news.

Needless to say, the story made quite a splash.

Unfortunately, it went on to become accepted fact, so well believed that it lost much of the legend style in the retelling. Not that this would have been a bad thing—if there was any evidence at all that it was Bundy's car Harry actually escaped from! While it's possible, anything is possible in the right circumstances, and modern air travel can get a person around rather quickly, there's absolutely no evidence Bundy was ever in New York City, where Harry's frightening experience took place!

In the course of their investigations, law-enforcement officers traced huge periods of time in Bundy's life, trying to make connections with murders across much of the country. Despite their attention to even the minutiae of his life, they simply can't place

him anywhere in New York State. No one is suggesting Harry's tale is in any way contrived, just that she, like many others, became caught up in the bizarre life of a man capable of almost anything.

Lauryn Hill, member of the Fugees, suffered the fate of many celebrities when a round of urban legends attributed a particularly nasty racist quote to her, claiming that in an MTV interview Hill had proclaimed, "If I'd known white people were going to buy my last album, I never would have recorded it."

Anger carries such rumors faster than any others. Within weeks, Hill found herself in the uncomfortable position of defending herself against an incident that no one had actually seen or heard, a statement that no two people quoted consistently, and that, left undenied, could have serious consequences for her career.

That no one, including the MTV program from which the quote was supposedly taken, could produce any evidence that the rumor was based on fact, meant nothing. Eventually, all Hill could do was continue her denials, challenge her accusers to produce proof, and hope the whole thing would fade away.

But how did it start? Without an originating incident on MTV, how did the rumor erupt simultaneously over such a huge area? There's likely no one answer, but the event that spread the rumor farthest, turning it into a full-fledged legend, was probably the discussion engendered by a call-in question to

> The Rolling Stones were so upset by the way the documentary film *Cocksucker Blues* represented them that they sought a court injunction to prevent its release. By judicial order, it can now only be shown if its director, Robert Frank, is physically present!

The Howard Stern Show asking if Hill had ever made the comment!

Michael Jackson, with his constantly changing features and surgical-mask fetish, seems a perfect candidate around which to build all manner of urban legends, but the one legend that really stuck to this celeb was incredibly innocent, even naïve. According to the myths sweeping American high schools, Michael Jackson's phone number was hidden in plain sight in the first seven digits of the UPC on his *Thriller* album! Nearly everyone with that number, regardless of area code, received calls asking for Michael Jackson! That anyone could believe this recluse would possibly chance giving away even that small a part of his privacy makes us believe there must be people out there who still believe in the tooth fairy and the Easter Bunny!

KISS, the band of heavily made-up rockers, is but one of many groups that have stirred curiosity and controversy with their choice of name. "Kings in Satan's Service," "Kinky Intercourse, Sadistic Sex," and "Keeping It Simply Sex" remain some of the *least* offensive meanings suggested as possible acronyms.

"Lucy in the Sky with Diamonds," more than thirty years after its release, after some fifty denials by Beatles and their buddies, and after the death of John Lennon, is still dogged by an urban legend to the effect that the title was a sly reference to LSD.

For the record, Lennon, who stuck by his story for all his foreshortened life, maintained the song title was inspired by his son Julian's picture of his classmate Lucy. The picture, produced for inspection at the time this legend first dusted up, certainly supports that contention. So do the first-person accounts of Lennon's friends and family. If the legend is true, the question remains: Why would a man whose other contributions were admittedly based on things like corn flakes lie?

Charles Manson, notorious for the murders he inspired, seems an unlikely candidate for membership in the society of musical urban legends, but, remarkably, he figures in two different tales and is only completely excluded from one of them!

Deciding whether truth or fiction is stranger, especially in the life of a psychopath like Manson, isn't easy, but we'll begin with a tale that contains more than a shred of truth.

After Manson's Helter Skelter night, rumors began surfacing that Manson had recorded an album with the Beach Boys, that one of their songs actually predicted the deaths to come! That's not true, of course, but Manson did share a house with Dennis Wilson, the Beach Boys' drummer, and did compose one of the songs the band later used on the flip side of a popular single. He did not, however, perform with the Beach Boys, did not collaborate on any album project, and in the one song he did compose, not even another psychopath could find references to Manson's later monstrosities.

Another legend arising at the same time was that Manson had once auditioned to be one of the Monkees! The tale, as is, is patently impossible. He didn't, he couldn't have, he was in jail at the time! But even here, there's the kernel of another truth. Manson did fancy himself something of a performer, even if no one else seemed to, and once auditioned for the producer of a famous group of that period, the Byrds.

Jim Morrison of the Doors ended up in hot water with the Federal Bureau of Investigation for stealing all the soap from the lavatory of an airplane.

True!

It was November 1969, and, additionally, Morrison was also written up for insisting on finishing his cigar while the "No Smoking" signs were illuminated.

• • • • • • •

Mike Nesmith, one of the Monkees, was already a multimillionaire before making it big in music; his mother was a famous inventor.

Not exactly, but close. Bette Nesmith created a unique product later known as Liquid Paper, and did eventually sell it for nearly $50 million to the Gillette Corporation in 1979. It was a long time coming, however. The product began in a very small way (less than twenty individuals made up the client base) in 1951, but didn't manage to show a profit until 1963!

The Ohio Players' "Love Roller Coaster," the song featuring a scream guaranteed to take years off your life, became notorious shortly after its release when a DJ suggested the band "must've killed that chick" to get a scream like that out of her. The dense dead air following that statement led listeners to believe there just might be more to that shriek than met the ear!

A variety of explanations floated around during 1996: The song had been recorded in one of the band members' apartment. The scream was the sound of his neighbor being assaulted. The model from the album cover, injured seriously enough during the photography to destroy the rest of her career, rushed the control booth during recording and attempted to kill the band's manager. For his part, he killed her in self-defense. Her death scream was captured in the process. Another version suggests the band was completely unaware of the added sound effect. That story holds that a couple of strung-out groupies who snuck into the recording studio to spy on another group due to record in the morning, got into a fight overnight—after playing with the equipment to amuse themselves. One killed the other and the entire screaming death scene was recorded on one track of the band's master.

None of those things happened. The scream wasn't even that of a woman! Ohio Player Billy Beck provided the sound effect by simply moving a ton of air through some really tight vocal cords!

Ozzy Osbourne, whose heavy-metal act was so heavy they need to reinforce the floors of most stages, must have known he'd attract legends right from the start, but even he couldn't have known how wild they'd get!

Ozzy threw Dalmatian puppies into the audience, then refused to play a single note until all the puppies died.

Ozzy, in a game of "Who's Got the Biggest Ones," defecated in the middle of the stage, then dared anyone in his audience to do worse. A fan leaped to the stage and ate it.

Ozzy had sex with a goat onstage.

Ozzy once bit the head off a live bat.

As Ozzy himself once pointed out, "This isn't news, it's been said of dozens of heavy rockers before me, and it'll be said of even more after me." The man could have been a folklorist!

Of all the things attributed to Osbourne, only one is true. He once bit the head off a live bat. Of course, when the bat was thrown onstage, it just lay there like a rubber bat,

which is precisely what Ozzy thought it was! When he chomped into it and realized it wasn't a toy, wasn't even dead, he ran for the wings, threw up, and ordered a tetanus shot! As one of his roadies once commented, "It's bad enough to have the Christian fundamentalists picketing you all the time, but ain't nobody wants Greenpeace slapping their stickers all over the bus, ya know?"

Elvis Presley, like most young performers, dreamed of hitting it big his first time out, perhaps forgetting that his first real audition would likely be more nerve-racking than any other to come. Still, he figured he had some talent, and probably wasn't expecting a rejection quite as strong as, "Stick to driving a truck, you'll never make it as a singer!"

According to popular legend, that's precisely what Sam Phillips, owner of the Sun Records label, said after hearing the rockabilly stylings of a young man with a handsome face and hips that wouldn't stop.

Like most celebrity legends, the story is only half true. The putdown didn't come from Sam Phillips. It came from Eddie Bond, a professional bandsman who auditioned Presley for a singing spot in his own group. After hearing Presley's first nervous renditions, he uttered the famous words and watched Presley drive off in Crown Electric's delivery truck.

When, months later, Presley's first Sun Records song hit it big and Bond asked Elvis to audition again, Presley sent a polite thanks-but-no-thanks reply.

The other famous quote associated with Elvis Presley is one he supposedly made himself on a respected talk show, Edward R. Murrow's *Person to Person:* "The only thing a nigger can do for me is buy my records and shine my shoes."

Presley never appeared on *Person to Person.*

Presley spent thirty years working with people of all colors and faiths. Not one of them ever heard him disparage anyone on either count. No one has ever come forward to provide a first-person account of the incident. In short, he never said it.

"Puff the Magic Dragon," made famous by Peter, Paul, and Mary, has long been held up as an example of the era's barely hidden drug culture references. "Little Jackie Paper" became a reference to the cigarette papers used to roll the day's drugs of choice. Puff himself stood for smoking whatever was rolled in "little Jackie Paper." "The Land of Hannah Lee" turns into Hanalei, Hawaii, the site of some really primo marijuana. And the imagery goes on and on—if you're looking for it.

Peter Yarrow, the Peter of Peter, Paul, and Mary, wasn't looking for such images when he wrote a tune to accompany a poem, "Puff, the Magic Dragon," by Leonard Lipton. Lipton claims he wasn't interested in drug imagery, either, when he based his poem on an even earlier rhyme by Ogden Nash, "The Really-O Truly-O Dragon." And Nash, like Lipton and Yarrow, was writing about child-hood lost.

Remembering that this song was widely performed in the sixties, why would anyone need to encrypt a drug song anyway?

Frank Zappa's appearance in any town invariably sparked renewed interest in two legends. The first contends that, sometime in 1964, Frank Zappa and Alice Cooper were performing on the same London stage when the two found themselves engaged in an impromptu gross-out contest. Cooper managed to stick his tongue up his own nose; Zappa topped that by sticking his tongue up Cooper's nose. Back and forth it went, each outdoing the other and pulling deeper groans out of the audience. Eventually, Cooper turned around, dropped his pants, pulled his cheeks apart, and proceeded to defecate in the middle of the stage. Zappa eyed that performance for a minute as the audience screamed. Then, without missing a beat, he walked over, scooped up a handful, and ate it!

The screams turned to low retching.

Cooper shook his head and backed off. "You win, man, you win."

Excuse the pun, but this whole story is nothing but crap!

Cooper and Zappa both denied it, no one's ever come up with the particulars, such as date or location, and no one can even recall an occasion when Zappa and Cooper could possibly have engaged in their "contest." Remember what Ozzy said?

7
CAMPUS CAPERS

ontradictions characterize the college experience. We leave home with high hopes and deep fears. From top dogs at high school to low men (or women) on campus is the matter of just a few months in time, but a world in experience. Anxious to break free. Homesick. Scared. Urban legends grow from just such contradictions. In one sense, the campus legends form a microcosm of all the others. There's a little sex, a little horror, a lot of humor. Still, they remain unique in their ability to illuminate our relationship with authority.

During our childhood, our ability to flout the rules is extremely limited, first by our parents. Our next tyrants, grade-school teachers, carry our parents' authority *and* add their own certainty that no student could possibly harbor any insight deeper than their own. College, then, is for most of us our first opportunity to insist the world deal with us on our own level. The resultant pushing and pulling as roles are established, and new limits drawn, create situations that could happen nowhere else, and certainly not with as much humor!

IN THE CLASSROOM

University classes are never quite what students—or instructors—anticipate, and, when those expectations clash, legends arise.

Just getting the professors and students in the same room can be a challenge, as "The Ticking Prof" proves.

Freshman students at Cornell were reputedly left wondering if they'd found the right classroom when, ten minutes into the class's time period, their instructor had yet to make an appearance. Many watches were looked at again, many pens rapped rhythmically against desktops, and loud sighs periodically punctured the crowded silence until one student, clearly older than his classmates, stood up and headed for the door.

"Time's up on this guy!"

What?

"Well, if he was a full professor, I'd have to wait twenty minutes, but since he's only a contractual instructor for us lowly frosh, we've only got to wait *ten*. After that, he can't mark us absent, but we can go."

Really?

"Oh yeah. Check the handbook."

No one checked, but they all trooped out following the older and presumably wiser scholar.

The next day, as they filed in to take seats in front of a clearly infuriated instructor, one freshman decided to take the bull by the horns and challenge the instructor on his tardiness the day before. The student lived to regret it, barely, as the instructor erupted into a tirade about education at this level being about "wanting it," not being "forced into it like kindergarten children." The student's suggestion, that the professor read the handbook before tearing into his students, provoked the expected anger—and an unexpected comeback!

In preparation for its twenty-fifth reunion, the Harvard class of '26 mailed a confidential computer punchcard questionnaire to its members and asked them to participate in a survey of sexual habits. One male alumnus returned his card promptly, but with this marginal comment. "In my opinion, sex is a subject to be discussed with women, not with an International Business Machine."

"There's a reason they call it the *student* handbook, young man. If *you'd* bothered to thumb through it, you'd know that *all* instructors at this institution receive *fifteen* minutes' grace—exactly the same amount of time we give *students* before declaring them AWOL from that class!"

The older student had slunk out at the beginning of that conversation.

As it happens, students across the United States are equally guilty of falling for this particular legend, which is trotted out at the beginning of almost every semester as students and professors discover how badly the administration has mucked up the room allocations. Few students have ever read their handbook—most can't even find it when asked!

Brunvand, the grandmaster of urban folklore, quotes a version of this tale that has a harassed professor rushing back to his office for a forgotten item and leaving his hat on the desk. The next day he chastises his students, and at the next class he arrives to find a classroom of hats on desks, but no students!

The film *Real Genius* takes the distance between student and professorial expectations one step further, and reverses the process when the fictional semester ends with a professor leaving his tape-recorded lecture running while students tape it onto their own machines! There's absolutely no one in the classroom!

"The Big Mouth" emphasizes the distance between generations as well as expectations. One professor, known for his chauvinistic comments, spent the better part of a semester alienating his female students while trying to buddy up with the guys in the class. Eventually, unable to contemplate yet another session of snide remarks and sexist jibes, the women of the class decided to exit en masse at the first incident of the next class. Their individual protests hadn't garnered much attention, but they hoped a show of concerted displeasure might get through to him.

The next day the female students sat calmly until he came out with, "I've heard there's a huge shortage of prostitutes in Russia since the breakup of the old Soviet Union . . ."

The girls, as agreed, rose together and headed for the door.

Their protest didn't turn out quite as expected when the professor immediately called out, "Hey, come back, the next flight isn't until tomorrow!"

Though this tale pervades many campuses, in many variants other than the example above (a relatively recent one overheard at MIT), it isn't a complete myth. Students in Minnesota trace this one back as far as the turn of the century to a Dr. A. C. Hadden. There have been shifts in focus over time. In the Hadden accounts, the anthropology professor was discussing a tribe in Africa whose men reputedly thought a fifteen-inch penis in the erect state was perfectly normal. When a clutch of women got up to leave, either because they found the incident offensive or because they simply had somewhere else to be, he called out something to the effect that boats to Africa only left once a week! In the earlier variant, the women weren't necessarily protesting anything.

Another student who didn't quite manage to be in the same classroom as his professor—at least not at the same time—features in "The Impossible Homework." George Dantzig, a math student at Stanford, arrived late, very late, for his statistics class while taking graduate classes at UC Berkeley. Seeing two problems on the board without any accompanying solutions or notes, he assumed they were the assignment set for that class. He copied them, and struggled with them a bit more than usual, but eventually completed both problems and slipped them in the prof's assignment drop box.

When the professor rang him that evening, the student could have been excused for expecting the worst. Who ever heard of a professor calling to *praise* a student? Then again, who ever heard of a student solving the examples his professor had put up as "impossible" to solve?

And this one's no myth! Dantzig is a real student who really solved the problems that had been deemed impossible by the best mathematicians. His solutions were written up in respected publications. Any scenario where the student outwits the establishment, startling the professor into actually noticing the student, naturally gives students everywhere, including those who have no hope of ever accomplishing anything so grandiose, a nice warm glow. That it's a true story only makes the glow that much more comforting.

Of course, being *in* the class doesn't guarantee that anything will go smoothly. The heroes of "Salt on the Rim," a genuinely interested student and her enthusiastic biology professor, both managed to find the classroom and were actively participating in the learning process. That day's topic, sperm and their survival ability, seemed pretty innocuous. Longer tails made sperm better swimmers, more likely to succeed in reaching the egg first. A heavier coating of specific enzymes made it easier for sperm to break down the outside of the egg and penetrate it, more likely to succeed in fertilizing the egg. A substantial amount of sugar stored in semen provided a ready food source for the sperm, enhancing the sperm's chances of surviving and reaching the egg.

The student nodded as each of the first two points was made, then frowned at the last.

The professor, seeing her confusion, asked if she had a question on any of this material.

She nodded, "Yeah, if semen is full of all these available sugars, so the sperm can use it, why does it taste so salty?"

Only when dead silence descended did she realize what she'd revealed about her own biological experiments! Face flushing wildly, she raced from the room.

This one is apparently nothing more than a highly amusing myth, though it's been repeated as having definitely happened to every friend of a friend who's ever been to college.

Another oldie but goodie is "The Biology Lab," which also features a seriously intent young female student and a helpful instructor, if in a slightly different setting. One of the earliest lab demonstrations in human physiology or general zoology asks students to observe the properties of a single cell. Freshman students, however, don't always have the skills required to separate cells from one another without destroying them. To overcome this little technicality, lab instructors long ago discovered that scraping a toothpick along the inside of the cheek and stirring it about in a little saline solution produced enough intact cells for study without having to teach these first-year students a whole new set of skills—or lopping off any really important cells!

So, as the earnest student stared through her microscope, she was delighted by the large swirl of intact cells on her slide, but startled by one oddball cell swimming right through her field of vision!

Calling her instructor over, she pointed at the microscope and asked him to identify whatever was moving around there.

He leaned over and looked down. For a very long time he stood there, just leaning and looking. After a while she tapped him on the shoulder.

"Do you know what it is?"

A muffled "Yes."

Still he didn't stand up or look her in the eye.

"Well, what is it?"

"Sp . . . mumble, mumble . . . cell."

"What?"

Another long pause, then he stood, looked her straight in the eye, and said, "That is what's known as a sperm cell. I'm making no comment on how it might have gotten there."

Face flushing wildly, she too rushed from the room.

Sex, as chapter one illustrates, is often the focus of urban legends. The difference between the usual sex legends and college legends about sex is that the college legends actually tend to be more, not less, innocent.

The classroom has been described as a crucible, a place to break down old beliefs and replace them with knowledge. Sometimes, however, as in "The Finger," it's simply a place to learn that things aren't always what they seem. This tale has been set in at least fifty different venues, but my personal favorite, as it's set close to my own home (and isn't it accessibility that makes these tales so enduring?), appears in *Sir Wilfred Grenfell, Forty Years for Labrador*:

"A Glasgow teacher, in order to emphasize the value of observation, prepared a little cupful of kerosene, mustard, and castor oil, and, calling the attention of his class to it, dipped a finger into the atrocious compound and then sucked his finger. He next passed the mixture around to the students, who did the same with dire results. When the cup returned and he observed the faces of his students, he remarked, 'Gentlemen, I am afraid you did not use your powers of observation. The finger that I put into the cup was not the same one that I stuck into my mouth.'"

In later versions, the mixture changes to urine for diabetes testing and all sorts of equally disgusting mixtures. The scene shifts from Glasgow to nearly every American university known. The warning to students, to watch out for the sneaky tricks of wily professors, remains inviolate. To folklorists, the tale also reveals much about the inner workings of the student mind—and what a paranoid place it must be to concoct such a lesson for unsuspectingly innocent scholars.

Even in collegiate urban legends, however, a touch of horror can still be found. "The Reunion" features one of the few places on campus that might qualify as a horrific setting—the gross anatomy lab. Not familiar with this corner of the campus? It's the place where medical students contemplate their first cadavers. Everyone in the medical field knows how notoriously difficult it is to obtain corpses for these young students to use. What isn't as well known is that the very best gross anatomy instructors teach their students not only the clues to be found in death, but a deep respect for the dead themselves.

Gallows humor, which serves to relieve tension, is quickly differentiated from simple, crude disrespect toward those whose generosity provides the bodies so necessary to qualifying a well-educated physician.

So, to a medical student, few things could be worse than, upon having been assigned one of the rare cadavers available for study, to discover that the body is that of someone he has known!

This isn't as unlikely as it might appear. Bodies donated for scientific study aren't shipped all over the country when they can go to local facilities. In many cases the deceased may have actually specified which medical school would benefit from the donation. Students are more mobile, but even so, the expense of out-of-state tuition in a field already costly would dissuade at least some from moving too far from home to pursue

> **To explain infinite distance more clearly to his physics class, a professor used this example: "It is that distance which the dean of women would like to use to separate the men's dorms from the women's dorms."**

their education. With both students and bodies staying close to home, the odds of meeting someone you know on the autopsy table certainly increase.

Several famous fictional students have encountered cadavers they previously knew as living, breathing characters, but the field is also rife with accounts of real medical students being reintroduced to acquaintances and family members after death. The real story of William Burke and William Hare goes back to the earliest days of gross anatomy classes, when the practice wasn't all that legitimate, and when bodies were often obtained by simply digging up the person most recently interred at the local cemetery.

Burke and Hare got into the body-snatching business almost accidentally. One of their lodgers died owing them rent and, to redeem the debt, they sold his corpse to a local anatomy professor. Then they helped a few other lodgers along, including a very popular prostitute from the area, Mary Patterson. Her dead body was identified by two medical students—no one asked how they knew her that well—and the whole setup was exposed!

In modern times, medical schools attempt to avoid presenting anyone with a relative or friend by posting the names of that session's cadavers ahead of time. Even this can't prevent all the accidental encounters, but it has cut down on them.

AT CENTER STAGE— PROFESSORS

Because the majority of college legends are generated and circulated by students, not professors, you'd expect to find tales painting these illustrious if somewhat intellectually snobbish men and women in less than their best light. And you will. Something else you might expect to find in tales where students finally get the upper hand of their professors is the trace of malicious retribution found in so many urban legends. You won't. As the next tales illustrate, college legends are more likely to paint professors as *too* human rather than godlike.

Take "It Takes Three?," for example. According to this legend, registration at Texas Christian University used to be much more complicated than it later became. At most colleges and universities, registration is a hectic round of students attempting to fit all the classes they need into the slots available while avoiding those early-morning classes, the toughest professors, or any slot that leaves you sitting in some lab late on a Friday night! Little things like filling in your name, address, date of birth, sex, and student number on dozens of forms as the day progressed were just the usual inconveniences—except for TCU students. When it came to the box marked "Sex," students could check "M," "F," or "U"!

"U"?

Registration at Texas Christian obviously required the student to have a degree *before* registration, or so goes the legend non-TCU students pass around as they stand in long lineups looking for a silver lining. At least *they* don't have to figure out if this is a trick question on the first day!

Though this one sounds suspiciously apocryphal, and a look at the last registration form for Texas Christian certainly doesn't have any spaces for "U," there's a hint of truth to the whole thing, a hint that can be traced back to a very human professor.

It seems Texas Christian University was one of the earliest colleges to begin switching their records, admissions, and student evaluations from manual systems to a new-fangled computerized system. To make the whole thing work, all the professors had to develop at least basic skills in this new area. Like students, professors aren't always delighted with being forced to learn new things—especially when learning the new thing takes a huge chunk out of an already jam-packed schedule.

To make the changeover a little less painful, the university sponsored free classes for all staff members. Within a short time the majority of teachers could check a student's past transcript, record new marks, and plot a graphic representation of class achievement, all before finishing that second cup of morning java—all except one. No matter how much effort he expended on this new system, one tenured professor just couldn't get a handle on the technology.

One day, after listening to his colleagues rant on about the new insights they were gaining from the ability to access student records instantly, he decided this might be the best way to tackle a question he'd been curious about for years, but for which he'd never had an easy way to gather the necessary data. He wanted to see if his male students or his female students were more likely to do well in his program of studies, and if that program of studies reflected how well male students and female students did overall. With a computer to handle the statistical analysis, he should have had an answer within days.

Should have.

When the computer, using the professor's programming, finished sorting the students by sex and achievement, he had *three* sets of data: Male, Female, and Undecided!

By casting the professor in the role of frustrated student, this legend lets the student body view eminent scholars as people, people with better benefits, but people nonetheless.

"The Yard" tackles that same issue from a different perspective. Harvard, like most large established universities, has sprouted many legends. Some, like the tale of students shooting at the university's bell to fool professors into letting them out early, are hard to prove. Some, such as the fact that Leonard Bernstein's piano is stuffed away in a clock tower, are easily confirmed. Some, like the one recounted here, have gotten a little twisted over time.

A senior student was walking with a freshman one beautiful fall afternoon, generally showing her around her new campus and filling her in on all the information that doesn't come in the students' handbook. As they passed the duck pond, he pointed at the season's migrating birds, then to several that waddled back and forth between the pond and some manmade hutches.

"Those birds belong to the student body. They were injured at various times and adopted. They stay here year-round."

The freshman smiled, said how nice it was to know students here were active in animal rescue, and then moved on. In a short time they came to a cow roaming through a nearby field.

"That cow belongs to the student body. It used to be some team's mascot, but, well, it's ours now!"

The freshman smiled, commented on the pranks she'd heard were pulled around this school, and suggested it might be time to send the cow home.

The senior shrugged, and after watching the cow calmly chew its cud for a few

How many teachers would you like to have set this table for?

moments, the pair moved on. Before long, they were walking across the Yard, one of Harvard's more recognizable landmarks, when another cow wandered by.

"Oh no!" the freshman exclaimed. "Pranks are pranks, but exactly how long have you been stealing cows from that team!"

"Oh, we didn't steal that one. Only professors are allowed to keep cows in the Yard!"

This is one of the multitude of ways that freshmen are introduced to Harvard's many rules, including those as outdated as the one that stipulates that the only cows to be kept in the Yard shall be those of its distinguished professors. Other places might rank their staff by how close their parking spot is to their offices, but this is Harvard!

Although most students avoid the tough professors like the plague, one legendary professor, a chemist from Harvard, had to beat them away from his classes with a stick. It wasn't that he was popular for his personality or his subject matter. His course wasn't a prerequisite for medical school, or for anything else. He was a perfectionist who expected the same from his students. His exams came back "bleeding" from the amount of red ink he doled out to unfortunates who fell short of perfection.

So why would students have vied for spots in his classes?

Because, according to legend, he once had to make good on the boast that "If any one of you ever catches me in an error, I'll eat my shoe!" No one had actually seen the last shoe go down, of course, but the chance to serve up a shoe, without ketchup, to any professor, was worth the price of admission to the class. So, each semester, students crammed into his class to see if they wouldn't be the next one to catch him in a mistake. Most left the class well versed in the principles of chemical theory, but none left a professor with only one shoe behind them. At least not until Bobby Vinny. Bobby wasn't a chemist at heart, as his marks proved, but his classmates would come to love him when, one deeply depressing February afternoon, it was Bobby who finally caught his professor in a boo-boo!

Of course, it wasn't a chemistry boo-boo (it had something to do with the engine size of a 1989 Ford Bronco), but it *was* an error and, as Bobby rightly pointed out, the prof hadn't said it had to be an error of chemistry.

The next afternoon, though still drab and dull, seemed glowing with sunshine to the 202 students who filled the lecture hall to watch their professor eat his shoe.

The professor, however, wasn't about to let such a captive audience leave without imparting some morsel of knowledge, and he was ready for them when they arrived. They, for their part, were more than a little confused by the array of glassware and chemicals topping the demonstration bench. They'd been expecting something a little simpler, like a knife and fork, maybe a plate.

The professor, however, would have the last laugh. As his students watched, he dissolved the shoe in a strong acid and then explained how this might then be neutralized with an equally strong base. When this reaction resulted in a neutral precipitate, the professor scooped it up, spread it on a bagel, and downed the entire shoe in just a few gulps!

As long as students perceive themselves as the "us" against the "them" of professors ranked against them, one-upmanship tales like this are frequent candidates for being passed along at the next keg party.

"The Errors," a tale of a professor who doesn't need students to engage in a one-upmanship contest, delights students as it proves beyond a doubt that profs can be as stupid as anyone.

The star of this legend is a history profes-

sor who, for over twenty years, was considered the top man in his field. He'd lectured widely, had written several books viewed as bibles by his students and senior scholars alike, and was now enjoying spending his last few years before retirement at a prestigious western university where his teaching duties were light and the perks many. It was to this distinguished man that the editors of the *Encyclopaedia Britannica* sent one of their articles that hadn't been updated for some time.

The article came back by return post, nearly covered in changes and notations, along with the professor's letter, which condemned the piece as being "as badly organized and full of errors as anything I've ever seen from a freshman!" Stunned by this harsh denunciation, the editors began digging through their records to discover just who might have been the first author.

Since this is an urban legend, you already know who wrote the first piece, right? The same professor who'd just condemned it!

The image of the forgetful professor is, of course, a staple in college legend—though usually portrayed with a bit more sympathy than in that last tale. There's something endearing about the Disney version of the absentminded but adorable professor who keeps forgetting his own wedding in his quest for knowledge. Everyone who has passed through the ivory towers has probably wished for teachers so enthusiastic about their subjects that they could put their students first in their eagerness to share what they've learned. All too often, students feel they come very low on the priority list of professors who only teach in order to be eligible for grants at the end of the year.

Students at the Massachusetts Institute of Technology must have thought they'd gone to heaven when one of the world's real absentminded professors agreed to teach there. Norbert Wiener, who wrote *Cybernetics* and became one of the most respected men in his field, was heading across a Cambridge quad when a student hurried up to catch him and ask a question. Wiener stopped and discussed the answer at length until the student was perfectly comfortable with the material. Wiener's only question to the student was, "Can you tell me which way I was going when you stopped me?"

The student blinked, then pointed. "Um, you were walking *that* way, sir."

Professor Wiener nodded, smiled, and murmured, "Oh, then I've had lunch, I guess," and continued on his way!

A different sort of professor and a different style of students appear in "The Pavlovian Professor." Ivan Petrovich Pavlov was the physiologist who pioneered the study of conditional reflexes. By ringing a bell every time he fed a group of dogs, he helped them form a mental and physical connection between being fed and the sound of the bell. Eventually the dogs began associating the bell with food, and salivated whenever they heard the bell ring. Psychologists

claim that by rewarding subjects positively for desired behaviors and negatively for unwanted behaviors, they can condition those subjects to behave in certain ways. One class of psychology students decided to conduct their own experiment in this area—with their professor as the guinea pig!

Together they decided to start with something simple. When the professor stood on the left side of the room, the students leaned forward, appeared intently interested, and responded often and enthusiastically to the professor's comments. When he stood on the right side of the room, they leaned back, became silent, and appeared generally apathetic. Much to their delight, they discovered that by midway through the semester, their professor walked into the classroom, dropped his gear on his desk, and headed straight for the left side of the classroom, where he stood for the entire ninety minutes! They'd done it!

Flushed with success, they decided to try something more complicated. For the next several weeks they responded well to the professor whenever he leaned against the windows on the left side of the classroom, and less well whenever he moved away from the windows. At the end of the semester, as spring was changing to summer, the psychology professor's typical teaching pose had devolved into his sitting on the wide window ledge, leaning back against the pane with his notes piled to either side of him.

Deciding that their experiment was a success, the students brought in a video camera to the last class of the term to record this behavior and then present the results to the professor. The film was rolling when the professor bounded into the classroom, crossed hurriedly to the windows, and hoisted himself up on the ledge. It was still rolling when the professor leaned back. Unfortunately, his students never got to give him that tape. The warmth of approaching spring had encouraged the previous occupants of the room to open the tall windows! The professor flipped backward before he said a single word, falling three stories straight down to his death!

The professor probably learned little from the whole experience, but his students learned a great deal about doing anything carelessly or without cause!

According to the legend, the tale can't be pinned down to a particular college or university, not because it didn't happen, but because the students couldn't admit to it without implicating themselves in the professor's death!

Of all the legends about professors, this one is the most variable. As in this example, it serves as a warning not to mess with another's head. In the examples where the professor doesn't die, but simply becomes the butt of an elaborate student joke, the message that professors aren't above human frailty comes to the fore. Other examples don't even rib the professor too severely and seem designed to prove that with the appropriate student achievement, students could establish themselves as

equal to, if not a little brighter than, their teachers.

A variety of behaviors have been attributed to the tale's victim. In one version the professor doesn't sit on a window ledge, but is "encouraged" to turn a wastebasket upside down and stand on it! Another is taught to write on just one side of the board, a behavior that continues to be honed by student response until he's writing in a tiny corner in script so small that no one could ever read it anyway! As with all tales, a certain percentage of these behaviors tend to make the professor appear ridiculous, while the majority do him little or no harm at all, all depending on the intent of those telling the tale.

The tale that brings professors and students closest, however, doesn't depend on student effort at all. "The Robin" tells the story of a class that, like many others, found it difficult to concentrate as spring unfolded around them. Soft air coming through the windows carried the scent of new growth, and the students stirred restlessly. Still, they tried to pay attention out of respect for their professor, an eminent man who'd done well by them all term.

When a robin landed on their windowsill, however, it was the *professor* who suddenly and unexpectedly gave his class the rest of the day off by going AWOL with the simple excuse, "Gentlemen, I have a date with spring."

If it sounds like some student fantasy, the sort that gets turned into a legend of fairy godmothers setting imprisoned students free, remember that professors fantasize, too! In April 1912, philosopher and teacher George Santayana was working at Harvard when a robin really did land on his window! The rest is legend, and truth.

THE EXTRACURRICULAR LIFE

If college life were nothing but classes and eccentric professors, no one would go. It's the rich experiences promised at those beautiful campuses that lure students to them. Almost anything can happen at college, or so students are led to believe—and so urban legends continue. No institution runs without administration and paperwork by the cartload, to which pranks and other minor acts of rebellion are a natural counterpoint, so there are dozens of such legends. College, being a little world unto itself, however, also spawns tales of celebrities, horror, and, of course, sex!

The Registrar, supposedly a real, living being, has, at most schools, turned into nothing more than an office, a name on a check, or the address on the envelope carrying an application. With the arrival of computerized registration, many students have come to believe the Registrar is nothing more than a workstation tucked away in some corner of the administration building. Which explains an urban legend like "The Zoo."

A professor walked into his first class of the semester with a stack of papers to hand out and a list of students in this section. Nothing unusual at all until he started reading out his roll call.

"Jennifer Byrd . . . Malcolm Fox . . . Herbert Lamb . . . Christian Wolf . . . Mark Renard . . . Philip Lyon . . ."

Every person in the section was named for some sort of animal! The Registrar, that contraption in the corner of the offices, had a sense of humor!

Unfortunately, for the legend at least, this probably couldn't happen today, as students are much freer to chose their own schedules and preferred time slots than when this legend first began its rounds. A similar tale put all the place-names, such as Chelsea and Bingham, into one class while the names of occupations, like Cooper, Hooper, Joyner, Weaver, Baker, and whatnot found themselves as classmates in the next room. In every case, the students are stunned by the realization that real people make up that faceless body known as the Administration.

That *individuals,* even those working at the highest levels of the ivory tower, could possess something as intrinsically human as humor has been accepted for some time, of course, especially if the individual's own stature was enough to overshadow even his lofty university position. It was just such an individual, Woodrow Wilson, who incited a brief belief that Princeton, in an effort to outrecruit its rival, Harvard, was offering a money-back guarantee with every student!

It wasn't true, but the story that inspired it

most certainly is, and illustrates just how well developed a sense of humor some administrators bring to their job.

It was a crisp day on the Princeton campus when Wilson decided to take a stroll about and see for himself how the fall registration was progressing. He was barely out of his office door when the mother of one of his new freshmen spotted him and proceeded to give him a piece of her mind.

It seemed that her father and her grandfather before him were Harvard men, and she'd always assumed any children of her own would also attend that prestigious school. Fate played a funny trick on her, however, and she ended up married to a Princeton man who'd insisted on sending their only boy here. She wasn't convinced they were doing the right thing. Could Wilson offer her any assurance that the education the boy was about to receive would "mold him for great things"?

"My dear madam," Wilson, who knew a thing or two about "great things" himself, replied with a straight face, "We guarantee satisfaction, or we return the boy!"

Even dorm assignments provide opportunities for humor, as was the case in "The Foreign Exchange Student." A young man from New York was accepted at Cornell and soon received the forms he'd have to return in order to receive his room assignment. One of the questions asked how he would feel about sharing a room with a foreign exchange student. The student quickly assured the questioner that he'd be delighted to room with a foreign student as it would give him the opportunity to experience a different sort of education.

On arrival, he found himself sharing with another freshman who seemed quite friendly and enthusiastic about the arrangement. For several days the two settled in and took care of the remainder of the registration process. During that time our student from New York was sure he could detect some accent when his roomie spoke, but couldn't place his home country based on that or any of his other habits. Eventually he couldn't resist and, just before they turned in on their third night together, he finally asked, "Where exactly are you from? I can't place the accent."

Startled, the other student looked up quickly. "You know, I was about to ask you the same thing!"

"Well, I'm from Queens—that's in New York City. You?"

"Brooklyn."

It seems the dorm director thought it was a great joke to take two boys from NYC, both of whom showed every willingness to share with a "foreigner," and see how long it took them to figure it all out! Though this tale is told at several universities besides Cornell, it may have a grain of truth to it as well. A letter to *The New York Times,* purportedly written by one of the two students, tells the story with every indication of its being a first-person tale and predates the first verifiable instances of its appearance at Cornell.

A penny saved is a penny earned—or put away for college.

One young man in "The Doctor" wasn't laughing when, because of a computer glitch, his degree and his transcript for the many courses leading up to that degree seemingly disappeared—just when he needed copies of those documents to present to a prospective employer!

Catching a cab across town to the campus administration office ate up most of the cash in his pocket that day. Arriving to find the counter staff on yet another of their seemingly endless coffee breaks, and being forced to wait twenty minutes for service, did little to improve his temper. Over the next two hours he was passed from administration office to administration office, then along to several of his old professors, before finally receiving a copy of the transcript and degree. He was racing for a bus, and tearing open the envelope to see, for the first time, his brand-new degree, when he almost ran in front of a taxi.

"You jerk!" the driver yelled.

At that moment the envelope finally gave up its treasure and, for just a second, the young man stood staring at it, continuing to block traffic. Finally, with the first serene smile of his day, he looked at the cabbie, tipped his hat, and replied, "That'll be *Doctor Jerk*, if you don't mind," before continuing on across the street to the bus stop.

Though likely apocryphal, this tale has been attributed to Jonas Salk.

The young man in "A Penny a Day" was more concerned with the fiscal practicalities of obtaining his degree than with the spiritual satisfaction he hoped it might one day bring. To that end, he placed ads in several major papers:

STUDENT SEEKS EDUCATION
Can you spare a single penny?
That's all it would take to
help put me through college!
I've worked hard all summer,
but I'm coming up short.
Please help!

Over the next few weeks the enterprising young man was delighted to find himself buried in envelopes containing the pennies he'd asked for, and a few larger donations, too. Before he knew it, he had the equivalent of nearly one *million* pennies, more than enough to get him through.

As a fairy-godmother story, with the twist of a little added innovation on the part of the lucky recipient, this legend works beautifully as is, and would certainly appeal to the many students who work their tails off just to stay in school. Discovering that the story is *true* just adds that much more fairy dust.

In 1987, Mike Hayes was a chemistry freshman in desperate need of money to get on with his education. He didn't take out ads, but he went one better. He persuaded a *Chicago Tribune* columnist, Bob Greene, to ask his readers to send the boy a penny. They

did—2,800,000 of them. When converted to $28,000, Hayes had the money he needed. He went on to graduate from the University of Illinois with a degree in Food Science. Not a bad return on couch droppings.

Some donations, of course, come with strings attached, as did the $5 million donation Mrs. Eleanor Elkins Widener once made to Harvard, though those strings have nothing to do with the "Ice Scream Patron" legend that's entrenched itself fairly firmly there. A lot of students arriving at Harvard are impressed by the quality of food available on campus, especially in the dorm dining halls.

One item in particular always seems to stand out, though it's neither rare nor costly—ice cream. Harvard's students can have ice cream with both their lunch and evening meal, seven days a week, if they want. Over the years this cool treat has gone down with many murmured thanks to Mrs. Eleanor Elkins Widener, but she isn't responsible for it. Yes, she did donate all that money, and put some restrictions on its use, but she didn't insist the school serve ice cream. It's on the menu because students have consistently shown their approval of it by coming back for more!

Much of Mrs. Widener's money has actually gone into that perennial administration project, the building fund. It seems every campus in America insists on erecting new buildings wherever and whenever possible, rerouting traffic every so often, and generally confusing staff and students. Since no topic is taboo for legends, even this aspect of collegiate life is immortalized in one tale or another.

At Columbia University, walkways seem to have been uppermost on the building committee's joint mind for some years now. Every spring the birds would return, new grass would be sown, and "Keep Off the Lawns!" signs would sprout quicker than the most enthusiastic crocus! Students racing from class to class ignored the signs. Before long the university was enforcing the message on those signs, requiring students to make long detours for the sake of this grass. Naturally this upset the students, and before long, administration and students were experiencing some rather heated discussions in the middle of those same lawns. Eventually the buildings and grounds committees brought it to the attention of the then-president of the university General Dwight D. Eisenhower.

Ike duly went out to inspect the troops and, after nodding for a bit as the students raced by him, turned to the committee head and said, "Have you ever noticed how much quicker it is to head directly where you're going? Why not let the students take whichever route works, then build the walkways over the bare patches?"

The kids walked, the committees watched and eventually built more walkways, and for some time now, Columbia University's campus has been recognized as one of the most conveniently arranged campuses nationwide.

Historic significance isn't, despite appearances to the contrary, always recognized by building committees. It's the lapses that are unusual, so, not surprisingly, it's the unusual incidents that find their way into collegiate legends. For example, it's widely believed that John F. Kennedy, while a student at Harvard, and living in Weld Hall, had to bunk in the bathroom! One tour guide at Harvard actually confirmed it while leading a bunch of Japanese tourists past the building!

It's not true. When JFK lived at Weld Hall, Room 32 was Room 32, not a bathroom, not a closet, not a storage room, nothing but a rather ordinary college dorm room. Pictures of him taken there show walls and a window, but no plumbing!

So how did the legend arise?

A building committee, of course. Having toured the building sometime after 1940, when Kennedy spent his freshman year there, someone suggested that extra bathroom space might be a good plan. To that end, when the building was next remodeled some years later, just after the end of the war, Weld Hall 32 became another women's bathroom. So, yes, there's some truth to the legend, if you ignore the intervening six or seven years. It didn't stay a bathroom for that long. Yet another building committee decision suggested it might be a more convenient building if it had an elevator to save students some of those stairs. Again, they looked at the overall plan and decided the space that used to be Weld Hall 32, and was now a bathroom, could easily be spared to accommodate an elevator shaft. So it would be equally true to say that JFK, while living at Weld, lived in the elevator!

What does it say about that legend's audience that we will believe the future president of the United States would willingly live in the ladies' loo, but we can't quite picture him living in an elevator?

The building committee features rather prominently in yet another Harvard myth, the "Upside Down Hall," which insists that the distinctive Carpenter Center, designed by French architect Le Corbusier, was built upside down! Le Corbusier apparently had no idea what had become of the plans as he was still in France while the Carpenter Center was being built and it was only his arrival for the dedication ceremonies that alerted Harvard that something was distinctly wrong!

(Of course, there are those who would argue that, right side up or upside down, it's *still* an ugly building.)

As it happens, the Carpenter Center wasn't built upside down.

So why would anyone believe builders *would* construct a building upside down, or backward, or in any of the other misaligned positions claimed of the Carpenter Center?

Because it *has* happened to other buildings on other campuses!

The Queen Elizabeth II Library and Resource Center at Memorial University of Newfoundland and Labrador, at St. John's, Newfoundland, was intended to be a marvel of solar heating, costing nearly nothing to run even through the cool winters. And it would have been—if the builders had turned it the right way around. As it stands now, backward to the architect's intent, the building roasts students all summer and leaves them freezing through the winter!

Students could be forgiven for thinking this was yet another prank pulled by the administration! There would be a certain justice in that, considering the number of pranks students regularly pull. At least the backward library only affects the students inside it. Student pranks tend to cause chain reactions involving guilty and innocent alike.

"The Dorm Room Picture" certainly began innocently enough. A magazine came to Rutgers to do a photo layout of student life, everything from what today's bright minds were thinking about, to how they spent their off hours, to how they decorated their dorm rooms. It was this last bit that started a chain-reaction response. The picture, of a typical fraternity room with its occupants lounging about amid the chaos, turned out to be an opportunity for any number of people to *un*prank themselves.

It seems the decorations in that dorm room had attracted the eye of a merchant in New Jersey. The sign hanging over one student's bed, the one with the merchant's name stenciled across it, used to hang on the front of his shop. He wanted it, or the fifteen bucks he'd paid for it, back!

Then the Hudson River Day Line, the regu-

lar ferry across the river, got in on the act.
They couldn't help noticing that one of the
life preservers dangling from the dorm room
wall belonged to them. They'd like it back.
How did they know it was theirs? Well, it
might have had something to do with the
name of the ferry, *Peter Stuyvesant,* stenciled across the front of the floating ring.

And Rutgers had thought this little photo
op might be good for the school?

Not after Standard Oil contacted them.
They couldn't think of any good reason for
their Esso globe to be dangling from that
dorm room's ceiling, and several hundred
very green reasons why it should be sent
back to them posthaste!

Though that particular story is nothing but
myth, we find it easier to swallow than many
other collegiate tales, even those based on
fact—which says a lot about our feelings on
student morality!

"The Surprise in the Dorm" brings back to
the collegiate legend some of the risqué elements other categories have in abundance.
It begins with a young man who's waiting for
his girlfriend to arrive in town for the weekend. Naturally he wants to look great, so he

gets out of class, drops his gear in the dorm
room, asks his roommate to let him know if
the girl arrives, and races for the showers.
While he's down there, the girl does indeed
show up—along with her parents—and the
roomie insists they wait here in the room
instead of down in the lobby. While they sit
and chat, the roomie can't help noticing, and
noticing, and noticing again, just how attractive the young woman across from him is. So
engaged is he in his contemplations that he
totally forgets to tell his buddy she's arrived.
When the young man arrives back at the
room, his girlfriend and her family are
shocked to see him leap through the door,
his towel wrapped around his head like a
bandit, his penis in hand, yelling "Bang!
Bang! You're dead!"

The roommate, who's been treated to this
display before, and returned it as well, during
the semester, isn't nearly as surprised by
this entrance. He's the only one capable of
laughing at all the red faces around him!

Strictly speaking, this tale could be set in
locations off campus as well, but in defense
of its position as a collegiate legend, exactly
where else would anyone be able to stand
naked *outside* his room door, towel around
his head instead of his hips, and not incite
screams outside the room as well as in?

Pranks, and the legends about them, satisfy the collegiate legend's need for humor,
but all good categories of legends also
include a little sex and horror, which is visible in these last three extracurricular tales.

"The Dead Roommate" gained considerable notoriety when the film *Dead Man on Campus* was released. It recounted the belief of many students that, as some sort of compassionate compensation, the roommate(s) of any student who killed himself or was murdered would automatically receive straights A's, or a 4.0 GPA.

In *Dead Man on Campus,* two roomies who are about to flunk out decide to take advantage of this "regulation" and set out to locate a third roommate who can be tipped over the edge and convinced to kill himself!

This tale clearly illustrates the differences between the student view of marks as being "awarded" and the professorial view that marks are "earned." To the student, a grade is arbitrary, much as the choice of which nominee is to take home an Oscar is arbitrary. They still believe in something for nothing. Their instructors work quantitatively, adding up points for each item on a predetermined list, counting off the points for items in which the student has somehow managed to demonstrate some mastery. The two systems are clearly incompatible, which is precisely why no college anywhere has ever had any such a policy. It's a real myth.

For a little extra horror, we can turn to "The John and the Coed." A man comes into town on business and decides to surprise his daughter, who's attending a college in that community, by stopping by her dorm and taking her out to supper. When he arrives,

however, her roommate informs him that the girl is working a part-time job to cover the higher costs at the college this term, and won't be back until quite late. She will try to get his message to her.

Left with nothing to do in his hotel room that night, he's flipping through the yellow pages when he spots a number for an escort service. He calls them up and is anticipating a very cozy evening as he showers up. He's just out of the bathroom when the doorbell rings. Peeking through the security peephole, however, he sees his daughter! Evidently the roommate managed to reach her after all. Very aware that his "escort" is also about to arrive, he hesitates to answer the door, then, figuring he can quickly call the service and cancel, he pulls the door open.

It's the shock in her eyes as she discovers her father in the room that makes the whole situation clear to him. She had no idea he was in *this* room! She's the escort the service sent, and *this* is her part-time job.

"The Scream Session" combines sex with horror in a way that clearly illuminates the fears that often hide behind the wild behavior attributed to college students.

Anxiety, especially around exam week, is a very real problem for students. Although some colleges provide counseling to stressed students, most simply leave it up to the individuals to find their own safety valve. From the tradition of extending the "quiet hours" on campus during exam week has grown a second tradition, the "group scream." At campuses across the United States, exam week begins when students throw open their windows, lean out, and scream at the top of their lungs for ten or fifteen minutes. It's supposed to make the enforced quiet of the next few weeks easier to bear, and to calm student nerves before they begin cramming.

For some students, it even seems to help.

The legend contends that at a northeastern college, this traditional scream led to a horrible rape-murder. A psycho waited calmly for the beginning of the scream, then grabbed his victim and dragged her into the minimal cover provided by some hedging. Her desperate cries for help were overwhelmed by the two thousand screaming voices of her fellow students.

That something awful will happen to those who let themselves go emotionally, or who allow themselves to indulge in too much fun, may be Victorian in outlook, but it's a dominant theme on American campuses, and this tale warns against any activity that allows us to let down our guard for even a moment.

MAKING THE GRADE

While students and colleges alike expound on the value of the "college experience," the experience doesn't seem to count for much without a degree at the end, and the sheer number of exam and term-paper legends reflects the anxiety every student feels as professors prepare to judge their competence. Their diversity reflects the ingenuity both students and teachers bring to the process.

Second only to final exams on the stress scale are the elaborate term papers that may take most of the semester to complete. Hundreds of hours of meticulous research are taken almost for granted, but, to propel a paper into the "A" realm, professional-quality charts, graphs, tables, and illustrations have become almost standard academic accessories.

One student, in "Whale of a Tale," spent hours preparing her term paper for marine biology. In addition to a brilliant paper on the feeding habits of large cetaceans, she included an elaborate illustration of a whale to help the reader follow along with her theories. When her UCLA professor returned it, she was delighted to find she'd earned an A for her efforts. When she returned home for the summer break, she kept her term paper and tucked it into her memory box.

A few years later her younger sister, now also at UCLA in the same program, came upon the paper and, figuring to do her bit in the national recycling scheme, rewrote it in her own handwriting but, not having her sister's artistic ability, simply included the original illustration completely unchanged. Though she had a few nervous moments, the professor didn't seem to notice anything untoward and she, too, received an A for the paper.

A few years after that, the younger sister was packing up her dorm room when she came across the paper. Since her roommate was planning on taking the same marine biology program next semester, she made her a gift of the thick paper, which would only take up space in her bags. Again the paper was rewritten to match the student's previous handwriting samples, but, concerned that the illustration was simply too distinctive, the roommate decided to omit it.

When she received the paper, she was disappointed to discover that, this time around, it was only good enough for a C! The mystery was explained when she found this comment on the bottom of the last page: "I liked it better with the whale!"

The lack of a marine biology department doesn't impede the spread of this legend. In liberal arts colleges, it's a history paper, with a detailed line drawing of a whaling ship. At Montreal's Polytechnic, a circuit board is the distinguishing diagram.

Another college legend of the same period, "A Good Read," began in a fraternity house where one of the good turns frat brothers did for one another was to leave copies of all their papers in a group archive. While the papers were intended only to form a reference work for other house members, it was inevitable that someone would notice the dates and, assuming that no one could remember a paper written twenty years ago, simply copy it to hand in as his own work. That, of course, is exactly what did happen, though the outcome doesn't include the tragic endings common in non-collegiate tales. Instead of being accused of academic

theft, plagiarism, the student got the paper back with this comment attached to his A grade: "I only got a C for this one when I wrote it. I always thought it was worth more!"

Presumably the frat brother realized how close he came to academic suicide, and showed better judgment in the future.

The last of the classic stolen-paper tales, "Again for Your Consideration," traces the path of a single paper through the hands of four different students. Each time the paper was sold by its present owner and resubmitted by the next owner, the grade went up! The first student received a C, the next a B, the third a B-plus, and the last an A. Attached to the A paper was the following note: "I've seen this paper four times now, and I like it better each time, but I just don't see where else it can go from here, do you?"

Needless to say, the paper was swiftly, and honorably, retired from active service.

The key element to these tales, which separates them and most other collegiate legends from mainstream stories, is that despite the perception that students expect the worse from professors, *none* of the cheaters in those three tales was ever reported for academic theft! Where a mainstream tale could drag any one of those stories into larger dramas wherein a cruel professor holds the plagiarized paper over the student's head for eternity, collegiate tales are content to live in the moment and move on, much like the students who star in them.

A definite "in the moment" tale is "The

Little Quizzies." A professor at Rutgers became well known for descending on his various classes with pop quizzes that rivaled any other teacher's full-scale exams for the sheer quantity of content expected. This habit did not find favor with his students, and the entire situation was only exacerbated by the professor's irritating habit of calling these unexpected exams his "little quizzies." It's bad enough to have your poor study habits exposed on a regular basis. Having them exposed by a test with a name like this seems just one stoke of humiliation too many. At least that's how it felt for one student, who, exasperated at the announcement of yet another "little quizzie," remarked, loudly enough for all to hear, "Well, if this is a 'little quizzie,' I don't want to see his 'little testies'!"

In good urban-legend style, the student, having realized exactly what she'd just said, flushed furiously and raced from the room.

It's tales like that one that encourage students to ascertain as early as possible in the semester just what a given professor's feelings on pop quizzes might be. Students in the journalism school of Toronto's Ryerson Polytechnical Institute were patting themselves on the back for choosing the right professor when he assured them on the very first day of class that he never sprang pop quizzes; all his graded tests would be announced the week prior to the event.

Imagine their dismay, then, when on arriving at class as usual, they were informed that their quiz would start in five minutes! Hey, they protested, what happened to the promise of a week's notification for graded assignments and testing?

Without a word, the professor held up the previous week's student paper, a periodical produced, sold—and presumably read—by the journalism school itself, and calmly turned to the ads. There, at one-quarter-page size, was the announcement of the quiz!

With a concerted groan, the students reached for their pencils.

Another group of students, this one at the University of Florida, figured they had it made when their professor promised he would never set foot into the classroom with a pop quiz in his hand. The Ryerson students, having been burned already, would probably have taken a second glance at that comment, but the Floridian students simply grinned happily and went blithely forward into the rest of the term. Just before March break, they were horrified to watch as their professor came through their classroom door with his briefcase held between his feet while he walked on his hands to his desk. Yup, you guessed it, the pop quiz was in the briefcase. Turns out the professor spent his off hours living in one of the small communities occupied almost exclusively by retired circus performers!

Several other versions of "The Circus Professor" have circulated outside Florida, where the lack of a large population of circus performers apparently forced the tale to mutate into some bizarre forms. One version suggests that a professor who promised never to walk through the door with a quiz instead squirmed his way inside the classroom through the tiny transom above the door. Another claims that the professor simply walked into the classroom through the ground-floor windows. Yet another says that the professor came down a chimney/air-conditioning vent/air exchanger vent, Santa style! The most bizarre version belongs to the army, whose take on this tale has an instructor rapelling down the side of an eleven-story building to reach the classroom window!

The message in each of these cases is obvious: Don't expect things to be as they appear!

One proven way of avoiding test anxiety is, of course, not to take the test at all. This method can, however, become rather bothersome come report time, when professors start handing out incompletes to students who haven't turned up for anything. Still, even if you can't avoid all the tests, goes one theory, it might be possible at least to determine *when* you'll take them by concocting a great excuse for absenteeism on the day of the exam!

Such was the plan of the four students in "The Flat." They knew they had an important exam scheduled for Monday morning, but since the powder was soft and one of the kids could get a cabin for the weekend, the four decided to skip the study sessions for a couple of days of skiing, drinking, and, if they got lucky, a little sex to warm up with afterward. The weekend was everything it had promised to be on Friday evening, and by Monday morning, all four were suffering the miseries of hangovers.

Hours after they were supposed to take the exam, the four stumbled into their professor's office and proceeded to tell him how sorry they were to have missed the exam, but they'd gotten a flat on their way home the previous night, and because they had been in an area where the sidewalks were rolled up at six, they had simply been stranded until they could get hold of someone in the morning. Even with the tire replaced, it had taken them a further two hours to drive back, so they couldn't possibly have arrived in time. Could they *please* take the test the following day?

The professor sympathized with their problems and agreed to fit them in the next day. Well content with having gotten their weekend without sacrificing their chance at the exam, the four settled in with goodwill for a long cram session that night.

Things weren't looking so good the next day. Instead of their usual classroom, the professor took them to one of the language labs and scattered them about in the listening booths until it was impossible to

One in every eight thousand students worldwide will commit suicide this year.

exchange so much as a wink. Then he handed out the exam itself. It consisted of just two questions. The first, worth 5 percent, was a theory question so basic that all four of the students could have answered it without ever attending a class. The second, worth 95 percent, was also simple: "Which tire?" Unfortunately, it was an all-or-nothing sort of answer; either they all got it right or they all got it wrong. When the four students responded with three different tires, none of them was given credit for their response.

The student in "Dear Mom" had, if the legends are true, considerably better luck with his scheme to cheat his way through at exam time.

Patrick Kelly took one look at the essay examination given in English literature at the University of Ohio in the fall of 1952, and knew he was in over his head. Though the exam was of the "pick one question and answer fully" type, and he had two questions to chose from, Pat didn't know the answer to either one. As he sat there with lots of time on his hands, he came up with a unique plan and quickly put up his hand to request a second blue book.

In the first one he wrote a long letter home to tell his parents that he'd just finished his exam and had high hopes of doing very well this semester. He also mentioned that the reason he was writing in this blue book was that he'd finished his exam early and had given himself time to look over it again, but was still waiting for his buddy to finish up so they could leave together. Just before the end of the exam period, he wrote both questions in the second blue book, handed in the first, and left with the second book under his coat. No one stopped to search him on the way out. There simply seemed no point in sneaking something *out* of the exam room!

Once free of the examiner's eye, he raced back to the dorm, yanked out his textbook, and answered one of the questions. He then went to the campus post office and sent the second book to his mother.

He wasn't surprised by his professor's call later that evening, though he certainly put on quite a show when asked what in the hell this thing was he'd handed in. After some begging and sobbing, the student convinced the instructor that there must have been a mixup in the books—which meant his exam was currently winging its way to his mom! The professor, sympathizing with all this student angst, agreed to grade the exam if the student called his parents and had them forward the unopened envelope directly back to the prof.

Of course the student agreed, called his folks, and waited.

The professor, on receiving the intact envelope with the date of the exam postmarked across its front, conceded that a mistake might have been made and marked the exam. The clever student walked away with an A!

The student in "The Longest Day" evidently had an even more criminal mind. He'd stopped by his professor's office for a little pre-exam help when he discovered the office door open, the tests stacked neatly on a side table, and the professor missing from the scene. Without a qualm, the student nabbed one of the test papers and quickly hustled himself far away from the scene of the crime.

While the student was home working on the stolen exam, the professor, a conscientious if slightly obsessive person, was counting the exams once more to make sure he had enough to go around the next day. Much to his surprise, and that of the department secretary who'd confirmed the correct count with him this morning, they discovered they were now one exam short. Realizing he'd left to go to the washroom without locking up his office, the professor was forced to admit the possibility that someone had stolen a copy.

But how to prove it? Or identify the culprit?

It was too late to prepare another exam and have it approved by the university, so the professor would have to come up with something on his own. Marking the papers in any obvious way might tip off the student. Since this wasn't the FBI, he couldn't very well paint the things with any special dyes or anything. Eventually he snipped the very bottom edge off every sheet of legal-sized paper. When the exams had all been handed in, it was a simple matter to pull the long one from the pile and flunk the student whose name appeared on the first page.

Students who don't know better always assume an open-book exam is the equivalent of being able to cheat legally on an exam. They forget that the instructor *knows* he's given the student a tremendous advantage, and that the prof will now simply make the exam all that much harder! So, when a University of Washington professor announced that the last exam of the term would be an open-book exam, his students couldn't believe their good fortune and kept asking such questions as, "Anything we like, or just the textbook?"

To all these queries, the professor assured them they could consult with anything they could carry in on their backs.

General merriment ensued.

The next morning, depression set in for all but one student. Despite being able to bring all their notes and textbooks with them, the students were discovering just how hard this "easy" open-book test was going to be. The instructor wasn't asking them to repeat facts or dates, or to answer essay questions based on the material they'd covered. No, he was asking them to take all that knowledge a logical step further and apply what they'd learned to a completely different field. Only one student in the group felt up to the task. He was the one who'd left his books home and, instead, carried in a graduate student!

As in the case of the professor who spent most of his spare time at the circus, this tale depends on both students and professors agreeing to take everything their opposite number says completely literally. That in itself should be enough to reveal the legendary nature of these exam tales, but as with most legends, it simply doesn't work that way and the tales continue to spread.

A tale of a different stripe, "Do You Know Me?," is set in a military college in Quebec where nearly four hundred students were taking the same exam in the college's gymnasium. Rules and regulations being a little stricter there than at a civilian school, one student quickly found himself in hot water when he continued writing for a few seconds after the command to finish up.

When he attempted to pass in the test, the examiner refused to take it. Pointing out that since he'd been farther back in the row when the exams were handed out from the front, and therefore had probably been a few seconds later starting than those in the front, wasn't cutting the mustard.

Eventually the frustrated student leaned in close to the instructor and asked, "Do you know my name?"

"No, cadet, I don't, but I fail to see what difference that makes."

"To you, none. To me, a career."

With that, the quick cadet shoved his paper deep into the pile with the others and raced out the door, back into the folds of anonymity!

That the moral of this tale focuses on the growing distance between professors and their increasingly large classes is obvious, and setting the tale in a military college where uniforms and strict codes of behavior serve to make students even more faceless, only serves to emphasis that aspect of the story. What isn't totally clear is whether the tale is telling students this is a good thing or not!

The infamous blue booklets used by so many colleges at exam time surface once again in "The Missing Blue Book."

When young Tim Taylor took a seat for the final of his History of Native Peoples course, he was startled to see that the entire examination consisted of only two essay questions. This wouldn't have been a bad thing except Tim had absolutely no idea what the answer to the first question might be!

Staring at the paper for another few minutes, he came up with an ingenious plan. Turning back to the cover of his blue book, he wrote his name and then "Book 2" in large letters. On the first page of this book, he wrote a single sentence that might, if read the right way, well have seemed like the concluding remarks for question number one. Skipping down a few lines, he then proceeded to answer question number two, a question for which he was prepared, in considerable detail. About halfway through the class, he asked for a second blue book.

When the exam period came to an end, he slipped the second book under his jacket and handed in the first with its prominent "Book 2" on the cover!

Some time later, he receives his marks and a letter from his professor. He'd received an A on the exam, and an abject apology from the professor, who, as intended, was absolutely guilt-stricken at the thought that he might have lost a student's final exam!

Every department has exam tales that are specific to its subject matter. A biology exam legend has students attempting to identify birds by nothing more than their beaks or feet. History legends also tend toward the minutiae of study. One exam reputedly asked students to provide a list of twenty famous individuals born between eight and nine o'clock in the morning! A phys-ed test required students to identify three winter sports that *weren't* played with some sort of special equipment, for example skis or skates, on the athlete's feet.

My favorites of this type both come from the field of theology. The first, "In My Name," traces the efforts of some twenty theology students to struggle through the entire New Testament in a single semester "with particular care and attention to the words and lessons of Christ." Not a small task.

By the time the day of their final exam arrived, several students were starting to show the strain of reading, examining, and commenting on hundreds of pages in just a few short months. One of the last things they needed on the morning of their exam was to arrive and discover the test had been shifted to a different classroom, all the way across the campus!

The absolutely last thing they wanted that morning was to be accosted by a vagrant en route, which was exactly what happened.

When they arrived at the other building, the instructor was sitting at his desk with a small walkie-talkie nearby and a stack of papers in front of him. The students quickly found seats and waited for the instructor to hand out the exams. Instead, as if he had all the time in the world, he chatted for a few moments about their change of venue, then asked if they had any difficulty making it to the new room.

Several students commented on the "beggar" who'd slowed them down on the way here. At least two other students agreed that the "drunk" shouldn't be allowed to "panhandle" on campus. Few students had no complaint to make. Their instructor, however, seemed less than impressed with their difficulties, and, after a few moments of listening to them, pushed the stack of papers into the garbage basket and proceeded to hand out little slips with letters on them.

The confused students asked what the slips were for.

"Those are your grades."

"But we haven't taken the test yet! You just threw it in the garbage!"

"That? No, that wasn't the test, that was some old forms we don't use anymore. I was cleaning out my desk and thought it was about time to get rid of them."

"Then where's the exam?"

"Out there." As he pointed toward the door, the scraggly-looking man from the quad walked in and took a seat in the back of the class. The professor asked him, "Did you ask any of these people for money?"

"No, sir, I did not."

"Did you suggest you needed money?"

"No, sir, I did not."

"Have you been drinking this morning?"

"No, sir, I have not."

"What exactly *did* you ask these people for?"

"Help."

"Nothing else?"

"No, sir."

"Your exact words?"

"Help me, please."

"Did any of these people stop to help you?"

"No, sir. Not one."

"Thank you." And, to the class, "It is apparent to me that not one of you has actually understood the teachings of Christ."

Variations on this tale go back some time, and in at least one case a version of this "test" was actually perpetrated on a group of students engaged in a social psychology class at Princeton University. In addition to restating the often prickly relationship between professors and students, the tale warns us against our natural tendency to pull away from those we perceive as different.

In "The Unprepared Student," another group of theology students were taking their exams at Brown University in 1941. The previous evening had been homecoming, and, like the rest of the student body, these students had been attending the game and enjoying the celebrations afterward instead of studying. Thus it was that one student looked at his exam paper and realized he hadn't a clue how to answer its single question!

After much internal debate, he wrote, "It seems to me that this is the sort of question to which the appropriate response can only be 'God knows!' Have a merry Christmas!"

Apparently, even in the theology department, students are required to do a little more than invoke God's name in order to pass. The professor's response? "God gets an A. You get an F. Happy New Year!"

Many of these specific legends only arise after a more general legend presents itself. It's entirely possible, for example, that "The Unprepared Student" is an offshoot of this older exam legend, "Why?"

A philosophy instructor spent four months trying to convince his students of the absolute need to question everything. His final exam reflected that broad approach to life in its brevity and simplicity. The only thing written on the test paper? "Why?"

While some students scribbled madly from the beginning of the test period to the last moments, when monitors almost had to drag their papers away, one student wrote briefly, then sat back to watch his fellow students. His answer? "Why not?"

The student with the brief response received an A, the others failed!

Dozens of variants for this one attest to its popularity:

"Why?"

"Because."

"Prove that this chair exists."

"What chair?"

Sometimes the point of a collegiate legend isn't to praise the simple answer, but to force students or professors to admit that simply finding *an* answer isn't enough. Even the *right* answer isn't the real solution. No, sometimes, the only right answer is the one the professor wants to see on the paper. Such is the case in "The Barometer."

In this tale, a physics professor in Chicago asked students taking his final exam to explain how a barometer could be used to determine the height of a skyscraper. The "right" answer, the one the professor wanted to see, was to detail how it could be possible to take a barometric reading at the base of the structure and another one at the top of the structure, and, by comparing the two readings, deduce the height of the structure.

Students being students, the class in Chicago seemed compelled to arrive at their own answers—using *five* completely different methods and without once resorting to the solution their professor wanted!

- One student dropped the barometer from the top of the building and, by counting "one-Mississippi, two-Mississippi, three-Mississippi . . ." determined how long it took for the barometer to hit bottom. Then, as he knows a falling object hurtles downward at thirty-two feet per second per second, he determined the building to be 312 feet tall or, assuming approximately twelve feet per floor, that the building was twenty-six stories tall.

- Another student assumed that direct observations would always be superior to inferred results, so, tying a string to his barometer, he too threw it off the top of the building, though he was much gentler as he lowered it to the ground, marked the string when the barometer touched bottom, and then measured the string. His direct observations led him to believe the building was 318 feet tall, approximately twenty-six commercial stories high.

- A third student had a similar idea but no string, so, starting at the top of the building's emergency exit stairwell, he proceeded to mark off barometer lengths on the walls as he walked down. By his observations, he determined the building to be 421 barometer lengths tall. As the barometer appeared to be eight inches long, he deduced that the building was approximately 316 feet or twenty-six stories tall.

- Yet another student took his barometer to the base of the building on a sunny afternoon, and measured the length of the barometer's shadow and the length of the building's shadow. By assuming the sun was at the same angle in both cases, the student was able to deduce the height of the building in comparison to the height of the barometer.

- The last student stood in the building across the street and watched his barometer until he was fairly sure a high pressure system was moving in. When he determined that he wouldn't need to go home and get an umbrella, he stepped outside and peered up at the building through the UV sunglasses that his observations of the barometer indicated might come in handy, and, without having to squint at all, counted the rows of windows. In short order, he determined there were twenty-six floors, which, at about twelve feet per floor, would indicate the building was approximately 312 feet tall.

Some students avoid all that stress and aggravation by entering the exam room in what they hope will prove to be a Zenlike state of near-trance brought on by the appropriate combination of large quantities of drugs. Their last-ditch effort is based on the belief that, in this tranquil state, knowledge, which they hope to have absorbed by osmosis rather than by actual study, will simply bubble up into the calm pool of their minds. Needless to say, this doesn't always work exactly as planned. The results have been amalgamated into the legend of "The Zen Test."

- The first student to receive her graded exam stared at it for a long time. Her professor nodded and said, "Yes, that was my reaction, too!" The entire blue book was covered with a single phrase endlessly repeated: "Do not exceed six tablets daily." Guess what her brain was trying to pass along?

- A second student was smiling broadly as he entered his professor's office to review the exam. He *knew* he'd written brilliantly, some of the best stuff he'd ever put together. Imagine his shock when, on opening the cover of his blue book, he discovered his pen had run out of ink less than halfway down the first page, a situation that simply hadn't sunk in during his altered state. A cryptologist and a graphology lab might have been able to deduce the rest but, as far as this prof was concerned, any great insights on this paper would remain mysteries.

- A similar fate awaited student number three. It's entirely possible that the altered-state experiment had worked beautifully for him, but with his entire response to the exam's single essay question squished into the white margins *outside* the lines, resulting in writing so small only one of those angels that hang out on pins could possibly read, this professor wasn't about to guess at the answers he'd provided.

• The last student seen that day, who'd watched all the others crawl out of the office, didn't hold out much hope for his own chances. Still, he was more than a little confused when a second professor came in and handed him his blue book. "Sir?"

It seems the student had written the entire exam in the wrong examination room! He was about to get a B in a course for which he *wasn't* registered and an F in the course for which he *was* registered!

The moral is clear, certainly clearer than the minds of the students taking their tests that day: There are no shortcuts! Still, this next tale, "The Times They Are A-Changing," seems to prove only that no student could possibly be prepared for any exam, not really.

An alumnus was in his old economics professor's office one day near the end of term to borrow some reference books and generally shoot the breeze. Glancing at the teacher's desk, he saw a copy of that semester's exam. He frowned for a moment, then turned it around for a better look. Eventually, after looking at all the pages, he said, "Sir, is this the exam you plan to offer this term?"

"Yes."

"But this is the same exam I took when I was a student here. Don't you realize that students bank exams for other students to study in future years?"

"Of course, I did it myself."

"Then how can you give the exact same exam twice?"

The prof's eyes twinkled. "Haven't you figured it out yet? In economics, we change the *answers*!"

Determining who, if anyone, wins the day in the old college legend "Cakes and Ale" is rather hard to determine. It begins at Cambridge University when, about halfway through a long final, a student turns to a hall monitor and asks for cakes and ale. The monitor, naturally, refuses the request and suggests the student get on with his exam.

The student refuses, citing the university's ancient rule, still on the books, which stipulates that "gentlemen sitting examination may request and require cakes and ale."

After some hurried discussion with the rest of the hall monitors, the modern-day equivalent, a Coke and two burgers, is brought to the student. He eats and finishes his exam, pleased to have finally put one over on the administration.

The administration isn't quite finished with this student, however, and when his degree should have been mailed to him, he receives instead a notice fining him for "failing to wear your sword to the examination room"! His degree will, of course, be conferred as soon as this little matter is dealt with. Looking at the bill again, he's horrified to see that the fine is the equivalent of the ancient and honorable amount assessed back then, adjusted for inflation. The student owes the college £1,200!

Of course, many colleges include what we might consider strange practices in the rites that permit a student to emerge from university with a degree in hand. One of the oddest is attributed to several universities and colleges, including Colgate. According to "The Donation," students attending Colgate had better arrive with their swimming gear in hand. It seems one of the college's more generous patrons insisted that every student learn to swim before being allowed to graduate. The reason? The patron's own child, once a member of the college's student body, had drowned while attending a school-sponsored beach party. This patron was determined that no more needless deaths should occur if she could prevent it.

Most students, assuming the test to be a holdover from a bygone era, don't bother to take the test. It's only when they apply for their degrees that they're informed the regulation is still firmly in place and that they'd better haul themselves over to the pool if they want to graduate!

Like most really good college legends, there is some truth to this one. Yes, Colgate and a few other colleges do still insist that all their graduates be able to get from one end of the pool to the other, but not because

of any stipulations in any of the donations made to the colleges. In most cases the requirement is a remnant of a World War I–era program in which the Red Cross tried to ensure that every American learned to swim. Colgate and other colleges seem to have taken the position that the Red Cross's plan was a good idea then and remains one today. If some of their students have turned up for graduation ceremonies a little damp after their last-minute swim, well, students really should read their handbooks, right?

The final two college legends present two ends of the examination stress spectrum. The first, "The Pencils," is set in Britain where, if anything, the layout of the collegiate year exerts yet more pressure on students sitting their finals. In most British colleges, students take courses in both the fall and spring, but take *all* their exams *after* the spring term. As American students who take exams every few months know, it's difficult enough to remain current in one semester's worth of classes; remaining in "testing trim" for an entire year's material is a truly daunting task. Add to this the fact that many British courses are graded almost solely on the final, and you've got some seriously high stress levels to deal with.

From time to time, students have simply dropped out without even bothering to take the finals at all, but the most extreme case of student depression certainly belongs to the British student who, after staring at his exam for nearly ten minutes, took his sharp new pencils, bought just for the exams, reversed them, stuck the sharp ends up his nose, and then slammed his face onto his desk, driving the pencils through his brain and, well, ending his exam anxiety rather permanently!

An American coed had a decidedly different way of handling the news that her grades were about to fall through the floor. She could handle it, and was quite willing to simply repeat the course work until she got a handle on the material; it was her parents who were likely to be suffering some anxiety as they watched an entire semester's tuition go up in smoke!

So, on a sunny afternoon, the coed found a comfy spot on the campus's sprawling lawns and wrote a letter to her parents:

Dear Mom and Dad,

I realize it's been some time since I've had a chance to write, so I thought I'd take this afternoon to catch you up on all my news. All I ask is that you sit down, now, to read this letter. Please? Please, sit down.

All in all, I've recovered pretty well. The skull fracture and concussion I received while jumping out of the burning dormitory gives me little trouble anymore. The two weeks in hospital were actually a rather nice break, and I can see perfectly well out of one eye now and have high hopes for the other. The headaches only get excruciating if I'm in bright light.

Fortunately for me, one of the college janitors was walking home when I jumped out the window and he did call for an ambulance and, later, the fire department. He's been very kind, visiting me in hospital and all. He even let me move in with him while we're waiting for the dorm to be rebuilt! Well, one thing led to another and I'd also like to make this letter my invitation to our wedding. We haven't set a date just yet, but don't worry, it'll be sometime before my pregnancy becomes too obvious. We'd have the license already, but, well, it seems we both have a little infection to clear up before we can retake the blood tests. A course of antibiotics should take care of it soon.

Now that I've brought you up to date on all the important things, I guess I should now point out that there really wasn't any dorm fire, I didn't jump out the window, I didn't nearly kill myself, I didn't take up with a janitor, and am neither pregnant nor infected with any sexually transmitted diseases. I am, however, about to fail both math and science and wanted you to be able to put these events in their proper perspective.

Your daughter,

Grace

Perspective is a wonderful thing.

CORPORATE CONVOLUTIONS

ho hasn't, at one time or another, felt like David to some mega-conglomerate's Goliath, like a very long account number with no name?

As with other legends, corporate legends attempt to level the playing field just a little, with tales of huge firms making the most boneheaded mistakes, of the little guy whose small idea became a treasure trove, and of the bright boys of Madison Avenue advertising firms bungling million-dollar accounts. What distinguishes some of these legends, however, is malice. In most legends, little lasting harm is done to anyone beyond ego bruising. One category of corporate legend takes the revenge tales to a new level, actively seeking to demolish corporate

and personal reputations. These legends, often hiding in the guise of a supposedly selfless product warning, actually serve no one's interests—least of all the buying public's. Before delving into the darkest side of corporate mythology, though, we'll start with some of the more humorous blunders these monster companies have made all on their own. Feel free to enjoy them with just the right amount of satisfaction.

THE BIGGER THEY COME . . .

Big companies are, in the public mind, perennially guilty of two major crimes: not knowing their market, and not caring about their market. Impersonal service is the number-one consumer complaint and legends reflect that frustration, rejoicing in those rare incidents when it's the company that's left with egg on its face. "The Pepsi Resurrection" is a classic of this type.

According to this legend, Pepsi-Cola, confident in its history of catchy slogans, assumed that expanding into other markets would be more a matter of "Americanizing" their market than adapting their product, or their ad campaigns, for a new, foreign audience. So, instead of concentrating on their new Japanese customers' culture and experiences, they simply hired a translator and had "Come Alive! You're in the Pepsi Generation!" made into its nearest Japanese equivalent. Secure in their prior success with this phrasing, they simply sat back and waited for more revenues from the new market to roll in. This being a legend, you naturally already know that no such thing happened. The campaign bombed—big-time.

Why?

The Japanese version of the campaign, when someone finally stopped long enough actually to look at it, threatened to "Bring your ancestors back from the dead with Pepsi"! Hardly an appealing promotional plan!

The appeal of this particular story lies in the fact that even with all their resources to draw on, a huge company with marketing gurus and million-dollar advertising agencies behind them made the same sort of stupid mistake usually attributed to the most foolish tourist.

> **Advertisement in the Three Rivers, Michigan, *Commercial*: "GE Automatic Blanket—Insure Sound Sleep with an Authorized GE Dealer."**

The "Just Do It!" legend also trades on the language barrier scenario, and leaves yet another company, Nike, blushing, but for a very different reason.

You've probably seen the commercial in which Samburu tribesmen trek across Kenya in their Nike hikers. At the end, one man, supposedly pleased with his dandy shoes, leans toward a zooming camera lens and exclaims excitedly in his native language. Across the bottom of the screen, a little subtitle reads, "Just do it!"

Sadly for Nike, who, like the producers who assumed American moviegoers wouldn't know pig-German from real German, they were caught in a huge linguistic boo-boo! America is much more of a mosaic than the melting pot it was just a few decades ago, and it was a cinch that someone in a 200-million-person audience was bound to know at least a little Maa.

As was pointed out, at Nike's expense, in *Maclean's, The New York Times, Time,* and dozens of other high-circulation papers and magazines, you really *can't* fool all the people all the time. Just weeks after the ad began airing, anyone with the price of a newspaper could discover that Nike's

Kenyan spokesman actually said, "I don't want these. Give me big shoes!"

Considering how much companies like Pepsi and Nike reap each quarter, and how little your average second-language teacher or history professor gets paid, it's hard to understand how such blunders make it to air. Then again, considering how bizarre some translated product instructions can become, maybe it's something in the air at mega-conglomerate offices?

Like most writers and teachers, I've taken on some pretty strange jobs to put bread on the table, but for sheer perversity, nothing tops the summer I was hired to translate English into English!

The Taipei Import Company, apparently more sensitive to the language issues than either Pepsi or Nike, realized that while "Tab C into Slot A please be putting" sort of looks like English, it certainly doesn't make the grade for native speakers. Considering that's one line from a 305-line instruction booklet, you can imagine the level of frustration generated by the time a customer got to line 299 and was confronted with "Easy to do slotted nail gentle to Guide 11." So, for a long, leisurely vacation, I translated instructions like those into "Insert Tab C in Slot A" and "Finger-tighten the screw in Hole 11." While I earned enough to eat, and take in a few movies, I was also the laughingstock of my small circle of writing confidants, who, to this day, continue forwarding me their most obtuse product assembly instructions includ-

ing this, my all-time favorite, from an Internet site, www.snopes.com, the Web site of the San Francisco Valley Folklore Society.

Instructions included with the novelty toy
TOUNGE OF FROG, made in Taiwan:

Frog. If it is thrown with full of your strenght, it will spit out the tounge, which is like the genuine one from the frog.

INSTRUCTIONS FOR TOUNGE OF FROG:

- *A product has the stickness and is just like a soft rubber band with high contractility. It can be played to stick the remote objects.*

- *Inspite of it is sticky, it is never like the chewing guns which is glued tightly and cannot be separated.*

- *If the stickness is not good enough, it can be washed by soap. After it is dried, it cab be used continously many times.*

- *The packing paper has printed the bug picture, which can be cut as per the black frame and place on the table; then you can stick the picture with your tounge of frog.*

- *The key point for throwing far away is the same as the throwing of fish rod, i.e. to throw out slowly with full of your strength. Separate it with two hands, then release one hand, throw it with full of your strength.*

Nary a New Coke in sight.

- **No matter what you make a round ball, it will recover the original shape.**

  CAUTIONS:

- **New throw out the other person's head.**

- **Keep away from fire.**

- **Inspite of it is non-toxic, it cannot be eaten.**

- **Never pull out tounge of frog hard, as it might be separated.**

- **Its content has the oil, so if it touches on cloth, precious object or wall, the stains will remain if you don't care about it.**

- **Never put on surface of any object, shall keep in polybag.**

Just in case you still haven't figured it out, the toy, a frog, has a sticky tongue with which, presumably, you attempt to pick up paper bugs.

Legends have grown from tiny incidents, but one corporate tale, "Reverse Psychology," operates on a huge scale—in direct conflict with all known facts. If business myths are to be believed, then Coca-Cola always knew New Coke would be a flop. However, as Pepsi was gaining on them in market share, Coca-Cola decided to try a little reverse psychology on its customers. They figured that, like artwork following the artist's death, there's nothing as much in demand as something that'll run out soon! So, when they announced the end of Coca-Cola production, they were already planning to release their stockpiled product a bit at a time, letting Coca-Cola addicts panic at the thought that their next bottle might be their

. . . and the steps of the New York Public Library, and the rivets in the Confederation Bridge, and the garbage in a hundred municipal landfills . . . Coca-Cola, that is—if by "rot" you mean make great big cavities in any or all of those things.

The claim that Coca-Cola will rot your teeth or anything else, however, doesn't make it bad. Orange juice will do it, tomato juice will do it, and so will any number of beverages—anything containing sugar and phosphoric acid—to almost anything!

last until demand grew so huge, they could relaunch the old product with all the splash and hype of something completely new! Something they didn't even have to pour research and development money into!

Quite a daring scheme—if it worked. And if it were true.

Facts, and the company's own admissions, however, make it highly unlikely that Coca-Cola was playing head games with its market. Production of Coca-Cola ceased entirely within days of New Coke's arrival into the marketplace. No one was hoarding the product. When trucks rolled away from Coca-Cola headquarters, only New Coke and Diet Coke sloshed around inside. The rush of support for the original Coca-Cola would have warmed the hearts of even the hardest executives—if there had actually been any plans to continue marketing the product! Shock, even panic, set in quickly, and a mere seventy-four days after throwing their entire weight behind New Coke, company executives were admitting their gigantic error and assuring everyone that Coca-Cola would soon be back on the shelves, not because they had any stockpiles to cover the demand, but because production was starting again.

This legend is unique for leaving the moral of the story in the truth instead of in the legend! "Reverse Psychology" proves just one thing: it's hard for the average person on the street to believe they've got more on the ball than a company as big as Coca-Cola—even when they do!

That businessmen as savvy as those on Madison Avenue or at the Yale Business School could be fooled really shouldn't come as such a huge surprise, not if you know the "Fedex Exed" legend.

According to that tale, Frederick Smith, who would eventually create the company that guarantees overnight delivery to something like 90 percent of the globe, was just working out the theory behind such a huge enterprise while he was a student at Yale. Clearly, point-to-point transport of individual packages wouldn't be feasible, so he devel-

CORPORATE CONVOLUTIONS 265

oped a system of central collection points with feeder lines in and expedited shipping out, in bulk. When he submitted it to his Yale economics professor, the expert didn't seem to see the potential.

The report earned Smith a very mediocre C!

Don't you just love the true tales? Especially the boy-makes-good variety?

If revenge is a dish best served cold, embarrassment definitely goes down better in the most public settings possible, so, when a company's best blooper is on its labels, well, there's another saying about birds and bushes that seems to cover it. It's one thing to relate a legend, another thing altogether to be able to point it out in living color!

That's the situation Dial Corporation found itself immersed in when an angry art director decided a picture was worth a thousand words and incorporated his vengeance into the packaging for Dial's new product, Renuzit's "Fresh Cut Flowers"–scented air freshener. Turn the container all the way to the left, next to the overlap. Now look closely. See something . . . phallic? So did a lot of other people, who called, wrote, and sent out cyber messages pointing out the graphic gaffe.

As it happens, Dial isn't aware of any disgruntled employees among its staff. According to them, downsizing is the real culprit. The images on this scent appeared on prior products without causing any outrage at all. On the earlier, larger containers, the rest of the "phallic" image also appears, making

it clear that the "offensive object" is actually just one petal of a larger tulip! Only when a perfectly normal photo is cut in half to fit a small package does it look like anything else.

Sometimes a cigar is just a cigar, and sometimes the company is innocent.

Was M&M's, or rather its parent company, Mars, Inc., "innocent" when it participated in a campaign to market its product to a different, older, demographic by insinuating that green M&M's were aphrodisiacs? That's what an e-mail message dated January 25, 1993, was asking "concerned parents" to consider:

Would you want your children buying a product that puts money in the pockets of pornographers?! If your children eat M&M's, that's exactly what you're doing! A judge recently ruled that M&M's must "cease and desist" its latest campaign, which features models in suggestive poses with the product!

Half-naked women pushing candy! Is that what you want for your innocent children?

Don't let pornography become part of the advertising that entices your children! Don't support companies that resort to such tactics. Vote with your wallets! Contact your congressman!

The origins of many legends remain murky, untraceable to even rumor or conjecture. Others, like this one, appear to prove how flawed human memory, mismatched facts, and half-heard television reports can combine to create myth.

Mars, Inc., the makers of M&M's, did

indeed find itself in court over green candies in 1992, but they weren't the ones ordered to "cease and desist"! That honor belonged to Cool Chocolate, Inc., which manufactured a candy very similar to M&M's called The Green Ones, an apparent play on the existing legends that green M&M's, or green Smarties, or green Skittles, almost any green candy, were actually an aphrodisiac. The ruling had nothing to do with pornography. Mars, Inc., and the judge, believed The Green Ones too closely resembled M&M's, and it was Cool Chocolate that was ordered to cease and desist.

So where did the pornography claims come from? It's a little convoluted, but may stem from a photo of Cool Chocolate's owner, Wendy Jaffe, that appeared in *People* magazine. Jaffe, not some anonymous model working for Mars, Inc., did appear in what many might consider a sexual pose on a bed covered in her green candy. Jaffe's whole marketing strategy was based on the notion that her candy was sexy, not exactly an unusual ploy, but it was her campaign, not anything undertaken by Mars, Inc., that seems to have incensed the author of the e-mail warning.

The important issue for many, however, remains "Are green M&M's really aphrodisiacs?"

On that one, the jury is still out, though you won't find too many M&M-green walls In jails, either!

In real estate, everything is "location, location, location." In business, it seems to be more "timing, timing, timing." Products that flub on a first introduction often take off on a second. Some products, apparently timely, never get off the ground. The next tales leave us to wonder how much "success" is "luck," how much "hype" is "hoopla," and how much "image" would be better described as simple "accident" anywhere outside the corporate circle.

Take Post-it notes. Everyone uses them. Most office workers would feel disabled without them. They generate huge revenues. But, according to a persistent legend, they were really nothing more than an accident for which the 3M Corporation eventually found a use! It's true!

The original developer, a gentleman named Spencer Silver, was working for 3M when he found himself with a product that wasn't quite sticky enough to be called a glue, too sticky to use as a tack cloth for fine carpentry or something similar, and, to all appearances, useless. Not seeing the immediate solution to the problem he *was* working on, Mr. Silver put the light adhesive aside.

It was some time later when Art Fry, another researcher, was frustrated by a bookmark that refused to stay put in his hymnal, that a glimmer of something, some use for Silver's not-quite-sticky-enough glue, began to take shape. He stuck it on the backs of little pieces of paper, found that the resulting product could be easily moved about and reattached, and took it to the 3M executives.

Okay, so now they had a *product,* other than straight glue, that didn't really stick. Ah, but imagine you've never seen a Post-it pad, and try to describe that product! Paper with glue that won't really keep two pieces of paper together? Sort-of-sticky notepads? Doesn't sound too impressive, huh? The company evidently had something of a marketing problem on its hands.

The solution?

Send the product out into the real world, let people use it, let them discover how convenient it is, how unlikely to blow off desks with the slightest breeze, how easy it is to become accustomed to having those little bits of paper around! Which is precisely what they did. Timing, and a company willing to market something they couldn't really describe, in a creative way, leaves them with a mega-hit product and us drowning in little pieces of paper that don't really stick!

This tale, and others in the corporate category, illustrate another function of urban legends, to preserve small slices of history that reflect the human elements of otherwise impersonal corporations and institutions.

Anytime a company puts a number in its product name, it's going to stir public curiosity. Pepsi One, its diet product, reflects the single calorie found in each can—and incidentally plays into the consumer's habit of associating the number one with "the best," "first place," and other good things that any company would like to attach to its products. "Old Number 7" on the Jack Daniel's bottle

likewise reflects a fact about its production history: the bottled liquor is from the seventh recipe tested. That seven is often seen as a lucky number in Western cultures is a pleasant coincidence. Heinz 57, 7UP, and other products repeat this pattern.

So, when Rolling Rock Beer came out with a big "33" on its label, people wanted to know what it meant. In this case, however, the company seemed reluctant to answer the question—which only served to make more people more curious! In the absence of an "official" answer, legends quickly popped up, most based on experience of other numbered products. One suggested it took thirty-three attempts for Rolling Rock to get the right formulation. A much later assertion was that it was Rolling Rock's way of marking the year in which Prohibition was finally repealed.

None of this is true.

It was a typo!

In trying to decide which bit of patter to put on the *back* of the bottle—and several were under consideration—a note was made on each sheet to indicate the number of words in each version of the back label text. The one eventually chosen had *thirty-three* words! The printers didn't understand the meaning of the numbers on the top of the page and printed it as part of the product name! Small wonder they didn't want to explain that 33!

Image is, of course, important to corporations large and small. Why else would the

Professional Golfers of America, the vaunted PGA, buy out www.pga.com, a Web page address, from the Potato Growers of Alberta?

Trademark infringement, copyright protection, and the careful cultivation of proprietary phrases have led companies to send warnings to nearly every major publisher, newspaper, and magazine. Huge sections of writing journals are taken up by ads advising writers they can no longer write, "The tawny-haired boy shoved his feet into his sneakers, flicking the Velcro strips across before stomping into the backyard." No, now they must write, ". . . flicking the Velcro® brand hook-and-loop fasteners across . . ." before letting our young protagonist stomp off anywhere!

Hmm.

The Rollerblade company tells us there are no "rollerbladers" in parks, just "in-line skaters."

W.L. Gore & Associates, Inc., informs us that Gore-Tex isn't complete on its own. It's an adjective. We should follow it with "waterproof/breathable fabric," "gloves," or "outerwear." Somehow I don't think too many protagonists will be pausing to get into their "Rollerblade® brand in-line skates" or their "Gore-Tex® brand outerwear" either. While writers understand the importance of copyright and trademark issues, it's highly unlikely they'll interrupt the flow of that final chase scene to accommodate clumsy descriptive legal language.

The lengths to which some companies will go to preserve their corporate image is best exposed in "Lawyers 'R' Us," which incidentally is also an invasion of trademark! This tale starts in offices of the Toys "R" Us general attorney's office. The morning coffee hadn't quite finished bubbling through the percolator when an assistant came in and dropped a pile of papers on his desk.

"What's this?"

"That's the list of infringers who've appropriated our trademarks in the last twenty-four hours."

"All these?" He lifted the stack. There were at least a hundred clippings, magazines, books, videotapes, and cartoons to go through.

"Well, that's not everything," the aide admitted. "The stuff our researchers found overnight won't be ready for you until about two o'clock this afternoon."

"Wonderful!"

As the assistant left, the lawyer started sorting through the pile and dictating into his tape recorder.

"Dear Blah-blah: It has come to our attention here at Toys 'R' Us that your store is operating as Kids 'R' Us. We feel this to be an infringement of our trademark and would appreciate it if you would desist from this practice immediately so we won't have to pursue this matter in the courts. The ' "R" Us' part of our brand name is reserved to us so that we can apply It to our own future subsidiaries if we so choose. Your use of the ' "R" Us' designation impedes our ability to exercise our full legal rights. Yours, Blah-blah."

Down through the list he went, dictating letters to anyone who'd used the "'R' Us" format in any way. Rockets "R" Us, Explorers "R" Us, Computers "R" Us, and so forth and so on. Eventually he stopped cold and called out to his assistant.

When the aide came in, he held up a note with "Coffins 'R' Us" and an address written across it. "You aren't serious?"

"Completely, sir." The aide pulled another typed document from the bottom of the pile. "I thought this language, in addition to our usual, might be in order." With that, the assistant left again.

The lawyer began speaking: "Dear Blah-blah, As I'm sure you are aware, your business name, Coffins 'R' Us, bears a strong resemblance to our trademarked and copyrighted business name, Toys 'R' Us. You must also be aware that the similarity might lead consumers to assume, incorrectly, that our firms are affiliated. The ' "R" Us' part of our brand name is reserved to us so that we can apply it to our own future subsidiaries if we so choose. Your use of the ' "R" Us' designation impedes our ability to exercise our full legal rights. To avoid such situations, we are asking that you voluntarily desist from operating under that name and avoid further legal entanglements. Sincerely, Blah-blah."

Work continued for another hour or so. Eventually the lawyer came across yet another company name and address on a scrap of note paper and called the assistant once more. "You really think we should attempt to stop this store from using this name?"

"Of course, it follows the same pattern as all the rest."

The lawyer sighed. "Yes. However, I don't really see how we, a children's toy company, can honestly claim that we would ever use this company's name for one of our own subsidiaries!"

"That isn't the point, sir, is it?"

"Perhaps not, but do you really want to go into a public courtroom and, in front of dozens of reporters, claim that Toys 'R' Us wishes to reserve for its own future use the proposed subsidiary name 'Handguns and Rifles "R" Us'?"

"But, sir, the issue—"

"The issue is this company's reputation, young man, don't ever forget it! How many *toys* do you think we'll sell if we claim, under oath, that we also intend to sell guns?"

The deflated aide thought about that for a moment, then picked up the piece of paper, rolled it into a ball, and quietly dropped it into the garbage. "Perhaps you have a point, sir."

Perception plays a key role in the following tales of corporate blunders as well.

Early in 1985, an interesting tale, "Fish Out of Water," about a family who, having fallen on hard times, began buying unlabeled cans from a discount grocery, began circulating. (It would later find expression in two films, *Look Who's Talking* and *The Selvidges*.) It made meals in the mythical household rather interesting, but, for the

Bet you check every can of tuna you buy after reading "Fish Out of Water."

most part, didn't seem to do any harm. Needless to say, the whole family began noticing the packaging of labeled products that much more closely for clues to what might be in their mystery cans.

While the husband, the wife, and their two children were loading up their cart one morning, an elegantly dressed woman stopped to stare at them. The youngest child, a beautiful blond boy with angelic cherub cheeks, immediately stepped aside. "Sorry to block this side, you go ahead first, we've got lots."

The woman flushed, clutched her coat a little tighter around herself, and clenched her carry basket hard. "I wouldn't be caught *dead* in that bin!" To the mother, "How do you know you aren't feeding those poor children cat food—or worse?"

At that point the other child, a bright-eyed young girl, piped up, "Oh no, ma'am, we know which cans are which." She glanced at the woman's basket and said, "Though you probably shouldn't pick that up." She pointed to a can of tuna. "Not unless *you* have a cat!"

"What?!"

Without a word, the mother reached across, plucked the can of "Royal Premium Tuna" from the basket, and flipped off the first label to reveal a second one that read, "Perfect Heaven Cat Food—Tuna Flavored!" Beneath that, a *third* label, "StarKist Tuna," could barely be read under the brilliant red overmark: CONDEMNED! NOT FOR HUMAN CONSUMPTION!"

As a tale designed to point out that money

and position can't make you invulnerable to life's little unpleasantries, the story is perfect. As a corporate legend, the tale is eerily similar to true events that wouldn't completely unfold for several years after the legend's original appearance!

At the time when the legend first circulated, StarKist Tuna, a very real firm in New Brunswick, Canada, had indeed been discovered to have canned millions of servings of tuna that the Department of Fisheries and Oceans would declare unfit for human consumption. On a local level, it was known that the tins had been recalled and resold to a cat food firm, Seventh Heaven, in the United States, so it's entirely possible that those real-life incidents could also account for parts of the "Fish Out of Water" legend.

What's harder to comprehend is how a legend circulating in 1985 could predict that the "cat food" would eventually be repackaged and sold to Americans as simple tuna! Which is exactly what did happen to the real StarKist tuna—in 1992!

Folklorists, of course, would say that the tale simply anticipated the well-known greed of American businessmen who'd happily shell out the few cents for labels when they could realize as much as seventy cents a can by selling "tuna" instead of "cat food."

Another packer of canned fish had a real perception problem on his hands in "In the Pink." The exact nature of the fish varies with location. In British Columbia, Washington State, Oregon, parts of Maine,

Nova Scotia, and the north coast of Newfoundland, the canned seafood is generally salmon. In California the tale can also specify tuna, while along the east coast of both Canada and the United States, lobster occasionally pops up as the canned food of choice. One isolated telling of the tale in Halifax, Nova Scotia, evidently a descendent of the same legend, cast trout, smoked instead of canned, as the star of the fish tale. It seems that almost anything normally found with a dark pink hue or, in the case of lobster, covered in brilliant pink spots, will suffice.

In any case, the story invariably begins when one packer finds himself with a problematic batch of fish significantly paler than usual. When people buy salmon, even canned salmon, they expect it to be pink. The more saturated the color, the more favorably the product is viewed. What was he to do with all this pale salmon?

Shaking his head over the problem, the canner jots a quick note to his advertising agency asking their advice.

Their response? "Labels are cheap. Forget the product photo and add 'Guaranteed not to turn pink in the can'!"

The canner did just that and sold hundreds of thousands of cans of his "new" product.

His competition, naturally, quickly got wise to the scheme and soon retaliated with their own new labels featuring a brilliantly pink salmon steak on the front, with the claim, NO BLEACHING AGENTS USED! GUARANTEED!

By that time, however, the canner had rid himself of all his pale salmon, and the original packaging, full of pink salmon, was soon back on the shelf!

It seems our small-town businessman had considerably more savvy than his mega-conglomerate colleagues.

IF ONLY IT WERE SIMPLE

Marketing products and services isn't easy. The patent office receives thousands of plans, prototypes, and models every year. Only a tiny fraction of the ideas represented are actually made available for public consumption. Now, while that's actually a good thing in cases like the "tooth enamel polisher" that turned out to be a Black & Decker grinding tool with the abrasive bit thinned out, it's also indicative of just how difficult it is to match people with products. The process only gets harder when urban legends arise to place yet more layers of confusion between customers and commodities.

The Battle Creek Toasted Corn Flake Company began selling its product, Corn Flakes, to the public in 1906, and did so quite successfully for decades before picking up its first legend. Sometime around 1946, after soldiers began finding their way home from World War II, battlefield legends began attaching themselves to stateside situations. One of the first such transfers was "The Saltpeter Legend." For years, troops overseas believed their food was doctored with saltpeter to keep their libidos in check.

One of the products rumored to contain the anaphrodisiac was corn flakes, so, when the boys arrived home, they viewed even the domestic version with suspicion.

Why corn flakes?

Well, probably because corn flakes were known to be associated in some vague way with unusual dietary habits even before the war. Few people were consciously aware that the product's developer was Dr. John Harvey Kellogg, or that Kellogg was a Seventh-Day Adventist and a vegetarian. All they knew was that corn flakes were developed to address a particular dietary restriction. Coupling that with the saltpeter rumors made corn flakes a natural target. Luckily for the Battle Creek Toasted Corn Flake Company, the legend of the saltpetered cereal never firmly established itself as specific to its brand. Indeed, it sort of free-floated about the industry for some time, affixing itself to Quaker Oats products, Graham Wafers, and a variety of others in a sporadic fashion.

Having your product associated with purposes for which it was never intended could be a boon or a disaster, depending on public perception. Coca-Cola, for example, wasn't exactly delighted to discover that not only had urban legends in the United States long touted their soft drink as a *spermicide* of all things, but that women of developing countries, a huge market for Coca-Cola, were buying it for that purpose alone! Other uses, as an emergency windshield wash, a degreasing solvent for small auto parts, and, in a pinch, a paint thinner, weren't exactly in line with the company's advertising: "Who wants to *drink* windshield wash, or spermicides!"

Obviously these unauthorized uses weren't the basis for their next ad campaign, or something to be added to the Web page, or even acknowledged if at all possible!

However, legends are persistent, seldom fading away when there's anything there to titillate human curiosity. Eventually someone was going to investigate those claims and—in the process—start the legends on their way to the few people who hadn't yet heard them.

In Aurora, Ontario, a garage owner entertained the tourists with a window display of two beakers, each containing a grungy-looking automotive part, one beaker filled with the commercial degreaser used by the garage, the other with a twelve-ounce can of Coca-Cola. While you waited for your tank to fill or your tires to be changed, you were invited to swirl the beakers around a bit, confirming that Coca-Cola was at least as useful for this purpose as the real degreaser! Which product was used on your car was completely up to you—though the Coca-Cola from the vending machine only cost a dollar, while the actual degreasing agent was going to cost you $2.75 plus applicable taxes!

Its efficiency as a windshield wash was proven in New York City one muggy summer when half a dozen guys who made their living washing windshields at intersections switched from Texaco's washing fluid to Diet Coke. "Cheaper, works better!" they told their semi-reluctant, but captive, customers.

The Coca-Cola Company probably thought it was safe from at least one claim, that its product was a terrific spermicide. Who in their right mind would actually use lab time and resources to test such a thing? At it happens, a group of three scientists at Harvard!

Their findings?

Well, all of the Coca-Cola products tested (New Coke, Classic Coke, caffeine-free New Coke, and Diet Coke) killed some sperm, but Diet Coke killed the most sperm while New Coke destroyed the least. Classic Coke fans cheered to learn that their beverage of choice managed to out-slaughter New Coke five to one!

Coca-Cola's position on all these legend-inspired tests?

"We manufacture a carbonated soft drink, nothing else."

Of course, Coca-Cola should be used to answering questions about rumors attached to its products by now. With the possible exception of the Disney Corporation, few businesses have attracted more legends—right from the start.

The most famous legend is that Coca-Cola in its present form as a bubbly soda was a complete accident! It most certainly wasn't—as its creator's assistants should know. Dr. John Pemberton, who didn't have a soda-water dispenser at his home, deliberately sent them, repeatedly, to the local

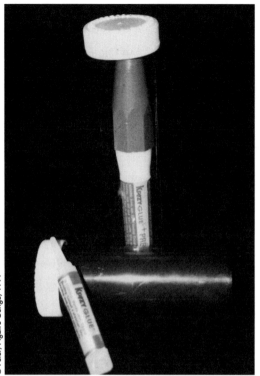

It really can do anything!

pharmacy specifically to have the soda water added to his syrup.

The makers of superglue, on the other hand, have no apparent objections to the legends surrounding their products—perhaps because, unlike "Coke-a-cide" jokes, the stories handed around about alternative uses tend to be less risqué and more likely to get even more people to buy their stuff!

"The Jigsaw Man," the tale of a patient who arrived at a South London hospital after being thrown through the windshield of his automobile—only to be put back together with superglue—doesn't actually contradict the product's intended use!

It's true; though shelved by several different scientists who all came up with versions of the product independently, it really has been used in place of stitches in certain instances, most notably cosmetic surgeries, where traditional sutures would only have further scarred a patient.

A second legend, that federal investigators never go anywhere without a tube of the stuff to use as emergency handcuffs—you simply glue a suspect's hand to something and come back to get him at your leisure—doesn't quite hit the mark. Yes, some federal investigators (some state and municipal investigators too) carry cyanoacrylates (the technical name of the substance) with them pretty regularly, but not to glue suspects to the scene of the crime. Used correctly, the compound can be used to lift fingerprints!

I suppose having your product even inadvertently associated with the healing of accident victims and the capture of the FBI's most wanted *is* just a tad more glamorous than being seen as something with which desperate young women might douche after an unplanned sexual escapade.

Some current corporate legends, however, are not only embarrassing and blatantly untrue; they have the potential power to force corporations to spend huge sums defending themselves in ad campaigns and aggressive legal action. When the following message circulated on the Internet and through the word of mouth of another large firm's agents, it cost Procter & Gamble more than a red face:

YOU CAN MAKE A DIFFERENCE!

The President of Proctars & gamble appeared on the Donahue Show in 1994 on March 15th. He'd decided that, what with gays and lesbians and everyone coming out of the closet, we, the public, could handle his alternative lifestyle decisions too. He's not gay. He's a Satanist!

What he does in his spare time is his own business but he also admitted that he's been using Proctors & Gamble Products as a way to raise money for his charity, the Church of Satan! I don't care what he does, but I sure don't want him using my hard-earned dollars to support that corruption!

Mr. Proctars & Gamble doesn't seem to care for our opinions. When Mr. Donahue asked if he wasn't afraid this admission might hurt sales, this man laughed! He says there aren't enough Christians in all the fifty states combined to make any difference to him or his company's profits!

I say we show him he's wrong!

I say we stop buying his products!

I say we let him know what Christians think of his kind! Now! Today!

Be part of the solution! Make a difference!

That mailing, which doesn't even spell the firm's name correctly, is clearly the starting point for dozens of other associated legends. One claims that Procter & Gamble's logo is a satanic symbol. The moon with the face, if turned sideways, could resemble Satan's horns. The thirteen stars inside the moon's curve represent the number of witches in a coven, the number of covens in a hold, not to mention the deviltry, supersti-

tion, and bad luck associated with the number itself. That the moon is only a sliver, with most of the area inside the trademark made up of dark sky, holds up the satanists' hopes that darkness will fall across the world and carry us to hell!

These myths, completely groundless, have plagued Procter & Gamble for nearly thirty years—despite not just one but nearly a dozen extended court appearances proving the tales had absolutely no basis in reality!

First of all, no president of Procter & Gamble ever appeared on *The Phil Donahue Show,* much less the Ides-of-March broadcast in 1994. No one associated with the firm has ever publicly claimed to be a satanist, or a member of the Church of Satan. No one from that firm has ever commented on the number of Christians—or Buddhists or Hindus or Jews or anything else—residing in the United States.

There isn't even the tiniest hint of a rumor that would support such claims. It's a complete fabrication.

"The Horns," the trademark legend, is equally slanderous, though at least it's based on contentions that can be argued.

The comment that the moon in the image is somehow linked to the Unification Church's Reverend Sun Myung Moon doesn't hold up. The mark predates the Moonies by several decades!

The horns? Well, a psychology class of forty-five students who were all shown the logo in the appropriate orientation found any number of possible symbolisms—none of which included Satan's horns or ram's horns.

The thirteen stars? Just to give you an idea of how many decades Procter & Gamble predates the Moonies by, consider this. Procter & Gamble was a well-established company back in the late *1700's*! You know, back when the flag still had thirteen stars!

As to the amount of light and dark in the trademark, well, that simply had nothing to do with Procter & Gamble. The trademark wasn't something the company actually planned. Back in the 1800s, crating and shipping of their products was sort of a customized thing. The company delivered the products in their packages to the dock. Dock packers bundled them into crates made on the spot to accommodate both the product and the ship that was to carry the crate. Just as roof thatchers of the time "signed" their work by twisting the topmost layers, those closest to the roof's peak, into distinct swirls and knots, these craters claimed their work by burning symbols into the sides. When it became obvious that plain crates were suspected of housing counterfeit goods, Procter & Gamble suggested the craters come up with one sign to burn onto all crates carrying their product.

The craters picked the symbol—not Procter & Gamble!

So, unless all those guys on that dock that day were also satanists, it's really hard to understand how they came up with such a fiendish symbol . . .

The truly unfortunate end to this story is that the man-in-the-moon symbol was eventually removed from Procter & Gamble products. That a malicious legend should force a company into discarding its own history, one of the more interesting bits of true corporate lore, is an irony of the crueler sort.

That similar circumstances could strike more than one company may seem hard to comprehend, but that old truth-is-stranger-than-fiction thing still works.

Snapple, the iced tea and soft drink manufacturer, was stunned to discover the legends circulating about it. One asserted that Snapple was a secret supporter of the KKK—a rather bizarre association, considering that Snapple is run by three Jewish partners in New York City, a considerable distance from the Mason-Dixon Line, but no one said legends must make sense. To "prove" their point, Snapple detractors, like the P&G detractors, turned to the product's packaging.

"See that little 'K' there on the side, that's an insider joke, a reference to the KKK. And this boat on the front, a slave ship bringing niggers to the States! Can't argue with what's put in front of you in living color!"

As it happens, Snapple could argue, very publicly. In the fall of 1993, the company ran a rebuttal ad campaign on both coasts. The "K," also found on many other products, stands for "kosher." The only insider joke here is that almost anyone *but* members of the KKK would know that! Pepsi, Coca-Cola, Dr Pepper, Hires Root Beer, and uncounted other companies also feature the little "K," making it easy for their Jewish customers to identify those food items prepared to rabbinical standards.

That boat, as the Associated Press reported in September, was a stock image from the largest photo collection in the U.S.A., the Bettmann Archive. The intended depiction was of the Boston Tea Party!

With those rumors shot down, the company's detractors resorted to a number of other equally common and equally false legends: Snapple products were packaged by underpaid foreign labor; Snapple supported Operation Rescue, an anti-abortion organization; Snapple products suffered from a variety of contaminants, including rat urine. While these charges, more nebulous than the earlier accusations, are harder for any company to disprove, debunking the previous legends certainly made it easier for Snapple to point fingers back. At present, Snapple is holding its own.

Considerably more lighthearted, at least today, is the mystery and legend surrounding the origin of the Curtiss Candy Company's most famous product, the Baby Ruth bar. While several soundly researched books have explored this legend and offer some startling insights that frequently contradict the official company line, producing virtual histories of the period in the process, we'll limit our discussion of this tasty treat to the two legends most often attributed to it. Run.

Ever since the bar was introduced in 1921, the public largely assumed it referred to the equally legendary ballplayer George Herman Ruth. Even those of you who aren't baseball aficionados have to recognize him by his better-known nickname, "Babe" Ruth! The company denied it, even claiming that Babe Ruth wasn't all that well known when the bar first came out. But Babe Ruth wasn't merely well known in 1921, he was more popular than the then-president, on more magazine covers than any other athlete that year, and *the* interview for any budding sports reporter to corral! Of course, using his name without his endorsement could well have gotten Curtiss Candy into a heap of legal trouble, which would explain why the company might deny the association.

The company's official position is no less curious than the one they've denied. For years they've asserted that the bar was named in honor of President Grover Cleveland's daughter, Ruth, who once visited the factory. Curiouser and curiouser. Ruth Cleveland died in *1904.* Remember, the bar wasn't introduced until 1921! Though Ms. Cleveland may well have been a memorable young woman, even at the age of twelve when she died of diphtheria, it's difficult to understand how her visit to a factory that didn't exist for another ten years could possibly have inspired anyone to name a chocolate bar after her, isn't it?

Some legends simply don't lend themselves to fact-checking, but once the facts have been lined up, it's certainly hard to ignore the contradictions.

The Avon Corporation wasn't initially sure what to do about the public image of its product Skin So Soft, that it was a better bug repellant than a skin moisturizer. It's not exactly a romantic image, or glamorous, but they were getting an awful lot of calls asking what was in it that kept bugs away. Their answer, "Nothing," wasn't satisfying anyone. So what do you do when fishermen become a key component of your market?

Repackage.

Keeping its original product in the original bottles, Avon created a new bottle and added to the Skin So Soft a sunscreen and a bug repellent. You can't sell something as an insect spray that doesn't actually contain insect repellent—even if it does work! Not wanting to get into the miasma surrounding the DEET repellents, which were recently acknowledged as carcinogenic—if incredibly effective—Avon stirred a little old-fashioned citronella, the same stuff in patio candles, into its product and went to the buying public.

The initial irony is, of course, that the bug repellent Avon is currently marketing actually has *less* of the ingredient everyone wanted than the original product still being sold as a moisturizer!

The last irony is that when tested against other existing bug repellents and moisturizers, Skin So Soft was less effective than any so-called repellent *and less effective than several other moisturizers to whom no bug legends have ever attached themselves*!

"Pucker Up" is a legend illustrating the opposite end of the product legend. According to this one, Carmex Lip Balm is just *too* good, so good it inspired a tale claiming that Carma Labs was secretly adding ground glass (or sand or asbestos or ground fiberglass) to its product. Users became "addicted" by applying the irritant again and again in hopes of healing their irritated lips! The U.S. Food and Drug Administration, however, approved the product without ever discovering anything in the least unusual in its preparation.

Heard the expression "There's no such thing as bad publicity"? Ford found itself in the perfect position to test this one in "The Gangster's Choice." According to this long-standing piece of urban folklore, the Ford Motor Company was once shocked to receive a letter from Al Capone complimenting them on the quality of their cars, their terrific acceleration in sudden, unexpected starts, and their nice solid construction. (Presumably those heavier side panels were better bullet-blockers or something.) Ford was in something of a quandary. Whatever else he might have been, Al Capone was a bona fide celebrity, a celebrity who was willing to endorse it's product without costing the company a dime!

What to do?

Eventually, deciding that not all publicity was good publicity, even if they did spell all the names right, they reluctantly set aside this golden opportunity.

True?

Almost.

The gangster in question wasn't Al Capone, but he was famous, and he did send the Ford Motor Company the following letter:

> Mr. Henry Ford
> Detroit, Mich.
> Dear Sir:
> While I still got breath in my lungs I will tell you what a dandy car you make. I have drove Fords exclusively when I could get away with one. For sustained speed and freedom from trouble the Ford has got every other car skinned, and even if my business hasn't been strictly legal it don't hurt anything to tell you what a fine car you got in the V8.
> Yours truly,
> Clyde Champion Barrow

Wonder if Bonnie got to pick the interior colors?

As the last photos of the pair and their bullet-ridden car prove, Clyde really did like to drive a V8.

It would be just too ironic if Clyde's Ford V8 happened to have a *Rand McNally Road Atlas* in the driver's door pocket that fateful day, especially as "The Road Less Traveled" already contends that the company's efforts at copyright protection, a little-known practice of adding nonexistent towns and fictitious streets to their maps, sent one young couple to their untimely death when they took what appeared to be the right turn on the road map, but ended up in the midst of a field where two Los Angeles gangs decided to mix it up one hot summer night. The pair was found the next morning by police, both shot, with the map on the wife's lap open to the nonexistent roadway.

Other variants of this one have the couple driving off a cliff in the fog one night, turning into a tough neighborhood and asking the wrong guy for directions, and sliding down into a swift river marked as a road on the map.

While some mapmakers do add fictitious landmarks to make it easier for them to identify cases of outright image theft, Rand McNally denies ever having done so. In any case, none of their maps has ever been implicated in any wrongful deaths.

Roadside maintenance agreements, though a fairly recent innovation in the world of domestic car sales, have figured prominently in "On the Spot," a legend about a legendary car and the lengths one company might go to maintain its image as the perfect luxury car.

It was a dark and stormy night (I kid you not!) when Janice and Jeremy Hopper of Great Neck, Long Island, along with their driver, Darrin, were driving back from an evening in New York City. The couple had some misgivings about the return trip. It was really dark and really stormy as they headed north. The driver, however, seemed unconcerned as he slid behind the wheel of the heavy Rolls-Royce his employer had bought the previous year.

"Don't you worry, sir," he said. "She's still under warranty!"

About an hour later they hit a guard rail as they swerved to avoid a fallen power line across the road!

The car refused to restart and, shaken, Janice opened the divider between them and the driver to ask what they should do now.

"You just sit tight, ma'am."

With that he pulled a small business card from the glove compartment and quickly dialed the number on the car phone.

"Yes, I'm afraid we've got a little problem here."

For the next few minutes he rattled off the car's registration information and their location. The couple in the back was rather concerned about comments like "as the crow flies," but the driver waved them off and finished up his call before sitting back with a big grin on his face.

"What are you so happy about?"

"You'll see."

"Shouldn't we call the auto club?"

"No, sir, you just sit there. I've got everything under control." The couple exchanged glances as their driver continued to smile as he stared out the window at the sky. "I've heard about this, but I've never actually seen it for myself."

The couple remained confused until suddenly the *whump-whump* of helicopter blades came within ear range. A brilliant beam of light surrounded the car, blocking sight of anything, until the chopper finally landed. Much to the couple's amazement, two mechanics with the Rolls-Royce symbol on the pocket flaps leaped from the helicopter, raced across the road, threw open the hood, crawled over, under, and around the car, and then, moments later, gave the driver the thumbs-up.

The car started immediately and the mechanics grabbed their gear and raced back to the waiting helicopter.

Jeremy let his breath out. "What was that?"

"That, sir," the driver beamed, "is the kind of service you get when a company like Rolls-Royce wants to make sure no one sees one of *their* cars on the side of the road. Bad for business!" As he pulled onto the road and turned back toward New York City, he added, "Image, sir. Image is everything."

The implication, that Rolls-Royce would go to incredible lengths to protect its reputation, is easy enough to figure out. Unfortunately, it isn't true, so keep those AAA numbers handy!

Some products came with built-in marketing problems. When the Kimberly-Clark company introduced Kotex feminine hygiene napkins, the first product of its kind, back in 1919, it couldn't even get magazines to carry its ads! Feminine hygiene products were too vulgar, they'd offend readers! Selling a brand-new product without being able to tell anyone what it was or what it offered the consumer was a major marketing problem.

It's possible that a small-scale urban legend actually helped save a product today's women wouldn't be without.

Almost as soon as the product became available, word circulated that Kimberly-Clark was marketing its wartime bandages as these new disposable sanitary napkins—which was true, sort of. The material inside the product was certainly the same, a processed wool that absorbed liquids better than cotton, twenty times better than the old cotton rags, but the heavy bandages used during wartime would not have been comfortable or appropriate in this new use. Kotex, originally marketed as "Cellunap," had been designed specifically for the women who'd use the product.

Still, the bandage legend had an unexpected side effect. Unlike hundreds of firms that provided products to the Department of Defense during the First World War, Kimberly-Clark *wasn't* looking to make a profit. This firm supplied millions of bandages to servicemen, through the government procurement program, *at cost*! Though not something the company had actively sought, this act of corporate generosity returned a certain goodwill. Claiburne Hume, a veteran, well aware of the Kimberly-Clark connections, was in the advertising department of Melton-Willis in 1919 when the first ads came across his desk. Despite the general reluctance to carry them, Hume gradu-

ally won them over with the legend's real history. Though Kotex would continue to be a hard sell in many locations, it hadn't been completely blocked out of the game.

THE PITS

For many years a legend has circulated in the form of a warning to parents to keep their tykes out of the ball-pit play areas of fast-food operations like McDonald's and Burger King. Why? Because snakes, including poisonous snakes, nest in the pits, hiding under those balls, waiting for an unwary child to tumble in!

Actually, snakes hate cold, dampness, and noise, things all too abundant in ball pits, and none have ever been known to get in there of their own volition.

Which is not to say ball pits are good places. Things that *have* been found in ball pits? Feces, both in and out of abandoned diapers, urine, rotten food, and vomit. Less disgusting but equally dangerous are eating utensils, sticks, and other pointy objects. Claims that used drug equipment, including needles and syringes, have also been found have yet to be confirmed.

Not all legends, though equally long-lived, are nearly as helpful. The Tootsie Roll candy company began marketing its new product, Tootsie Pops, a lollipop with a piece of chewy Tootsie Roll at the center, in the early 1930s. Like the Captain Midnight decoder ring, which everyone thought existed—largely because several other shows of the era had giveaway decoder rings—Tootsie Pops quickly became associated with a nonexistent giveaway promotion—because dozens of candy companies promoted *their* products the same way!

Diamonts, the Springfield Chocolate Company, and Mendelsen's Sweet Treats all ran promotions the year Tootsie Pops was introduced. Diamonts provided lucky youngsters with a free sucker if the child returned a wrapper with a star on the inside to the place of purchase. Springfield, a chocolate bar company, included a hidden inner wrapper in "about one in a hundred" of its Dandy Bars. This inside wrapper, with three large stars printed across it, included the company's address and instructions on how to get a free Dandy Bar! Mendelsen's Sweet Treats leased an early vending machine that they then kept stocked for pharmacies and soda shops. If a child was lucky, he'd find a candy with a silver star pasted on the outside of the wrapper. Mendelsen's left each shop owner a small box of "free prizes" to hand out for the stars.

So, clearly, a star on a junk-food wrapper had been fairly well established as meaning "free stuff" before Tootsie Pops hit the market. Even so, the company might have gotten away without becoming the star of "The Indian Star Legend" if *all* its wrappers were identical. They weren't. About one in three included an image of a young boy dressed as an Indian shooting an arrow at a star. Well, apparently customers thought this was another of the "lucky wrappers," and they started sending them to the Tootsie Roll people. Though the company did everything possible to squelch the rumor (including answering tons of letters individually, explaining that they weren't running any such promotion), it's stuck. Right up to the present, people continue to send in their wrappers!

Why?

Well, it seems, in some cases at least, that parents have been the culprits. Marie Woodson of Madison, Wisconsin, relates the story of how she had sent in a Tootsie Pop wrapper as a child—and received a free candy in the mail! So, when her own children began talking about the wrappers and collecting them, she encouraged them. It wasn't until they were about to send off a hundred or so that her mother, Gladys Cook, confessed that it wasn't the company, but Marie's father, who'd sent her the candy.

"When the company sent the letter, which clearly didn't have a candy inside, we opened it. Realizing how disappointed Marie would be, her dad bought a candy, put it in the envelope, and put it back in the mailbox.

Marie couldn't read yet, so she never knew the difference!"

While companies exert considerable influence over their customers through packaging, marketing, and their various promotions, some legend always seems to creep up out of nowhere and trip up even the most cautious companies. The introduction of new technology often sparks fear and legends, and even something as innocuous as a bar code can appear suspicious and corrupt in the context of a good legend. This one, "Raising the Bar," combines techno-fear with a little old-fashioned fire-and-brimstone sermonry by claiming that every bar code includes the superstition-fraught number 666, the mark of the Beast! As if that weren't bad enough, the biblical references to the number supposedly come from a passage in the Book of Revelation, and its appearance in Revelation clearly must indicate that the spread of the Beast's number is predictive of the end of the world!

Whew! All that from something so unreliable it can't even coax a little beep from the checkout scanner without forcing some disgusted cashier to key the whole thing in manually?

Leaving the debunking of 666 as being anyone's mark, much less the devil's, for another discussion, let's tackle the notion that the number even appears in "every bar code." Pick up anything with a bar code on it—which should be practically anything you own—and really look at it. There's a wider white streak at the beginning, which you don't notice because it's sitting on a white background. There's another wider streak at the end, which you also don't notice because it's sitting on a white background. There's at least one wider white streak somewhere in the middle, which you do notice because there are bars to either side of it! This is the symbol claimed to represent the number 6, so, if true, there would be a six at the beginning, the end, and the middle of every bar code—making the legend at least semi-true. Except this wider white bar *isn't* a six! See if there's a six in your bar-code example. Yes, there's a wide white strip. There's also a narrow bar to one side or the other. The six and the "guard" bars, those wider white bands you found earlier, which help the scanner align itself correctly, are two different symbols. Bye-bye, legend.

If nothing else can be said for "Raising the Bar," at least it wasn't biased toward any particular product!

One smidgin of truth in the bar-code legend has nothing to do with the story itself. In industry, elements set in motion by other parties can create legends as quickly as your own choices and decisions. Who could possibly have anticipated a connection between biblical prophecy and sticking an inventory-control number on the side of a product? Industry standards, it would seem, are as vulnerable to legend as products.

Ever wonder why a CD should contain precisely seventy-four minutes of recording time? Rather an odd number, isn't it? Sixty minutes make an hour, a nice round figure. Ninety minutes are an hour and a half, a fairly standard length for other recording media, such as audio tape. Why seventy-four minutes, an hour and a quarter less one minute? Doesn't seem to make any sort of sense.

That's basically the chain of thoughts that passed through most audiophiles' heads when Phillips and Sony got together to create a standard for the new compact disc format. Naturally, stories arose to answer it. Most were shot down fairly quickly. It's not an amalgam of the time available on a 33⅓-rpm album plus a 45-rpm single—too short. It's not the optimum size to encode the Bible in binary—too long. It's not even the same size or time span of the gold record sent out on the *Voyager* space probe, as yet others postulated.

The officially approved legend claims that seventy-four minutes was just long enough to capture the entire score of Beethoven's Ninth Symphony!

Which just leads to more questions, doesn't it? Why would the length of that particular piece be important? If it was, then whom was it important *to*? What Beethoven fanatic would have enough clout to affect an industry standard?

Well, depending on which version of those early negotiations you hear, one of three people. Was it Norio Ohga, then-president of Sony Corporation? Or was it Akio Morita, his

wife, who was so fond of the piece? Was it, as yet others claim, a famous conductor who directed the "classic" rendition of this piece and who suggested a size large enough to record it in its entirety?

Believe it or not, none of the principles in this little drama seem to know!

Though they all agree it had "something to do with the running time of Beethoven's Ninth," not one person actually involved in the decision has satisfactorily explained how the decision, which affected an industry worth several billion dollars, was made!

Even this explanation is suspicious to many musicians. Not only are most renditions of the piece sixty-nine minutes long, but the "famous" version, the one the disc is supposedly designed to accommodate, is only seventy minutes long!

If legends are supposed to impart some sort of truth, even if the legend itself isn't factually accurate, what sort of lesson is there in this tale? That human memories are shorter than we thought? The CD standard was only settled in the late seventies—less than twenty years ago! How accurate, then, can the rest of our "history" be?

To explore that question a little more closely, the last five tales presented in this section are considered "classics," legends that have been floating about the corporate world for so long they're more likely to be quoted than the *Encyclopaedia Britannica*!

"The New Hotel" proves that, unlike the folks at Phillips or Sony, some people have quite excellent memories. One such man was William Waldorf Astor. He had no difficulty remembering George C. Boldt, especially after Boldt, the manager of the Bellevue Hotel in Philadelphia, moved his family out of their suite at the hotel to allow him and his wife to spend the night. The hotel manager and the older man kept up a brisk correspondence over the next few years, and when the prestigious Waldorf-Astoria Hotel opened its doors for business, it was Boldt who became its first manager! Everyone loves a "Good Samaritan gets rewarded" tale, and when the reward is so wonderfully public, it's no wonder this legend continues to be shared by hospitality staff worldwide more than fifty years later.

As mentioned earlier, Coca-Cola, which began business back in 1885, has had plenty of time to gather legends. Some, like its later use as a spermicide, arose independently of the company itself, but others trace their way directly back to the real history of Coca-Cola.

The most famous is, of course, that even today people become so addicted to the favorite beverage because, as the name implies, trace amounts of cocaine, the same stuff the DEA is now trying so hard to keep out of the country, is an integral part of Coca-Cola recipes!

This was true in 1885, when the company advertised the medicinal value of two of its ingredients, coca leaves and kola nuts! But it hasn't been true since 1929, when the last vestiges of coca-leaf extract were removed from the product. The only ingredient in modern formulations that might be considered addictive at all is caffeine, which is available in dozens of other products, in considerably higher percentages!

The tale of the Coca-Cola Company's distinctive bottle's origin comes in several variants, the widest spread being that the bottle mimicked the curvy form of a woman's hips as they would appear in the then-trendy hobble skirt that almost managed to show off a young miss's legs by cutting in sharply at the hem, instead of ballooning out as previous skirts did. The bottle, therefore, many claimed, was a waist-down silhouette of a woman.

Coca-Cola denied it then and denies it now. According to their official history, the bottle was modeled after a biological drawing of a cacao nut, which has nothing whatsoever to do with the Coca-Cola formulations, but was used as a bottle model by mistake! Hmm. It's understandable that anyone looking at the bottle would fail to see the connection.

Though not quite so old, the legend claiming that the introduction of the Chevy Nova into the Mexican market was a flop because Chevrolet refused to abandon the Nova name (*no va* meaning "doesn't go" in Spanish) is perhaps one of the best known. It's not true. Though frequently cited in articles on product placement and marketing, the Chevy Nova performed as well as

YOU DON'T SAY!

You don't have to have a language barrier to make a company look stupid.
Here's just a sampling of the kind of copy that proves domestic and foreign product
instructions can be equally funny!

Do not use while sleeping.
—Sears hair dryer

This floodlight is capable of illuminating large areas, even in the dark.
—Komatsu grader manual of rear lights

Warning: Do not attempt to swallow.
—tag on a mattress

You could be a winner!
No purchase necessary.
Entry form inside.
—cheese snacks

Use like regular soap.
—Dial soap

Fits one head.
—shower cap box

Do not invert.
—bottom of Belgian chocolate tarts package

Caution: Do not use near power lines.
—on a toilet plunger

If you are having problems installing your modem, please contact us by e-mail.
—installation instructions for computer modem

Farm fresh *hen* eggs.
—on egg carton

Do not iron clothes on body.
—Rowenta iron

Do not drive car or operate heavy machinery.
—children's cough medicine

Warning: May cause drowsiness.
—sleeping tablets

Warning: Keep out of children.
—Korean kitchen knife

Cape does not enable user to fly.
—adult Halloween costume

Do not use to pick up anything that is currently burning.
—commercial wet/dry vacuum

For indoor or outdoor use only.
—Christmas lights

Instructions: Take with water.
—Pepcid AC Chewables

Not to be used for the other use.
—Japanese food processor

Warning: May contain nuts or nut oils.
—Elliot's Deluxe Roasted Nuts

Instructions: Open packet, eat nuts.
—American Airlines peanut packet

Do not use as an ice cream topping.
—hair dye package

Do not attempt to stop chain with your hands.
—Swedish chain saw

Warning: May be hot to the touch while in use.
—Boxwood Candles

Why not try tossing over your favorite cereal.
—raisins package

Serving suggestion: Defrost.
—frozen dinner

Chevrolet could have hoped for in its new market. Perhaps because of its stellar associations, or because of its similarity to the word *nueva,* meaning new, the car was very well received, proving that, as with legends, it's often the perception, not the reality, that's the most telling.

One of my favorite legends, "Scraped" tells the story of the Atlantic Mutual Insurance Company, which reputedly played on public perception of its business—but with a bit more fun than most!

The company library of the Atlantic Mutual Insurance Company in New York City has one of the most complete sets of records of marine disasters that exists outside of England.

The completeness is so legendary that someone once wrote in and asked Atlantic if it had a record of Noah's Ark. Within a short time, the inquirer received the following information from some naughty wag at the firm:

"Built 2448 B.C. Gopher wood, pitched within and without. Length, 300 cubits; width, 50 cubits; height, 30 cubits. Three decks. Cattle carrier. Owner: Noah and Sons. Last reported stranded Mount Ararat."

THE SCAMMERS AND THE SCAMMED

Not all relationships between companies and clients are as congenial as the one Atlantic Mutual evidently enjoyed with its customers. In modern times, connections based on thinly veiled suspicions, outright aggression, and the conviction that companies pick consumer pockets by charging high prices for shoddy goods or services seem to be the norm.

In that environment, it would be surprising if tales of consumers shafting companies and companies shafting consumers weren't part of the corporate-legend scene. "Shaft" legends, boycott legends, hoaxes, and petitions for hoaxes illustrate the full range from the absurd to the truly nasty side of corporate myth.

In "Express Books," Houghton Mifflin found itself swamped with "spam" e-mail after some cybernaut "adjusted" the details of the book publisher's Christmas promotion before sending it out into the wilds of the Internet once again.

Houghton Mifflin has for several years run online promotions, and this one started out as simply as the rest. For every twenty-fifth e-mail message the company received through its special "Polar Express Share the Spirit" campaign, Houghton Mifflin would send one of two thousand available copies of one of children's author Chris Van Allsburg's books to a children's hospital. The campaign would start on November 15 and run through the holidays until New Year's Day. What could be more in the holiday spirit than that?

Whether it was through a mistaken belief that where one e-mail was a good thing, hundreds would be better, and would ensure that all those books were given away, or whether it was a deliberate attempt to overload the system and ensure that no one benefited, is difficult to discern. In any case, the original message, chopped down to a chain letter encouraging everyone to send as many e-mails as possible to this Web address and send the same message to all their friends was quickly lost in the rising swell of mail rushing toward Houghton Mifflin's offices. A log jam resulted, the system was creaking, and though all the books had long been awarded (in fact, they added five hundred more copies to their donations), the frazzled company was still receiving tens of thousands of e-mail messages *per day!*

Even the end of the promotion didn't end the madness. At least one pared-down version of the legend failed to give any end date whatsoever for the campaign.

The average Joe probably doesn't see any harm in an e-mail message. Like any other junk mail, it just gets thrown out, right? Not necessarily. As savvy cyber-vandals quickly came to grasp—and twist to their advantage—that amount of traffic at a single site has far-reaching consequences for the company. Most Internet providers (IPs) can't handle that volume. What can't fit in an in-box gets bounced back to the sender, effectively doubling the traffic generated on all the systems between sender and receiver! The sender can't receive legitimate mail in the clogged mailbox, the IP's service slows (affecting more than one mailbox), and system resources are strained by the doubling

effect. And that's only the hardware end of it. Staff, real people who should be handling real jobs (little things like publishing books), are inevitably hauled off their current projects to deal with the crisis. Routines throughout the firm are disrupted, business slows, and eventually profits are affected. Which is what most cyber-vandals are hoping for.

What may seem little more than a prank can stifle business for days and weeks at a time, endangering the jobs of real people. In a situation like the Polar Express promotion, the cyber-vandals have one precious resource on their side: the basic goodness that would send an average person to his computer to send a message that might help a sick child receive a book. Of the half-million messages Houghton Mifflin received, all but a few would have been sent by people who honestly believed they were doing a good thing.

The Nike Corporation found itself the victim in a similar situation when this message swept not only the Net, but office bulletin boards, fax-machine baskets, and even grocery store corkboards:

"FREE NIKES!!!"

Ever done something nice for someone and received a thank-you card for your efforts? Great feeling, isn't it? Well, Nike is looking for your help now and they're giving away something much more useful than a thank-you card in return!

Did you know this huge multinational company is one of the most active in the arena of charitable causes? They are! The Re-use-a-Shoe Program is just one of their many current campaigns, one that helps churn old tennis shoes into the basic material to construct hundred of playgrounds and ballfields in underprivileged neighborhoods.

All you need to do to help make these dreams a reality is send in your beat-up old tennis shoes, even the ones the dog chewed up, along with your name and address. Your old shoes will go into the playground project and Nike will send you a brand-new pair absolutely free!

It doesn't even have to be a Nike product! What more could you ask?

Help Nike continue to make this program a success, help build those playgrounds, and help yourself too! Here's the address:

> *Nike Recycling Center*
> *c/o Re-use-a-Shoe*
> *26755 SW 95th Street*
> *Wilsonville, OR 97070*

Sound too good to be true? It was. Think about it for a second. Wouldn't it be a lot cheaper for Nike to bury its own new shoes than send them out in the mail to someone else? Nike does support a fair number of charities, but this just doesn't make sense.

That hasn't stopped people from sending in the sneakers.

There really is a program that turns sneakers into playground material, but Nike isn't sending you any shoes to reward you for your efforts. If you'd like to help out, by all means send in your shoes, just remember to send along a note telling them you don't expect anything in return. They already have too many people sending out letters of explanation and asking those hoping for free sneakers if they'd still like to donate theirs to the project.

Hoaxed product warnings not only cause indirect harm to the victimized company, they directly attempt to erode consumer confidence and force firms out of business. Nike's potential customers might have been disappointed to learn they weren't getting the shoes they felt they were promised, but most people can get over it and actually sympathize with the company's public-relations problems. What no consumer would ever forgive is the thought that a big company, for nothing but monetary profit, would deliberately endanger them or anyone they cared about.

In 1996, a hoax warning claimed that water-resistant sunscreens were blinding children. Once the product got in the children's eyes, the notice insisted, its water resistance prevented parents from quickly washing it away. Children would have to be taken immediately to the nearest emergency room, where doctors, well aware of the threat, would use special preparations designed to remove the lotion. Of course, unless parents realized the danger, they wouldn't get the children there fast enough and would have to bear not only the grief of seeing their child blinded, but the guilt of not having been aware of the danger in the first place!

In just a few paragraphs, this "product warning" not only scares parents half to death, but suggests that doctors, the media, and the companies producing waterproof sunscreens are conspiring to keep this information away from us in the hope we'll continue to buy their products!

If you believed this warning was true, would you buy this product? Of course not, and, in the absence of proof to the contrary, the average consumer doesn't have to believe it completely. Erring on the side of caution would be enough to destroy companies that hardworking individuals have spent lifetimes trying to grow.

That these warnings are more often than not deliberate efforts to undermine particular companies is evident in the victims they choose to display in their warnings. In the previous example, does it really make any sense that children using the product would be blinded, but not adults? Eyes are eyes; older eyes aren't any less vulnerable than younger ones. Picking on this segment of a product's market is a deliberate attempt to arouse anger and fear. If children aren't the immediate targets, then women, the "weaker sex," are the next choice.

In 1997, a warning circulated all along the West Coast that Tampax tampons contained asbestos, a substance included for the sole purpose of aggravating bleeding and causing the consumer to use yet more of the product.

The next year, companies that use sodium laureth sulfate in their shampoos and toothpastes were targeted with claims that this substance was a carcinogen, that the companies knew this when they used it, and were, frankly, willing to ignore the threat to public safety if they could get away with it.

Procter & Gamble was hit yet again the following year, when yet another false product warning declared that their Pot Scrubbers, specifically the "new and improved" ones in the antibacterial formulation, contained Agent Orange! Not just traces of it, either, but enough to kill pets and—you guessed it!—small children.

None of these rumored horrors is true, not one. There aren't even glimmers of truth here, as can so often be found in other corporate legends and in the wider scope of urban legends in general. The common denominator here is that these are all products purchased primarily by women. Sure, modern men do scrub dishes, they even pick up scrubbies in the store, but, as advertisers know, most men buy "whatever the wife uses" and that's that.

Tampax, clearly a product for women, does not contain asbestos fibers. Asbestos is a substance banned by the FDA and cannot be used in any products for human use.

Sodium laureth sulfate is used in many products. It is not a carcinogen. It can cause diarrhea if ingested in large amounts, but not even toothpaste is *meant* to be swallowed. Certainly not shampoo.

The Procter & Gamble tale, like most directed at the company over the years, is the most openly malicious and, again, completely off base. First of all, *they don't produce the Pot Scrubbers, in any variety, described in the warning.* Second, antibacterial formulations made by other companies don't contain Agent Orange either.

If so many of these warnings prove to be hoaxes, why does the public continue to believe and perpetuate them? Erring on the side of caution just doesn't seem a sufficient basis for the deep mistrust the average American has for big business. Certainly there must be some underlying cause.

Perhaps, though, in a roundabout way, this next anecdote also proves consumers are being well protected, even if it approaches the issue in a roundabout way.

"The Eyes Have It," which began circulating in the fall of 1994, is one case where the legend, which claims contact-lens manufacturers bilk their customers by charging more for regular lenses than for disposable ones—even though the lenses are identical—can be traced to a very public article in a major publication. In *Consumer Reports,* one of the magazine's highly respected product-testing articles concluded that "Bausch & Lomb markets essentially the same soft contact lenses under different brand names, at different prices, and with different recommended wearing times."

Pretty damning stuff.

According to the report, Optima F.W. soft

A WINDOW ON MICROSOFT

Techies have some of the best legends. And "GIGO," the acronym for "garbage in, garbage out," remains one of the most popular short legends about one of the largest corporations, Microsoft. If the legend is true, those of you with high-powered microscopes can look at your computer processing chips and see how the company's employees *really* feel about their boss.

Engraved in micrometer-sized letters: BILL SUX!

Wouldn't it be perfect if it were true? But this one is just a legend.

---

lenses, which were recommended for a year-long period of daily use, and which cost forty-six dollars per pair wholesale, were the same product B&L marketed as SeeQuence 2 lenses, which were intended to be disposable, used for only a couple of weeks, and which cost five dollars a pair wholesale! So why weren't consumers allowed to buy the SeeQuence 2 lenses at the cheaper price if they could clean and use them identically to the more expensive Optima F.W. lenses?

In this case, profit seems to be the only motive.

So why didn't this real consumer warning gather speed and zip across fax lines and the Internet with the same speed as the hoax about Tampax, if not actually faster? Several reasons. The danger isn't immediate. Yes, it hurts your wallet, but it doesn't blind or kill your children if you pay more than necessary for your lenses. Indignation, but no horror, is inspired by this tale. The information was already well spread. *Consumer Reports* is read by millions. The legend, coming after the article, wasn't a surprise anymore. It didn't spread as a legend because it had already spread as other factual information usually does. The perceived market for this product, evenly spread between men and women, is also different from that of the other products. Cheering for the minority, the oppressed, and the vulnerable is much easier than cheering for everybody.

And how does this tale, depicting a true scenario of consumers being scammed, actually reinforce our sense of safety?

Well, now you know, right? They can't do it again and you're going to be *appropriately* cautious the next time you buy this product, not scared without reason. Cautious people ask questions; scared ones simply avoid the situation.

DOCTOR! DOCTOR!

If ever there was a love-hate relationship, the doctor-patient bond must be it. Vulnerability, helplessness, anger, and impatience, stirred by fear and frustration, a surefire recipe for disaster stalks these associations to such a degree that both patients and doctors soon come to view the other with wariness and caution.

The concept of a "consultation" between patient and doctor always implied a certain equality. Patients recognized their doctors' study and skill; doctors treated their patients as treasured clients. Today the most common complaint among patients is that their doctors "have no time to listen."

Many patients find themselves jotting notes before their appointment, planning the upcoming encounter with as much care as any general ever gave to his battle strategy—a rather sorry state of affairs at a time when medical science seems poised to conquer so many long-standing ills.

Of course, any relationship is a two-way street, and doctors have their justifiable complaints as well: patients who can't seem to describe what's bothering them; insurance plans that won't put out for the one test that would offer a definitive diagnosis; patients who neglect to mention such things as preexisting diseases or conditions (one woman appeared in an emergency room complaining of severe abdominal pain, but didn't mention her sixteen-week pregnancy!) or allergies, or that they're habitual drug users.

Medical legends cover surprisingly wide-ranging territory, with tales evidently aimed at both health-care workers and patients, and with blame shared around almost equally! They differ from the other groupings in one important way: the inclusion of innumerable "old wives' tales." Whereas most legends consist of an elaborate setup followed by quick-and-dirty twisted endings, medical legends can be as structurally simple as "Masturbation makes hair grow on your palms!" Their simplicity might lead you to believe they aren't real legends at all.

Brevity aside, old wives' tales do satisfy the definition of a legend. They record, reveal, and impart a specific societal moral, often more bluntly and obviously than their more convoluted cousins. They have staying power, spreading quickly. They make good entertainment. They frequently combine the horrific and the humorous. They play on our senses, creating images that appeal to us on many levels. Sounds rather like an urban legend, doesn't it?

Even their brevity doesn't mean they're ignoring the other traditional quality of an urban legend, the narrative. In many cases the short, snappy old wives' tale is merely a stripped-down version of a longer tale, verbal shorthand for a tale the audience once recognized easily. I'm sure, with a little imagination, you can re-create some of the tales that might have been associated with young men and hairy palms.

Occasionally an urban legend becomes so well represented in the factual reporting of the day that the legend is no longer considered a legend at all. For example, in the first half of the twentieth century, legends of doctors amputating the wrong limb were in vogue. Likewise, tales of doctors operating on the wrong patient altogether proved popular as both medical legends and horror tales. They've become considerably less prevalent in the second half of the century, and two reasons for this have been put forward.

The first is that as surgical procedures of any sort became more common and supposedly safer, surgery lost the terror it evoked throughout the 1800s and into this century. In 1890 an attempted amputation had something less than a 30 percent chance of complete success. ("Complete success" was something of a misnomer even then, as one common procedure, cauterization with a hot poker or iron instead of the delicate stitching of today, left patients with grossly disfiguring scars.) The procedure, even when clearly indicated as necessary, was therefore seldom attempted. In 1990, amputation of a limb was better than 90 percent likely to prove completely successful. More procedures were performed, with better results. People were less afraid. The legends faded.

That's one theory. Another proposes that people have simply become so accustomed to reports of *real* medical bloopers that the legends aren't necessary to remind the audience of the horror and danger!

Two basically opposing theories, with perhaps more than a hint of truth in each!

One other thing that differentiates medical legends from others is the rich history that accompanies them. Although many areas, such as corporate history, have been neglected by scholars of all eras, medicine enjoys a rich written history that allows us to trace many tales to a specific source, or at least to put them in context for the time period in which they arose. Another, more obvious advantage of all those written words is that more *legends* have survived, giving us an extraordinary view into common beliefs and fears dating as far back as Aristotle!

Which is not to say that medical legends are heavy on dust or stuffiness, as you'll soon see.

OF MALADIES
ODD AND UNUSUAL

One of the most frustrating experiences for doctors and patients is the presentation of a patient with symptoms for which there seem to be no single best, or right, solution. Almost any doctor who's been practicing medicine for more than a few years has a story of one case that never was resolved. Sometimes the results are tragic and patients die. Often, even postmortem exams fail to turn up a specific cause. On other, happier occasions, the symptoms resolve themselves and the patient goes on without further difficulty, leaving a puzzled physician behind.

Legends of the "Betcha can't identify this illness!" type are peculiar to doctors and students, with older physicians frequently producing obstinate cases for their younger colleagues to attempt to diagnose, and rarely move into the general public domain. One exception is the "Bright Lights" legend, which begins with an anecdote supposedly dating to 1745. A young sailor who spent most of his time overhead in the rigging would, on occasion, usually just before sunset, and without apparent reason, plunge to the deck with all the symptoms of the "falling sickness," epilepsy. An older seaman who possessed some knowledge of medicine, enough to stitch wounds and set bones, knew as much about epilepsy as the next man, but had never heard of a case so predictable!

Confronted with the possibility that the boy might kill himself by falling to the deck or into the ocean, the older seaman and the captain ordered the boy to tie himself to something stable when working above. This wasn't entirely convenient, so from time to time the boy would unstrap himself and fall anyway. Eventually, two items became evident: the lad only fell into fits when it was sunny, and he would eventually kill himself if he continued. At the next port, a new sailor was brought aboard and the captain decided the first young man could work on the decks, in the captain's cabin, and below in the kitchens.

The problem never recurred, and the old sailor concluded that the boy had some strange aversion to the sun that caused his fits.

> Obviously there were no old wives working in watch factories when women were busily painting watch faces with radium to make them visible at night. If there had been, one of them would undoubtedly have said, "Hey, don't put that brush in your mouth!" and saved hundreds of those factory workers from dying horrible deaths from radium poisoning.

The next anecdote in the tale begins just outside London on a large estate owned by the Sedgwick family. The grand approach included a long, tree-lined drive down which the Sedgwicks' many guests glided in their carriages. All was well until, late one afternoon, the fiancée of one of the house's sons arrived to spend the weekend. Her carriage driver arrived flustered and panicked and raced into the main entrance to request that a doctor attend the young woman immediately. She'd fallen into a fit of some sort shortly after coming onto the Sedgwick property, and was now huddled in the bottom of the carriage!

When the doctor arrived, he examined the girl, who slowly came out of her disoriented state, and suggested she might suffer from epilepsy. The girl, however, had no history of epilepsy, nor did anyone in her family, and at eighteen years of age, she did seem a little old to develop the disease. A day went by and all was well. She, her fiancé, and his parents spent the next day in town shopping and enjoying themselves. On the way home, as they came up the drive, less than a minute after turning onto the Sedgwick property, the girl once again fell into convulsions! This time two doctors and the girl's parents were summoned—with similar results. Her parents confirmed the girl's assurances that she had no history of the disease; the doctors could find no cause for her ailment.

Eventually one doctor pulled the girl's father aside and gently suggested that, as the fits only occurred at the Sedgwick residence, perhaps the young woman wasn't as resigned to her upcoming marriage as everyone supposed? The other doctor, while all this was being discussed, pointed out to the boy's parents that a daughter-in-law with epilepsy might well pass on the disease to her children, their grandchildren.

After some further quiet discussions, the girl was escorted home, the engagement broken.

As she never again suffered from the fits of that weekend, her parents consoled themselves with the notion that the marriage, though excellent socially, obviously wouldn't have been to their daughter's liking. She eventually married someone else and lived happily ever after, without ever discovering what had caused the convulsions.

Skip ahead to Philadelphia in 1985, and the rec room of a typical suburban family.

Their youngest son, a game freak, is propped in front of the TV with his fingers darting across the paddle of his favorite video game. Without warning, he pitches forward and begins to convulse! Doctors examine him, but, like their predecessors, can seem to find nothing to offer him or his parents other than the suggestion that he be checked for epilepsy. A full battery of tests and a detailed medical history later, it seems unlikely that this nineteen-year-old has suddenly developed epilepsy, but there seems no other explanation. Days, weeks, eventually months go by and there's no further recurrence. Ready to put the incident behind them as a medical oddity, the family concludes the mystery will never be solved.

Then, at Thanksgiving, the entire family gets together, and with the women upstairs arguing with the turkey, the men retire to the basement, where the older crowd sips some good whiskey while the younger ones whoop and holler over the video games. Everyone is shocked when, once again, the youngest son falls onto his face and is racked by convulsions!

This time doctors have an explanation!

It's the flashing light of one of the video games! The light strikes the retina, causing a specific set of responses in the ocular nerves, a reaction that swiftly spreads to the brain. Chemical fireworks go off and an epileptic seizure begins! Of course, not just any old flashing lights will do it, but just those of a particular frequency: the frequency of a video game's lights, the frequency with which sunlight falling through a line of trees would strike a young woman's face with a horse pulling a carriage at a reasonable speed, or the frequency with which light from the setting sun might flicker along the leading edge of a topsail!

This rather unusual tale, which had been floating about the medical profession for a very long time, only became public, and a legend, when a real-life case of video-game-induced epileptic seizures made its way into well-distributed magazines and televised medicine shows.

The moral changed in the telling, too.

What began as a warning to medical students never to overestimate their ability to diagnose an illness became, when appropriated by the general population, a vague warning that doctors don't know as much as they think they do! A lesson in professional humility for one group became proof of professional snobbery to another! A complete reversal.

Later revisions—mostly mutations that lost the original text altogether—were appropriated by a specific subset of the population—parents—as proof that video games, in and of themselves, were dangerous! Not a hint of the history of, or science behind, the discovery of photic stimuli epilepsy remained. Such loss of meaning, the *devolution* of knowledge, is a fairly common theme in medical legends.

For a much shorter tale on the perils of simple light, there's "Sunlight Makes You

Sneeze!" According to the collected wisdom of generations of mothers who told children with an almost-there sneeze to "look at the sun," bright light of any type makes you sneeze. This seems easy enough to prove or disprove, too, doesn't it? Who doesn't know someone who sneezes every time he or she steps outside on a sunny day? Who hasn't looked at the window to rid himself of a reluctant sneeze? Walk into any classroom or other group of people and ask everyone who sneezes in sunlight to raise their hands. Guaranteed, someone will stick his hand up. Some will even tell you the sneezing is a symptom of their "allergy to sunshine"!

This seems pretty cut-and-dried. Unfortunately, while old wives' tales depend on things like observation and common sense, science and medicine depend on replicable testing, testing that can get pretty convoluted and take years to proceed through the experimental design stage, the testing, the publication, the peer review, the retesting, and, finally, the publication of *final* data.

All to prove that there is indeed something called the photic sneeze, an involuntary bout of sneezing on initial exposure to significant amounts of light—something the old wives already knew?

Well, yes, and to discover the why and how, and the implications of the discovery.

The old wives knew photic sneezing existed; the doctors told us three things: First, the whole photic sneezing thing is likely an inherited trait. It runs in families and

appears to be a dominant characteristic. It affects at least 20 percent of the population, but is most likely to affect Caucasians. Second, it may be caused by squinting, which forces tears into the nasolacrymal ducts, which tickles the nose and causes the sneeze. Third, it can happen under many circumstances, some more dangerous than others. Walking out your front door and sneezing is one thing; driving out of a dark tunnel into bright sunlight, sneezing, momentarily losing sight of the road ahead, and slamming into someone else is a serious situation.

A man whose case was reported in *The St. Louis Medical Journal* appears to prove yet another medical legend, "She Sneezed When Pleased!" According to this tale, which can be traced back to at least 1875, a person who reaches the absolute peak of sexual excitement will sneeze! Men who wondered if their women were really satisfied had only to give it their best shot and see if she sneezed! It seemed women had the same option, and when this tale became popular around Columbia University, dozens of "sneeze jokes" also made the rounds.

No one's gotten around to testing this tale yet, but the case in St. Louis gave it a new credence when an article on this supposed effect was published and one subject admitted that not only did he sneeze when pleased, he sneezed whenever he thought about sex! Erotic thoughts, anticipation, actual sex—almost anything—could set him sneezing! Needless to say, the article also left lots of couples listening for little sneezes in the dark.

In a neat bit of circular legend-making, it seems that for some individuals, sneezing leads to yawning, while, for others, yawning leads to sneezing. It's a little inconvenient, but less irksome on the whole than, for example, constant hay fever or an allergy to soap—for most. When yawning leads to *orgasm,* however, as it does for a specific portion of the population, a portion already identified in "The Best Side Effect," sneezing gets truly problematic! Sneeze, yawn, orgasm! It'd be enough to warp almost anyone's perceptions of socially acceptable behavior!

So what did the urban legend know that the scientists didn't? That some drugs, like Anafranil (clomipramine) or Prozac (fluoxetine), have an odd little side effect in some patients—inducing orgasm whenever the user yawns or sneezes! Considering that several users reported continuous yawning—and orgasms!—for up to two hours, the side effect wasn't inconsiderable. While dozens of scientific papers attempted to explain the why of this seldom-discussed side effect, the legend was racing ahead to reach as many laypeople as possible. Before long, the legend of a medicine that could make later drugs like Viagra unnecessary was bringing speculative sparkles to many an eye. If the legend-surrounding-the-legend was to be believed, doctors were rightly amazed by the sudden increase of psychiatric patients flooding their offices! Was the thought of their "normal" sexual lives getting them down? No! Fluoxetine and clomipramine were antidepressants, and everyone wanted the magical pills!

Not all medical legends are quite so risqué; some harken back to our childhoods. Remember this one? "Don't chew on your braids! You'll clog your intestines!" One expanded tale, told by a certain nun at Mary Queen of the World Girls' School, got considerably more graphic than you might expect from sanctified lips. In that version, the girls weren't getting their own hair in their mouths! Hmm. Maybe this legend is more risqué than it seemed at first glance.

In any case, the usual version of the tale, "The Rapunzel Effect," which has circulated pretty much unchanged since the early 1920s, details the life of a naughty little girl who, among all her other bad habits, chewed on the loose tips of her braids. No amount of censure from her mother, her nanny, or her teachers could break her of this nasty habit. In the urban-legend tradition of retribution for wayward girls, this little hoyden soon found herself griped by painful stomach cramps. At first she tried to hide her discomfort and avoid the "I told you so." Soon the pain left her doubled up in her seat. When her teacher called on her to finish a sum at the board, she collapsed halfway there and couldn't be roused!

The doctor, though told of her terrible habit, couldn't believe something so seemingly inconsequential might wreak such havoc on a young girl. For several days her physician sought other answers, but found none. In the face of the girl's rapidly weakening condition, and her mother's insistence that her daughter suffered from the human version of feline hairballs, he eventually agreed to open her up for exploratory surgery. Her mother was vindicated, her physician horrified, when he discovered a hairball as big as his fist lodged in the upper portion of her small intestine. Had he not given in to the mother's pleas, the young girl would surely have died!

As it turns out, a series of real-life cases, reported in journals as geographically diverse as the *Australian and New Zealand Journal of Surgery* and the *European Journal of Pediatric Surgery* prove the older legend may well have been based in fact. One trichobezoar—that's a fancy name for "people hairball"—weighed 707 grams, over a pound, and had grown so large that the young girl's stomach was completely filled.

"The Rapunzel Effect" isn't restricted to hairballs. In various forms, the same tale warns children about the hazards of ingesting any number of supposedly unnatural items. "Swallowing bubble gum will stick your insides together!" True, according to an article relating the medical difficulties of a girl who not only chewed on her hair but swallowed gum, which quickly collected all the loose hair in her stomach into a single huge, unpassable mass that also had to be surgically removed. "Too much chocolate will poison you!" Not proven true by medical study, but based on the high sugar levels that follow its ingestion, it's not all that unlikely, sugar itself being a metabolic poison.

What no mother anywhere has ever said, of course, is "Don't eat your oat bran, it'll stop up your intestines!" Children can, however, still hope. In 1989 the *New England Journal of Medicine* reported the case of a man who, after considerable agony, had an *oat-bran* bezoar removed from the depths of his digestive tract.

When the star of "A Little Liquor" presented himself to his local emergency room with bizarre symptoms that, while life-threatening, didn't add up to any of the usual maladies, doctors were stumped. For days they treated the symptoms while desperately seeking a cause and watching new symptoms pop up. Even when a full workup revealed that the man suffered from *iron poisoning,* no one could find a source!

This time there was no help from the only old wives' tale that seemed to apply: "Too much iron gives you arthritis." The man didn't have arthritis, and in any case the old wives' tale failed to provide even a suspected source for all that iron. He didn't live downstream from an iron-ore mine, didn't use an iron skillet, and hadn't mistaken anyone else's iron tablets for M&M's. There was nothing in his history to explain why an otherwise healthy man was at death's door!

As the man's condition worsened, his wife

snuck in several pints of his favorite beer. When the doctor surprised them in mid-slurp, the wife flushed, then shrugged. "Even the condemned man gets a last meal of his own choosing, right?"

Far from being concerned about the hospital's rules against bringing food or liquor in to patients, the doctor's first thought was, "Hey, that wasn't on the list of foods we tested!"

Grabbing a stubby brown bottle from the paper bag, he realized they weren't commercial. "His own stuff?"

"Yeah, he's been brewing for years. This is one of his best." Shyly, she offered him an open bottle. "You can have one if you'd like."

He took it, but not to drink. Moments later he was rushing back into the room to confiscate the lot. "It's the beer!"

"What?"

"Show me the still!"

The homemade brewery included one huge iron vat, untreated. The beer was the source of the iron!

The man's only comment as he was released from the hospital?

"And here I was thinkin' a few beers a day was just the ticket for my kidney stones!"

It was probably on a morning-after-the-night-before that someone once said, "Too much baking soda will make your insides explode!" As with many such short admonitions, there's also a longer legend, "Blown Away!," that provides all the gory details anyone could want.

Super Bowl Sunday, bowls of peanuts, yard-long hero sandwiches, beer, pretzels, and every form of chips imaginable combined into a roiling, acidic stomachache for one football fan. Finding he'd run out of his usual antacid, he spent the half-time break rummaging a box of baking soda out of the fridge. The box didn't come with medical instructions and smelled vaguely of onions, but that didn't stop the uncomfortable man from chucking a few spoonfuls into a glass of water and swigging it down.

Before the end of the third quarter, the man's stomach was rock-hard and aching worse than ever! Figuring it was time to knock off the nachos, he stirred up another glass and downed it before the first of the fizz dissipated.

He didn't get to see who won the game.

After a few moments of excruciating pain, he fell to the floor unconscious, and died en route to the hospital. Cause of death was found to be the violent explosion of a grossly distended stomach, which caused half-digested food and stomach acids to flood the normally sterile abdominal cavity, shocking his system beyond recall.

Tracking down this particular Super Bowl Sunday tale proved impossible, but a dozen similar stories are recorded in the reliable medical literature, certainly enough to justify the simpler tale, "Too much baking soda makes your insides explode!"

Remember the legend of the husband who found a pork-chop bone amid his obese

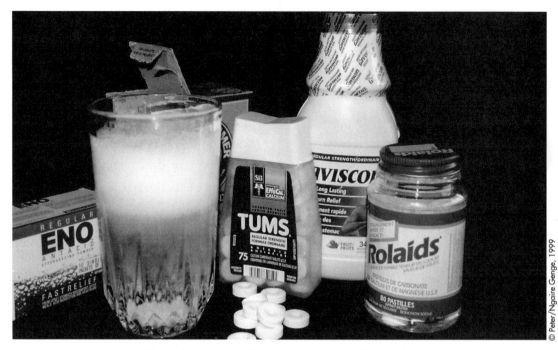

© Peter/Ngaire Genge, 1999

"One of these things is not like the others, one of these things . . .
should stay in the back of the fridge!"

wife's rolls of fat? Although that legend appears to be nothing more than a malicious little tale designed to denigrate, a series of interconnected events gave the tale a boost in 1989. For years, legends about swallowed objects turning up in odd places, usually body parts, formed part of the "body" of medical legends. Bullets lost inside soldiers only to turn up later by being coughed up, vomited up, sneezed out, or found sliding about under the skin some distance from the initial entry wound were featured in stories tied to numerous conflicts. One man, reputedly deaf in one ear for several decades, suddenly regained his hearing after a bout of sneezing, when a food stamp popped out of the ear. Another man, who swallowed a small coin as a child, but never passed it, was startled when his doctor found the coin in his left lung nearly forty years later.

None of those legends compares with the real story of a chubby woman from Hartsville, Tennessee, who discovered a four-inch-long pork-chop bone protruding from the cheek of her bottom! According to the woman's statement, it had been years since she'd last eaten a pork chop; she had no idea when she might have *sat* on a chop bone. Yet there's no other apparent explanation for the bone's presence. From the amount of tissue adhering to the foreign bone when it was removed, her doctor firmly believed it was just sitting in there for five years or more.

It wasn't long after this story broke into public awareness that the legend of the lost chop bone once again became popular.

A more recent medical legend, "Me Too!," begins in the elevator of a hospital where a very embarrassed young woman has just given birth to a handsome baby boy. Asked why she didn't come in earlier, the woman flushes bright red. "Believe it or not, I didn't know I was in labor."

Wrapping the baby up in a warm towel, the doctor attempts to console the new mother. "Well, don't feel bad. At least you got to the hospital. We had someone deliver in the middle of the lawn last year—and she didn't know she was *pregnant,* much less in labor!"

To the doctor's surprise, this only draws more blushes, even a few tears.

Eventually the new mother confesses, "That was me, too!"

What's a doctor to do when the *patient* doesn't notice *those* symptoms—twice!

Even patients who arrive safely and in time are the subject of two more medical legends. The first, "Flowers for My Love," details the experience of a young woman who, upon delivery of her first child, was inundated with flowers from the happy father. Roses, her favorites, arrived hourly by the dozen while pots of living mums began filling up the remaining space in the corners. Smiling at the man's enthusiasm and joy was easy for both the young wife and the staff, and when he began showering the nurses with chocolates and flowers of their own, well, he quickly found a way into even the hardest hearts.

When he'd finally left that evening, long

© Peter/Ngaire Genge, 1999

Yes, you can leave them in your bedroom overnight.

after visiting hours were supposedly over, the staff tucked in the new mother and her adorable little daughter and closed the door to the small room. The following morning, well before visiting hours, even before breakfast was served, they all saw the young man, arms heaped with presents for his wife and daughter, sneaking toward the private rooms. With a new box of chocolates on their desk, however, they were willing to turn a blind eye to the minor breach of hospital policy. They were shocked when, just seconds later, a high-pitched scream filled the corridor. Racing to the man's side, they discovered his wife and child both blue and cold—they'd been dead for hours!

The distraught man was hustled out of the room, the doctor on call summoned, and nurses ran in all directions to soothe the fears of other patients. When the doctor arrived, he took one look at the banks of flowers and turned on the staff!

"Don't you know flowers aren't permitted in patient rooms?"

"Of course, doctor, but it was only for one night! She was supposed to go home with a nurse today. We didn't see any harm. And they made her so cheerful!"

"Some good they'll do her now!" He returned. "They sucked every bit of oxygen out of the room! She and the child suffocated in their sleep!"

In good urban-legend style, the young father, believing himself responsible for his family's death, soon kills himself.

Of course, it couldn't have happened that way at all. While some hospitals have a no-flowers policy, it's usually to avoid inconveniencing patients with pollen allergies, not because anyone is likely to be suffocated.

The second tale, "Gas Out," features a much less sympathetic figure. A grumpy old man, the source of of an unending stream of nasty remarks, crude jokes, and wandering hands, manages to alienate most of the staff of his nursing home long before evening comes. By the time they can finally close his door that evening, it's with deep sighs of relief! Surprisingly, he makes it through the entire night without a single jarring buzz from his bedside call button. The nurses are almost willing to forgive him and start the morning off on a brighter note when they discover why he hasn't been bothering anyone.

They're just about to bring in his breakfast when his doctor arrives, inquires after the man's night, and starts to enter his room. The nurse following with the tray almost trips over the physician, who has been brought up short in the middle of the hallway, his mouth hanging open.

"Doctor, is anything wrong?"

"How long has his door been closed?"

"Why, all night, doctor. The patients find it easier to sleep if we close the doors."

"Oh no!"

Leaving the nurse standing in the hallway, he races ahead and throws open the door. Even from where she's standing, however, she quickly catches a whiff of the stench now emanating from the patient's room. With considerable trepidation, she lays the tray aside, covers her nose, and follows the doctor.

Inside, the patient is dead and the physician is throwing open all the windows.

"Doctor?"

"It's methane gas. This man was admitted so we could find the source of his problem—excessive flatulence!"

The patient expired from the inhalation of his own gas!

Of course, no such cases exist in the real world, though some wives would no doubt believe this one, based on their own nocturnal experiences with fragrant spouses.

The best medical-oddity legends are, naturally, those that add a fillip of embarrassment to the story recounted, which is certainly the case in "The Patch." In this one, the patient with the undiagnosable problem is a middle-aged woman in normally excellent health. Her usually robust state is threatened one morning when, for no apparent reason, she suddenly falls victim to a pounding headache, faintness that prevents her from standing, rapid heartbeat, and shortness of breath. Her husband, watching her stumble toward the shower, decides the situation is only getting worse and, without bothering to call for an ambulance, simply wraps her in several blankets, tucks her into the family car, and races to the nearest hospital.

An hour later, doctors can find nothing physically wrong, but agree the woman is in serious condition. As they continue testing and questioning, the woman slips briefly into unconsciousness and is taken to the intensive care unit, where every effort is made to gain control of her racing pulse.

Turning their attention to the husband while the patient is settled into her new accommodations, they ask all the usual questions: "Any allergies?" No. "Anything new in her environment?" No. "Any new foods?" No. "Has anything like this ever happened before?" No.

Frustrated, one young doctor asks, "Any unusual stress? Problems at work? Anything."

"No, not at all. In fact, this is the first day of our vacation. She was fine before we got out of bed." He flushes. "In fact, we had a wonderful late morning in bed that included a very active session of lovemaking that left us both very satisfied and relaxed."

At that moment, a nurse turns from her patient, whom they've been undressing and easing into the hospital's blue gowns that opened down the back. "That might explain how she came to have this stuck to her bottom!"

Everyone is left giggling as the husband realizes the skin-colored patch the nurse has just removed from his wife's posterior is his own nitroglycerine patch, which he applies to himself each night for continuous control of mild angina!

The patch is removed and the woman recovers completely.

TALES OF THE OLD WIVES

Though many old wives' tales survive as modern medical legends, some represent a completely different period in our understanding of human physiology, a time when even procreation wasn't completely understood. Without the illumination of science, people made what observations they could while searching for the elusive consistencies that might explain what couldn't be seen happening inside the human body. Some of these observations were startlingly ahead of their time. Others were, if anything, a step backward. Physicians were hard put to mine the golden nuggets of knowledge from "women's medicine," that odd combination of fact and superstition practiced by mothers and midwives in kitchens, fields, and bedrooms, all the places you weren't likely to find a doctor of any stripe.

"There's a good reason not to share a home with your mother or your mother-in-law," one bit of wisdom went. "When women live together, their natural cycles want to run together, and soon none of them will know when their time is coming!" At a time when birth control was dependent on the vagaries of the "rhythm method," anything that disrupted a woman's normal menstrual cycle was a matter of serious concern. If she didn't know when she'd begin or end her cycle, she had no idea when she was most likely to conceive—or least likely!

For generations, women accepted the fact that, by whatever means, women who lived together would, over time, find themselves on the same menstrual schedule. Science pooh-poohed the idea despite a long-standing anecdotal history and numerous first-person testimonies to its veracity—until women began speaking the language of science and put their belief to tests that met the criteria of the scientific method. It took only three studies to prove that women living in close proximity, or who spent considerable time in one another's company, would indeed experience "menstrual synchrony." Even before anyone knew what a pheromone was, the "old wives" had recognized group PMS when they saw it!

Menstruation, an essentially hidden process with no male equivalent, could be expected to engender tales that not only attempted to explain the phenomenon, but to cast it in a less-than-favorable light. Anything not well understood—and menstruation wouldn't be explained at all until the turn of the century—is usually feared, and things that are feared are frequently denigrated—especially in urban legends. So we have tales of menstruating women causing mirrors to crack or lose their polish, menstruating women turning milk sour, and even a few medieval contributions with menstruating women causing plague or pox!

Lactation, however, being an entirely visible process with an obvious purpose, would seem a much less likely target for myths. Wrong. At least a dozen tales, all centered on breast-feeding, continued to be passed along as recently as 1860. It's long been noted, for example, that newborn babies, male and female, occasionally leak tiny amounts of milk from their nipples just after birth. Known as "witch's milk," this substance was viewed with suspicion, as was the child who produced it, and the mother whose child would need witch's milk.

An even odder breast-feeding story is associated with an early Dutch version of "Rumpelstiltskin." In that variation, the evil gnome Rumpelstiltskin steals the young wife's firstborn child and refuses to return him unless and until the woman can discover his name. While he has the child, he holds it to his breast and eventually coaxes milk to form so he can feed the baby himself. A Caribbean tale contends that a man who stole the son of a cruel landowner before fleeing into the hills managed to keep the boy alive with milk from his own breasts until the child was old enough to drink properly. In Transylvanian folklore, a baby girl is stolen by wolves who kill her mother and severely injure her father. Disregarding his wounds, the man tracks the wolves for days, eventually finding their den, killing them one by one, and rescuing his daughter. Desperate to keep her alive, but with nothing to feed her, he presses her lips to his own breast and prays. Soon, milk flows and he manages to crawl back to civilization with her.

A significant number of folktales and fairy tales cast elderly women, long past child-bearing days, and women who have never had children in the role of desperate rescuer who must somehow feed a starving child. A Korean story features a great-grandmother who, with a little supernatural help, is able to feed forty-three children when war destroys her village!

What could possibly explain a societal need to shift breast-feeding tales away from childbearing women of average ages with normal children? Some folklorists claim it's a way of denying the average woman a unique ability, making her less valuable to society. Others take a differing opinion, pointing out that women themselves have often kept these tales alive. They feel that, like the menstrual synchrony tales, these stories of unusual breast-feeders are ways of recording observations that women who believed themselves familiar with all aspects of breast-feeding still couldn't explain.

While we now know that there's very little difference between male and female breast tissue itself, that the difference lies in the hormones acting on that tissue, and that hormonal activity can sometimes be induced by external physical stimuli, previous generations of women could simply observe some odd physiological similarities. They could, for example, recognize that men with lumps growing in their breast tissue were as likely to die of the lumps as women, even if they didn't recognize breast cancer per se in either sex. They could recognize that relactation, the process of encouraging a supply of

milk to come in without a pregnancy to stim-
ulate production, was possible in some
cases—even in men. With the discovery of
hormones and the mechanisms behind their
production, these tales eventually faded
from circulation.

As you've likely noticed, numerous old
medical tales revolve around reproduction
or the mysteries of various reproductive
organs. That trend continues in these next
few tales, though you'll likely find them more
amusing than insightful, as none of them
contain the smallest fragment of truth.

Recessed navels ("insies") versus protruding ones ("outsies") were of absolutely
no interest to early midwives. "Tying the
umbilical cord too close to a boy's tummy
will give him a short penis," warned the old
wives up into the sixteenth century. "Always
leave it a little long, and his wife will thank
you for it." A baby girl's cord, on the other
hand, was tied as close to the abdominal

wall as possible. Modern obstetricians and
midwives tie all cords a little less than two
fingers' width from the tummy, with no
observable consistency in the length of
penises.

In the days when left-handedness was
deemed socially unacceptable at best, and
demon-inspired at worst, determining a
child's handedness as early as possible was
considered advantageous, especially in the
case of a boy who might one day be
expected to write in public or join up for military service, two activities likely to highlight
handedness. If parents could know their little boy would be afflicted with this plight, so
the theory went, then they might well be able
to "train" him out of it before it became
apparent to anyone. To this end, midwives
and mothers closely inspected the newborn's tiny testicles. If the legends of the day
were true, boys with a lower right testicle
were likely safe from being "cory-fisted,"
while those unlucky enough to have a lower
left testicle would require early intervention if
they were to live a full and productive life.
That nearly two-thirds of all men have a lower
left testicle, while less than one-fifth of all
men are left-handed, seems to invalidate
that particular legend.

It wasn't just midwives who were looking
to a man's genitals to provide some clue to
his inner self, however. Physicians of the
same period also held the penis in high
esteem as a diagnostic tool. For many years
it was believed that the direction in which the

penis lay, left or right, on a patient lying flat on his back, would indicate the side of the body that was causing the complaint. So prevalent had this little bit of medical wisdom become, in fact, that a group of osteopaths at Charing Cross Hospital in London decided it was time to see if there was any truth in the old chestnut, and began a series of informal observations to test the hypothesis.

Deciding that a broken hip was certainly painful enough to warrant some attention, and could easily be determined as affecting the left of right side of the body, they began noting which way their male patients' penises were lying in relation to the broken hip. The old tale died a swift death when, regardless of how the data might be manipulated, it became clear that penises would lie where they lay without regard to the state of the hips on either side. Absolutely no correlation was possible.

Perhaps the most persistent old wives' tale of all also picks the penis as its body part of choice. "If you play with it, you'll go blind!" This Victorian tale, an obvious warning against masturbation, hasn't changed in over a hundred years, and, according to minutes of a meeting of school psychologists, is still making its way through school locker rooms in 1998. One wonders what the man who found himself the subject of a *New England Journal of Medicine* article thought of the old adage when, well into middle age, he abruptly developed an odd malady that left him blind in one eye whenever he reached orgasm! Whatever else he may have thought, it certainly wasn't that the situation should in any way dissuade him from sexual activity. In fact, according to the article, he'd been through the temporary blindness in excess of thirty times before deciding he might need to seek medical help!

Though sexual oddities of one type and another certainly take up a large portion of the older old wives' tales, the scope is actually quite broad, as the remainder of these legends prove.

Ever since domesticated cats moved into the home, mothers have regarded them with suspicion, and new mothers have been warned to keep them away from their newborns. "It'll lie across a baby's face to smell the milk on its breath, and smother it!" Though virtually all mothers hear this story, no one, for many years, was able to locate a single reported instance of a cat smothering a child. Since suspicious deaths get written up not only in the papers but in hospital records and police reports, the distinct lack of any mention of cats would seem a definitive mark in favor of these tales being nothing more than cautionary stories designed to ensure that new mothers kept on the lookout for dangers, even in unsuspected corners. Which is precisely how most young mothers took them—until 1995, when a New Zealand tragedy set all caregivers back on their heels and made cats persona non grata in nurseries once more.

According to the *New Zealand Medical Journal,* the victim was a three-week-old child that parents found in his crib with the family's long-haired cat lying across his face. Already blue from oxygen deprivation, the boy couldn't be revived by his parents or by an emergency medical team. Though this could have been a case of sudden infant death syndrome, the autopsy results found numerous cat hairs in the boy's mouth and larnyx as well as other classic symptoms of suffocation not found in SIDS results. The coroner, after examining the evidence and receiving the various related statements, concluded that the cat had indeed been responsible for the child's death.

A *very* old medical tale suggests that it wasn't all the chopping that made beheading so horrific. Even the guillotine, a considerable improvement over a headsman, who was likely to be drunk and unfocused for the occasion, couldn't resolve this problem. If "The Blinking Head" was given any credence, those unlucky enough to die by beheading weren't free of all their problems when the blade sliced through their necks. If the eyes of a separated head could still blink, so the tale went, then obviously the victim's brain remained alive and capable of receiving information even after the head flew off!

To a modern-day audience, this tale has all the horror of entrapment legends, paralysis nightmares, and suffocation phobias rolled into one! Imagine being caught inside your own skull, your eyes still receiving the vision of your body spurting its life away, while you remain cognizant enough to know you no longer have lungs to draw breath! Your vision slowly fades to darkness with nothing but the image of chortling faces to take into eternity! And yes, heads can blink.

The guillotine, a French invention, took a little time to be accepted in Britain, but, being a progressive people, the British sent many observers to report back on the new device and its level of acceptance among the general population. In the process, the possibility that some semblance of thought remained within the separated head evidently bothered these fine scientists and, as they would later document in the letters sent back to England, they devised some tests of their own to see how much "life" hung about a head separated from its body. Throughout these letters and reports are enthusiastic comments on the "neatness" and "efficiency" of the new device, the lack of "mangling noticeable in those beheaded by axe and sword." They also noted that an eyeball touched immediately after decapitation would blink! Though the eyes of most heads refused to respond as little as ten seconds after decapitation, one observer, a cleric and doctor, discovered, to his considerable consternation, that one eye blinked for as much as a "full minute" after the head was separated from the body!

Another legend that traces its roots well back in history states that, under the most trying or terrifying circumstances, a person could awaken to find his hair turned gray overnight. The most famous case is attributed to Marie Antoinette, who, on hearing she was to be killed in the morning, went completely white before she could be beheaded. That changes in the hair should be connected to stress isn't a new idea or even a novel one. Stress has long been linked to hair loss. Poor nutrition, a rather frequent condition for prisoners and terrified individuals, is often first diagnosed on the basis of hair loss. Even apparent changes of hair color are known to occur under special circumstances. Pregnant women frequently find themselves with a new crop of hair of a lighter or darker shade than their normal, pre-pregnancy color. An unusual condition, diffuse alopecia areata, which causes hair to fall out all over the head, especially normal hair, could, over time, give rise to the perception that a person's hair "went white" in a remarkably short period. The "overnight" part of the tale, however, remains legendary. That anyone could lose a significant amount of hair to diffuse alopecia areata without noticing a pile of hair on the pillow in the morning is certainly every bit as hard to believe as that hair could turn completely white in less than twelve hours.

Another old legend that harkens back to childhood claims that "summer ice cream gives you tummy aches, but winter ice cream won't." I can personally remember my grandmother telling me that on one of our rare wintertime excursions to her cozy home. Personally, the only ache I've ever gotten from ice cream is the stunning headache caused by shoveling in the sweet treat too fast for my own good, but, as usual, there's a perfectly reasonable rationale for summertime tummy aches.

Even today, in modern commercial freezers, ice cream is never actually "frozen solid." It's kept cold, but not necessarily frozen, which makes it easier for us to scoop it out into our bowls and cones—and easy for salmonella bacteria to survive! While many causes of food poisoning can be eliminated at even the relatively high temperatures best for ice cream, salmonella can't be. During the summers of even a few decades ago, when keeping anything cold was a tough task in a real ice box, ice cream that had been contaminated with salmonella never got cold enough to be really safe. In the winter, when ice cream became so stiff it had to sit on the counter for a while before getting soft enough to scoop out, the organisms died. So, "winter ice cream" didn't cause tummy aches!

As technology progressed, many of the oldest medical tales fell by the wayside. One, however, has only been made stronger by its complete resistance to new scientific methods and knowledge. Remember the expression "We can put a man on the moon, but we can't beat the common cold"? Well, in the main, it's true; we never have developed a defense that's proof against every one of the innumerable cold strains. What most people don't quite grasp is that developing a cure for the common cold is analogous to creating a cure for literally thousands of diseases, because the common cold is actually caused by that many different organisms!

The old wives, of course, have a different explanation. The scientists simply won't accept what they've been telling children for generations that "cold causes the cold"—specifically, going out in the cold with a damp head, or when it's raining, or after being in the heat too long, or after living in an overly well heated house. When scientists point out that hundreds of people have sat around in various temperatures, and varied amounts of dampness, just to prove the tale wrong, the old wives can rightly point out that, well, the scientists haven't come up with that cure, so maybe it's the testing that's wrong, not them!

NEW WIVES' TALES

The important thing to grasp in even this brief overview of the huge field that is folklore is that it's not done yet! New tales arise all the time in response to new situations. The more we learn about science and medicine, the more questions arise, the more technologies and knowledge there are to challenge us—or scare us silly. Our response to all this "new" stuff can be either global, in which we're threatened by everything, or local, in which we focus on minute items with a concentration verging on obsession, in order to avoid the global stuff that we can't quite handle.

New wives' tales, like old wives' tales, tend to fixate on everyday events and themes, including all things sexual. Unlike the old wives' tales, new wives' tales often concentrate on new medical techniques and possibilities, scenarios that couldn't arise without the existence of some innovative technological wonder. A certain amount of technophobia is evident in these tales, but so is an acceptance of gadgetry. Many tales focus on our new religion, health. We've been inundated with advice on how to "live healthy." Not surprisingly, many new wives' tales are backlashes against the new strictures that separate people from all the "bad" things they enjoy.

One new wives' tale is the notion that healthy people need to drink "eight glasses of water a day." Not tea, not coffee, not even "healthy" fluids like fruit juices. Eight glasses of *water*. All across America, parents are coaxing their children into drinking more water more often. Some people even tout this new Eleventh Commandment as a diet aid. Distending the stomach with a bucketful of water will prevent you from putting food down there, or excite the "full-tummy" enzymes to kick in earlier and make you feel less hungry. Unfortunately for the Church of the Eighty Ounces, this widely accepted maxim for health is based on a mistake!

Yup.

The annual guide to recommended daily allowance, as published by the Food and Nutrition Board in 1945, was supposed to read: "A suitable allowance of water for adults is 2.5 liters (83 ounces) daily in most instances. An ordinary standard for diverse people is 1 milliliter for each calorie of food. Most of this quantity is contained in prepared foods."

When this section of the book was reprinted in more than twenty different health guides, *the last line was left out*! So, on the basis of a misprint, millions of Americans have been nearly quadrupling their recommended water intake! Imagine how bloated a young child must feel with as much as eight times the water he needs floating about in his tummy!

The legend of "The Water Drunk" describes the use of water for an entirely different purpose.

For much of the 1980s, scattered tales of yuppies stumbling into an "altered state" by forcing themselves to ingest huge quantities of water circulated in Seattle, Chicago, New York, Cincinnati, and numerous other northern cities. At first, though reports of water-based highs were racing from town to town, it was mostly ignored by the medical community. How could water, that stuff you needed eight glasses of every day, possibly hurt you, or make you "drunk?"

Strictly speaking, it couldn't. What it did do was induce drastic changes in body chemistry. Blood volume swelled, then fell. Salts,

present throughout our 70 percent saltwater bodies, shift from areas of high concentration, like the insides of cells, into areas of low concentration, like the rapidly thinned blood already mentioned. They slosh around there for a while, then get excreted along with all the extra water racing toward the water-drunk's bladder. Salt wastage, the unusual loss of normal salts, can simulate many things, including intoxication, which is why the state caused by forcing all those fluids is frequently called "water intoxication."

Unlike normal intoxication, water intoxication doesn't always cure itself. In extreme cases, a particular type of paralysis occurs and victims can die before their bodies manage to right the chemical scales. It wasn't until 1991 that the first broad-response policies and procedures for addressing this bizarre self-inflicted illness were handed down.

Another water legend, this one not strictly a new wives' tale, attempts to convince us that boiling water and childbirth are natural partners. We've all seen movies and television programs where an unexpected birth is attended by the boiling of copious amounts of water, usually accompanied by enough steam to send non–water breathers outside for fresh air. Just how the legend started is hard to determine. Even harder to figure out is what all that boiling water was supposed to be for!

Obviously not to bathe a child.

Or to sterilize it.

Or to sterilize its mother.

Sterilizing anything else when the child is born into a normal household environment seems rather pointless. Whatever little bugs might have fallen onto a towel or a sheet are already falling on the baby itself as soon as it's born! And, if not to sterilize something, why would the water need to be "boiling" hot?

Maybe to make tea? Or perhaps to occupy those with no stomach for screams or blood?

You'd almost think that in the length of time that legend has floated around, someone would have noticed that when babies are born in delivery rooms, there's not a whiff of steam anywhere.

Hot water of a different type, the kind whooshing around your tired body in a hot tub, features in two new wives' tales. "Not in the Hot Tub!" is usually set in Aspen or Vail, or somewhere else vaguely alpine that might summon up visions of ski bunnies and hot toddies and, of course, a hot tub. Any sort of shared bathing arrangement is just a little suspicious to North Americans, so it's no surprise that the hot tub was subjected to early tales about a variety of diseases that might be shared in heated water. Those tales faded pretty quickly as bathers were assured that they were at least as safe as they'd be on a beach or in a public pool. The one that persists, however, is that because there's no chlorine in a hot tub, any sperm that might somehow find their way into the tub could live quite happily in the warm, rolling water—certainly long enough to find their way to whatever females might be sharing that tub!

That sperm can't live in a freshwater environment, no matter how cozy, has done nothing to slow the legend's spread.

A different variation suggests that the hot tub might well be the most comfortable birth-control contraption ever made, or at least that's what the coeds in "Some Like It Hot" hoped. The tale begins in Aspen with four couples from a Southern university skipping off for a naughty weekend. All but one of the eight young people knew the score and came prepared with their favorite contraceptive. The naïve member of the group, a young woman, was nearly in tears when she confessed to her sorority sisters that she wasn't on the Pill and hadn't thought of bringing anything with her. As two of the girls depended on IUDs and the third on the Pill, they had nothing immediate to offer her, but one quickly suggested she and her boyfriend take a nice long soak in the hot tub before having sex.

"Why? What's that going to do?"

"Well, think about it. When a couple is trying to have a baby, they encourage the guy to wear boxers, right?"

"Yeah?"

"That's to let his privates dangle more freely, keep them cool. Sperm die if they get too hot!"

"So the heat from the hot tub should . . ."

"Right!"

Delighted with the idea of solving her contraceptive problems while enjoying a little foreplay in the hot tub, the young woman spent the weekend alternating between soaking, making love, and swooping down the hills. The outing seemed a complete success.

Just a few weeks later the young woman began suspecting something was wrong. When she missed her second period four weeks later, she didn't really need her doctor's confirmation to tell her she was pregnant, but she couldn't really grasp her situation, either.

In a moment of panic-stricken honesty, she blurted out how careful she'd been to soak her boyfriend in the hot tub before each lovemaking session. The doctor stared for a second, then covered his mouth with his hand to hide a sudden grin. "Well, that's a high-tech sort of solution, isn't it?" Getting control of himself, he asked, "I don't suppose you know what normal human body temperature is, do you?"

"Sure, I'm not stupid! Ninety-eight point six."

"Right. Did you happen to check the temperature of the hot tub?" At her blank look, he shook his head. "Most of them never get hotter than your bathtub. Ever heard of bathing as a contraceptive measure?"

Darn! Another high-tech tale bites the dust.

While reproducing all the "modern" tales out there is clearly impossible, the following tales represent a good cross-section of updated fears are illustrated in these new wives' tales.

"The Inflatables" takes places within the rarefied circles of one of medicine's most controversial and commercial arenas, cosmetic surgery. Hailed for its ability to rescue some semblance of dignity for the scarred and disfigured, while simultaneously shunned as a money-making racket on the same level as last century's snake-oil merchants, cosmetic surgery both titillates and repels us. Somehow we can't always get our minds around the concept that surgery is as life-affirming for some as it is terrifying to others. Breast augmentation, usually through some form of implantation, is the procedure most often invoked by the words "plastic surgery," and it's this procedure that's found its way into a funny little legend.

Breast implants have a stormy history. In addition to eliciting strong emotional responses pro and con among women, the various medical procedures to accomplish this augmentation have also made waves from a therapeutic point of view. Implants of several types have been around since the 1940s: human tissue, plastic, water-filled rubber, and, of course, silicone implants, both the early solid models and the later silicone gel models. Some have worked well, others not. For women who held strong negative beliefs about implants, the flurry of legal activity surrounding "leaking" silicone

> **The average adult human passes gas fifteen times per day.**

implants provided an emotional vindication, the opportunity to say, "I told you no good would come of them!"

It almost seemed that the lawsuits gave society permission to poke fun at those who'd been "taken in" by an easy cure to their self-image woes. Implant tales ran wild.

"Did you know they swell up when you get on planes? Something to do with the air pressure."

"I heard that some woman in Maine refused to get hers removed after she fell over the side of a boat. She claims they saved her life!"

"*I* heard a woman in Arizona is suing the company that made hers. Says they burst in the heat while she was sunbathing!"

"Well, did you know they've come up with new ones now? Yeah, they've got little air pumps, like on the Nike shoes! You can adjust them to go with your outfit—or your date!"

As examples of our fear that technology is running ahead of our ability to evaluate our needs or desires, those new tales are as effective as anything the old wives could have dreamed up.

Anyone who's been in a diner lately has likely seen that little hand-printed sign, "Microwave in Use," propped up somewhere

in the establishment. Waves of all kinds have inspired fear and warnings. People near power lines worry about invisible emissions. Radio waves and television waves were once blamed for illness among sheep. X rays, once considered relatively safe, are coming under closer scrutiny, and pregnant women are now told that the big lead apron may not have been protecting them nearly as well as they thought. The fears aren't totally unfounded. Marie Curie, an eminent scientist of her day, was propounding uses for radium even as it killed her. When the first of the atomic bombs exploded over Japan, the "chain-reaction theorists" hadn't been completely silenced. Science has a long history of discovering new things, integrating them into our everyday lives, and *then* figuring out there were unforeseen hazards!

In the last few years, "emission" tales have filled the void once crammed full of food fears. Instead of worrying about how much fat might be lurking in our cereals, we worry about emissions from our computer terminals at work, radon and carbon monoxide creeping through our too-efficient homes, and outgassing from the upholstery in our cars and the chemicals used by our dry cleaners.

The latest emission tale?

Cell phones. According to warnings flooding the Internet, a medium being reached more and more often through wireless communication systems, cellular phones can cause brain cancer.

How?

With low-energy electromagnetic radiation. It's the waves again! According to cellular detractors, instead of leaving the radiation inside the microwave, we're now carrying it next to our hearts and holding it to our own heads.

Psychological hazards aren't exempt from new wives' tales, either, as the "Road Rage Buggie" illustrates. Road-rage legends in areas like Los Angeles seem almost natural. Take that many people and strand them in the middle of a big, smelly highway, snorting up everyone else's exhaust, and it would probably be more surprising if *nothing* happened. "Road Rage Buggy" brings the fears associated with the L.A. highway legends into an airport near you. Just as stories of women having their purses stolen from under the doors of bathroom stalls once swept airports, a new wives' tale claims that a baggage buggy, in the hands of a malevolent personality, is a dangerous weapon. To support that contention, they claim thousands of people are being hamstrung each year by enraged travelers who can't get the handle of that buggy in their hands without feeling an irresistible urge to ram it into the vulnerable calves of their fellow travelers!

Attempts to locate these "thousands" have so far proven futile, but before letting down your guard as you globe-trot, you might want to consult a tiny article in the *British Medical Journal*. Apparently some Israelis really need to talk out their issues before being entrusted with a baggage buggy.

SIMPLY BIZARRE

A wise man once said, "Sometimes stuff happens just to make sure you're paying attention." These last few cases might have been the inspiration for that observation.

For years following the first nuclear weapon test, stories circulated that a young blind woman had, at the moment of the explosion, called out "What was that flash?" Since she lived over a hundred miles away, in Albuquerque, her ability to see the flash would have been extraordinary in any case, but because she couldn't see *anything,* her physicians were floored by the incident. The legend insists that, even in 1995, a full fifty years after that first test, doctors continued to investigate the phenomenon without gaining one whit of wisdom. The girl remained blind to the end of her days and, after moving away from New Mexico, never again saw even the vaguest flickers of light.

It's a great tale, no doubt kept alive as much by our continuing fear that we don't fully understand the powerful nuclear forces we've continued to exploit as by the mystery of a single blind girl's moment in the light. Unfortunately, though it's based on a real incident, it's grown considerably in the telling.

The young woman was indeed legally blind—she had been for some time—but

Women pass gas as often as men.

legal blindness and the utter blackness most of us associate with blindness have little in common. In this case the woman, a student at the time, could distinguish light from dark, and since she was much closer to the explosion than Albuquerque, she could certainly have seen the brilliant light of the explosion without experiencing anything superhuman or unexplainable. As often happens, local radio stations passed the report from one to the other and, as pertinent details were lost, a legend arose.

"The Blast" details one of those instances that, after the fact, leaves everyone wondering why they didn't foresee the outcome much more clearly.

One of the classic campus legends recounts the story of four frat brothers who, with nothing better to do with their time, decided to while away an evening trying to create a "fireball" by farting over an open candle flame. Evidently none of the four went on to medical school. If they had, they could have applied the lessons they learned that evening to the remarkable medical tool known as the cauterizing scalpel.

Electrocautery in surgery has saved innumerable lives by immediately heat-sealing blood vessels as incisions are made. In thoracic and abdominal surgery, the technique ensures a clear field of view instead of forcing the surgeon to fumble about in a pool of blood for whatever he's trying to find while a second doctor or nurse shoves suction tubes ahead of his probing fingers.

What more than one doctor has failed to really appreciate is that something that seals with heat is, in effect, burning—that is, it's hot. That lesson was driven home with force to several physicians who combined the cautery equipment and the lower digestive tract—a source of methane, a material the frat boys had already proven was highly combustible!

Though this tale started as a sort of what-if scenario among medical students, it seems the students assumed these things had already occurred to their teachers and the doctors with whom they made rounds. They assumed wrong. The legend became fact when patients in Israel, France, and the United States exploded under the cauterizing scalpel!

Few individuals can contemplate the notion of letting even skilled probers poke around inside their bodies without some qualms. When the probing involves the insertion or replacement of artificial parts, the qualm factor naturally rises a point or two, and it would be truly remarkable if we didn't have at least one modern myth about the hazards of tinkering.

"Reduce, Recycle, and Reuse" is a policy the cash-strapped health-care system can get behind. While real-world tales of hospitals washing and reusing *disposable* medical equipment remain reassuringly few and far between, legends and the popular media can't get enough of them. Cardiac pacemakers are expensive pieces of equipment that are usually removed at autopsy (with many people being cremated, it's a hazard to leave one inside a body, since they tend to explode in flames). Human curiosity wouldn't be up to its usual standard if someone didn't ask what, exactly, happens to them?

An episode of the TV series *Law & Order* spurred on a young legend by suggesting that unscrupulous pathologists, doctors, or funeral home owners were making a little money on the side by "recycling" used pacemakers into unsuspecting patients. Since the batteries inside pacemakers have a limited life, the new owner would have no idea when it was time for his 100,000th-beat tune-up!

Though the program is well recognized for taking real issues and recasting them in a fictional light, used pacemakers aren't being recycled. At least not in humans. In at least six states, however, they find new homes inside dogs, where the shorter battery life is never a problem.

Of all these tales, the one that brings home our uncomfortable relationship with new technologies is "The 90 Percent Solution."

A young man, desperate, depressed, and determined to end his life, left a message on his ex-girlfriend's machine, went outside where he waved to a neighbor, and then into the garage. Closing the door tightly behind himself, he found a suitable piece of hosing, attached it to his exhaust pipe, ran it into the interior of the car, got in, and started the engine. Soon he felt tired and everything went black.

That might have been the end of the story if the ex-girlfriend hadn't arrived home an hour after the message was left and immediately called rescue personnel.

The EMTs were shocked, delighted, and confused to find the man in the exhaust-filled garage very much alive, if groggy.

The hospital staff were equally amazed, at first insisting the time on the message machine was wrong. Carbon monoxide poisoning is quick, killing in as little as six minutes. No way, they claimed, could he have been in that environment for nearly an hour and not died. Yet the patient was clearly not dead. In fact, it appeared he'd suffered absolutely no damage at all from his attempted suicide!

The mystery might have continued indefinitely had not one young woman, who actually read the owner's manual for her new car, not piped up with, "Excuse me, but those new three-way catalytic converters? Well, they remove better than 90 percent of dangerous carbon monoxide gas from the exhaust of modern cars."

So Much for Comfort Food!

 arning: What follows is not for weak stomachs.

For those of you who skipped the introduction (I know, I do it too.), this seems an appropriate time to remind you that urban legends are no different than any other form of entertainment in at least one important respect: They often include factual elements, such as the names of towns or people or companies, to make the story seem more real to the audience.

In the following tales, you'll see frequent references to real companies, like McDonald's or Taco Bell. The inclusion of a particular company name within a legend in no way implies that the legend is true, or that the company featured in the legend is guilty of anything other than being a household name. Pop legends, however, are as guilty of attempted brand-name recognition as any other form of storytelling.

That said, it's time to hold on to your stomachs!

Of all urban legends, it's the food tales that inspire real horror. Images of contaminated food, germs, and full-sized, visible-to-the-eye critters invading our bodies make up a large section of urban horror legends, leaving us no comfort from our favorite foods, no delusions of security.

McDonald's, Burger King, and Taco Bell frequently appear as the offenders, but, as expected in a primarily oral tradition, the restaurant associated with each event changes from telling to telling, usually to accommodate whichever restaurants are operating locally. Long-standing stories become generic tales when they've been assigned to so many chains that no one can trace them back to their point of origin.

Foods that naturally conceal themselves from sight, the chicken or fish wrapped in batter, the plate of food under its layer of gravy or hidden beneath a layer of cheese, are prime targets for contaminated-food legends.

One of the oldest tales was probably attributed to particular cooks or individual restaurants before migrating on to the cloned eateries springing up across the country. A housewife, running late, decides to grab a bucket of chicken from the nearest Kentucky Fried Chicken. Not wanting anyone to realize she didn't slave away in the kitchen all day, she hastily tosses out the bucket, arranges the chicken on her own tray, and, after laying the table, brings out the candles. The family arrives and tucks in.

As she eats, the housewife notices a distinctly odd taste to her piece, but the remainder of the family munches away with only her husband mumbling, "Not bad, honey." The housewife soon feels distinctly unwell.

"Did anyone else notice an odd taste to this chicken?"

"No, it's great, really. Best ever."

Leaving the rest of her piece on her plate, she picks at her food until the others finish and hastily clears the table. By now she's really sick, and her worried husband rushes her to the hospital. The doctors, convinced it must be some form of food poisoning despite the evident health of the rest of the family, sends the man home to locate any leftovers and bring them back for testing. The wife, nearly delirious, keeps muttering, "No, don't look in the garbage . . ." but no one pays attention.

The husband returns with everything he can find—including the half-piece of chicken his wife had been eating and the discarded Kentucky Fried Chicken bucket! It takes only a few seconds to identify the source of her sickness. Instead of chicken, the wife had been eating a piece of battered rat!

Following the chicken theme, a woman— who'd perhaps heard the KFC tale already— decided to get her chicken sandwich at a McDonald's drive-through. "A Coke and a McChicken, hold the mayo," didn't seem like a difficult order, but, as drive-through customers are all too aware, what you order and what you get can be two different things. So when she stopped and bit into her sandwich, she wasn't all that surprised to find they'd messed up the order. There was definitely something white and slimy in there. Since she'd parked in the parking lot, and still had her receipt, she decided that *this* drive-through customer was going to get what she'd asked for!

Marching back into the counter, she asked for a new sandwich because of the mayonnaise on the one she was served. The

"Gimme the special!"

manager quickly points to the big X across the mayonnaise symbol. It's hard to say who's more horrified when, on opening the sandwich to display the "mayonnaise," the customer discovers a thick white substance seeping from a huge growth on the chicken breast! It had been hidden by the batter.

Before you get the idea that chicken is the only culprit—and start feeling safe with your hamburgers and gyros—hold your stomach and harken to yet another urban legend of drive-through horror. This one begins at Burger King.

A young man pulls up to the window, orders a soda, large fries, and a Whopper, no pickles, no onions. He, too, pulls into the parking lot to wolf down his meal. Out of habit, he lifts the top of the burger before eating. Onions. Tons of 'em. All sending their distinctive scent aloft. Incensed, he storms into the restaurant and demands

another burger. Despite the staff's immediate apologies, the man continues to harangue the server loudly enough that no one in the restaurant *didn't* realize he hated onions.

Eventually a new hamburger is brought out, and the customer is reimbursed for the full cost of his meal. Far from being happy, he continues berating the staff even as he scoops up food and cash.

Out in his car, he once again lifts that top bun. As promised, no onions. Well content with his lunch and the money in his pocket, he bites into the burger with considerable anticipation—only to run into something round and chewy under the patty! He's halfway out of the car, ready for another round with the manager, over pickles this time, when he actually stops to look at his food. It's not a pickle. It's not even green, though the customer, who's just discovered his pickle is actually a condom, definitely is. And with all that mayonnaise swirling about, who's to say if its been used or not?

Perhaps it's xenophobia raising its head again, but, gross as these tales have been, foods perceived as "foreign" to the American market—basically anything other than fried chicken, hamburgers, and hot dogs—are the butt of even worse tales. At least all the things found so far were *dead.*

Taco Bell makes a natural target. Its menu includes many items that Americans, even now, can't recognize. Several dishes include sauces, which hide any number of sins, and pastes, which have absolutely no recognizable ingredients. Layers of food stacked on a plate provide infinite hiding places. Combined, those factors explain why stories like these have circulated since Taco Bell opened its doors.

One of the oldest ones, "The Furry Olive," obviously a south-of-the-border tweak, features a young couple about to try Mexican fast food for the first time. Not knowing a burrito from a burro, they ask the server to suggest a typical meal, pay for their food, then leave. Back home, they giggle their way through everything, trying to figure out what's in the entree. They're doing fairly well until the woman turns up something resembling a fat, furry olive in her salad. Shrugging, she splits it in half with the edge of her fork and pops one piece into her mouth before sliding the other section onto her husband's plate.

"What is it?"

"Haven't the vaguest."

"Well, what does it taste like?"

"Mmmm, not bad. Sort of like a kiwi on the outside, but crunchy. Pretty bland inside. Try it."

Hubby has just about reached the limit of his adventurous foray into foreign food, so he plays with it a bit. Suddenly he freezes.

"Did you swallow that?"

"Yeah, why?"

Without a word, he turns the thing on his plate around. From this angle, it's obviously the front half of a tarantula with its legs pulled close to its body in death!

A similar setup starts "Delivery!" Again, a couple, Robert and Sally, decide to broaden their culinary experiences by checking out the local Taco Bell. They know there's no burro in burritos, but that's it. Eventually settling on quesadillas, a layered meal of vegetables, corn-flour tortillas, and various sauces, along with ground beef and refried beans, they pick up their order and head home.

As they walk in, the phone is ringing and the trip to the table is temporarily sidetracked. The husband runs upstairs to grab a shower while the wife handles the call. The caller, Sally's mother, is a chatty sort, so Sally puts the takeout bags on the counter and starts setting the table. While wandering around at the extreme range of her telephone cord, she hears a faint scratching but can't locate the source. Moments later, something seems to move just out of the corner of her eye. Sally excuses herself from the call for a minute, but can't see anything! Again, the scratching sounds from somewhere in the kitchen. Telling her mother she'll call her back later, Sally yells upstairs for Robert. When he arrives, dripping, he can't hear or see anything!

Not about to be left alone until she figures out what's making the noise, Sally flips off the light and follows him upstairs, willing to wait on supper until he's dressed and dry.

Sally's just reached the point of laughing at herself when they troop back downstairs and head into the kitchen to get their supper at last. Robert flicks on the light and Sally

It might take two hours to soften up, but there are no spider eggs in there!

screams. Surrounding the bags containing their supper are a dozen shiny black cockroaches—*las cucarachas*!

In a similar story, but higher on the "ick" scale, the cockroach, by some bizarre biological feat, manages to disgorge hundreds of eggs when she is unintentionally eaten by the young wife. The eggs, by yet another miracle, manage to insinuate themselves into the woman's salivary glands. (As though eggs have the ability to seek out anything, much less salivary glands!) There they grow into huge lumps that must eventually be surgically excised if the woman doesn't want hundreds of little cockroaches digging their own way out of her face!

Both tarantulas and cockroaches are native to the United States, but, in this connotation, their symbolic value is in being *perceived* as commonly occurring south of the border. It's not a giant step to turn the insect invasion associated with Taco Bell into American fears of the immigrant Mexicans themselves.

So prevalent have contaminated-food stories become that some companies are forced to address the specific charges in the popular press. Responding to a charge that McDonald's was using worms in their hamburger patties, a spokesman felt compelled to point out that, per pound, worms cost six times what McDonald's pays for beef!

When nearly every grade-school child in New York City was wondering what exactly made Bubble Yum gum so soft and chewy (unlike, for example, rock-hard Bazooka, another local favorite)—and attributing the wonderfully tender texture to the inclusion of spider eggs in the recipe—Life Savers, the parent company, spent hundreds of thousands in advertising and press releases to combat the rumor.

Even such seemingly innocuous chains as Tim Horton's and Dunkin' Donuts attract their share of urban legends: How would you respond to suggestions that your cream-filled doughnut was semen-filled?

And, though fast-food restaurants remain the most popular targets, Bob Evans and other home-style restaurants like the Olive Garden, Applebee's, and Friendly's are victimized as well. Gravy, spaghetti sauce, and cheese toppings reputedly harbored bugs, spit, and semen!

Makes you wonder why anyone would consider eating anywhere but home, doesn't it? Of course, like the worms-in-the-burgers story, many legends simply don't make sense viewed in the light of day, so we can manage to convince ourselves that if one story is apocryphal, they are all apocryphal—just a little warning to be careful what you eat, right?

Sort of.

If you're of the opinion that if one apocryphal tale is actually true, then they could all be true, you'll be forced to reconsider your dining habits. Occasional, extremely localized incidents do pop up—and they're as bad as any fiction.

For example, Jeff Bolling, though certainly nowhere near as uncouth as the man in the Burger King legend, can certainly relate to that fictional guy's problem. According to the *San Diego Union-Tribune* and other very public media sources, Jeff Bolling sued McDonald's and the CLP Corporation, the parent company, for unspecified damages when he, too, found a condom impersonat-

ing a pickle in his Big Mac after leaving the drive-through window on October 6, 1995. Despite finding the condom in an unrolled and therefore probably unused condition, Bolling claimed extreme emotional distress that sent him back and forth for AIDS testing on a regular basis. Oh, and for some reason he can't bring himself to eat Big Macs anymore.

Robert Alfano probably isn't eating at Burger King these days. According to Alfano's story, which, like Bolling's, was widely reported, on July 29, 1993, he left work for a quick lunch at the local Burger King and had just chomped into his burger when he smelled something "really, really

© Peter/Ngaire Genge, 1999

At that price, it's cheaper by the pound to buy beef!

bad" and felt something rough stick into his throat. Looking down, he realized something was sticking out of his burger just as he began having difficulty breathing. He was taken to the local hospital, but not before he remembered to take the object from his burger along with him. The Nassau County (New York) Board of Health, on July 30, reported the object as "probably in the genus *Rattus*" and described it as a "skinless, dry, cooked rodent foot, probably the rear."

Alfano's claims when he filed his suit included a weight loss of over fifteen pounds, insomnia due to recurring rat nightmares, and a strong aversion to meat products—especially Burger King hamburgers.

Veronica Minor's experience may prove two points: first, that McDonald's chicken sandwiches aren't any safer than their hamburgers, and, second, that foreign-objects-in-the-Mickey-D's tales are as applicable to America's heartland as to the big centers on either coast.

Veronica, her husband, and their two children were out celebrating one of the kids' birthdays at a Menomonie, Wisconsin, McDonald's. She had ordered a chicken sandwich (guess she'd never heard about that *other* chicken sandwich), which looked perfectly fine until she bit into it and found herself chewing into yet another unpackaged condom! Reality *is* different from urban leg

end, however. After spitting out the condom, throwing up in the bathroom, and complaining to the manager, she and her family, including their two small children, found themselves being escorted from the restaurant by police officers!

Allegedly, the manager believed the Minors were trying to perpetrate a hoax!

A court decides which party was victimized later this year.

Believe it or not, Taco Bell, featured in the worst urban food legends, is nowhere near the top of the list of restaurants being sued. Of course, when you consider that a couple in Shirley, New York, was given a bag containing $1,940, the entire night's receipts, instead of their seven-layer chicken burrito, you could be forgiven for wondering what else might be sneaking into those cute takeout bags!

The important thing to recall—important if you want to eat out again, anyway—is that these are the actions of individuals, not of the restaurants themselves. No one orders "a box of mayo, two cases of ketchup, and a case of spider eggs."

On any scale of edible horror, discovering *half* a worm in the apple you're eating has always rated at least a nine-and-a-half. Hair, fingernails, fingers, and used Band-Aids, stars in other urban legends, blow the top clear off. No one wants to contemplate inadvertently ingesting such things.

AND IN CLOSING . . .

our hundred plus legends after page one, you might expect that we'd covered just about every area of human interest that might possibly inspire our colleagues and neighbors to remember—or *mis*remember—a story told by a "friend of a friend."

We haven't.

We're not even close.

From faxlore to cyberlegends, this book presents examples of every style and type of legend, but in order to squeeze everything into a volume that didn't come with its own forklift, focusing on a narrower list of topics quickly became necessary. Luckily for fans of urban legends, this collection is just the tip of the topic iceberg. There are also . . .

- **High-Tech Tales**—when the plumbing gets too complex
- **Low-Tech Tales**—Science 101 can't prepare you for this
- **Animal Antics**—everything the lemmings didn't do
- **Big Brother**—what you'd wish on your politicians
- **Bugs, Bugs, Bugs**—when zeros and ones don't compute
- **Politically Correct**—words you wish you could take back—or that you'd never said
- **Caught on Video**—the latest in invasion tales
- **Shrink Stuff**—the psychiatric side of medicine

- **Chemical Capers**—drugs, licit and illicit

- **Tearjerkers**—everyone needs a good cry now and then

- **Plain Gross**—tales designed to disturb your digestion

- **Body Human**—what you *do* know can hurt you

- not to mention *more* of everything in this book!

Another five hundred tales are already crowding my desktop. Dozens more arise every month. Singly, each tale is a complete story, an entertaining glimpse into the hopes, fears, and secrets of the people I pass on the street, at the water cooler, or under my own roof. Together, these modern myths reveal patterns of belief that have evolved over time within the mold of a specific location. The compelling narratives, amusing ironies, and warnings for a modern era continue to provide effective vehicles for these satisfying stories. Even if we could publish at the speed of light, we'd never catch up with the rapidly changing face of modern mythology.

But we're going to try!

If you'd like to contribute one of your region's tales, comment on any of the myths in this volume, or be put in touch with other contributors with like interests, Harmony Books and I would be delighted to receive your mail.